# PERSIANS

## AND OTHER PLAYS

AESCHYLUS lived from about 525 BC to 456. Throughout these years there was constant political upheaval in his home city of Athens as well as the threat to all of Greece from Persian invasions in 490 and 480. Aeschylus took part in the fighting and celebrated the final Greek victory in his *Persians* of 472, a uniquely surviving 'historical tragedy'.

Aeschylus competed in the annual dramatic festivals at Athens from about 500 until his death; in this time he wrote, and often produced, about eighty plays, three-quarters of them tragedies, for which he often won the tragedians' prize and which brought him wide fame in the Greek world. Only seven tragedies survive complete; one of these, *Prometheus Bound*, is generally deemed inauthentic. Of the six certain plays, three now stand alone: *Persians*; *Seven against Thebes* (467), the last play of an original thematic trilogy upon the extinction of the royal line of Thebes (the Oedipus story); and *Suppliant Women* (late 460s), probably the middle play of a trilogy handling dynastic conflict. The other three plays are those of the *Oresteia* (458), the only trilogy to survive from Greek Tragedy, which has been regarded since antiquity as one of its greatest monuments and is the culmination of Aeschylus' dramatic and poetic achievement.

CHRISTOPHER COLLARD is Emeritus Professor of Classics, University of Wales, Swansea. He has also translated Aeschylus' *Oresteia* for Oxford World's Classics.

## OXFORD WORLD'S CLASSICS

*For over 100 years Oxford World's Classics have brought
readers closer to the world's great literature. Now with over 700
titles—from the 4,000-year-old myths of Mesopotamia to the
twentieth century's greatest novels—the series makes available
lesser-known as well as celebrated writing.*

*The pocket-sized hardbacks of the early years contained
introductions by Virginia Woolf, T. S. Eliot, Graham Greene,
and other literary figures which enriched the experience of reading.
Today the series is recognized for its fine scholarship and
reliability in texts that span world literature, drama and poetry,
religion, philosophy and politics. Each edition includes perceptive
commentary and essential background information to meet the
changing needs of readers.*

OXFORD WORLD'S CLASSICS

AESCHYLUS

# *Persians*
## *and Other Plays*

Translated with an Introduction and Notes by
CHRISTOPHER COLLARD

OXFORD
UNIVERSITY PRESS

# OXFORD

UNIVERSITY PRESS

Great Clarendon Street, Oxford OX2 6DP

Oxford University Press is a department of the University of Oxford.
It furthers the University's objective of excellence in research, scholarship,
and education by publishing worldwide in

Oxford New York

Auckland Cape Town Dar es Salaam Hong Kong Karachi
Kuala Lumpur Madrid Melbourne Mexico City Nairobi
New Delhi Shanghai Taipei Toronto

With offices in

Argentina Austria Brazil Chile Czech Republic France Greece
Guatemala Hungary Italy Japan Poland Portugal Singapore
South Korea Switzerland Thailand Turkey Ukraine Vietnam

Oxford is a registered trade mark of Oxford University Press
in the UK and in certain other countries

Published in the United States
by Oxford University Press Inc., New York

© Christopher Collard 2008

British Library Cataloguing in Publication Data

Data available

Library of Congress Cataloging in Publication Data

Data available

Typeset by Cepha Imaging Pvt. Ltd., Bangalore, India
Printed in Great Britain
on acid-free paper by
Clays Ltd, Elcograf S.p.A.

ISBN 978-0-19-283282-5

17

# Preface and Acknowledgements

First in this volume are the three plays—the only three—which survive complete from Aeschylus' work earlier than the trilogy of the *Oresteia*, his final masterpiece. Inevitably they have been always in its shadow. They are very different from one another; each has moments or longer spans of brilliance, and each is of great dramatic or poetic interest, *Persians* most of all, perhaps, for it is the only historical—and near-contemporary-historical—Greek tragedy we have. *Seven against Thebes* is important as a clear forerunner in many ways of the *Oresteia*'s techniques, and has an air of its grandeur. *Suppliants* dramatizes timeless religious and social issues. Fourth in the volume is *Prometheus Bound*, ascribed to Aeschylus but believed by the great majority of modern scholars to be in some or even large part inauthentic. The truth is unlikely ever to be known, but its protagonist is a theatrical figure of huge power fully worthy of Aeschylus' imagination. The impact of Prometheus' myth upon the modern arts through this play has been enormous.

The volume follows the pattern of my Aeschylus, *Oresteia* (2002); and I have repeated a small part of its Introduction, that on Aeschylus' dramatic form and language, revised where appropriate for plays of very differing content and manner. I have again thought it useful to begin the volume with brief summaries of the plays, above all because these four, except perhaps *Persians* and *Prometheus*, are less frequently read (or performed). In the Introduction, and in the individual essays upon the plays, I have had space to discuss only their more important features and aspects. Here, I give rather more guidance than I did for the unified *Oresteia* to secondary literature listed in the Bibliography and Further Reading. Many of the works there direct readers to both older and newer interpretations; not everything in the Bibliography gets a citation in the rest of the volume, and conversely. The Maps show as many as practicable of the places named in the plays, in the hope of giving readers a general idea of ancient geography, historical and mythical. The Explanatory Notes are again very full, and I have been as factual and objective in them as I can. In both Introduction and Explanatory Notes I have provided a large number of cross-references within the individual plays, and not a few between the plays, from a strong belief that they should be interpreted in the first instance from within themselves. The line-numbers given in the Introduction and Notes are those of the Greek text, from which those of the Translation sometimes differ by one or two: this is because English sentence-structure and word-order are often irreconcilable with those of poetic Greek. I hope, as before, that readers will be able to let their eyes slide past these references if they wish. There is occasional duplication of matter between parts of the Introduction and the Notes, and even within both, but it is intended to be helpful.

I suggest to newcomers to these plays that for each they read first the summary and then the translation, and only afterwards the sections Introduction 1 and 2; and that they use the Explanatory Notes (which include analyses of each play's major scenes or parts) at any point as they find best.

I have gratefully taken the opportunity to include an Index in this volume, and to incorporate in it references to my earlier *Oresteia* (2002, above).

I have the pleasure of thanking again those who encouraged or helped me with my earlier volume, and repeated their generosity for this one: first, Hilary O'Shea (whose suggestion it was), Classics Editor at Oxford University Press, Judith Luna, the Press's Oxford World's Classics Editor, and Paul Smith, the Press's copy-editor; second, Bill Allan, Elizabeth Craik, Patrick Finglass, Doreen Innes, and James Morwood, who read all or part of the volume, and whose comments were as invaluable as they were numerous; and third, most fittingly, as the best possible agent of the Saving Zeus (*Suppliants* 26) whom I often invoked, my wife Jean, for her support and love.

*Oxford 2006*                                   Christopher Collard

# Contents

# Abbreviations: Play-Titles and Works Frequently Cited; Other Abbreviations

Pers.    Persians

Seven    Seven against Thebes (Greek Hepta epi Thebas, Latin Septem contra Thebas)

Supp.    Suppliants (in full, Suppliant Women; Greek Hiketides, Latin Supplices Mulieres)

PB    Prometheus Bound (Greek Prometheus Desmotes, Latin Prometheus Vinctus)

Ag.    Agamemnon

LB    Libation Bearers (Greek Khoephoroi, Latin Choephori)

Eum.    Eumenides

The titles of Aeschylus' fragmentary plays are not abbreviated. Other Greek authors sometimes abbreviated: Eur(ipides), Hom(er), Soph(ocles); the titles of their works are not abbreviated, except for Homer's Od(yssey).

CCGT    P. E. Easterling (ed.), The Cambridge Companion to Greek Tragedy, 1997

CHGL    P. E. Easterling and B. M . W. Knox (eds.), Cambridge History of Classical Literature, I: Greek Literature, 1985

Collard (2002)    C. Collard, Aeschylus, Oresteia, 2002

Conacher (1980)    D. J. Conacher, Aeschylus' Prometheus Bound: A Literary Commentary, 1980

Conacher (1996)    Aeschylus: The Earlier Plays and Related Studies, 1996

Csapo-Slater    E. Csapo and W. J . Slater, The Context of Ancient Drama, 1994

Gantz    T. Gantz, Early Greek Myth: A Guide to Literary and Artistic Sources, 1993

Gregory, CGT    J. Gregory (ed.), A Companion to Greek Tragedy, 2005

Rosenmeyer, AA    T . G . Rosenmeyer, The Art of Aeschylus, 1982

Sommerstein, AT    A. H. Sommerstein, Aeschylean Tragedy, 1996

Taplin, Stagecraft    O. P. Taplin, The Stagecraft of Aeschylus, 1977

West    M. L. West, Aeschylus, Tragoediae, 1998[2]

Reference to other works listed in the Bibliography is made by author's name, a section-number there, where necessary a date, and page-numbers, e.g. Wiles (Bibliography §5, 2000) 123.

## Other Abbreviations

| | |
|---|---|
| Introd. | Introduction (numbers point to section(s), e.g. Introd. 2.3) |
| Bibl. | Bibliography and Further Reading (§ and §§ point to divisions of the Bibliography) |
| EN | Explanatory Notes (the abbreviations n. and nn. cross-refer within the Explanatory Notes, or point to notes in the Introduction) |
| fr(s). | fragment(s) of an author, followed by a number |
| s.d. (often italicized) | stage direction |

# Summaries of the Stage-Action

## PERSIANS

THE play is a historical tragedy, set in the year 480 BC. The scene is the Persian court, near the tomb of its previous king Darius. The Chorus of elderly counsellors anxiously await news from Greece, where Darius' son Xerxes has gone with a huge army and navy to compel its subjection—just as Darius had attempted ten years before, only to fail at the battle of Marathon (490 BC). Anxiety is confirmed by a dream which the Queen, Darius' widow and Xerxes' mother, reports to the counsellors. They advise propitiatory offerings to the gods, and in particular to the dead Darius to secure his favourable intervention. The Queen agrees, but first enquires about the Athenians who have always been the Persians' greatest enemy among the Greeks.

A Messenger brings a lengthy description of Xerxes' defeat in the great sea battle of Salamis. There has been huge loss of Persian ships and crews, and the land army has been almost destroyed by natural disasters during its retreat; but Xerxes himself is alive and will soon return. Amid lamentation the Queen nevertheless prepares her offerings to the dead Darius; in fact, his ghost is 'raised', in the hope he may explain the catastrophe and advise how to prevent worse; it is, he reveals, due to the young, rash, and arrogant Xerxes' desire for aggrandizement, who defied natural and divine law in bridging the Hellespont so that his army might march from Asia into Europe, disregarded his father's own example as a safe king, but also committed sacrilege in Greece. Before Darius goes, he advises the Queen to console and counsel her son at his return, and to be ready with fine and proper clothing for him, since he has been reduced to unkingly rags.

Thus the play's end is prepared, for it is all continuous lamentation, first by the Chorus alone, then shared with Xerxes; he has entered on foot, is unattended, and, as Darius foretold, now wears rags. Their joint laments become wilder and wilder until they stop abruptly.

## SEVEN AGAINST THEBES

The 'Seven against Thebes' are about to attack the city: they are helping the dead king Oedipus' son Polynices to recover his share in its throne and in his inherited possessions, from which his brother Eteocles has expelled him. The play is set within the city, where the burden of defence sits solely and heavily on Eteocles; he alludes briefly to his father Oedipus' curse, that his two sons might fight over their inheritance, for he fears that Thebes may be totally destroyed in the attack.

A Theban Scout has already informed Eteocles that an assault is imminent, and undertakes to report how the Seven will each be allotted one of the city's seven gates to attack. Eteocles' attempt to make a concerted and disciplined defence is threatened by panic among Thebes' young women, who form the Chorus; but he quietens them, and directs them how best to share his own prayers for safety. Then he leaves to appoint seven Theban champions to the gates, including himself as seventh. The Scout returns, together with Eteocles; the Scout names and describes the Seven and their individual arms, and how they boast of victory, so that Eteocles may designate apt opponents. The Chorus follow each pairing with fears and prayers; tension increases until the seventh attacker is named as Polynices, and only Eteocles is left to confront his brother. Eteocles recognizes the working of Oedipus' curse, but also the 'justice' of the inescapable duel; despite the Chorus' appeals, he is not to be deflected from the probable fratricide. The Scout reports that the city has been saved, but that the brothers have indeed killed each other; either side of his report, the Chorus sing with powerful emotion of the accursed family's history.

The play ends with protracted and ever more frantic grief for the brothers' cruel fate; it is sung by the Chorus alone, who divide into two groups each increasingly evoking the fate of one brother.

[The end of the play suffered considerable interpolation probably in the fourth or third century BC: see Introd. 2.2, p. xxxv.]

## SUPPLIANTS

Danaus and his daughters, the suppliants of the title who form the play's Chorus and are its dominant characters and voice, have fled

from Egypt to Greek Argos, the homeland long ago of their ancestress Io. As a girl Io was desired by Zeus, and tormented by his
jealous wife Hera through transformation into a cow and harried
round the remoter world by a cattle-fly until she reached Egypt; there
Zeus restored her form and impregnated her, and she gave birth
to Danaus' grandfather. Now Danaus' brother Aegyptus, the king
of Egypt, wishes to enforce marriage between his sons and Danaus'
daughters; they have fled from this threat, detesting any such violent
marriage, and marriage in general, and expect pursuit.

The play is set at Argos where they come ashore at a collective
shrine of all the city's gods; it offers them sanctuary until they have
persuaded Argos' king Pelasgus to save them from their pursuing
Egyptian suitors. The daughters, not Danaus himself, plead their case;
they use the two arguments of common ancestry and the universally
inescapable duty to Zeus who protects all suppliants, but they also
threaten suicide within the shrine if their appeal is not granted. Pelasgus reluctantly concedes their case, despite the certainty of consequent war between Argos and the Egyptians; then he leaves to consult
his citizens, and to ensure their support, after sending Danaus ahead
to make the fact of supplication known. Danaus reports Pelasgus'
success with his citizens, and all seems safe. The Egyptian pursuers
are now sighted, however, and Danaus again leaves to fetch Pelasgus'
aid. The Egyptians send men, cast as a second chorus, who attempt to
drag Danaus' daughters to their ships, amid cruel threats and panic.
Pelasgus comes in time to repulse the Egyptians temporarily with
words, but war looms. His renewed assurance to the suppliants of
protection, and promise of homes in Argos, are joyfully confirmed
in a further report by Danaus—only for a third chorus, comprising
Men of Argos who nominally welcome the new residents, to warn that
marriage will in any outcome be the daughters' natural and inevitable
destiny as women; for why else did the gods permit the Egyptians to
reach Argos? The play's end thus forebodes the unwelcome marriages
already twice prevented.

## PROMETHEUS BOUND

The Titan Prometheus joined Zeus, the new ruler of the gods
after deposing his own father Cronus, to defend his throne against

Prometheus' own brother Titans whom Prometheus could not dissuade from aggression; they were crushed, and Prometheus then helped Zeus distribute prerogatives among all the gods new to power. Zeus, however, wanted also to destroy mortal mankind; only Prometheus opposed him, protecting and benefiting men, particularly with the gift of fire and its associated skills, which he stole from the gods.

Now Zeus retaliates upon Prometheus by fettering him eternally to a cliff face in the remote Caucasus; the play begins with this vivid action, carried out by the artificer-god Hephaestus under the direction of Power and Force. The noisy hammering is heard from afar by the daughters of the god Oceanus, whose water bounds the world's remotest edge. They arrive aerially to sympathize with an embittered Prometheus, and form the play's Chorus; but Prometheus counters with an assurance that he knows how Zeus is to be deposed from his throne, and that he will not reveal this knowledge before Zeus frees him; Prometheus' name implies foreknowledge, and he has it in part from his prophetess mother. In the following episode Oceanus himself arrives, riding on a griffin; he offers vainly to intercede with Zeus for Prometheus' release—if Prometheus will humble himself; but Prometheus resists, and Oceanus goes away. After Prometheus recounts to the Chorus his gift of fire and its skills, and of other benefits, to mankind, the wretched Io bursts in on them, in the course of a frenzied wandering round the world: this is the maiden whom Zeus desired and who was vengefully transformed into a cow by Zeus' wife Hera and tormented by a cattle-fly (cf. the summary of *Suppliants*). To all these visitors Prometheus emphasizes his increasing and obdurate anger against Zeus, dwelling on and eventually revealing to Io and the Chorus what he knows of Zeus' fall. The cruel fate of Io particularly moves him; she too is a victim, if indirect, of Zeus' tyranny, and in foretelling the end of her wanderings he discloses how her son by Zeus will have a later descendant destined, ironically, to free Prometheus of his bonds, Heracles. Io's frenzy suddenly resumes, and she rushes away. Prometheus' subsequent and most extreme restatement of defiance is interrupted by a last visitor, Zeus' emissary Hermes; he demands that Prometheus should reveal his secret knowledge, or he must face still worse agony: collapse of the cliff upon him and crushing by its weight in endless dark, to be ended only by return to the light and daily rending of his body by Zeus' eagle. Prometheus is contemptuously dismissive; as Hermes leaves, the cataclysm begins, when the Chorus make the ultimate gesture of sympathy and go down with him.

# Introduction

## 1. AESCHYLUS AND HIS EARLY PLAYS

A few details are known of Aeschylus' life (c.525–456 BC: see the Chronology, p. lxxxv). The three plays in this volume which are certainly his are the earliest which survive complete from a total output of perhaps more than eighty. These and the three plays of the *Oresteia* are in fact all that survive; moreover they come from the final third of his career; the dates are *Persians* 472 BC, *Seven against Thebes* 467, *Suppliants* probably the late 460s, *Oresteia* 458. It is a small but perhaps just adequate basis for an appreciation of his creative range and development.[1]

With very simple resources Aeschylus created compelling drama. The earlier plays were conceived for a largely featureless performance-area bare even of a backcloth, and for male performers comprising not more than two speaking actors and a chorus of singing dancers. Subsidiary choruses could be used for short scenes, and mute extras for any duration. By the time of the *Oresteia* a third speaking actor was available, and the theatre's physical facilities had been developed, enabling busier plots and some striking visual effects.[2]

*Persians* is the most straightforward play, because it is the only one that is self-contained, and not part of a linked or sequential trilogy; its dramatic premiss is fully worked out, and its issues resolved. *Suppliants* is the first play of a trilogy, the rest of which has almost wholly

---

[1] For surveys of Aeschylus' career, see Rosenmeyer, AA 369–76 (with good references to earlier treatments); Sommerstein, AT 13–32; and in *Oxford Classical Dictionary*, 3rd edn. (1997), 26–9.

[2] It is a frustrating aspect of Greek Tragedy's survival that the early careers of all three of its great poets are unrepresented except in fragments; few things would be more illuminating than the recovery of one at least of Aeschylus' very earliest plays, especially since Aristotle in his *Poetics*, ch. 4 records that he raised the number of speaking actors from one to two (a major step in Tragedy's development). I discuss most aspects of the individual plays, including the theatrical, in Section 2 below, and their compositional elements in Section 3. I handle *Prometheus*, which I follow most scholars in believing not to be a fully authentic work by Aeschylus, mainly in Section 2.4, and incidentally elsewhere.

disappeared but can be guessed in very broad outline; it completes the first stage in a long action, and increasingly points forward to the remainder, provoking questions and anxieties for the characters as well as for the audience. *Seven*, probably a little earlier than *Suppliants*, is the final play of its trilogy, and the near total loss of the two earlier plays makes appreciation of it more difficult, for we cannot know well enough how far it depended upon or alluded to them. It is inevitable that Aeschylus' one complete trilogy, the *Oresteia*, should influence appreciation of both *Suppliants* and *Seven*, because its techniques of continuing plot, characters, and issues are wholly visible; and yet the *Oresteia*'s own skilfully varied dramatic economy simultaneously invites assumptions about these earlier plays which may be unsafe (see Introd. 2.2 and 3).

*Suppliants* and *Seven* are therefore semi-detached, like the first and last houses in a terrace of three; yet they are as satisfying structurally and emotionally as the wholly detached *Persians*. In this play the outcome is already determined and wholly outside the characters' control, and at first also their knowledge; anxiety and supernaturally aided foreboding are swiftly confirmed by report of the disaster, before it receives supernatural explanation by Darius' ghost and its full tragedy is revealed in the play's lamentation-filled ending. The outcome of *Seven* too is foreseen, and almost certainly predetermined, in the events of its trilogy's first two plays, but this is more than a play of inexorable situation; its protagonist fears a double catastrophe, to his city and to his own life, but in trying to avoid the first helplessly brings on the second. Their full causes and meaning are exposed only in the last third of the play, which in this respect has roughly the same proportions as *Persians*; the exposure in *Seven* is through the recollections and reflections of the Chorus, who recapitulate events from the trilogy's first two plays, rather than through supernatural interpretation, but the endings have similar style, climactic and exhaustive lament. *Persians* and *Seven* are plays which act out the strains of gradual realization and bitter acceptance. In *Suppliants* there is an initial threat of disaster, but also hope and a way for its avoidance through effort; and when the threat becomes physical danger, enough has been done to survive it (at least for this first play of the trilogy). The tension here is different from that of *Seven*, because the suppliants are not fighting the inevitable (as is the protagonist of *Seven*), and they are arguing their case, and arguing it face to face with a potential saviour.

The *Suppliants* can hope, while the characters of *Persians* and *Seven* for the most part can only fear; and these suffer within their plays' limits. Yet enough is hinted in *Suppliants* that the feared suffering will later become reality, whether or not as the result of human weakness or wrongdoing, or because Aeschylus adds to those the predetermination by god which is visible in *Persians* but overpowering in *Seven* and, even more clearly, in the *Oresteia*. The sufferings of the *Seven* and *Oresteia* are extreme, the imminent annihilation of a family's male line—extreme, but right, given their self-destructive tendency to do wrong, even if their responsibility can seem ambiguous. The danger may appear to be the same in the *Suppliants* trilogy, if the conflict between the two sides of the family in the first play led to bloodshed in the subsequent two, as other mythography told. The outcome is right too in *Persians*, where maximum offence to the natural constraints upon human power earns maximum catastrophe from the gods. The majesty of the Persian empire is humiliated, the Theban royal line in *Seven* is extinguished: here are bleak, logical finalities. In the *Oresteia* the royal line survives, through combined human and divine justice, but only because the gods relent; the message repeated throughout the trilogy is 'The doer suffers—and learns' (*Agamemnon* 177, 250, etc., *LB* 313, 1009, *Eum.* 520–1). Knowledge thus won is meaningless, however, unless it embodies understanding and acceptance: this is the implication of *Persians* 827–31, 904–5 and *Seven* 719, 743–4 (with which compare *Agamemnon* 1485–8, 1562–4).[3]

These patterns of punishment by the gods in Aeschylus repeat those of earlier Greek epic poets, Homer and Hesiod especially. Order or 'justice' in the gods' own closed and immortal world is largely the same as in that of mortal men: anything is punished that threatens the stability of house and family under their ruling heads, divine or human, and among men endangers their broader society, either within communities or between countries. Man must learn, observe, and safeguard the laws of gods and men which control all conduct. He may implement or attempt his own or society's justice, but he knows that he does so under the just eye of Zeus himself, supreme

---

[3] On these issues, see Collard (2002), pp. xxxviii–xlii.

among the gods as he is over all mortal existence (in *Suppliants* alone
see this prominence for Zeus at e.g. 1, 26, 139, 402–6, 437, 478–9,
627–9, 671–3). In this knowledge man recognizes Zeus' justice when
he suffers it (e.g. *Pers.* 739–42, 827–31, and the passages from the
*Oresteia* cited above), and regularly invokes it in his cause. In *Seven*
the gods and especially Zeus are invoked to save the besieged city
(8–9, 69–72, 116–19, 265–79; Zeus e.g. 301–3, 485, 520, 614, 630)—
which they do, and are acknowledged (823–5); but the invocation is
against a godless and unjust attack, recognized as such by one of the
attackers himself, the seer Amphiaraus (580–6), and condemned by
the defender Eteocles (414–16, 590–614, 662–71). There has been a
much grimmer invocation of supernatural powers in the city's past,
however: Oedipus' prayer-curse upon his sons (first mentioned in
this play at 70). The curse leads to their mutual fratricide and to the
extinction of the family's male line; it is the special work of the Fury
(700, 791; Greek *Erinus*), as in the *Oresteia* (*Ag.* 992, 1190, etc.)—
indeed Curse and Fury are equated at *Seven* 70 as in *Eumenides* 417.
Oedipus pronounced his curse in consciousness of his own transgressions, parricide and incest, although he committed both in ignorance,
and of his father Laius' disobedience of the god Apollo in fathering
him at all (741–57, 779–91: see Introd. 2.2). So men's offences draw
sure punishment by the gods, inexorable if delayed (*Seven* 744–5,
766–7, 840–2, cf. *Ag.* 59, *LB* 383). In *Suppliants* Zeus is called upon to
uphold the principles of sanctuary and supplication which are prized
by both god and man (83–5, 190, 347, etc.) and to protect his own
descendants from persecution (40–6, 206, 527–8, etc.). Punishment,
or retaliation for defiance of Zeus, dominates the *Prometheus*, but
upon god by god for an offence confined among the gods (PB 8–9,
29–30, 37, 92, etc.). Zeus punished this harshly, and made justice his
own possession (187): so the play can be read as a drama of absolute
power abused, rather than as a tragedy, with this first obvious
implication for human morality, and a second in the sympathy
shown towards Prometheus for his benefits to mankind, and towards
the wretched mortal Io, victim of both Zeus and his wife Hera.[4]

---

[4] On the gods in Aeschylus, see esp. H. Lloyd-Jones, *The Justice of Zeus* (1983[2]),
79–103; and (Bibl. §7.4, 2003); Rosenmeyer, *AA* 259–83; Sommerstein, *AT* 355–91;
Sourvinou-Inwood (§6, 2003) 201–63; S. Said in Gregory, *CGT* 223–6. For dreams,
oracles, and divination as intimations of the gods' will, see n. 14 below.

Greek tragic drama is set in the world of myth, and the tragedians' success depended largely upon their individual representations of it and upon the fresh meaning they gave it for their contemporaries. Euripides was the most varied, both benign and harsh in his view of man's condition under god; Sophocles in some plays, such as *Women of Trachis* and *Oedipus the King*, was even bleaker than Aeschylus in *Seven* and the greater part of the *Oresteia*. It is very difficult to see much of the poets' individual personalities behind the plays; ancient biographical anecdote and interpretation were based mostly on the play texts themselves, and we risk the same danger from incautious inference. For Aeschylus, however, we can have a certain confidence in linking the poet in his particular time with one marked aspect of his plays: their patriotic and political dimension. First, one of the firmest traditions about him was his pride in having himself fought against the Persian invaders of Greece, certainly at Marathon in 490 and possibly also at Salamis in 480; an epigram composed for his tomb in Sicily commemorated him only for this, not for his tragedies.[5] Second, there is *Persians* itself, the only tragedy with a basis in history not myth. The choice of this play subject, seven or eight years, but not immediately, after the historical event, is evidence enough of Aeschylus' public voice upon the greatest issue of his day (see Introd. 2.1). Similarly, in *Eumenides*, the last play of the *Oresteia*, he 'changed' the myth to 'invent' history, when he moved the trilogy's climax from Orestes' Argos to his own Athens, and had Orestes judged by a jury court of its citizens, established by Athens' patron-goddess; at the same time he maintained the supreme control of the family's fate by Zeus and the gods which he had set out forcibly at the trilogy's start. Here he was lending art's support to the contemporary liberalization—or 'democratization'—of Athenian justice.[6]

[5]     'At Gela, rich in wheat, he died, and lies beneath this stone:
        Aeschylus the Athenian, son of Euphorion.
        His valour, tried and proved, the mead of Marathon can tell;
        The long-haired Persian also, who knows it all too well.'

The ancient *Life of Aeschylus* 11 = T 162 in *Tragicorum Graecorum Fragmenta* 4, p. 107, as translated by Sommerstein, *AT* 24. The ancient attribution to Aeschylus himself is questionable.

[6]   For the *Oresteia* and contemporary Athenian politics, see Collard (2002), pp. xv–xx, and the bibliography cited there; add Pelling (Bibl. §.5, 1997), 167–88.

Third, there is the character of Argos' government in *Suppliants*: its king Pelasgus resembles a constitutional monarch, much in the style of King Theseus, the mythical founder of Athenian democracy (see the EN on *Supp.* 963, and Introd. 2.3). The apparent 'anachronism' is more striking precisely because Argos is not Athens, and Pelasgus is not Theseus. Even though the historical Argos of the mid-fifth century had a form of communal rather than fully democratic government, Aeschylus may well have styled his Argos and Pelasgus this way to put a contemporary political slant upon the timeless moralities of saving refugees from violence—and to offer support to Argos' government (compare the allusion to the historical Athens–Argos alliance of about the same time in lines 289–92 and 754–74 of *Eumenides*). In *Seven* too there is a distinctive portrayal of the Theban king, and his conscientious duty to the safety of all his people amid his preoccupation with his own.

These three early plays differ much from one another in matter and manner; but they have individually many features of dramaturgy, theatre, thought, and language which foreshadow the mature mastery of the *Oresteia*. By then, Aeschylus had developed and combined them to achieve a consistent grandeur of expression and a profundity of meaning at which only *Seven* of these early plays really hints.

## 2. THE PLAYS IN THIS VOLUME

### 2.1. Persians

[For a summary of the action, see p. xi. In this Section 2.1 all references to the Bibliography are to §7.1 unless stated.]

The *Persians* of 472 BC is the only surviving 'historical' Greek tragedy, but we know of at least two others inspired by the Greek–Persian conflicts of 500–480; both were by Aeschylus' approximate contemporary Phrynichus.[7] In his *Capture of Miletus* Phrynichus had

---

[7] *Capture of Miletus* (or *Persians*: title uncertain), which dramatized the Persians' sack of this place in Ionian Greek Asia Minor in 494 and was probably produced in the late 490s; it so distressed the Athenians that they fined Phrynichus and forbade reperformance (Herodotus 6.21). Aeschylus alludes in *Persians* to the subjection of Ionia, ll. 880–900; the Greeks at Salamis collectively fight above all to keep their freedom, 402–5. Also, Phrynichus' *Phoenician Women*, which had an Eastern setting and dramatized King Xerxes' defeat in 480, is recorded as having been adapted by Aeschylus for *Persians* (see also EN on l. 1); it was produced in 476 and financed by

made a Greek defeat into a Greek tragic drama; Aeschylus 'mythologized' history in *Persians*. He commemorated a Greek victory as extraordinary as the Persian attack had been unprecedentedly dangerous, in the triumph of a smaller, disciplined, and skilled force over huge numbers; but he represented the defeat of Persia entirely through the fears and distraught reaction of Persian characters. At the same time he was recreating history in a way vivid to the Greeks' and especially the Athenians' own remembered experience, and suggestive to their present imagination. Furthermore, *Persians* is almost certainly the earliest surviving tragedy of all; and it differs importantly from Aeschylus' other complete plays, all five of which were part of connected trilogies.[8]

The major interpretative issues it raises are the mingling of the factual and the contemporary with the universal (in this respect not unlike Aeschylus' later *Eumenides*); for the historian proper, the play's value as evidence;[9] and Aeschylus' antipathy (or sympathy) towards the Greeks' great enemy before and after the Persian defeat.

An important thing to note is the interval of seven years between the historical events and the play's production.[10] While the drama is one of retrospect, hostilities between Greece and Persia continued after 480, and the Athenians had inspired, and now in 472 led, a

Themistocles, the great Athenian commander against Persia in 480 (as had been the *Capture*).

[8] For the plays which accompanied *Persians* in 472, see the ancient *hypothesis* on p. 130.

[9] The play's historical accuracy can here be treated only in passing. There are summary reviews by Broadhead and Hall in their commentaries (Bibl. §3.2, 1960 and 1988), and detailed analysis of the battle of Salamis itself, especially through comparison with Herodotus and other ancient historians, most recently by Lazenby (1988) and Wallinga (2005): see Map 3 (p. xcii). The Persians named in the play are considered by Ebbott (2000), and the whole historical and contemporary background by Sommerstein, *AT* 410–13 and, most widely, Harrison (2000); cf. also S. Said in Gregory, *CGT* 220–2 and P. Debnar, ibid. 7–9. Aeschylus omits mention of the earlier battles of 480, Artemision (sea: Greek defeat) and Thermopylae (land: Greek defeat); and he times Xerxes' return to Persia before its final defeat at sea at Mycale (479), also unmentioned; but the land-defeat at Plataea (also 479) is 'forecast' by Darius (l. 817; see EN on 681–851). For Aeschylus' knowledge of past Persian kings, and comparison with that of Herodotus and with the historical king Darius' own inscriptional record of them, see EN on 765–79.

[10] See esp. Pelling (1997), 9–13.

defensive alliance of Aegean cities.[11] Despite its great defeat, Persia remained a great danger, and still occupied much of Ionia. Recent scholars in particular find an ideological purpose within the play which accords with this political time and need: to confirm Greek, and especially Athenian, superiority over an arrogant, aggressive, and culturally inferior foe. There is debate whether a seeming emphasis upon the Athenians as Persia's ancient and dangerous enemy (231–45, cf. 348–9, 473–5, 716, 824, 976) and upon their tactics and skill at Salamis (285), is unfair to the united Greek effort. In the other direction, the Greeks' ruse before Salamis, to split the Persian fleet, is known to have originated with the Athenian Themistocles (Herodotus 8.75–6), but Aeschylus attributes it to an anonymous Greek from the Athenian fleet (355–62); and the gods give victory to the Greeks collectively (454–5—as Persia's opponents are consistently named throughout 338–452). Scholars write of ethnic 'stereotyping', which contrasts Greek moderation with 'Oriental' extravagance, and collective and disciplined organization with individual, instant authority. The Persians are shown as preoccupied with wealth and its acquisition (4, 163–4, 250, 252, 709, 755, 826—but they speak defensively of it at 168, 842). They are uncontrolled in its enjoyment (543), so that when riches and lives are lost they collapse into excessive, unmanly grief, both their women (135, 541) and their men (1072, cf. EN on 943). The long, antiphonal lament which the Chorus of elders and Xerxes share (908–077; see EN) becomes ever more extreme in a form of grief which the Greeks accepted principally from their women alone (e.g. at *Seven* 874–1004).[12] And yet: the play is no less a retrospective tragedy, because everything is presented as the defeated Persians perceived it. The Greek victory shines brightly at first, and the Messenger observes Xerxes' failure to foresee deception or disaster (361, 372–3, 454). Aeschylus, however, from the start shows Persian fear of the human cost (93–137, the end of the Chorus' entry-song) and its anguished realization (249—330, etc.); he

[11] The Delian League (a modern name), dependent originally upon mutual support by sea; Athens' natural hegemony after Salamis soon became what was perceived as its 'empire', Thucydides 1.96, cf. 97.2, 118.2, etc.

[12] For such cultural polarities in the play, see esp. Hall (Bibl. §3.2, 1988), 5–6 and (1989), esp. 76–98; Goldhill (1988); Pelling (1997), 13–19; Harrison (2000); all with further literature.

qualifies disparagement of the Persians with sympathy, stirring pity that they suffer and grieve so immoderately. Critics are torn between resistance to this plain implication of the play text, and recognition that pity is intrinsic to tragedy as one of Aristotle's chief postulates for it (*Poetics* ch. 6).[13]

The victory of the heavily outnumbered Greeks (337–44) indeed shines, on a day of appropriately brilliant sunlight (386–7; see the end of this Section 2.1, at n. 22). They deceive the Persians into splitting their fleet, anticipate Persian plans to deny them safety on land, and deploy and move their ships with boldness and superior skill (355–464). The Persians expect victory from their mere numbers (341–4, cf. 89–92), but their mass prevents responsive manoeuvring (412–6); they obey an absolute king (369–71), initially with sound discipline (377–83), but quickly lose self-control in defeat (423)— as does Xerxes himself (468–70). Their consequent disorder lasts into the army's land-retreat (481), compounding its destruction in a land and climate hostile by nature to invaders (480–512). Xerxes' misguided campaign has been faulty throughout, and until Darius appears this appears to be the only explanation of the disaster. It has been pointed out that Xerxes' conduct illustrates Aristotle's doctrine of the fatal 'error' which precipitates tragedy (*hamartia*: the Greek word-root in fact occurs at 677, unfortunately in a badly corrupt text, immediately before Darius appears with his deeper explanation).

Extremes mark the Persians, not merely in their wealth and its enjoyment (above), their vast numbers (8–133, 337–44, etc.) and the immensity of their losses (251–5, 721, 728–32, 1014–15), but earlier in their aspirations for the widest possible conquest, both in their campaign against Greece (75, 102–7) and historically elsewhere (762–4). Xerxes' father Darius was hugely successful (852–902) and Aeschylus has the Persian mourners gloss over his defeats (652–6, 662, 722–5, 780–1, 855, etc.: see EN), even that by the Athenians at Marathon in 490 BC (474–5, cf. 236, 244). He may have wished to emphasize the supreme Athenian contribution to Salamis over the more distant and collective Greek victory (above); his clear intention is to make the son's disaster so far beyond Persian precedent (782–6), and so in contrast with the father's achievements, that Darius

---

[13]  See S. D. Goldhill's review of Harrison (2000) at *Classical Review*, 51 (2001), 10.

responds by spelling out what has been implicit before the news of disaster comes. Xerxes had succumbed to reproach for cowardice and failure to increase his father's wealth, the Queen first tells Darius (753–8), but then became 'furious for war' (718, 754, cf. the Chorus earlier at 74) and overconfident in his numbers (352); he wished above all to punish Athens (473–4). Darius explains that the rashness of youth drove Xerxes to defy the gods (744); it was a 'disorder of the mind' (750–1; cf. EN on 722–5) which brought him to offend them by bridging their 'sacred' Hellespont and so 'enslaving' it (745–6: contrast the Chorus' earlier pride in this feat, 65–73). Another folly was the Persians' subsequent sacrilege in Greece (808–12, 831). Such extreme arrogance towards heaven has brought its inevitable punishment in ruin (821–3, 827; cf. Introd. 1 above, p. xviii), in the most shattering form for Persia's royalty, damage and loss to its great wealth (751, 826, cf. 163–4, 251–2). Persia's fortunes are inseparable throughout from those of its royalty. Anxiety for Xerxes individually begins the play (5–12, 144–9, 176–214); when the Queen is advised to seek Darius' help against her dream (215–25: see n. 14), her departure and return to hear his explanation are contrived (521–31, 598–626), so that the mother's concern for her son may be shared with the father (733–8). She does not, however, return in time to meet Xerxes, despite her intention (849–51, cf. 834 and the 'stage-direction' at 852), so that her son's misery in his isolation is total (1000–1, 1025; cf. 734). The contrast between the son's disaster and the father's unfailing success (above) has begun to dominate the play (548–57, 619–786, 852). Xerxes' almost first, broken words on return are an acknowledgement of the harm he has done to his country (932–3); in his grief, however, he is distressed as much by the misery he has dealt himself (908–10, 932, 943), signalled by the loss of retinue and by his now tattered garments (1019–37: see EN on 198–9). It is a selfishness which bears out his mother's intense concern for him from the start (168–9, 211–14, 299–300, 473–7, 529–31) and her shame for his impaired dignity— which Darius shares (832–8 before her 846–51).

Darius' explanation, the offence to heaven, appears to match the Persians' earlier and immediate attribution of the disaster to a 'divine power' which tilted things the Greeks' way (346, cf. 282–3, 294, 354, 373, 454–5, 472–3, 514, 515); the gods' support of the Greeks is perhaps implied in the naming of Pan as the deity inhabiting Salamis

(449). From the start the Chorus have mixed their expectation of
Xerxes' success with anxiety that a god too often deceives men's
hopes (93–100, cf. 10). The Queen later speaks of a 'god' cooperating
with Xerxes' wrong purpose (724–5, repeated by Darius at 742), and
Xerxes names one too (911, 921, cf. the Chorus at 1005). The gods
are also seen working through the Queen's dream that Xerxes may be
thrown by a Greek chariot-horse (181–99) and through the following
omen of an eagle attacked by a smaller hawk (205–10). Darius links
the disaster with an old oracle predicting defeat for Persia (739–
41, 800–2)—he means, the disaster was long foreseen, and perhaps
brought about, by the gods.[14] There is a gulf, moreover, between
simple attribution by the Chorus, the Queen, and the Messenger to
a malignant, hateful deity (354, 472, 515) and the reasoned combination of human fallibility and divine punishment which Darius
offers as explanation (725, 742–51, 782–3, 808, 820–8). He identifies
an older and deeper involvement by the gods which anticipates the
manner of *Seven* and *Oresteia*.[15]

   The play may seem largely static; and its even proportions help
to express its measured emotional progression: fearful, disbeliev-
ing anticipation, culminating in the Queen's dream and anxious
questions about Athens' power (1–245); confirmation of disaster
(246–531); lamenting and searching for explanation and comfort

---

[14] Dreams and oracles in Tragedy are usually omens of certain disaster; cf. esp.
Clytemnestra in *LB* 32–41, 523–53, who tries to avert fulfilment of her dream, that
she will be killed by her son Orestes in vengeance for his father Agamemnon, with
offerings to her dead husband (44–8, 84–163, etc.), just as in *Persians* the Queen
is invited to invoke the dead Darius' aid (215–25). With her bitter realization of
her failure at *Pers.* 518–19, cf. Clytemnestra's at *LB* 928–9. Io's dream at *PB* 645–57
portends no disaster, although its inevitable fulfilment has that outcome. A vague
dream of disputed interpretative importance is found at *Seven* 710 (see EN and n. 25
below).
   Other intimations of the gods' will are given through oracles, consultation of seers,
and divination (*Seven* 24, 230–1, 379, etc.; *Supp.* 450; *PB* 484–99). Darius does not
state the motive for the Persian oracles, but at *Seven* 618 the seer Amphiaraus has
consulted his patron god Apollo when he misgives the attack upon Thebes. Laius
sought, and then disobeyed, Apollo's guidance, *Seven* 747. Io's father had to consult
many oracles after her dream—and this difficulty was itself ominous, *PB* 658–72.
[15] Aeschylus has Darius uses the word arrogance (Greek *hybris*) of Xerxes' and the
Persians' conduct, 808, 821, cf. 820, 827–8; see esp. Winnington-Ingram (1983), 8–13.
The word's confinement to the Darius scene has been stressed by Garvie (1999), 30–4;
but Conacher (1996), 6 n. 7 and 24–6 sees it as consistent with the general morality of
Aeschylean drama, crystallized in *Ag.* 750–72. See Introd. 1 above, pp. xviii–xix.

(532–851); renewed, climactic lament (852–1077). The first three parts accumulate linked revelations: the Queen's dream (176–214); the Messenger's reports (349–514); Darius' explanation and prophecies (739–831); only grief can follow.[16] The play is nevertheless strongly visual and theatrical.[17] It calls for exotic costuming. All the individual characters make striking entrances and exits (the Queen twice); there is the Queen's initial entrance in a carriage, and then her sombre reappearance on foot and alone (EN on 607–8). The ritual summoning-up of Darius' ghost is vividly effective.[18] The contrast between the luxury, the spectacle, and the ostentatious catalogues of Persian might, with which the play begins, and Xerxes' humiliation at its end, is complete; spectators and readers may, however, wonder whether his self-pity (above) impairs the pathos of collective tragedy.[19]

The play's language is aptly varied. It is sonorous and often exotic when describing the majesty and numbers of the Persian forces, especially in the Chorus' entry-song (1–139), in the roll-calls of their commanders both alive (21–53) and dead (302–28, 967–1001), and in the catalogue of Darius' conquests and tributaries (865–902). It also conveys extremes of distress and despair in the laments (548–83, 931–1077). All of those passages (except 302–28) are lyric, enhanced in the original by appropriate metre: solemn or elevated for much of the majesty paraded (65–101) and in imagining the deaths at sea (568–97), as elsewhere for the ritual summoning-up of Darius (633–72) and evocation of his conquests (852–907). The final lament (908–1077), despite its apparently uncontrolled emotion and extraordinary antiphonal effects, employs chiefly the much less complex metre characteristic of such scenes elsewhere (as in *Seven* 874–1004,

[16] Cf. Michelini (1982), 72. Adams (1952) uses the analogy of a symphony for these three 'movements'. Other analyses of the play's structure, esp. built-in pointers to the disaster such as the intimation of deceit by the gods as early as 99–100, are examined by Conacher (1996), 15–16 and (the Chorus' prime function of articulating the tragedy), 160.

[17] A point well made by Hall (Bibl. §3.2, 1988), 30.

[18] How Darius' appearance was realized in the ancient theatre is discussed in Introd. 2.5 and EN on 623. This omniscient voice from the grave, in probably the earliest surviving Greek tragedy, inverts the function of gods 'on high' in many later ones, especially of Euripides; see Rehm (Bibl. §5, 2002), 246, citing Broadhead (§3.2, 1960), pp. xxviii–ix. For ghosts in Tragedy, see EN on *Pers.* 681–851.

[19] On these last points, see Clifton (1963) and Said (1988).

for example).[20] Very colourful too, but often marked by precise order-
ing of detail, are the narratives of the Messenger (353–514: see EN on
290–514) and of Darius (759–838); more deliberate in language are
the Queen's longer speeches (176–214, 517–31, 598–622). There are
only two intense dialogues in stichomythic form, but they are of the
greatest importance: the Queen's apprehensive interrogation of the
Chorus about Athens after her dream (226–48; see EN) and Darius'
questions to her about the disaster he has been summoned to explain
(715–38); both are set, moreover, in scenes which use the rarer dialogue metre, apparently expressive of urgency, trochaic tetrameters.[21]

   Amid the rich language some uncomplicated images and repetitions of vocabulary stand out (for the role of imagery in Aeschylus
generally, see Introd. 3.4. below). Insistence on the Persian intention
to yoke the Greeks into slavery (50; cf. 242) immediately precedes
the literal yoking of the Hellespont (72, 130); and the Greeks' triumph in thwarting the first enslavement is reported before Darius
explains the gods' hand in punishing the second, an 'enslavement'
of their own 'sacred' Hellespont (745–6, cf. 722–5 and above). Note
too the Queen's dream at 196, when Xerxes' chariot-yoke, broken by
the Greek horse, symbolizes the larger disaster to come; so too her
omen at 205–10 when an eagle is overcome by a smaller hawk. There
is repeated emphasis on the multitudinous Persian fleet and army
(126–9 they swarm like bees, 434–6 they are like a catch of tunny-fish
beaten to death); many bare words for 'mass' occur (20, 366, 413, etc.)
which magnify the enormous loss both of men (272, 329–30 ending
the catalogue of 302–28, 431–2, 435–43, 508–10, 729–33, 800–3, etc.)
and of huge wealth (250–2, 751–2, 826, etc.). The reports of Salamis
are articulated by the day–night–day progress of the battle;[22] the sun
shines brightly for the Greek victory (386–7), just as later it melts the
ice to cause the Persians' further loss of men (502–5). The Queen is
the dominant and unifying figure of the play: images of motherhood
and loss are appropriately frequent in her words.

[20] For these metres in *Persians* and other plays, see EN on *Pers.* 65, 532–97, 623–80,
852–907; for *Pers.* 908–1077 see EN on *Seven* 822–1004; cf. also n. 61 below.
   [21] Tetrameters are studied for *Persians* by Michelini (1982), 41–64; see also Section
3.2 and EN on 155–531.
   [22] See esp. Pelling (1997), 2–5. For the narrative strategies designed by Aeschylus
to give the Messenger's reports transparency and authority, see Barrett (1995 = 2002).

2.2. Seven against Thebes

[For a summary of the action, see p. xii. In this Section 2.2 all references to the Bibliography are to §7.2 unless stated.]

An ancient record (see the start of EN, p. 160) states that *Seven* was the third play of a trilogy which began with *Laius* and *Oedipus*. These first two plays, which are lost, dealt, it is safe to say, with the tragedy of Laius, who defied Apollo's oracle that any child he had would kill him (*Seven* 741–9); but he fathered one. This was Oedipus, whom Laius then exposed but who was saved and grew up elsewhere, and in ignorance of his identity killed his father and had children by his mother (750–7). His later self-discovery and hideous realization brought him to curse his own two sons, that they should divide their inheritance, the kingdom of Thebes, with the sword (778–91). The *Laius* took these events as far as Oedipus' killing of his father, the *Oedipus* as far as the cursing; they are recapitulated in the third play by the Chorus at the places given; but this is only after fulfilment of the curse by Oedipus' son Eteocles has become inevitable, through his decision to duel with his brother Polynices (712–19). Further recapitulation and comment follow news of the mutual fratricide (822–47; see also the Chorus at 893–936).[23]

The problem for us is to judge Eteocles' path towards his decision in the first two-thirds of the play (1–719). At its start Aeschylus shows him aware of the curse (70), but it then goes unmentioned while he plans the city's defence, and appoints seven champions, including himself, at its gates (282–4: see EN, and on the 'Shield-Scene' 369–676).[24] When he learns that the seventh attacker will be

---

[23] In the choral ode 720–91, ll. 734–57 link Oedipus' parricide and incest (also 779, 782–3) with the ancient transgression of Laius (744) in fathering a son despite Apollo's oracle that his own and Thebes' safety depended on his obedience (745–9, cf. 800–2); 744–5 state that the ' penalty ... remains to the third generation'—the generation of Eteocles and Polynices. Eteocles' statement of the gods' hatred for the family (653) and of Apollo's (691, cf. EN) appears to relate only to this defiance by Laius. Mentions of the curse surround this central passage (724–6, 766, 785–7), but Oedipus' immediate motive is given as 'anger they had not sustained him' (786 and EN). There is no hint in *Seven*, and we know nothing of the *Laius* and *Oedipus*, that the whole family had been accursed since Laius' own lifetime: in some later mythography Pelops had cursed Laius for the rape of his son Chrysippus (see EN on 689–91, and Lloyd-Jones, Bibl. §2 [2005], 33).

[24] It is a mistake to find allusions to the curse when the Chorus address Eteocles with the formula 'son of Oedipus' (205, 372; they use it later, too, at 677), and in

Polynices, who positively wishes to fight him (632–8), it seems certain that Eteocles will instantly name himself as his brother's opponent. Instead, Aeschylus has him burst out with a recall of the curse, in realization of its fulfilment (653–5): 'Oh, the family of Oedipus, and mine, maddened by the gods, and their great detestation, and all the tears to shed for it! Oh, alas for me, now my father's curses are brought to fulfilment!'

Here Aeschylus at last works the power of the curse into the overriding duty to defend Thebes which has pressed upon Eteocles since the play began. He states it himself (1–9), together with his determination to exercise command (20, 196–200, 224–5); the Scout confirms it as his duty (62–4, 650–2); the Chorus rely on it when they accept obedience to him (260–3, cf. 287). His obligations are to organize the stoutest defence (10–20, 30–5); to learn the attackers' plans (24–9, 36–8) and later oppose them (200–1, 282–4, 369–676); to quell the inhabitants' panic, which the Chorus embody at its extreme (182–202, 232, 237–8, 285–6); to keep the support of the city's gods by prayer and sacrifice (14–15, 271–9), in which he orders the Chorus to join (265–70). All this he does.

It is this sense of duty to his native city which carries Eteocles forward into the duel with his brother. It combines with the curse in forming the resolve he makes in his speech at 653–76. In 659–71 he rejects Polynices' claim upon the goddess Justice who is the emblem on his shield (645–8; cf. 659–61): she never has allied herself, and will not now, with a well-named 'man of strife' (658: see EN on 576–8), a demented and reckless invader (661, 671) of his native land (668): 'Of this I am confident, and I will stand against him myself: who else can do so more justly? Leader against leader and brother against brother, enemy against enemy, I will take my stand' (672–5). There is, however, no further mention of the curse in this speech after its opening lines 653–5: that comes when the Chorus in response warn him against

the mention of the Sphinx at 540 (which Oedipus had overcome, 775–7); similarly in Eteocles' own words at 415 when he refers to 'the justice of blood-kin' which drives the Theban defender Melanippus forward (cf. the Justice to which both Polynices and Eteocles appeal, 646, 667, and the horror of their mutual slaughter evoked by the Chorus at 681, 940); also, in the unrelated 'Fury' of 574 (see EN).

For the problematic implication of ll. 282–4 see EN there and on 369–716 (1) at end. The best discussions and help are in Sommerstein, *AT* 104–6 and Conacher (1996), 65–8.

the pollution of kin-killing (681–2). His determination nevertheless to avoid the shame of failing his city (683–5) brings them to charge him with a mad, ruinous lust for blood (686–8); the madness recalls that of the curse, 653, with 725 and 780–7 to follow, and the wildness of Polynices, 671. His reply voices again (but for the first time fully) the gods' irresistible will for his family, its destruction (689–91; again, cf. 653–5 and the earlier 69–72), and the compulsion of the curse (695–7). The Chorus try to deter him from fulfilling it (698–701, 705–8); but just as the gods are implacable (702–4) and his dreams how his father's goods will be divided are now all too clear (709–11), so he is inflexible in his soldier's duty (715, 717). Above all, the gods have abandoned him; they require his death (702–3); their will is inescapable (719, recalling both 689 and 702).[25]

The gods are present throughout the play. Their statues may have been visible in the theatre, for the Chorus cling to them (99, 211–12). Their ultimate determination of fortune is repeatedly stressed by the besieged Thebans (4, 23, 35, 217, 226–9, etc.); worship and protection of their shrines are necessary if they are in turn to protect the city (14–15, 70–7, 85–181 repeatedly, 211–35, 253–5, 266–79, etc.); in the outcome, joy mixes with sorrow that the gods save the city at the cost of its now extinguished royal line (814–17, 822–8). Both sides in the siege depend upon divine favour, which they consult through seers (Thebans 24–9; attackers 42, cf. 378–83) or try to wrest to their advantage (Thebans 402–6, 609–11; attackers 639–41—or discount, 427–9, 469), or resignedly find to be against them (Thebans 808, Amphiaraus the attackers' seer 587–91, on whom see below). In fact almost all the attackers except Amphiaraus dishonour the gods (EN on 596).

The heart of the play's structure and meaning lies in the 'Shield-Scene' (369–719) which achieves considerable tension before its

---

[25] For a most persuasive exposition of how Eteocles's deep sense of the duty to which he had bound himself combines with the irresistible working of the curse, see Long (1986). Others too have combated the older view that Eteocles' decision to fight his brother, or his 'self-sacrifice' to save his city, is predetermined by the gods or fate; Conacher (1996), 69–70 analyses the history of this discussion. In other readings of this crisis, the significance of Eteocles' dream about his inheritance when he suddenly realizes its implication (710–11) can be overstated; some readers contrast the man of patriotic duty in 1–652 with the man in fatalist despair at 653; 'fatalism' is an interpretation shared by Sommerstein, *AT* 109–15.

climax in the sequence 631–719. The Scout's first entry at 39, when
Eteocles must face the imminent attack, gives much greater importance to his second entry at 369, when his successive reports bring
Eteocles to the limit of his duty as defender and to his destiny as
accursed son and brother. The early mention of the curse (69–72)—
which the audience would remember from the preceding *Oedipus*—
sets them to fear the outcome once Eteocles announces that he will
himself be one of the defenders (282; see EN on 282–6). Then, Eteocles reveals their names, each particularly appropriate to the attackers
as the Scout sketches them; Eteocles' choices serve only to aid the
closing of the trap as he postpones naming himself.[26] Aeschylus' art
makes the sixth attacker the brave and wise seer but reluctant com-
batant Amphiaraus (568–96), the only good man caught up among
bad (Eteocles at 597–619); he is the only attacker whose shield bears
no device at all, let alone an arrogant one (EN on 591–4, 595–6). How
could Eteocles post himself against such a man? Instead, he appoints a
plain, valiant defender to oppose Amphiaraus' bravery (616, cf. 569,
592). The placing of this sixth pair of speeches, with its distinctive
and doomed attacker, foreshadows the imminent catastrophe of both
the reckless Polynices and the disciplined Eteocles. Also, Amphiaraus
condemns not only Tydeus on his own side (571–4) but, more importantly, Polynices for attacking his native city (576–86), precisely the
intention Polynices will claim as just (639–48) and Eteocles will con-
demn as unjust (660–71). Implicitly, it seems, Eteocles sympathizes
with a good man caught in an inescapable fate. Amphiaraus knows of
his doom, and will fall as a soldier should (587–9; cf. 617); Eteocles
too will soon himself resolve to fight honourably in accepting his own
doom (683–5, 704, 715, 717: above).[27]

The effect and meaning of the 'Shield-Scene' are increased by the
two scenes of 'persuasion' which bracket it. In the first (182–286) the
safety of the city is the issue and in the second (677–719) that of Eteocles. Eteocles quells the Chorus' damaging panic, contemptuously

[26]  For this effect, see esp. Roisman (1990).

[27]  This special function of Amphiaraus was set out fully by the French scholar A.
Moreau in *Bulletin ... Association ... G. Budé* (1976), 158–81. I offer a fuller analysis
of the Shield Scene in EN on 369–719. Some extremely complex and improbable
interpretations of the shield devices have been offered, first by Vidal Naquet (1981):
see the criticisms by Hutchinson (§3.2, 1985), 106 and Conacher (1996), 49 n. 29.

at first (182–202) and then more methodically but still impatiently (250–63 after 202–49), before he associates them with his prayers for the city; in the second scene the Chorus attempt, but fail, to dissuade him from the duel (677–719). The gender-roles are surprisingly reversed. Both scenes have the same form, which helps to make the second a suggestive parallel or 'mirror': they begin and end with speech, passing through excited, mixed exchanges (203–63, 686–711: 'epirrhematic' structure: Introd. 3.3, p. lxii).

Despite the Chorus' illumination of Eteocles' and Polynices' tragedies through recall of the events which led to Oedipus' curse (above), scholars ask whether the trilogy may have had the same structural principles as that of the *Oresteia*, which survives complete. Would the last play there, *Eumenides*, be adequately appreciated if *Agamemnon* and *Libation Bearers* were lost? In an obvious way, yes, because of the continuing presence of Orestes (as also of Clytemnestra, but as a ghost) and constant retrospection to the past kin-killing still to be punished by the visible Furies. In part, not so well, because of the play's changed setting; because of the innovative and literally forensic re-examination of the issues of the entire trilogy; and because of their remarkable resolution, part-divine, part-human, and its 'political' accommodation within contemporary Athens (see Introd. 1, p. xx). Rather than attempt reconstruction of *Laius* and *Oedipus* backwards from *Seven* by applying a model from the *Oresteia*, it is more profitable to find in *Seven* itself some anticipations of the later trilogy's design and techniques. First there is the uncanny working of a curse, directed to the killing of kin; in *Seven* it has a comfortless finality which Aeschylus mitigates in *Eumenides* by offering justice to both persecutors and persecuted. Second, *Seven* has clearer signs than *Persians* and *Suppliants* of cumulative dramatic power and intensity. The long sequence from Eteocles' prologue of communal crisis to its culmination in his own tragedy which he embraces achieves its tension through the calculated aptness of the opposing champions and the moral ideas embodied in the Shield-Scene (369–676). This scene makes concrete the already vivid fears of the Chorus in 78–180; its climax opposes Polynices to Eteocles, preparing for the ever more powerful images and meaning which Aeschylus accords their confrontation in the Chorus' odes 720–91 and 822–47 (see below). In *Persians* there is pictorial splendour in the Messenger's reports but his episode is heavily one-sided, despite contrasts between Greek and Persian behaviour; in *Suppliants* there is tension, and formal variety, in the long scene of persuasion between the Chorus and Pelasgus (Introd. 2.3, p. xxxviii). In its intense dynamism, however, the whole central episode of *Seven* (369–719) looks forward to such powerful spans of theatricality as those between Clytemnestra, Cassandra, and Chorus in *Agamemnon*, the invocatory lyrics of Chorus, Orestes, and Electra in *Libation Bearers*, and the great trial scene of *Eumenides* between Orestes, the Chorus of Furies, Athena, and Apollo. Third, the choral odes *Seven* 287–368, 720–91, and 822–47 and the further lyric sequence 874–960 strike levels of poetic richness and authority equalled only by the majestic lyrics of the *Oresteia*. Last, there are signs in *Seven*, again stronger than in *Persians* and *Suppliants*, of maintained figurative language used to support dramatic meaning. There is nothing to match the prominently thematic images of the *Oresteia* such as those from hunting, the law-court, and ritual sacrifice, but there is the insistence, for example, on a motherland's soil and the duty of its sons to defend it (16–20, 72, and throughout the Shield-Scene). In support are less frequent but sometimes more striking pictures like the ship of state and its captaincy (2–3, 62–4, 208–10, and the critically placed recall in 652); the chance lots and the designed allotment of persons, fortunes, or property which characterize the appointment of attackers and defenders (55–7, 127, 282–3, 376, 395, 408, etc.) and the inescapable confrontation and death of the brothers (690, 727, 789, 816, 906–7, 914, 916) and the iron sword so ruthless in the curse's bloodshed (730, 788, 817, 883, 911).[28]

---

[28] Thalmann's study (1978) of the play's imagery is much the fullest and most successful (see his 'The importance of imagery', pp. 142–5, and the review by O. Taplin, *Journal of Hellenic Studies*, 100 [1980], 215–16); in particular he shows how its use aids the shift from war and city in the play's first half to curse, house, and family in the second (yet Eteocles fears for both in 180, and Polynices desires both in 647–8); for imagery from the sea, see Thalmann's pp. 32–8, from the soil, 42–50, from lots and allotment, 63–75. As effective for the original audience, perhaps, was Aeschylus' frequent, skilful mingling of actual Theban topography known to them (and revealed to us by archaeology) with local details drawn imaginatively from the Epic tradition (Berman, 2002): see the map of Thebes on p. xcii. Edmunds (2002) notes how the theatrical effect of both the Chorus' initial panic (78–181) and their final lamentation (848–60, 874–1004) is constantly aided by non-verbal effects like sounds, groans, and music whether described or made during performance.

*Seven* has the quality and feel of an independent play, above all in its concentration upon the hero in his crises both political and personal, and in his isolation in facing them. No other Greek tragedy has so short a cast-list, in which only one other individual, the Scout, and the Chorus introduce new pressures upon the protagonist (even *Prometheus Bound*, with its immobile hero, is more diverse). The prologue-scene (1–77: see EN) sets out the crises, and presents the hero Eteocles in all necessary detail; the action intensifies and his danger alters; his fated decision quickly becomes fatal; the end is extinction for him, his brother, and his royal line (805–13, 827–8, 951–60) but not for his city (793–8, 814–15, 826, etc.) as had been feared at the start (71–2) and which the Chorus still fear before the fratricide (764–5). The tragedy of such a doomed hero—and of his brother—can close only with extremes of lamentation which overwhelm its only witnesses in the play, the Chorus. In this respect the grief-filled ending of *Seven* is truer to the play's meaning (and to the course of the trilogy now completed) than the formally similar end of *Persians* (on which see Introd. 2.1, p. xxvii).

[Appendix on the play's inauthentic ending, 1005–77—for so the great majority of scholars regard it; West deletes it in his edition (see his *Studies*, Bibl. §2, 1990, 6 n. 8; Sommerstein, *AT* 130–4; Conacher (1996) 71–4 has a history of the problem). Producers and actors reviving the play may have wished to 'complete the story', by bringing in Polynices' sister Antigone defying an interdict upon his burial as a traitor. Hutchinson (§3.2, 1985, 209–11) argues that this happened under the influence of Euripides' *Phoenician Women*, which in the mid-fourth century became more popular in the theatre than Sophocles' *Antigone*; both dramatized this part of the myth. That too is the time towards which the verbal style of 1005–77 points. If *Seven* was revived for performance on its own, rather than in its trilogy, it would have been tempting to return to the issue of the city's well-being which dominates the play's first half; but the trilogy can end only with the protracted and climactic lyric lamentation of 822–1004: see also the EN on these lines and 1005.]

2.3. Suppliants

[For a summary of the action, see p. xii. In this Section 2.3 all references to the Bibliography are to §7.3 unless stated.]

Until about 1950 *Suppliants* was generally believed the earliest play of Aeschylus to survive, because of its apparently archaic features; these lay in its dramatic technique and verbal style, and particularly the Chorus' dominant role both as lyric voice and as protagonist in the action, which made it seem close in form and time to the origin of tragedy in a purely choral performance. In 1952 a very damaged papyrus text of about AD 200 was published which stems from a scholarly *hypothesis* or 'introduction'; it reproduces a small part of the fourth-century BC Athenian official record of the play's first production, when Aeschylus was victorious in the dramatic competition. The text is defective where the date-year was given, and conjectural restoration is uncertain. More important is that Sophocles is named as coming second to Aeschylus. Since Sophocles either competed for the first time, or, as some scholars interpret other literary evidence, won his first victory, in the year 468, it was concluded that *Suppliants* was first produced in the middle to late 460s, later, that is, than *Seven* with which Aeschylus was victorious in 467.[29] A recent re-evaluation of the evidence both documentary and literary for Sophocles' first production, however, sets this in the late 470s; an accompanying reconsideration of *Suppliants'* structural and stylistic features suggests a date for it either side of the *Persians* of 472. The question is unlikely to be resolved without new evidence. In this volume the later date is accepted.[30]

---

[29] Oxyrhynchus Papyrus 2256, fr. 3, ll. 1–5, supplemented on the model of similar records as 'in the arch[onship of (*name missing*) in the (*number missing*) year of the (*number missing*) Olympiad]; Aeschylus was victorious [with *Suppliants, Egyptians*,] *Daughters of Danaus, Amy*[*mone*: satyric)]; second was Sophocles; [third was] Mesatos [...' The Athenians counted their official years through the name of the chief archon, or elected magistrate, in each. This reading of the first line leaves speculation about the date-year free. An alternative but more contentious reading supposes the omission of the formulaic phrase 'in the archonship of' before the archon's actual but damaged name, and that the name here itself began (like many Greek ones) with the letters 'Arch-'; it is supplemented from other contemporary records as '...in the archonship of Arch[edemides in the *numbered* year of the *numbered* Olympiad]'. Archedemides held office during the official year 464/3.

[30] Late 460s, and probably 464/3, Garvie (1969¹) and Friis Johansen and Whittle (Bibli. §3.2, 1980) II. 21–9; near 472, Scullion (2002). Sommerstein, *AT* 152–8 and

Most scholars believe that *Suppliants* was the first play in a trilogy, followed by *Egyptians* (of which we have only one certain word) and *Daughters of Danaus* (very fragmentary); the Oxyrhynchus papyrus indeed names this last as the third play, but both preceding play-names are missing (see n. 29 above). This order fits the mythical outline reconstructed from later accounts; for nothing substantive survives from an earlier epic poem *Danais* or from a tragedy *Daughters of Danaus* written by Phrynichus (for whom, see p. xxi above).[31] *Egyptians* would show how Pelasgus' promised defence of the Danaids (*Supp.* 940–53, 963–5) had failed in a battle in which he was killed; how they submitted to forced marriage with their hated cousins; and perhaps how Danaus planned that they should kill their bridegrooms on their wedding-night (cf. *PB* 853–63). The content of *Daughters of Danaus* can be conjectured with some confidence: these killings had been carried through, but one daughter, Hypermnestra, had spared her new husband out of a suddenly conceived love. She was at risk of being killed (by Danaus? perhaps after some judicial process at Argos), but the goddess Aphrodite appeared and saved her, upholding the procreative function of marriage (*Daughters of Danaus* fr. 44). All the daughters were thereupon reconciled to marriage, so fulfilling the warning they receive at the end of *Suppliants* (1034–5, cf. 1050–1) that marriage is women's normal lot, and sanctioned by Zeus and Hera. The outcome will have been a new royal dynasty at Argos named for their father Danaus (cf. *PB* 869–70).[32] A thematic continuity

403–9, and (1997), and Bakewell (1997) argued for the very late 460s on grounds of affinity with contemporary political phenomena: see n. 35 below. In the face of Scullion's arguments, Garvie (2006[2]) pp. ix–xv still favoured 464/3 but conceded that '470 is a *possible* (his italics) date'. Earlier, Taplin, *Stagecraft*, 195 had also suggested the early 470s, and received some support from the Dutch scholar S. L. Radt in a paper of 1988 (repr. in A. Harder (ed.), *Noch einmal zu...*, Mnemosyne Supplement, 235 (2002), 358–61). West in his edition leaves the date as uncertain.

[31] For the mythography, see Gantz, 198–208.

[32] For this order of plays and reconstruction (much simplified here!), see in Bibl. §6.1, esp. Winnington-Ingram (1983), 55–72, and in §7.3 Garvie (1969[1]), 185–6 and (2006[2]), pp. xviii–xix; also Gantz 204–6, West, *Studies* (Bibl. §2, 1990), 169–72, and Conacher (1996), 104–11. The implications of *Supp.* 1034–5 and 1050–1 that the women will inevitably marry are perhaps supported by Danaus' anxiety about their attractiveness to all males, 996–1005 (see EN on 966–1073). The minority view, that *Egyptians* was the first play, and dramatized the persecution and flight of the Danaids from Egypt to Argos (*Supp.* 8–15), is argued again most recently by Sommerstein (1997); cf. n. 34 below. The satyr-play *Amymone* (Sommerstein, *AT* 151–2, Conacher

throughout the trilogy is thus probable, in the women's resistance to marriage. A recent suggestion is that a polarity in both ethnic and ethical terms between 'civilized' Greek values and 'barbaric' foreign ones also pervaded the trilogy: thus in the first play the refugees put their trust in Greek values, particularly concerning supplication, which Pelasgus upholds (*Supp.* 411–14, 478–9, etc.); in the second play the Egyptians' victory threatens to overturn such values, and Danaus' consequent plan for his daughters to kill their husbands itself employs the violence which typifies the Egyptians (e.g. *Supp.* 741, 821, 830; 'barbaric' at 914); in the third play, the goddess Aphrodite helps restore a civilized normality.[33]

Even a cursory reading of the play strikes home the cardinal feature of its dramaturgy: the Chorus of suppliants are the protagonists. They voice 60 per cent of the text; their role is greater than that of the Chorus of Furies in *Eumenides*. They begin the play; their entry march and song, the *parodos*, are longer even than that of *Persians*. They displace their father Danaus when the crucial appeal is made for Argos' and Pelasgus' aid in a lengthy and varied episode (176–523). They are left alone to face the arriving Egyptians (776–907) and, when Pelasgus has saved them, the Chorus on their own voice celebration and face the new anxieties which end the play (1018–73). Earlier, their passionate odes of hope (524–99), grateful prayers for Argos (625–709), and fresh panic (776–823) are spaced only by brief scenes which mark their safety (600–24) and then again threaten it (710–75). Their movements into and out of the collective shrine are the most important of the play, for they accompany their fortunes: early in the play they carry their suppliant boughs into it (207); after they win Pelasgus' help, he persuades them to leave it, although some of their boughs remain as witness (506–8); they move back into the shrine as the Egyptians threaten (at or after 725), only to be pulled

(1996), 108–9) told of this further individual Danaid whom a satyr tried to rape and the god Poseidon saved, taking her himself (the story is known from elsewhere); the incident replicated the attempted violence of the Egyptians in *Suppliants*.

[33] The ethnic and ethical 'polarity' is suggested by Turner (2000); see also n. 36 below. There appears to be nothing in *Suppliants* or its whole myth to make this trilogy apt for the techniques of constant anticipation and retrospection which are so effective in the *Oresteia*. There, events are predetermined jointly by the gods and a curse, and men get warning by omens and prophecy (cf. on *Seven* in Section 2.2 above, p. xxxi–xxxii); this is well brought out by Podlecki (1975).

away (885) before Pelasgus rescues them (924–5, 940–1, 955). So self-interested are their words from the beginning of the play, both lyric and spoken, that Aeschylus gives them very little room for general moralizing (only 86–102: contrast the similarly protagonist Furies at *Eum.* 526–65 within their ode 490–565, and the rich didactic tone of *Eum.* 321–96). The suppliants' passionate and aptly lyric voice nevertheless enhances and varies two important scenes in which they participate, alternating with a single speaking character ('epirrhematic' structure: see Introd. 3.3, p. lxii): with Pelasgus throughout the critical argument of 347–437, and with Danaus in alarm as the Egyptians approach (734–61).

In short, this chorus carries its play; and yet there are two subsidiary choruses, the Egyptians (vocal throughout 825–65, possibly present till 953) and the Men of Argos (1034–61: see EN). Aeschylus opposes his main chorus with these two further collective voices, simply but effectively. Amid them all, three individual figures move in and out. Briefest is the appearance of the Egyptian Herald, who articulates (882–953) the earlier crude violence of his countrymen (825–65); he is dismissed contemptuously by a resolute Pelasgus (911–65). The handling of the second figure, Danaus, is complex. He has been the director of the suppliants' flight (11), and now he advises his daughters how to address their supplication with the utmost reverence and propriety (176–233); but he falls silent while they do so, and succeed, until he asks to follow up their success by taking their suppliants' emblems to the city itself, and to its shrines (490–9); Pelasgus will use him there to help persuade the citizens (517–19). It is the first of Danaus' two absences: the Chorus sing during the first (524–99: see EN for the ode's character); on his return they hear his reassuring report from the city (600–24), sing again in gratitude (625–709), and face new alarm when he spies the Egyptians approaching (710–75), only to leave them alone in doubtful sanctuary when for a second time he goes to the city, to fetch armed help (772–5). His second return comes only when Pelasgus has saved the Chorus from the Egyptians. He then has a single long speech (980–1013; he is silent after it till the play's end), and it is oddly self-congratulatory, as he instructs his daughters not to disgrace by any immodesty his new dignity in Argos, which is marked by his new, armed attendants (perhaps Aeschylus is preparing his significant role in the rest of the trilogy). The most noteworthy aspects of his part in *Suppliants*, however intermittent, are that he is twice used to signal imminent crises, the approaches first of Pelasgus (180 ff.) and then of the Egyptians (710 ff.), and that his silences and absences expose and isolate his daughters dramatically.

The third and most important individual is Pelasgus. In his two scenes, 234–523 and 911–65, and in Danaus' two reports of him, 605–24 and 980–4, the two dominant issues of the play are fully brought out: the suppliants' attitude to marriage and the difficulties of undertaking the protection demanded by their ritual entreaties. The confrontation between the Chorus, the seeming protagonist of the play (above), and Pelasgus, who has the responsibility and the power to decide their safety, turns him into the actual protagonist. His own city's safety is endangered by his decision, in potential (342, 355–7, 397–401, etc.) and in the event (938–51). The Chorus are single-minded, Pelasgus is divided. His dilemma in itself draws our sympathy, and this is increased by the kinder feelings he shows towards the women-suppliants after he decides (504–16, 954–65). Danaus' concern for them becomes overshadowed, for he seems as much preoccupied by his own safety and dignity (490–9, 772–5, 983–97, 1012–13).

The suppliants are fleeing from an arrogant and offensive suit by their Egyptian cousins (8–10, 104–10, etc.); it is presented as unlawful (37, cf. 360), requiring a just prevention (77–8, 82, 343, 385, 404–6), and even as impure (227–8). The suit's violent prosecution is objectionable, but marriage within a local people was not; indeed it was the norm for both Greeks and 'barbarians' (see EN on 387–91). Danaus planned flight from Egypt as the best way to escape the violence, and decided upon refuge in his ancestral Argos (15–20, cf. 274–5, 323–31, etc.); he is given no other motive than concern for his daughters.[34] As the play progresses, they reveal their antipathy to marriage altogether, a hatred of the 'male' (141–3 = 151–3, 392–3, 487, 643–5, 790; cf. 426, 528, 818); the issue returns at the end of the play (1017, 1050–1, 1063: see above).

---

[34] Some later versions of the myth told that he wanted to avoid marriage for his daughters because he had received an oracle that he would die at a son-in-law's hand (Gantz 206). Those who argue that *Egyptians* was the first play of the trilogy place this oracle within it: see Sommerstein, *AT* 143–7 and (1997) 76, and cf. Conacher (1996), 109–11 and n. 32 above.

Such suppliants are indeed difficult for Pelasgus to handle: they are foreign in appearance and behaviour, but claim native ancestry (above) and adopt Greek modes of supplication (191–6, 222–4, 241–3, 333–4), knowing well how to exploit its extraordinary power over the supplicated (345, 348–437). If Pelasgus receives them, he will risk disputes within his own city (356–8, 415) and war with the Egyptian pursuers (342, 439, 474–7), which indeed results (950–3); it is a harsh dilemma (376–80, 397, 407–17). His first, correct reaction is to fear the wrath of Zeus, the god of all suppliants, if he irreverently rejects these in particular (340, 346–7); then the Chorus press his fear home (345, 359–64, 381–6, etc.). His way out is to link his community's approval to his own, if he can get it: it is equally the citizens' responsibility to answer the supplication (365–9). The Chorus, who have experienced only royal absolutism in Egypt (335, 906–7), attempt to quash this excuse, saying that leadership in both the city and its religion is his own (370–5); but he holds firm (398–9). His further evasion, a resort to divinatory sacrifice to the gods, in order to find a solution (449–54), is met by a threat of suicide within the shrine (465, cf. 159–60), which would pollute it (473), and he at last gives way. Aeschylus' 'anachronistic' creation in a mythic Argos of 'democratic' constitutional procedures like those of contemporary Athens is bold, but no more so than the similar 'foundation' of another Athenian institution, the Court of the Areopagus, in *Eumenides*.[35] There is, however, a deeper purpose to this 'anachronism' than inviting the favour of the Athenian audience or of the judges in the dramatic

---

[35] On this 'anachronism', cf. Section 1 above, p. xxi. Many have pointed out that *Supp.* 604 ('the people's sovereign hands voted in majority') has the first explicit reference to 'enfranchised democracy' in Greek literature, in that it links the two words *dem-* 'people' and *krat-* 'power' (cf. also 942 and 963–5). Lines 601–14 (see EN) echo Athenian democratic institutions and vocabulary most strongly, and there are looser allusions at 366, 370, 398–401, 517–18, 698–701, 726, 739, 942, 1010. Pelasgus nevertheless rules with an authority like a Homeric king or lord, both consulting and directing his people (e.g. 615–22, cf. 963–4); public debate is available to him as it is for king Agamemnon returning to Argos from Troy, *Ag.* 844–6. In Euripides' *Suppliants* Theseus is styled like Pelasgus, a king in a democracy who consults his people, but more readily: cf. ll. 350–3 and 404–6 there with our 368–9, 398–9. For the 'Areopagus', see *Eum.* 681–710 and e.g. Collard (2002), pp. xvi–xix. Sommerstein (1997), 76 observes that *Suppliants* is like *Eumenides* in dramatizing the acceptance of 'immigrants' ('metics') into a community (609, 994, and EN; *Eum.* 1011); similarly Bakewell (1997), who adds the point about the Areopagus: cf. n. 30 above.

competition: Aeschylus aims at a contrast of measured, open consultation and persuasion of the people, and reverent responsibility, with foreigners' violent self-assertion, whether that of the Egyptian suitors or the suppliants' own manipulative threat of suicide.[36]

The play is strongly visual. The setting is a collective shrine to Argos' gods (189–222), perhaps with statues (on which the suppliants threaten to hang themselves: see Introd. 2.5. at n. 53). Against such a commonplace background, the exotic costuming and appearance of the suppliants (234–7, 278–89) and their pursuers (825–953) help bring home Pelasgus' difficulties in dealing with these two sudden threats from abroad. The one significant stage-property is the suppliants' emblematic boughs, first mentioned at 22, which they place symbolically in the shrine (191–3, 241–2) and some of which Danaus takes away into the city (480–2). Pelasgus' armed attendants (500, cf. 180–5; 911, cf. 774) and the two subsidiary choruses make for spectacle from crowded movement; the Egyptians also bring menace, their violent words matching their terrifying appearance and actions (825–71). The Men of Argos (1034–61; present with Danaus from 980) afford protection (985–6) and celebration (1022–4), but also give warning for the future (1043–51). Unmentioned till 977 are yet further stage-persons: the women attendant upon Danaus' daughters and silently present from the start.[37] For the play's final scene the *orkhêstra* was thus filled with persons, in numbers unique in surviving Tragedy; they conveyed to the audience how the trilogy would develop: Egyptian suppliants and Argive hosts are now united, but the certain war (950–3) will endanger them all.

Searches for consistently figurative language in the play have been largely unsuccessful. Many images associated with the suppliants' flight and predicament have analogies in the story of their ancestress Io (291–315, 538–89). She is more than a simple lever to move Pelasgus' pity, however. The suppliants use Zeus' pursuit and ultimate

[36] These aspects of Pelasgus' dilemma and actions are well expounded by Burian (1974) and Meier (Bibl. §5, 1993), 84–101; see also Zeitlin (1988), although her emphasis is on issues of gender in the suppliants' case. For other 'suppliant dramas', see EN on 348–437. Many 'ethnic' issues in the play are discussed with full comparative background by Hall (Bibl. §7.1, 1988), and the portrayal of the Egyptians as non-Greeks by M. Ebbott in Gregory, *CGT* 372–5; see too Mitchell (2006).

[37] See EN on 977, 1034.

release of her in pleading for their own liberation, both to Pelasgus (323–4, 331, 401–6) and to Zeus himself (26–9, 524–36, 590–9); moreover, they remind both Pelasgus and Zeus of Io's ordeal where it began, and where they themselves are now in danger, in Argos (292, 350–4, and esp. 538–42; cf. 15–22, 50–1).[38]

The play has always been the least read of those by Aeschylus, and perhaps by any Greek tragedian. It has the most corrupt text. Its plot, characters, issues, and dramatic styles have lacked general appeal. The extraordinary dominance of the chorus in all these respects seems to have been a further barrier to modern sympathies. Recent years have brought it new attention, however, if seldom for its dramatic and poetic interest; like all Greek tragedies it is now studied increasingly as a significant social document of its time.

## 2.4. Prometheus Bound

[For a summary of the action, see p. xiii. In this Section 2.4 all references to the Bibliography are to §7.4 unless stated. The play's authenticity, date, and relationship to other Prometheus-plays attributed to Aeschylus, and aspects of its staging, are discussed in an Appendix at the end of this Section.]

The only surviving and substantive accounts of Prometheus earlier than that found in this play were by the seventh-century poet Hesiod. In his *Works and Days* 42–105 Zeus punishes Prometheus' theft of fire in order to bestow it upon men by imposing on them Pandora and her jar of evils (cf. EN on 248–50). Hesiod's *Theogony* 521–720 has a narrative closer to the play. When Prometheus tries to trick Zeus into taking the fat and bones of sacrificial animals so that men may keep the meat for themselves (cf. EN on 82–4, 493–9), Zeus retaliates with the (apparent) substitution for fire of the gift of woman, which is disastrous for them (*Theog.* 570–602); and his punishment for Prometheus is that of the play: eternal fetters and the torturing eagle (521–5, 616). In both poems Prometheus' trickiness

---

[38] For the play's language, and the passages about Io, see esp. Garvie (1969[1], 2006[2]), 69–72 and Sommerstein, *AT* 163–8. There is discussion of the play's imagery by Fowler (Bibl. § 6.2, 1967), 10–23, cited by Conacher (1996), 80 n. 13. Mackinnon (1978) argues that hunting images assist the suppliants' hostility to the marriage which the Egyptians pursue violently (the image is used again at *PB* 858).

and benevolence to men offend Zeus, who is impossible to outwit (*Theog.* 613, cf. *WD* 105: unmistakably echoed at *PB* 62; see also below). To Prometheus' punishment Hesiod at once subjoins Zeus' harsh treatment of the Titans who rebelled against his power; he does not mention Prometheus' aid to Zeus in his victory over them (which may have preceded the theft of fire), but in *Prometheus* it is part of Prometheus' bitter complaint that Zeus not only betrayed his benefactor but punished him cruelly (199–225, 239–41, 304–6, etc.), just as he had his fellow Titans (347–72).[39]

Zeus' harshness (*PB* 34–5, 94–8, 186, 240–1, 324, 952, 980) and Prometheus' defiant favour of mankind (11, 28, 123, 506, 613, etc.)[40] are the poles between which this unusual tragedy plays out. Since its hero was to be immobile from the beginning, for any development the dramatist had to contrive plausible visitors to him, and plausible exchanges with him; and since Prometheus is both a god and a prisoner remote from the human world (1–2) he can expect only divine, or supernatural, visitors, not mortal ones.[41] The dramatic sequence is one largely of sympathy: first, from Hephaestus, despite Power's scorn, in the prologue-scene, where he is compelled to fetter Prometheus (36, 66, 69); then from the Chorus, whose motive in coming is friendship (128), who weep constantly for him (144–6, 160–2, 395–400, etc.), and who in the end voluntarily endure the cataclysm with him (1058–70). The Chorus nevertheless quickly urge moderation upon him (178–80), and this prompts Prometheus to explanation and self-justification (197–276). He maintains this attitude so firmly that he rejects help from Oceanus who shares his pain (288, 297), like the Chorus urges moderation (307–24), and offers to plead for his release (325–39, 381–5). Further explanation and justification (to the Chorus, 436–525) begin to harden him before the long and perplexing Io scene (561–886) turns him to obduracy (908–40).

[39] For the mythology, see Conacher (1980), 3–20 and Gantz 154–66.

[40] 'Favour of mankind': the Greek word *philanthrop(os)* occurs for the first time in ll. 11 and 28 (but not quite in the modern sense of 'philanthropy').

[41] Similarly in Aristophanes' *Birds* of 414 BC (which reflects the *Prometheus*: see Appendix below, p. l), once the action has moved from the earth to Cloud-cuckoo-land, new entrants can be only birds and gods.

Io's arrival is fortuitous, extraordinary because she is a mortal, but plausible given the far remoteness of her supernatural wanderings (577, 591); and it has only allusive links with the rest of the play. Io's response to the sight of Prometheus is instant sympathy (562–4, 614, 685). Her sense of her own persecution by Zeus and Hera (566–603) nevertheless makes her from the start think primarily of tapping his prophetic knowledge of her future (604–8); and his immediate readiness to tell her (609–11) is surprising after so long a preoccupation with his own condition; when he resists her questions about himself she turns wholly to her own destiny (622–30). His prophecies to her are, however, delayed once the Chorus insist that she first tells her own past story (631–86); this sequence is dramaturgically a loose repetition of the earlier passages of question and narrative between Chorus, Oceanus, and the victim Prometheus. Io describes her suffering as a result of Zeus' passion for her (671–2, cf. 590–2, 649–52) and Zeus' failure to protect her from Hera's jealousy (earlier at 578–81, 599–601). Her account appears to strengthen Prometheus' indignation; he partly discloses to her his secret knowledge, how Zeus' planned new marriage will destroy him (761–8, later repeated in full to the Chorus in 907–40).[42] His prophecies eventually link Io's destiny with his: a descendant of hers will free him physically from his fetters (771–4, recapitulated at 871–3). Zeus will release Io from her torment (848–9), just as he will ultimately be compelled to release Prometheus, to save himself (769–70). The Io scene holds true to the main plot only in these few essentials, as one of protracted suffering at the hands of Zeus, directly or indirectly, which Io shares with Prometheus, and of anticipated but very distant relief; and, still, of sympathy.[43]

---

[42] There is possibly an ironic allusion to the splendid 'marriage' with Zeus which had been promised to Io (648–52) and which had only a bitter outcome for her (739–40)—as the prophesied marriage will have for Zeus himself (764). Just before the Io scene the Chorus sing an ode (526–60) deprecating Zeus' absolute power as exemplified in his punishment of Prometheus, a sight which causes them to recall their participation long ago in Prometheus' wedding (555–60).

[43] The Io scene divides critics: e.g. Conacher (1980), 161–8, applauds its imagination, Sommerstein *AT* 301 finds the links tenuous, and suggests that its main purpose is to look forward to the following play, *Prometheus Unbound*. An unexpected and bizarre human visitor does achieve impact, although some readers question the length given to the two narratives of Io's past, her own (640–86) and then Prometheus' (823–43: see EN), and then to his prophecies of her future (700–41, 786–818), which only at their end mesh with his own (844–86).

Io's abrupt relapse into frenzy and sudden departure (877–86) herald the yet harsher torment which is now imminent for Prometheus. After she goes he can only repeat his confidence in Zeus' fall (907–40); and the only further plausible development for the play is Zeus' discovery of the secret, and reaction. Hermes' sudden appearance as Zeus' emissary, to extract its details (944–50), is the ultimatum necessary to precipitate Prometheus' final disaster. When he will not heed it (988–1006), he must suffer still worse; and a long future of agony is not just threatened (1014–29, including the eagle in Hesiod's account), but at once begins, with the cataclysm. The play ends with uncompromising violence, just as it began with the cruel fettering; Zeus' brutal harshness is confirmed, and it is represented as so extreme that only the spectators' imagination will compass it (see Appendix at the end of this Section).

Hesiod in his two poems (above) gives no reason why Prometheus benefited mankind, except as part of his attempt to outwit Zeus. In the play he has done it when Zeus not only took no account of men's wretchedness but wished to annihilate them and create a new race (231–3). Only Prometheus pitied them (239), saved them (234–6), and bestowed benefits on them: he removed their fear of death (248) before giving them fire (252) and its related crafts (254; later he lists both material and intellectual skills: see EN on 436–525). His pity for men is matched by that for his similarly persecuted fellow Titans, Atlas (347–8) and Typhon (352), and now by his sympathy with Io (628, 637–9, 696–7, 743–4, cf. Io herself at 684). This pity for men, the most human of feelings but absent from Zeus, draws pity for his own consequent suffering: and especially from Io, whose pity as the only human and mortal in the play is an automatic return for his benefits to men (613–14). The mortal girl Io is innocently feminine (645–57), just as the Chorus, the young daughters of the divine Oceanus, are innocently modest and reserved (134), so that they help to accommodate Io's pathetic self-portrayal and helplessness, as part of the contrast with Prometheus' obduracy. Despite their divinity, both the Chorus and their father Oceanus are human in their sympathy; Oceanus' offer of help to Prometheus seems to mirror Prometheus' aid to mankind. All this pity is contrived for one who is immortal (752–3, 933, 1052), and so he is punished with endless pain (26–7, 93–100, etc.). Prometheus, however, seems to scorn the pity, as inappropriate to his fortitude (263–5, 298–303, 342–3, 373–6, 383, 436–8, 752, 928–40). Hermes accuses him of luxuriating in his torment (971). In his frighteningly obsessive obduracy before divine inexorability Prometheus a little resembles Eteocles in *Seven* (683–719).

Prometheus is a god who has betrayed his fellow gods (29) by giving men in fire a prerogative unique to the gods (30, 37–8, 82–3); for this 'wrong' (9, 112, 260, 266, 945) he must pay their punishment (9, cf. 112). He resents it so strongly (he explicitly terms it 'unjust' only as late as 976, 1093, after earlier descriptions of its cruelty at e.g. 92–7, 169, 176, 240–1, 306 etc.) that his defiance (172–4, 258, 320, 375–6, etc.) turns into total obduracy (752–6, 932–40, 963, 987–96, 1001–6, 1052). He relies upon Zeus' overriding desire to preserve his own rule, and therefore to learn his secret, as the key to his release from torment; his gradual revelation of it gives the play its slow progress, and keeps pace with his growing intransigence (168–71, 188–92, 511–25, 755–70, 907–40, 987–98, 1040–52) and with his associated confidence (e.g. 257–8, 871–6, 958–9); Hermes confirms Zeus' anxiety at 947–8, 984. Concealment of his secret is also the last throw of Prometheus' cleverness (Hermes at 1011), which has always overreached itself (Power at 62, Oceanus at 308, 328, Hermes at 944). His own admission that it is failing to secure his release (469–71) chimes with Power's ironic jibe to the same effect, that he has proved to lack the forethought explicit in his own name (85–6 and EN).

The play's theology is bleak, presenting the supreme Zeus of earlier poetry (and of Aeschylus' plays), but here in a rule of absolute repression unrelieved by the usual concern of such poetry to associate the gods with disinterested justice for men. This has no part in *Prometheus*: men are simply wretched under god (231, 249, 442, etc.), or are pitied and relieved by Prometheus (234–6, 248, 251, 267, etc.). Instead the play depicts mistrust, warfare, embitterment, and violent retaliation between gods alone. Prometheus' wrongdoing is described as a betrayal of godhead, first in his aid to men (9, 112, etc.) and then in his defiance of Zeus' supremacy (10–11, 309–10, etc.): Zeus has made justice his own possession (187, 403, cf. 324). The play has accordingly been seen as theologically bankrupt, a study of power asserted cruelly between immortal gods, a tragedy without ordinary human values, and unedifying, one which bars sympathy.

The question is asked: when the protagonist is a god and there-fore immortal, how can he be a 'tragic hero'? Yet Prometheus is a superhuman figure recognizably human in fallibility who embraces his suffering (again not unlike Eteocles in *Seven*: above); compassion for him is instinctive, despite his obduracy. There is also the pathetic Io. Furthermore, the play offers some reassurance in the hints that Prometheus' release by Zeus is eventually certain, and that this will implicitly sanction the progress and values which Prometheus bestowed on men. The Zeus who punishes offence against himself relentlessly, and crushes Prometheus, may in the end be as capable of relenting as the severe Zeus of the *Oresteia* who ends by 'acquitting' the matricidal Orestes through his spokesman Apollo (*Eum.* 797–9, cf. 616–24). On the other hand, the cruel treatment of Io by Hera, and neglect by her suitor Zeus, are analogues of Prometheus' misery as the price of helping a mankind neglected by gods preoccupied only with themselves: such a depiction is frightening for men. [44]

Lastly, two comments on the play's language. First, many of the spoken parts have a vigour like that of Aeschylus: for example, Prometheus' narrative expositions at 197–241, 446–71, 476–506, and Io's at 645–82. There are echoes of his 'geographical catalogue' style in the lyric 406–30 (cf. *Pers.* 865–97, *Supp.* 538–73); and 'geographical narrative' bulks out Prometheus' prophecies at 707–35, 790–815, 827–52 (so fully that the scene's momentum suffers: see n. 43). [45] There are some effective dialogues, even the superficially formalized and therefore slightly stiff 36–81 (see EN; Introd. 3.2 p. lxi). Most of

[44] For the conflict between the clever Prometheus and the tyrannical Zeus, see esp. Said (1985); it has often been observed that the play affords one of the earliest characterizations of tyranny in Greek tragedy. For the absolutism of Zeus towards mankind (which Prometheus must endure with them), native to early Greek thinking, and the theology of Zeus in the play, see esp. Lloyd-Jones (2003) = (2005), with references to his earlier work; Gagarin (Bibl. §6.1, 1976), 132–6; Conacher (1980), 120–37; see also n. 48 below. As to the play's comfort for men: White (2001) argues that Io's journey through a primitive and barbaric world to an Egypt where she will be the forebear of a saving civilization (869) perhaps symbolizes progress, in that Zeus' release of her from torment (848–9) portends also his eventual benevolence and justice towards Prometheus.

[45] Studies of the geographic detail have led to differing judgements, that the vagueness of description in e.g. 406–30 matched the imprecise knowledge of the fifth century (EN on 420–4), while the occasional precision of 708–815 could have come only from the fourth century, so that 'interpolation is to be suspected': respectively S. R. West (1997) and Finkelberg (1998).

the stichomythic exchanges are convincing in their measured progress (e.g. 246–62, 757–81); in contrast, there is suitable irregularity in 377–96, helping to express mutual disillusion. The formally unusual 'lyric dialogues' of 128–92 and 1040–93 are striking, and probably intended to mark dramatic high points. Second, an action which keeps its protagonist fettered is often supported (unsurprisingly) upon language of harnessing, yoking, and binding, some repetitiously literal and repetitive (as in the prologue-scene and *parodos*), some metaphorical: for example, Io is yoked or harnessed to agony (579, 672) just as Prometheus is (e.g. 5–6, 71, 108, 562, 618, 1009–10)— and, ironically, unless the effect is unconscious, just as he himself yoked animals to serve mankind (462). It is hard to find other imagery used prominently and often enough to suggest a thematic purpose, although medical language in particular has been identified, for example, in the passages 224–5 'this vice (literally, "sickness") not to trust one's friends' and in 375–84 ('sickness' in multiple metaphor, cf. 977–8, 1070) and 471–83 (both metaphorical and literal); these figure respectively 'disease' in Oceanus' failing attempt to help Prometheus and then his own inability to 'cure' his troubles in contrast with his gift of 'cures' to men. There may be a link between the description of Prometheus' 'sickness' in 472–5 and that of Io in 597, 606, 698; note, too, Io's medical 'self-diagnosis' (879–85 and EN).[46]

### Appendix to Prometheus Bound

*Authenticity and Date* The issues of authenticity and date remain unresolved, and perhaps irresoluble, although recent intense study has led to a majority opinion: that the play is possibly, even probably, Aeschylean in concept, but was built upon material which Aeschylus left incomplete at his death. Certainly the play's power is characteristic of his imagination. Scholars have nevertheless found many features to be untypical of his dramatic and compositional style, and of his 'thought': these are mainly the long dramatic prologue; the Chorus' entry-song shared with Prometheus' individual voice;

---

[46] Figurative language in the play has been weighed by Fowler (1957: general) and Mossman (1996: harnessing, binding, medicine). Griffith in his edition (Bibl. §3.2, 1983), 20–1 is concise and judicious.

the Chorus' very small lyric role overall, and its lack of robust-ness;[47] the sometimes clumsy construction of scenes, especially those with Oceanus, entirely unconnected with the earlier arrival of his daughters, and with Io (see above); a monody (Io's), unparalleled in Aeschylus; very numerous un-Aeschylean usages in metre, dic-tion, syntax, and style; theology lacking profundity, or in conflict with that of the other plays; the status and depiction of mankind. Furthermore, there are things which point to a date in the second half of the fifth century, after Aeschylus' death: there is influence from Sophoclean and Herodotean ideas, and from sophistic think-ing with its increasingly anthropocentric quality; some geographical details (above p. xlviii and n. 45); apparent demand upon theatrical resources not yet developed in Aeschylus' lifetime (below). All these pointers are strong. Defenders of authenticity argue that many of the features just listed are nevertheless compatible with Aeschylus' authorship, and that the play came from his very last years, written during his final visit to Sicily (see the Chronology, p. lxxxv; they cite especially the description of Mount Etna at 363–72). Defenders also point out, and condemners acknowledge, that the play's authentic-ity was never questioned in antiquity. Unmistakable near-quotations from it in Aristophanes' *Birds* of 414 BC (line 1547 echoes *PB* 975, and 685–7 echo 547–9) not only confirm the play's currency at that time, but 'Aeschylus' as the target for paratragic humour (forty years after his death; the fashion lasted at least until Aristophanes' *Frogs* of 405: see Introd. 3.4 below, p. lxiv). A suggestion from the 1930s has recently been strongly revived, that the play was reworked and produced between 440 and 430 by Aeschylus' son Euphorion, known to have won victories at the dramatic festivals of Athens with his father's unperformed plays.[48]

[47] Very few of the lyrics hint a true Aeschylean colour, although Io's monody (561–608) aspires to pathos. For the Chorus' role in the action see Scott (1988).

[48] See in particular West, *Studies* (Bibl. §2, 1990), 68–71 and Sommerstein, *AT* 321–7. West's arguments are questioned esp. on grounds of 'theology' by Lloyd-Jones (2003) 52–71 = (2005), 184–202, who holds that Aeschylus' authorship is 'likelier' but 'not certain'. When Lloyd-Jones edited T. C. W. Stinton's *Collected Papers on Greek Tragedy* (1990), on p. vi he recorded that Stinton, who had begun an edition of the play, was unconvinced of its inauthenticity (pp. 91–7 reprint Stinton's largely sympathetic review of Herington (1970), a principal defender). For full reviews of the argument and its progress, see Griffith (1977) and more briefly in his edition (Bibl.

*Part of a Trilogy?* The second issue, that of a possible trilogy, is equally difficult. A *Prometheus Unbound* is also attested for Aeschylus which followed directly upon *Prometheus Bound* (ancient commentary on *PB* 511 and 522), so that some scholars have thought of just two linked plays, a 'dilogy'; unfortunately, *Unbound* survives only in a very fragmentary condition (see n. 49). A further play, *Prometheus the Fire-Bearer* (sometimes translated as *Bringer of Fire*: the play is lost except for one line), is attributed to Aeschylus in an ancient catalogue, and a trilogy of these three plays has therefore also been suggested. In such a structure, the title 'Fire-Bearer' might imply that it was the first play, dramatizing the theft of fire to carry to men; but *Prometheus Bound* itself contains much narrative of the theft and re-examination of its cause and circumstances, which would seem to be superfluous if the play followed *Fire-Bearer*. Accordingly, some hold this to have been the third play, and its title to connote Prometheus' whole story, but particularly his reconciliation with Zeus (foreseen at *PB* 190–2) and the institution of his later cult at Athens with a festival, the Prometheia, which celebrated his fetching of fire to man through a symbolic torch-race; a comparison is made with the reconciliation of the Furies to Zeus' merciful justice at the end of the *Oresteia*, and the institution of their cult too in Athens (*Eum.* 778–1047). There are difficulties with supposing either a trilogy or a dilogy, then; and the latter would not have complied with the regulations of the main Athenian dramatic festival. The problems about the extent of Aeschylean authorship of *Prometheus Bound* remain, and necessarily stretch also to the other plays.[49]

§3.2, 1983), 31–5 (inauthentic); Conacher (1980), 141–74, cf. 23–4 (Aeschylean); West (above), 51–72; Bees (1993), esp. 4–14, 252–3 (inauthentic); Podlecki (Bibl. §3.2, 2005), 195–200 (Aeschylean). De Vries (1993) argues that new fragments of an Attic vase of about 370–60 BC reflect a production of *Prometheus*, possibly of a trilogy, in Athens at that time, and, it may be inferred, in the name of Aeschylus.

[49] For the evidence and arguments about a trilogy see West (1979) and *Studies* (1990), 67–72 (a trilogy beginning with *Fire-Bearer*); Conacher (1980), 98–119 (*Fire-Bearer* as the third play); Griffith in his edition (1983), 281–305, with texts of the fragmentary plays, translation, and commentary (the same trilogy favoured); Lloyd-Jones (2003), 67–70 (sceptical of a trilogy, unless *Prometheus Bound* is its first play, and the third was the genuine but very fragmentary *Women of Etna*); Podlecki in his edition (2005), 27–34 (similar scepticism). Yet another Prometheus play is attested for Aeschylus, *Prometheus the Kindler of Fire*; this is thought to have been the lost satyr-play entitled simply *Prometheus* which completed the heterogeneous tetralogy

*Aspects of Staging* How was *Prometheus Bound* staged in the ancient theatre? An answer depends much upon the supposition that a back-cloth or even stage-building existed when it was first produced; if a post-Aeschylean date is right, the latter is very likely (cf. Introd. 2.5, p. lv). If it had been painted as a cliff-face, Prometheus could be fastened to it, and at play-end his disappearance in the cataclysm managed by removal on the *ekkyklêma* or 'wheeled platform' through the central door (hesitantly, Taplin, *Stagecraft*, 273–5; rejected by Wiles (Bibl. §5, 1997), 81–2). As to the major stage-effects implicit in the text, it seems wrong to suppose that they were realized literally, and then to reconstruct the means. In Aeschylus' own lifetime, and probably throughout antiquity, one at least of the two aerial entries described in the text would have been impossible, for even with the later 'crane' (or *mêkhanê*) the arrival by air of a chorus of at least twelve (and probably fifteen) persons, whether riding each in separate winged vehicles or all together in one, could not have been achieved; the crane might, however, have been able to carry Oceanus on his griffin. Besides, three fully aerial entries for the Chorus, Oceanus, and then Hermes would have been excessively demonstrative, and the last, an anticlimax. With or without a stage-building and machinery, all these entries could well enough be made at ground level. The Chorus might wheel in, if not ride in, lightweight replicas of a winged vehicle,

of which *Persians* was part (EN p. 130); papyrus fragments from it, including a lyric hymn, were published in 1952 (frs. 204a-d). Some suggest that *Fire-Bearer* may have been a variant title for *Kindler*.

Here is a synopsis of *Prometheus Unbound* (frs. 190–204): Prometheus is still fettered in the Caucasus (fr. 193.28) but has been returned to the daylight from beneath the cataclysm which ends *Prometheus Bound*. He is now rent by Zeus' eagle (forecast by Hermes at *PB* 1020–5). As in *Prometheus Bound* the play's Chorus comprises visitors who come to view his agonies, and no doubt to sympathize; this time they are male (fr. 190.3) and probably fellow Titans. The action had these main turns: Heracles came by on his quest for the Golden Apples of the Hesperides (a fortuitous visitor like Io in *Prometheus Bound*, but male here, like the Chorus). Heracles slew the eagle, but in fear of Zeus did not unfetter Prometheus (ancient commentator on Virgil, *Eclogues* 4.62). Prometheus gave him directions for his quest (frs. 195–9; cf. his prophecies for Io) but revealed his secret knowledge, how Zeus would lose his throne (in *PB* first at 170–1); Zeus somehow learned it and freed Prometheus (commentator on *PB* 522 and Virgil). It is possible that Chiron the Centaur, a benefactor of mankind like Prometheus, took his place, sacrificing his immortality (the story is in Apollodorus 2.85 and 119; a substitution is mentioned at *PB* 1026–9). Most of the fragments are descriptive and hardly fill out this outline.

or follow a single such vehicle on foot; the words 'in formation' in line 128 suggest that they entered severally. Oceanus could enter in a wheeled vehicle also, perhaps drawn by a horse got up to look like a griffin. Hermes too could enter on foot (at 941 Prometheus contemptuously calls him a mere 'runner', and there is no indication that he flies). Io makes a crazed, running entry (self-description throughout 566–608); supernatural speed is implicit in her bizarre, unceasing torment (e.g. 643, 673–5, 681–2).

Some simulation of the final cataclysm might have been attempted, with suitable noise but hardly with physical illusion, let alone the 'disappearance' of both Prometheus and Chorus (and Prometheus' final words imply only the cataclysm's noisy beginning, with quaking, thunder and lightning, dust-clouds and wind-storms). After these words, the play might have ended acceptably with simple silence, an effect reversing that of plays which began with tableaux silently assembled in sight of the spectators. Conversely, the prologue scene, with four figures entering at once, among them Prometheus who is then fettered, was easy enough to stage, and vividly enough, with impressive costuming and stage-properties (see EN on 1–87). While the actor's subsequent endurance of immobility may have been a problem, he had at the same time an opportunity to show virtuosity with the voice alone.[50]

## 2.5. The plays in the ancient theatre

It became regular in Aeschylus' later lifetime for tragic poets competing at the Great Dionysiac festival to present a tetralogy in a single

---

[50] Some of these suggestions go back many years. The long debate between proponents of fully attempted realization and those who 'leave all to the spectators' imagination in response to the words' is reviewed, for example, by Taplin, *Stagecraft* 240–76, who favours imagined effects except for a single aerial entry by Oceanus, and by Conacher (1980), 175–91; see also Davidson (1994) and Wiles (Bibl. §5, 1997), 81–2, who suggest a Prometheus fettered to the altar in the *orkhêstra*, with the Chorus entering unseen behind him, with or without a backcloth. If he were fettered to a backcloth or stage-building, however, spectators could readily accept that he does not at first 'see' the Chorus entering (114–26), just as in *Libation Bearers*, for instance, they could accept that Electra does not 'see' Orestes and Pylades standing by (from *LB* 20–1 to 212, when they reveal themselves). A final silent tableau might have resembled the start of *Seven* (EN on line 1, *s.d.*, and Taplin, *Stagecraft* 134–6); but a tableau is rejected by Wiles (above), 115.

Wiles (Bibl. §5, 2000), 183–9 discusses (with illustrations) how the famous 1927 Delphi production of the play approached all these problems.

day—that is, three tragedies and a concluding satyr-play (a shorter piece, a burlesque of myth in which the chorus always comprised satyrs: the half-human, rebellious, sexy, and drunkenly excitable followers of the god Dionysus).[51] We do not know if Aeschylus was the first dramatist to exploit this compressed timetable by basing all three tragedies, let alone a complete tetralogy, upon a single myth, but he perfected this approach. In the tetralogy of 472, which included _Persians_, all four plays dramatized differing subjects; in 467, when _Seven against Thebes_ was performed, the three tragedies made a connected trilogy upon the Oedipus family-story, and the satyr-play burlesqued an incident in it, Oedipus' victory over the Sphinx (see _Seven_ 775–7, cf. 541); the tetralogy to which _Suppliants_ belonged (probably the late 460s), dramatizing the myth of the Danaids, was similarly thematic; and then there was the celebrated tetralogy which comprised the _Oresteia_ and its loosely associated satyr-play _Proteus_.[52]

The performance-space of the Theatre of Dionysus at Athens was large; it had two parts which in Aeschylus' day were becoming conceptually separate but were probably still on one level and flowed easily into each other, giving mutual access. The first was an area enclosed on three sides by terraced seating, the _orkhêstra_. The name means roughly 'dance-place', and the area was created originally for any performance of song, danced or stationary; in tragedy it was already on the way to becoming a preserve of the chorus. At its centre was a small permanent altar to Dionysus, which perhaps served to represent the 'common altar' of the gods at which the suppliants take refuge in _Suppliants_ (222, cf. 189 etc.) and Darius' tomb in _Persians_.[53] There was access to the _orkhêstra_ from both sides, between the outer ends of the seating and the second area. This was a long, rectangular, and transverse space used mostly by the individual actors but sometimes also by the chorus, especially when it had an active role in the plot and dialogue (in _Persians_ and _Suppliants_, especially).

[51] For satyr drama, see P. E. Easterling in _CCGT_ 37–44; R. Seaford, _Euripides: Cyclops_ (1984), 1–48; B. Seidensticker in Gregory, _CGT_ 44–9.

[52] Aeschylus' known tetralogies and trilogies are discussed by Sommerstein, _AT_ 53–70. For _Proteus_, see Collard (2002), p. xliii n. 23.

[53] For such use of the altar in _Suppliants_, see e.g. Wiles (Bibl. §5, 1997), 196, who argues that it must have had statues nearby from which the suppliants hang their boughs (354) and later threaten to hang themselves (465); cf. the next n. Its use for the tomb in _Persians_ is more problematic: see EN on _Pers._ 623.

In part terraced out towards the rear, it may at first have had no backcloth, the spectators looking across it and above the naturally falling ground behind. This seems to have been the state of things at the time of *Persians* and *Seven*; and *Suppliants* would have played as well in it. By the time of the *Oresteia*, however (458), the second area was confined at the back by a wooden structure faced with canvas, the *skênê* (in modern terms, the 'scene' or 'stage-area'); in later antiquity a raised stage developed upon the part-terrace, although its beginning cannot be certainly dated. The structure came to serve as a house-front (in the *Oresteia* at *Ag.* 3, *LB* 653) or temple-front (*Eum.* 3–4), or a background for any outdoor location (*LB* 4); for *Prometheus* it could provide the cliff face to which Prometheus is fettered (*PB* 55; see Introd. 2.4, Appendix p. lii). With no backcloth at all, or a plain one, a change of scene, or closer refocusing of the initial one, could be managed, and merely indicated or implied in the characters' words: for example, in *Persians* (598 ff.), where the Queen brings propitiatory offerings to her dead husband Darius, coming from the palace specifically to his tomb (659) rather than to the general area in front of the council-chamber (141) where the play begins.[54] Stage-properties were straightforward, such as the Queen's offerings or the emblematic boughs in *Suppliants*. Costume was enhanced or varied for special effect: for example, for the dead Darius' royal splendour or the defeated Xerxes' ragged dress in *Persians*; the Egyptians in *Suppliants* needed darkened skin and masks (EN on 154–61), and Io in *Prometheus* a horned cow's head (EN on 588). The use of costume and actors' movements are inferred from the play text to give the 'stage-directions' inserted in the Translation.[55]

This plain theatre could accommodate some striking physical effects, like the Queen's chariot (*Pers.*150: see EN on 607–8), almost certainly drawn by live animals, or the 'raising' of Darius' Ghost (*Pers.* 629–80).[56] Its very bareness could enhance the isolation of

---

[54] Wiles (Bibl. §5, 1997), 117–19, suggests that in *Seven* the bare space might successively represent the centre of the city, with gods' statues to which the Chorus cling (99 above); the front of the royal house, when the Chorus sing of its dire history (700–19); and both the house front and, again, the centre of the city when the dead Eteocles and Polynices are brought in.

[55] See e.g. EN to *Pers.* 598–622, 908.

[56] Ghosts are not rare in Greek Tragedy: see EN on *Pers.* 681–851.

the suppliants at the altar, their imminent violation, and their final rescue (*Supp.* 189, 825, 911), the isolation of Eteocles in *Seven*, and the obduracy of the fettered Prometheus, which grows until the cataclysm engulfs him (*PB* 1080–90). Other effects were ordinary enough but nevertheless brought out meaning with some power, like the silence of Danaus the suppliants' father while they conduct the plea to Pelasgus (*Supp.* 234–524, except for 490–9), the protracted, hopeless lamentation which closes both *Persians* (852–1077) and *Seven* (822–1004), and the frenzy of Io as she bursts upon Prometheus (*PB* 561). A further stage-effect was perhaps developed in Aeschylus' time or soon after his death, the *mêkhanê* ('machine') or 'crane' to simulate aerial entries; for its possible use in *Prometheus*, see Introd. 2.4, Appendix p. lii.[57]

The performers available for the three certain plays of Aeschyus in this volume were all male: two speaking actors and a chorus of twelve dance-singers.[58] The chorus' leader might join in spoken or sung exchanges with an actor: for example, spoken at *Pers.* 159–248, with a long speech at 215–25 for the leader, and throughout *Supp.* 204–347; both spoken and sung at *Seven* 686–719. In *Prometheus* three actors were required (this number had become available by the time of the *Oresteia*, 458 BC), but only in the opening scene where a silent Prometheus is fettered to the cliff during a tense exchange between Power and Hephaestus (1–87; Prometheus begins to speak only at 88, after they have left). These performers were supplemented occasionally by mute persons to any number (attendants upon royalty in *Persians*, *Seven*, and *Suppliants*; women-servants of the suppliants in that play; Force in *Prometheus*); and by an additional chorus (of unknown number) for single scenes—in fact by two such bodies in *Suppliants*, the Egyptians at 825–65, and the Men of Argos at 1034–73 (see EN).

---

[57] For clear descriptions and illustrations of the theatre in Aeschylus' time and immediately after, see e.g. J. Gould in *CCGT* 263–81; Green (1994); Green and Handley (1995); Wiles (1997), 23–62 and (2000), 99–127; and J. Davidson in Gregory, *CGT* 194–211 (from the Bibl. §§5 and 6.4). General discussions of Aeschylus' handling of his theatre may be found in e.g. Rosenmeyer, *AA* 45–74, Sommerstein, *AT* 217–41, and above all Taplin, *Stagecraft*.

[58] It is not known when the number went from twelve to fifteen (twelve were still used in the *Agamemnon* of 458 BC: see ll. 1346–71), but the increase was attributed to Sophocles. If *Prometheus* was of the 430s, it would have used the higher number.

In *Seven* one of the two actors is used heavily and continuously for the principal character, Eteocles—indeed this play has the shortest supporting cast of any surviving tragedy, the only other character being the Scout. In *Persians* the Queen would be played throughout by one actor, having exchanges with the Chorus, the Messenger, and Darius, but not with her son Xerxes, whose voice is heard only in lyric dialogue with the Chorus at the end of the play; it is possible that the Queen's actor took his part too, if he was very versatile. In *Suppliants* the chorus itself is effectively the protagonist, rivalling the principal individual character Pelasgus (see Introd. 2.3, p. xl). Once more *Prometheus* is distinctive in its conception, in which the principal character never moves after the prologue, and speaks to a series of individual visitors. The Chorus is such a visitor itself, making small contributions to these successive scenes; when it itself exchanges lyric and speech with Prometheus, his is by far the dominant voice. In fact this chorus chants or sings barely 100 lyric lines in all—and it has a lyric rival in Io, who sings a monody, a feature unexampled in Aeschylus' authentic plays.

In the fifth-century theatre entries and exits, movements, and a few portable properties not only gave visual support to the all-important words, but the entries and exits articulated the plot significantly. The Queen comes and goes twice in *Persians*, before and after her dream and the Messenger's reports which confirm it, and before and after her offerings help raise Darius' Ghost to explain the disaster; her anticipated return in a third entry to meet Xerxes (see 849–50) is forestalled by his arrival, so that he becomes the sole theatrical and emotional focus at the play's end. In *Seven* the Scout's two successive entries and reports bring Eteocles to his crisis of duty and destiny (see Introd. 2.2. above, p. xxxii). In *Suppliants* the Chorus' movements into and out of the collective shrine mark fluctuations in their safety (see Introd. 2.3 above, p. xxxviii). Such corresponding scenes measure out the drama effectively for the eye as much as for the ear. *Prometheus* is set in a world literally apart and far away, beneath a bare cliff face, as bleak as the hero's future; the play's theatricality is created by the nature of his visitors and the manner of their successive entries; yet here too these arrivals from outside, and not less their departures, help reveal and progressively harden his stubbornness (see Introd. 2.4. above, p. xliv).

The chorus is visibly active throughout *Persians* and *Seven*—in the first supportive, in the second obstructive initially, dissuasive later, filled finally with uneasy sympathy; in both it has an exceptionally theatrical role at the end, in the first participating in protracted lyric grief, in the second voicing all of the grief. In *Suppliants* it is dominant, orchestrating its own predicament and rescue, chanting, singing, dancing, arguing, panicking, and rejoicing (see above). In *Prometheus* the chorus' role may be small but it is important visually and emotionally; its growing sympathy for Prometheus paradoxically accompanies the increase in his obduracy.

## 3. DRAMATIC FORM AND LANGUAGE IN AESCHYLUS

### 3.1. Dramatic form in general

A Greek tragedy moves forward in spoken episodes (serving rather like play acts) which alternate with lyric song or chant; they may themselves include brief song or chant, or passages mixing speech with song or chant. Including the prologue-scene or final movement, they range in number from five to seven. They can be very brief, with no more than a single speech from one character (the Queen at *Pers.* 598–622), or the briefest of exchanges (Danaus and Chorus *Supp.* 600–24). They regularly begin with an entry and close with an exit, and may comprise one or more scenes also delimited by entries or exits: *Supp.* 176–523 contains the movement of Danaus and Chorus into sanctuary (176–233) and the arrival and departure of Pelasgus (234–523); there are long spoken exchanges between Chorus and Pelasgus, which are interrupted by mixed spoken and lyric dialogue (347–417) or purely choral lyric (418–37), and briefly by words of Danaus (490–9). The very long central episode of *Seven* (369–719) is unique in all surviving Tragedy, for it consists largely of seven pairs of speeches by the Scout and Eteocles, spaced by three pairs of brief responding choral stanzas; the Scout may leave after his seventh speech at 652, effectively turning Eteocles' seventh (653–76) into a monologue; the episode ends with a mixed spoken and lyric exchange between him and the Chorus (677–719). The singular conception of *Prometheus* led to episodes in each of which only one other individual character appears, and then leaves—or to no entrant at all, the episodes 192–276 and 436–525 being shared just by Prometheus and the already present Chorus. These variations in form and length are in themselves a means of dramatic expression, indicating moments of realization, or crisis, marking significant developments or conveying shifts of feeling.

Plot and action advance for the most part in these episodes, in which individual characters converse with one another or with the chorus, or use monologue. In *Persians, Seven*, and *Suppliants* there are never more than two characters speaking together, and two actors can perform all the character-parts. In these plays variety and forward movement in the action may consequently seem more limited, but the formal spareness usually shapes an individual's progress with great concentration: Eteocles is the supreme example here (like Clytemnestra in *Agamemnon* and Orestes in *Libation Bearers*), but Prometheus matches him.

Aeschylus' chorus is very prominent: it chants, sings, and dances on its own or exchanges song, chant, or speech with one of more of the characters. The major lyric parts never exceed six in number, and the purely choral songs vary in length and number; there are four in each of *Persians, Seven*, and *Suppliants*. Both song and chant may voice the specially strong emotions of the chorus, at first or second hand, immediate or prospective; in this latter respect they often herald imminent disaster (*Pers*.140–9, *Seven* 790–1) or crisis (*Supp.* 808–23), all at the end of odes. The functions of these lyric parts, both pure and mixed, are discussed in Introd. 3.3 below.[59]

## 3.2. Speech and spoken dialogue

The episodes often appear to be dominated by long speeches, sometimes from one person: for example, from Darius throughout *Pers.* 681–842, Pelasgus throughout *Supp.* 234–523; and Prometheus is

---

[59] P. E. Easterling, *CCGT* 151–65 gives an excellent general account of the resources, forms, and modes which Greek Tragedy employs; there are good treatments in Gregory, *CGT*, by L. Battezzato on Lyric (148–66), M. Halleran on Episodes (167–82), and P. Wilson on Music (183–93). For a full review of these phenomena see M. Heath, *The Poetics of Greek Tragedy* (1987). M. L. West, in his *Studies* (Bibl. §2, 1990), 3–25, 'The Formal Structure of Aeschylean Tragedy', relates its elements and course to the dynamics of the plot.

inevitably the principal voice of his play. Such long speeches only seldom receive a long reply (mostly in Aeschylus' last work the *Oresteia*), for the exchange between Scout and Eteocles in *Seven* is unique (Section 3.1 above); short replies, or a series of them, are regular: for example, of the Queen to the Messenger throughout *Pers.* 290–531. Long speeches in particular often introduce new information to which the chorus or another character reacts. They may be narratives like those of the Messenger in *Persians*, or Danaus' forebodings when in *Suppliants* he sights first the approaching Argives (176–203) and second the approaching Egyptians (710–33). They are typical of all drama in tracing the formulation, or change, of thought, particularly in preparation for action: for example, in Eteocles at *Seven* 264–86 or Pelasgus at *Supp.* 438–54.

Important dramatic encounters contain more than one form of speech (or of mixed exchange), foreshadowing in technique the heavily charged scenes of the *Oresteia*: for example, that between Athena, Apollo, the Furies, and Orestes at *Eum.* 566–777. So the episode between Darius and the Queen at *Pers.* 681–842 includes his long speeches (above); a brief mixed exchange; a long stretch of dialogue in the rarer spoken metre, trochaic tetrameters (including stichomythia; on both see below); and a slightly irregular spoken exchange between Darius and the Chorus.[60] An even better example in these early plays is the varied exchange, untypical in that the chorus is one of the partners, in *Supp.* 234–523 (see Section 3.1 above). There are a few short irregular spoken exchanges: for example, between the Queen and the Messenger at *Pers.* 433–46 and between Pelasgus and the Chorus at *Supp.* 323–34. Much the commonest form of intense spoken exchange is line-by-line (stichomythia); in Aeschylus' early plays it is used chiefly for question-and-answer (*Pers.* 715–38, *Supp.* 291–322, etc.; cf. *PB* 246–58) or persuasion (*Seven* 245–64, *Supp.* 506–16, etc.). So it can precipitate a long speech, often of decision: for example, *Supp.* 455–67 where Pelasgus gives in after the Chorus' threat of suicide in the sanctuary, cf. *PB* 613–30, where Io's questioning of Prometheus persuades him to foretell her further suffering; it can develop a speech: for example, *Supp.* 204–21, where Danaus' advice to

---

[60] For speeches and dialogue in Aeschylus, see Halleran (previous n.) and Rosenmeyer, *AA* 188–210, including 201–5 on stichomythia.

his daughters leads to their identifying the gods they must supplicate; or it can complete a scene: for example, *Pers.* 232–45, the Queen's anxious questions about Athens after her dream, or *Seven* 712–19, where this form of dialogue powerfully crystallizes Eteocles' terrible decision. *Prometheus* contains a remarkably effective—and lengthy—alternation of double-line with single-line speech, as Power compels Hephaestus to fetter Prometheus; the rhythm of the dialogue perhaps suggests the interrupted hammering of each fresh fetter (36–81). The most passionate exchanges in the three plays, however, alternate one speaking voice with a lyric one: see Section 3.3 below.

The verse line of speech in Greek Tragedy is the iambic trimeter, described by Aristotle, *Poetics*, chs. 4 and 22 and *Rhetoric*, Book 3, ch. 8 as closest to the rhythm of everyday speech. Its general character is the alternation of 'long' (or 'heavy') and 'short' (or 'light') syllables, quantitative rather than dynamic or 'stressed'; but this pattern has some internal subtleties, especially in the placing of word- or phrase-divisions, and is therefore flexibly expressive. 'Trimeter' denotes a verse of three *metra* or 'measures'; the iambic *metron* consists of a variable syllable preceding a group comprising 'long–short–long'. When such a group is followed by a variable syllable, it makes a trochaic *metron*; and trochaic tetrameters ('four-measures') are used for speech in these early plays at *Pers.* 215–48 and 698–758, two scenes of urgent foreboding and of deep feeling (see Introd. 2.1, p. xxviii n. 21). The trochaic rhythm gave the impression of quicker movement than the iambic (Aristotle, *Poetics*, chs. 4 and 24; *troch-* is from the Greek word for 'run').

### 3.3. Choral song and lyric dialogue

*General.* Lyric is most commonly sung and danced by the chorus in 'odes'. They are arranged in pairs of metrically equivalent or 'responding' stanzas called *strophe* and *antistrophe*. We assume that the musical accompaniment, played on a pipe, similarly 'responded'. Rhythmic variety within stanzas is very great, often appearing subtle and delicate, but we lack almost all information about how to relate any particular metre or variation to mood. Most stanzas are self-contained in sense and syntax, however, each moving to fresh illustrative matter or a new topic; continuity across stanzas, however, sometimes occurs: for example, at *Pers.* 871–2, *Supp.* 62–3.

Sometimes a pair of such responding stanzas is followed by a free stanza, or they are separated by one. *Seven* 375–630 offers the most extended example in Tragedy of responding choral stanzas punctuating spoken scenes; there is a single pair of such stanzas at *Pers.* 694–6 = 700–2. Paired stanzas, especially in Aeschylus, sometimes have individual words, phrases, sounds, and even ideas also 'responding' exactly or approximately, often with rhyme or assonance (see too EN to e.g. *Pers.* 694–6 = 700–2, 1002–3 = 1008–9, 1038 = 1046). The phenomenon (which transfers with difficulty into English) originated in hymnic and sacral ritual and creates solemnity or a marked emphasis; final lines can be repeated at an interval, giving the effect of a refrain: for example, at the end of a stanza (*Sept.* 975–7 = 986–8, *Supp.* 890–2 = 900–2); whole stanzas respond at, for example, *Supp.* 118–21 = 129–32 and 141–3 = 151–3.

Lyric may also be sung antiphonally, in 'dialogue', between the chorus and one or more play-characters. An archetypal form and the best Tragic example is the *kommos* ('beating'), a rhythmic lament accompanying physical striking and tearing of the face and body (see EN on *Pers.* 908–1077). Xerxes joins in it with the Chorus at *Pers.* 931–1077, while at *Seven* 874–1004 the chorus divides in two for such lament. In a scene of extreme excitement at *Supp.* 825–65 two different choruses sing in contrast, and again in a tense and important exchange at 1052–61. Lyric dialogues which alternate choral singing with a chanting individual are quite rare (e.g. in the *Oresteia* at *Eum.* 916–1020; also *PB* 128–92), but antiphony between a lyric chorus and a speaking individual, the so-called 'epirrhematic' structure ('with speech afterwards'), is a marked feature of Aeschylus' whole work, from the earliest *Pers.* 256–89 through *Seven* 203–44, 686–711, *Supp.* 348–417, 734–61 into the *Oresteia* (e.g. *Ag.* 1072–113); these exchanges regularly mark a peak of emotion, or a crisis. There is no example, however, in *Prometheus*.

Other choral lyric may appear as a simple sequence of verses with varying rhythm; good examples of such free lyric are *Seven* 78–107, the entry of the panic-stricken chorus of young women, and *Supp.* 825–42, the violent entry of the Egyptians and the chorus' panic in response. The *Prometheus* affords two examples of an individual character singing (not chanting) when Prometheus briefly voices his amazement at the imminent aerial entry of the chorus (114–19), and when the god-maddened Io enters chanting at 561–5 before singing freely in 566–73 and then changing to responding stanzas in 574–88 = 593–608, in a solo aria or 'monody'.

Then there is chanting, in the regular anapaestic rhythm which can accompany the chorus' pacing steps at first entry into the *orkhêstra* (*Pers.* 1–64, *Supp.* 1–39, and *Ag.* 40–103). This rhythm also marks a degree of emotion or involvement greater than that voiced in ordinary speech, but not fully 'lyric' in intensity: so, for example, *Pers.* 140–54, 532–47; in *Prometheus* it is used also for individuals at entry (Oceanus at 284–97, Io 562–5)—or when the final catastrophe begins (1040–93, shared by the three voices of Prometheus, Hermes, and Chorus).[61]

*Lyric in Aeschylus' early plays, and in* Prometheus. Lyric is as extensive in the three early plays as in the later *Oresteia*, although in this trilogy the choral odes, some very long, have an extraordinarily suggestive and emotive quality in addition to their profound meaning. Aeschylus' manner in the early plays is not so consistent. In *Suppliants*, the first play of its trilogy, the Chorus are preoccupied throughout with their future, and they are allowed hardly any general interpretation (only 86–102 stand out). *Seven*, the final play of its trilogy, has a similar emphasis, upon personal and communal anxiety, until Eteocles has resolved to duel with his brother, saving his city but simultaneously fulfilling his father's curse; only then do the Chorus turn to historical interpretation, reviewing the action of the first two plays to draw out the full meaning of the third. The two odes *Seven*

---

[61] Note on this *General* section. 'Odes'; the Greek word is *ôidai*, 'songs', but the odes of Tragedy acquired the technical name *stasima*, 'things (performed) in (their) station', in the *orkhêstra*. The single stanzas sometimes attached to a pair of stanzas are termed 'epodes' or, if they are refrains, 'ephymnia'; if they stand between paired stanzas they are called 'mesodes'. These terms appear in the Translation, where corresponding stanzas are signalled with Str.(ophe) and Ant.(istrophe) in the margin. The ancient evidence upon all these lyric phenomena is collected by Csapo-Slater, 289–326. For some notes on individual metres see nn. 20 and 21 above, and EN on *Seven* 78–181, 287–368, 720–91; *Supp.* 1–175, 710–75, 825–907; *PB* 397–435, 526–60.

The 'ethical' aspects of music (and therefore of lyric metre) are discussed by P. Wilson in Gregory, *CGT* 186–90; see there also L. Battezzato, pp. 159–65. For lyric and the chorus in Aeschylus, see Rosenmeyer, *AA* 145–87, Sommerstein, *AT* 204–7, Conacher (1996), 150–76, and Battezzato 148–66 (152–3 and 161–3 on the *kommos*, 152–3 and 157–8 on 'epirrhematic').

720–91 and 822–47 have a profundity like many of the *Oresteia*; in 874–1004 there follows the Chorus' lengthy antiphonal lament for the dead brothers which analyses their uniquely tragic fate (the long lyric lament which closes *Persians* is not so illuminating morally because the principal sufferer Xerxes is still alive—and participates in the lament).

In *Prometheus* very little space is made for conventional choral commentary; it is the hero himself, constantly in view, who narrates the past, defending his thoughts and intentions, as well as prophesying his own and Io's future, and the significance of all these. The Chorus are sympathetic hearers, occasionally in conversation with him, both in lyric (128–192) and in speech (193–276, 436–525, 906–40), but only the last of their three very slight odes enters upon universals (397–435, 526–60, 887–906; see also Introd. 2.4, p. xxxiv).

### 3.4. Language and imagery

*General.* The 'Note on the Text, Translation, and Explanatory Notes' (pp. lxxi–lxxii below) describes the great difficulty of translating Aeschylus' poetry, because of its profuse verbal effects. These can require sustained concentration from a modern audience or reader— in the early plays very frequently, everywhere in the *Oresteia*. We have only a few hints how the ancients themselves responded. Aristophanes' comedy *Frogs*, performed in 405 BC, some fifty years after Aeschylus' death, evokes the lasting impression made by his language, especially in the *Oresteia*: comic exaggeration represents his diction as distinctively sonorous, especially in his lyrics, and as not readily intelligible to the ordinary man in the audience. Much later ancient writers who describe Aeschylus' style as direct, heroic, and full of sound are rhetoricians and literary educators, not theatregoers, and they mix admiration with reservations about what taste in their own day perceived as lack of discipline or refinement.[62]

---

[62] Aristophanes, *Frogs* 923–6, cf. 833–4, 902–4, 1016–18, 1261–97, 1365–7. Even if comic distortion is here in play, the difficulty of comprehension was presumably real enough. Among other writers these stand out: the Greek critic Dionysius of Halicarnassus (late 1st cent. BC), *On the Arrangement of Words* 22; the Roman rhetorician Quintilian (1st cent. AD), *The Institution of Oratory* 10.66; and his near-contemporary the Greek intellectual Dio Chrysostom, *Oration* 52. These and the Aristophanic passages are handily available in translation in D. A. Russell and M. Winterbottom, *Ancient Literary Criticism* (1972). For the 'reception' of Aeschylus

Throughout Aeschylus, if most clearly in the *Oresteia*, some qualities are especially his own. Simplicity and concision contrast with lengthy mixing of ideas, images, and clauses; and their sometimes extraordinary compression makes them densely suggestive. Then there are the deliberate effects of sound particularly noticed by the ancients, which are often enhanced by the deft juxtaposition or interlacing of words which characterizes the high style in an inflected language like Greek. In support is a vocabulary of the widest provenance. Aeschylus uses, echoes, and imitates words and formations from his predecessors in epic and lyric poetry, Homer above all. His own inventiveness appears to have been remarkable, in all registers of diction; his plays are crowded with rare or compound words which occur nowhere else, or only where they are obviously imitated by later poets. Because his tragic poetry is the earliest which survives, except in minute scraps, we cannot measure his debt to earlier dramatists; but it is clear that he was a great shaper of his art and its diction, with a stature like that of Shakespeare in English literature. As a poet with words he is grand, magisterial, craggy, sonorous, colourful, brilliant; but he is also delicate, natural, everyday—at times so everyday that the mere contrast with the richer styles can make him seem almost pedestrian or colloquial.

### Imagery

Many lengthy descriptions maintain a pictorial brilliance. The Messenger's report of Persian disasters in Greece (*Pers.* 353–531) is consistently vivid, with highpoints like the first clash of ships at Salamis (408–28) and the fatal crossing of Strymon's ice (495–507); Aeschylus relishes the effect of Persian names throughout the play, and particularly at 21–44, 302–28, 955–1001. Warriors are effectively individualized through their shield-devices in *Seven* (375–652). There is much Aeschylean colour in many long descriptions in *Prometheus*, for example, of Typhon and his destruction (351–72) or Io's wanderings (707–35, 790–841: see Introd. 2.4, p. xlviii). Single pictures regularly bring sudden illumination to a stage-moment, like Pelasgus' attempt

by both his contemporaries and later antiquity, see the survey by S. Halliwell in Gregory, *CGT* 399–412.

to find comparisons for the suppliants' exotic appearance (*Supp.* 279–89) or Danaus' anxiety that their young beauty may undo them (996–1005); the outlandish appearance and behaviour of the Egyptians is depicted in detail throughout 825–902, a scene extraordinarily vivid to both eye and ear.

In the *Oresteia* it is easy to see—it is inescapable—that recurrent images link and enhance meanings; they give point to narrative, accompany action, and often confirm prophecy.[63] In the early plays sustained, cumulative, and forceful imagery is seldom evident; but scholars find images from one broad field which stand in loose association and varying detail, and argue that they provide a continuity important to the play's whole effect. A few examples (some are handled with different emphasis at the ends of Introd. 2.1–4 above): 'yoking' is a prominent image of *Persians*: the Persians try to throw a yoke over Greece (50), just as they yoke the Hellespont with a bridge (72, 130, 722); both yokings are doomed (725, 745–6). In *Seven* the ship of state, captained by the Theban Eteocles (2–3, 62–4, 652, allusively at 32–3, 208–10), must weather the storm of attack or capsize (114–15, 795–6; allusively 690–1, 705–8, 758–65); in this play much is made of constant reference to the Theban defenders' duty to their motherland's soil and gods; but, as in *Persians*, these are naturally figurative terms, not strong, deliberate images; and they are barely avoidable in such a plot. It has been well observed, however, that in *Seven* there is a shift in prominence from the city to the single, royal, and doomed family once Eteocles finds he must duel with his brother (after 653).[64] In *Suppliants* the early and extended image of the suppliants under threat from the pursuing Egyptians like doves from hawks is powerful (223–8; it is reused for them at *PB* 856–9); but critics associate too many casual, brief, and independent phrases with it (e.g. 30 swarm, 510–11 winged serpents, 751 sacrilegious ravens, 796 a mountain vulture).[65] *Prometheus*, for all its verbal colour, seems to lack images which consistently focus the issues, but some recur

---

[63]  See Collard (2002), pp. lv–lviii.

[64]  Thalmann (n. 66 below), 78–81; cf. n. 28 above.

[65]  Conacher (1996), 132–3, well says that searching for thematic imagery in *Suppliants* 'perhaps fails to do justice to the particularly rich and imaginative use of figurative language throughout this play'.

sufficiently to merit attention, such as yoking and fettering, and medicine.[66]

## 4. AESCHYLUS NOW: 'RECEPTION' AND PUBLIC RESPONSE

Aeschylus' plays were first translated into English in the later eighteenth century, and became widely accessible only in the mid-nineteenth. Until then they were read in the original Greek only by learned men and a few university and school pupils using Latin translations and commentaries which concerned themselves almost exclusively with the immediate meaning of the text. Commentaries with English notes which considered questions of form and poetic style began to appear from the 1840s. These and later nineteenth-century studies, however, hardly touched the theatrical aspects of his plays and their deeper issues: these had to wait until the second half of the twentieth century.[67]

[66] For an assessment of 'key' images in *Prometheus*, see Griffith (Bibl. §3.2, 1983), 19–21 (cited at the end of Section 2.4, n. 46).

A most helpful and level-headed general approach to imagery in Aeschylus (in all six authentic plays, and the *Prometheus*) may be found in Conacher (1996), 115–49, with an evaluation of the scholarly literature; similarly judicious is Garvie (Bibl. §7.3, 1969[1] and 2006[2]), 64–72; Rosenmeyer, *AA* 117–42 ranges widely. The fullest collection of material is E. Petrounias, *Funktion und Thematik der Bilder bei Aischylos* (1976), who often, unfortunately, exaggerates thematic linking in these early plays. The study of figurative language in a single field, intellectual activity, by Sansone (Bibl. §6.2, 1975) has a complete list of examples which reveals some remarkable clusterings of such imagery, e.g. *Pers.* 205–27, *Supp.* 438–73, *Seven* 280–90, 554–618 (the latter describing the seer Amphiaraus), *PB* 866–86 (but what else in a play where the protagonist is clever even beyond his fellow gods?—see e.g. ll. 18, 62, 308, 328, 944). Individual plays: *Persians*, Anderson (Bibl. §7.1, 1972) and Hall (§3.2, 1996), 22–3; Conacher (above), 120–4; *Suppliants*, Garvie (above), 69–72, Conacher 132–9; *Seven*, Thalmann (1978), 31–81, Vidal-Naquet (1981), Zeitlin (1982), all in Bibl. §7.3; Conacher 124–32; *Prometheus*, Griffith (above), Conacher (1980), 145–9, Mossman (§7.4, 1996).

[67] The first complete translation was into verse, by R. Potter (1771, etc.). Very literal prose translations ('cribs') started to appear in the 1820s; further verse translations came after 1840, including Robert Browning's of the *Agamemnon* (1877), again made famous by Terence Rattigan's play of 1948. Translations into European languages began at about the same time, only France having a slight lead over England. Aeschylus was much slower in reaching modern translation than the other surviving Greek tragedians, Sophocles and Euripides. The first complete commentary in English was F. A. Paley's (1855).

Detailed critical appreciation of Aeschylus as a poet of the theatre began in Britain only with Gilbert Murray's *Aeschylus* of 1940 (he had earlier translated some plays for performance), although Gilbert Norwood had treated the poet less fully in his *Greek Tragedy* (1920). The USA was a little quicker, with e.g. H. W. Smyth's *Aeschylean*

In England at least Aeschylus began to inspire graphic artists earlier than he attracted theatrical producers;[68] in the twentieth century this direction was almost completely reversed. Painters were drawn chiefly to the *Oresteia*, and in its shadow infrequently to the other plays, from the 1860s; somewhat earlier to the *Prometheus*.[69]

The myths which yielded the plots of *Seven*, *Suppliants*, and *Prometheus* first became known through the recovery of Latin literature, chiefly the poets, in the early Renaissance of the twelfth and thirteenth centuries. In England Geoffrey Chaucer translated or adapted incidents in them from Boccaccio's retelling; later poets like Spenser, Milton, and Blake alluded to them. *Persians* was very late in receiving attention of any kind. There appear to have been few performances of any of the four plays anywhere in Europe before the advent of translations. *Prometheus* led the way on the Continent, and as early as 1609. The earliest production certainly known in this country was also of this play, in 1775 in London, two years after H. Morell had published a translation of it. Incidents in the Danaid myth beyond those told in *Suppliants* were burlesqued by T. F. Dibdin (1821, in London) and in F. Cooper's *Hypermnestra* (1869, also in London). There were burlesques of *Persians* (1843, in Oxford, but probably not performed) and of *Prometheus* (1865, in London). Some of the earliest 'true' performances were of the *Seven*, in the USA at the end of the nineteenth century—most remarkably, since this play has always been one of the least performed of all Greek tragedies. Isadora Duncan nevertheless danced some of its lyrics on the Continent soon after 1900.

Apart from *Prometheus* (above) it appears that only *Persians* was given a straightforward production in Europe before 1900, in 1889. Subsequent modern performances of our plays, or of adaptations, began at Delphi with *Prometheus* (1927, repeated in 1930; filmed in part) and *Suppliants* (1930, in possibly the first production of

---

*Tragedy* (1924). The greatest recent advance is due to Oliver Taplin, especially his *The Stagecraft of Aeschylus* (1977), a pointer in many fresh directions, not only theatrical.

[68]  See F. Macintosh, *CCGT* 284–8.

[69]  The most significant earlier works were thirteen drawings to illustrate the *Oresteia* made by John Flaxman in 1793–5; in these same years he made three or four drawings each based upon *Suppliants* and *Prometheus*. Shelley's *Prometheus Unbound* was published in 1820.

modern times) and with *Seven* at Syracuse (1924). During the 1990s, however, productions became more numerous, if still rare, but some were notable: *Persians* by P. Sellars (1993, in Salzburg) and *Seven* by E. Schleef (but in a 'double bill' with Euripides' *Suppliants*, entitled *The Mothers*: 1986, in Frankfurt). *Suppliants* was produced by C. Mee in a reconstructed trilogy entitled 'Big Love' (2000, in Louisville). *Prometheus* inspired Tom Paulin's *Seize the Fire: A Version of Aeschylus' Prometheus Bound* (1989) and a TV film by T. Harrison (1998). *Seven* had been translated by A. Arrufat in Cuba in 1968 but was suppressed; it was republished in 2001 and given its first performance in Glasgow in the same year.[70]

---

[70] For the 1927 Delphi *Prometheus*, see Wiles (Bibl. §5, 2000), 183–9. Sellars's *Persians* and Harrison's *Prometheus* are fully discussed, with illustrations from performance, by E. Hall in Hall, Macintosh, Wrigley (Bibl. §8, 2004), 176–85 and 185–93. In the same volume Schleef's *Seven* is discussed by E. Fischer-Lichte at 355–9, Mee's 'Big Love' by H. Foley at 107–8, and Arrufat's *Seven* by L. Hardwick at 222–4; an Italian film by M. Martone based upon *Seven* (1998) is treated by P. Michelakis at 199, 205–6. Paulin's *Seize the Fire* is discussed by F. Macintosh, *Amid our Troubles: Irish Versions of Greek Tragedy* (2002), 54–7. W. M. Calder III, 'Aeschylus, *Prometheus*: a DDR interpretation', in his *Theatrokrateia* (Collected Papers), ed. R. Scott Smith (2005), 31–40, throws interesting light on the play's meaning for East European Communism in 1968.

Other details in these paragraphs have been drawn from works in Bibl. §8: Hartigan (1995), Burian (1997), Macintosh (1997), Garland (§5, 2004), Hall and Macintosh (2005), Macintosh, Michelakis, Hall, Taplin (2005), together with J. M. Walton, *Living Greek Theatre* (1987) and H. Flashar, *Inszenierung der Antike: Das griechische Drama auf der Bühne der Neuzeit, 1585–1990* (1991). The three works here by Hall, etc. (2004, 2005) and Macintosh, etc. (2005) impressively augment the bibliography I was able to give for productions of the *Oresteia* in Collard (2002), pp. lxi–ii; see too A. Wrigley, 'Aeschylus' *Agamemnon* on BBC Radio, 1946–1976', *International Journal of the Classical Tradition*, 12 (2005), 216–44.

The most comprehensive guide to the artistic 'reception' of Aeschylus remains J. Reid, *Oxford Guide to Classical Mythology in the Arts, 1300–1990* (Bibl. §8, 1993): see pp. 323–5 'Danaides' for *Suppliants*, 594–9 'Io' for *Suppliants* and *Prometheus Bound*; 923–37 'Prometheus' (930–5 for *Prometheus Bound*); 989–92 'Seven against Thebes' for *Seven* (cf. 'Oedipus', 754–62).

# Note on the Text, Translation, and Explanatory Notes

## TEXT

The basis of Aeschylus' Greek text is precarious. Only seven plays attributed to him survive complete from his estimated total production of more than eighty; of these seven, only three are preserved in any considerable number of medieval manuscripts which have independent importance (*Persians, Seven,* and the almost certainly inauthentic *Prometheus*), while the other four (*Suppliants* and the three plays of the *Oresteia*) depend variously upon a very few quite closely related manuscripts or even upon one alone. This one manuscript of supreme authority for *Suppliants* has suffered physical damage and, like all other manuscripts of Aeschylus, frequently offers a text so corrupt that editors cannot reconstruct the poet's original words with any confidence; instead, they are often forced to make the best diagnosis they can of a corruption, and to emend it as best they can by conjecture.

The Greek text translated here is that edited by M. L. West (Bibl. §2, 1990[1], 1998[2]). It is acknowledged as the most thorough and authoritative modern edition in describing and evaluating the manuscripts; and its critical apparatus is generous in reporting manuscript readings and editors' corrections and conjectures. West's edited text is often adventurous in conjecture, but sometimes also surprisingly conservative where he retains what many other editors have condemned and emended. He is consistently honest in marking as desperately corrupt the numerous words or passages which he believes have yet to receive plausible conjecture, let alone convincing emendation. My translation replaces this corrupt wording with what seem to be the soundest conjectures from his apparatus (I have listed these in the Textual Appendix after the Explanatory Notes). Places where text has been lost are signalled in the translation with '*words missing*' or the like enclosed by square brackets; where there can be little doubt of the sense of the words lost, I supply it inside these brackets. I think it important that users of this translation, whether able to read the original Greek or not, should know the degree of authority for what they read and be careful accordingly when they interpret both drama and poetry. Many of these places, and some others where West's edited text is less secure but still problematic, are therefore discussed in the Explanatory Notes.[71]

TRANSLATION

The varying reliability of the Greek text adds to the difficulties of translating a poet as individual as Aechylus. First, the primary meaning even where the text seems entirely secure and straightforward is often fiercely contested, and not only because the surrounding context may sometimes be ambiguous or damaged: Aeschylus is often abrupt in expression, and in changing ideas or topics, and the precise implication of a sudden new one can be hard to fix. Second, Aeschylus' verbal style is flexible and daring, sometimes clear and easy, especially in speech, sometimes complex, dense, and full of suggestive imagery: an attempt to describe it is made in Introd. 3.4 above.

Can this singular richness be reproduced in translation? The translation which I offer here is not a poet's. I have tried to make it as accurate and readable as possible; but even with allowance made for the state of Aeschylus' text, there will be many places where my translation can and will be disputed, and where other interpretations are not disprovable. I have tried to reflect the general tone and flow of the language, in particular the broad variations in diction and style which follow from the alternation between speech and lyric. I have been as consistent as possible in the translation of words and ideas which regularly recur and have thematic importance; and I have reproduced many close repetitions of words which may be not so much deliberate as unconsidered or even unconscious (the Greeks were apparently much less sensitive than we are to this kind of repetition). I have tried not to go too far from the imagery or idiom of the original if it can be kept without unnaturalness in English. I have occasionally adjusted the limited style of ancient Greek pronunciation to the more flexible

---

[71] For a description of Aeschylus' manuscript and editorial history, see Rosen-meyer, *AA* 11–28 or Kovacs in Gregory, *CGT* 379–93; cf. Garland (Bibl. §5, 2004), 89–91.

English kind, particularly by using exclamation marks; but I have very
seldom changed its location, and then only to make clear the emphasis and sequence of ideas. Parenthesis is marked by dashes; I use
square brackets to indicate or to supplement brief textual defects (see
'Text' above); round brackets enclose many of the italicized 'stage-
directions'.

The translation of spoken dialogue, and of spoken verses set among
lyric, is into prose (some of the first examples of the latter to be
encountered are *Pers.* 260–1, 266–7, etc., cf. e.g. *Seven* 208–10, 216–
18). Those verses which were apparently intoned or chanted, in an
almost regular anapaestic rhythm, I have rendered line-by-line, but
with no attempt at imitating the rhythmic regularity (*Pers.* 1–64, for
example). I have been more ambitious—or self-indulgent—in translating lyric. I have translated pure song differently, whether choral or
antiphonal between chorus and actor (*Pers.* 930–1065, for example),
in an attempt to show its distinctive nature and emotional intensity,
and the importance of many choral songs to the action and meaning
(see Introd. 3.3 above). This pure lyric is for the most part shaped
by Aeschylus into stanzas in pairs which have identical form and
rhythm, every line 'responding' between *strophe* and *antistrophe* (also
3.3); in these stanza-pairs I have tried to achieve near-responsion in
the number of syllables in the English lines, and, where I can, also
approximate rhythmic expression in stressed and unstressed syllables.
There has been some loss in the lyric, however: achieving readability
in our language has often brought some sacrifice of exactly those
effects of compression, juxtaposition, and sound described above as
individual to Aeschylus. I disclaim any pretension to have made these
lyric parts more 'poetic' than the remainder of the translation: if they
appear and read 'differently', that achieves my main object.[72]

Lastly, I must record a few special difficulties in translating Greek
Tragedy over which all translators agonize. Words describing or

---

[72] See Edith Hall's assessment of H. D. F. Kitto's very successful translation of
Sophocles, made upon approximately similar lines: *Sophocles: Antigone, Oedipus the
King, Electra* (1994, also 'World's Classics'), pp. xxxiii–iv. So too Peter Burian in his
translation of *Suppliants* (Princeton, 1991), pp. xi–xviii.

In his early life Gerard Manley Hopkins experimented with translations of
*Prometheus*; if only in his poetic maturity he had translated the whole of Aeschylus,
for in his own work he came perhaps nearer to Aeschylus' verbal brilliance than any
other English poet!

evoking social or moral values and behaviour, injury, outrage, and suffering; their physical and emotional impact; and reaction to them in pain, anger, resentment, grief, and lamentation—these are the life-blood of Tragedy. Greek is rich with these words, and some individual ones appear in differing contexts which occasionally force on them differing translations in English; here any translator must choose as best he can from the idiom of his own day. In particular, English is losing from everyday use many words which seem appropriate for a vocabulary of extreme suffering: these are such archaic-sounding or almost self-conscious literary words as 'woe' or 'evils' and the exclamation 'alas!', and I have for the most part tried to avoid them. Commonplace and ritualized ancient reactions to hurt like constant tears and loud, demonstrative grief are also obsolescent in much of the modern English-speaking world and its culture; literal translation of the Greek terms inevitably sounds strange or exaggerated to the modern ear, and more than strange in its insistent repetition. Greek had also many exclamations, some of them apparently inarticulate; in Tragedy those of pain and grief naturally predominate. I have sometimes reduced these from their full and impressive sonority to a mere 'O-o-oh!' or the like; or I replace or accompany them with an articulate meaning such as 'Sorrow!' or 'No!', or with an itali-cized 'stage-direction', much as a modern dramatist might use, like '(*shrieking*)'.[73]

Line-numbers are those of the Greek text, placed in the margin at the point of approximate correspondence.

The 'stage-directions' depend as far as possible on modern con-sensus on how the plays were probably performed in the ancient theatre. Practically all are safe inferences from the text about the moments of entry and exit and their manner, and about costume,

---

[73] There is a huge international literature on the difficulties of translating Greek Tragedy. In addition to the remarks made by all translators themselves, see for English esp. P. Green, 'Some Versions of Aeschylus', in his *Essays on Antiquity* (1950), an essay reprinted more than once; K. J. Dover, 'The Speakable and the Unspeakable', *Greek and the Greeks* (1987), 176–81; P. Burian, 'Translations Yesterday and Today', *CCGT* 271–6 (and n. 72 above); Wiles (Bibl. §5, 2000), 196–201, 236; P. Woodruff, 'Justice in Translation: Rendering Ancient Greek Tragedy', in Gregory, *CGT* 490–504; Macintosh, Michelakis, Hall, Taplin (Bibl. §8, 2005), 189–251 (various authors, including translations for the stage); J. M. Walton, *Found in Translation: Greek Drama in English* (2006).

movement, posture, and gesture. Special problems are discussed in the Explanatory Notes.

In reproducing the names of persons and places I have generally followed the comfortable tradition of preferring familiar Latinized or Anglicized forms to the more accurately (and now modishly) transcribed Greek ones—for example, I use Oceanus rather than Okeanos, Athens rather than Athenai. In the usual pronunciation, all single vowels are voiced, especially final −*e*, which is long as in (e.g.) Aphrodite (an exception is English monosyllabic Thrace). Adjacent vowels should be pronounced as a diphthong unless the second is marked with diaeresis, as in (e.g.) Acheloïs. The commonest diphthongs are *ae*, which in English convention varies between *i* as in *high* (e.g. Perrhaebians) and *ee* (e.g. Aegyptus); *au* as in *noun* (e.g. Aulis, but many say 'Awlis'); *eu* as in *deuce* (e.g. Zeus); *oe* as in *subpoena* (e.g. Euboea). Both initial and internal *c* and *ch* (representing Greek *k* and *kh*) are normally hard, as in (e.g.) Cadmus (Greek *Kadmos*), Achaea (Greek *Akhaia*); but both initial and internal *c* are soft before *e* or *i*, especially in Latinized names, such as Cilicia. The Greeks frequently personified abstract concepts as gods or powers; I have rendered these as far as possible with a capitalized English translation: for example, Justice for *Dikê*, Fate for *Moira*, Fury for *Erinus*. (In the Explanatory Notes Greek names and words are sometimes transliterated in underlined italics to serve etymological clarification.)

## EXPLANATORY NOTES

In all four plays the Notes include summaries of the action and its development, with comment on issues, persons, form and structure, and tone. They handle successive episodes or scenes, or such elements as choral odes, dialogues, or long speeches. If they are read consecutively, they offer an analytic résumé of the play which greatly expands upon the play summaries beginning the volume; in *Persians*, for example, they stand under the line-numbers 1–154, 155–531, 231–45, 256–89, 290–514, 532–97, 598–622, 623–80, 681–851, 759–851, 852–907, 908–1077.

For the rest, the Notes range very widely, in the hope that explanation or brief comment will help fuller appreciation of the plays.

There are many cross-references within individual plays; occasional note is made of comparable matter and language in the other plays of Aeschylus, and in Homer's *Iliad* and *Odyssey*, but very seldom in other Greek drama or authors. Purely textual notes are enclosed in square brackets, and where possible given the final place in an extended discussion of a line or passage.

# Bibliography and Further Reading

ITEMS listed are mostly recent books and articles, almost all in English or in English translation. They are all important or useful; many contain their own bibliographies, so that readers may have a number of starting-points to follow up their own interests. Items in each section are arranged in chronological order; those which require a good knowledge of Greek are asterisked, but apart from text-critical works and linguistic commentaries (mostly in §§2 and 3), hardly anything is listed which will not yield most of its value to someone armed with this or any other translation which gives the line-numbers of the Greek text.

1.1. *Complete English translations of Aeschylus.* R. Lattimore in D. Grene and R. Lattimore (eds.), *Complete Greek Tragedies,* vol. 1, 1953: still the 'standard' complete translation. H. W. Smyth, 2 vols. (Loeb Classical Library), 2nd edn. 1957: includes the great majority of the fragments (a new complete Loeb translation is being prepared by A. H. Sommerstein). M. Ewans, 2 vols. (Everyman), 1995–6 includes major fragments and is directed at a 'performance' text, with notes accordingly.

1.2. *Translations of individual plays in this volume. Persians*: J. Lembke, C. J. Herington, 1981 (with brief notes); A. J. Podlecki, 1991 (a 'companion' with translation); E. Hall in §3.2 below. *Seven against Thebes*: C. M. Dawson, 1970 (with commentary). *Suppliants*: P. Burian, 1991 (with brief notes). *Prometheus Bound*: C. J. Herington, J. Scully, 1975 (with brief notes); A. J. Podlecki in §3.2 below.

2. *Critical editions of the Greek text. Surviving plays*: *D. L. Page, 1972 (Oxford Classical Texts); *M . L. West, 1st edn. 1990, 2nd edn. 1998 (Teubner Series), supplemented by his *Studies in Aeschylus,* 1990. Both these editions have introductory matter and critical apparatus in Latin; West's two volumes have full bibliography of text-critical work. Review of West's two volumes by Sir Hugh Lloyd-Jones, *Further Academic Papers* (2005), 163–80 (first published, 1993). Fragments: *Tragicorum Graecorum Fragmenta*, vol. 3: *Aeschylus*, ed.

S. L. Radt, 1985: exhaustive critical edition, with some interpretative matter, in Latin. English readers have Smyth (§1.1 above), vol. 2, pp. 374–521, with Appendix by H. Lloyd-Jones, pp. 525–603 (Greek text, English translation and brief introductory notes) and Ewans, vol. 2 (§1.1 above, where see also Sommerstein).

**3.1.** *Complete commentaries on the surviving plays.* *F. A. Paley, *The Tragedies of Aeschylus*, 4th edn., 1879: Paley's common-sense makes his work still useful. *H. J. Rose, *A Commentary on the Complete Greek Tragedies of Aeschylus* 2 vols., 1957–8. J. Hogan, *A Commentary on the Complete Greek Tragedies of Aeschylus*, 1984 (based on the Lattimore translation of 1953, §1.1 above).

**3.2.** *Editions and commentaries of the individual plays. Persians:* *H. D. Broadhead, 1960 (major work); E. Hall, 1996 (excellent; contains translation); Sommerstein, *AT* 71–96 (a brief 'running' commentary). *Seven against Thebes:* *G. O. Hutchinson, 1985 (major work, but concise); Conacher (1996) 39–64 (a 'running' analysis); Sommerstein, *AT* 92–134. *Suppliants:* *H. Friis Johansen, E. W. Whittle, 3 vols., 1980 (almost entirely philological; a huge repository of information); Sommerstein, *AT* 97–134 (a 'running' commentary); see also A. F. Garvie in §7.3 below. *Prometheus Bound:* *G. Thomson, 1932; Conacher (1980) 32–81 (a detailed 'running' commentary); *M. Griffith, 1982 (major work); A. J. Podlecki, 2005 (excellent; contains translation, brief commentary and very wide-ranging introduction).

**4.** *Bibliographical surveys of Aeschylus.* Writings upon Aeschylus are numberless and beyond concise survey. The most helpful starting point for all enquiries is now Sommerstein, *AT* 447–79, who categorizes and briefly evaluates a large range of publications. *CCGT* 355 has a list of Texts, Commentaries, and Translations of Aeschylus, and on 359–79 a list of Works Cited in the entire volume. S. Ireland, *Aeschylus* ('Greece and Rome' New Surveys in the Classics 18), 1986, surveys the principal aspects of Aeschylean tragedy, with good bibliographic annotation. The very large bibliography for all Tragedy in Gregory, *CGT* (2005) provides useful updating to these works; similar but less full, although categorized, is Storey and Allan (2005 in §5 below), 296–304.

**5.** *General studies of Greek Tragedy in English.* J. P. Vernant and P. Vidal-Naquet, *Tragedy and Myth in Ancient Greece*, 1981 (original

French edition of 1973). O. P. Taplin, *Greek Tragedy in Action*, 1978. A. Lesky, *Greek Tragic Poetry*, 1983 (the bibliography remains as in the original German edition of 1972). W. B. Stanford, *Greek Tragedy and the Emotions*, 1983. *CHGL* (1985), 258–345 (various authors). S. Goldhill, *Reading Greek Tragedy*, 1986. C. Segal, *Interpreting Greek Tragedy: Myth, Poetry, Texts*, 1986. P. D. Arnott, *Public and Performance in the Greek Theatre*, 1989. C. B. R. Pelling (ed.), *Characterization and Individuality in Greek Tragedy*, 1990. J. Winkler and F. I. Zeitlin (eds.), *Nothing to do with Dionysus? Athenian Drama in its Social Context*, 1990. B. Zimmermann, *Greek Tragedy: An Introduction*, 1991 (original German edition of 1985): a brief student's handbook. R. Rehm, *The Greek Tragic Theatre*, 1992: concentrates on 'performance'. C. Meier, *The Political Art of Greek Tragedy*, 1993 (original German edition of 1988). R. B. Scodel (ed.), *Theater and Society in the Classical World*, 1993. Csapo-Slater, 1994: the ancient evidence translated, analysed, and annotated. J. R. Green, *Theatre in Ancient Greek Society*, 1994. R. A. Seaford, *Reciprocity and Ritual: Homer and Tragedy in the Developing City-State*, 1994. *CCGT* (1997): studies by various authors on the historical context of Tragedy, on the plays, and on Tragedy's reception since antiquity. C. B. R. Pelling (ed.), *Greek Tragedy and the Historian*, 1997. D. Wiles, *Tragedy in Athens: Performance Space and Theatrical Meaning*, 1997. A. P. Burnett, *Revenge in Attic and Later Tragedy*, 1998. B. Goward, *Telling Tragedy: Narrative Technique in Aeschylus, Sophocles and Euripides*, 1998. S. Goldhill and R. Osborne (eds.), *Performance Culture and Athenian Democracy*, 1999. J. Griffin, 'The Social Function of Attic Tragedy', *Classical Quarterly*, 48 (1998), 39–61, with a debate in response by R. A. Seaford, ibid. 50 (2000), 20–45, S. Goldhill, *Journal of Hellenic Studies*, 120 (2000), 34–56, S. Scullion, *Classical Quarterly*, 52 (2002), 102–37, and P. J. Rhodes, *Journal of Hellenic Studies*, 123 (2003), 104–19. L. McClure, *Spoken Like a Woman: Speech and Gender in Athenian Drama*, 1999. D. Wiles, *Greek Theatre Performance: An Introduction*, 2000. C. B. R. Pelling, *Literary Texts and the Greek Historian*, 2000. P. Wilson, 'Powers of Horror and Laughter: The Great Age of Drama', in O. P. Taplin (ed.), *Literature in the Greek and Roman Worlds: A New Perspective*, 2000, 88–132. H. P. Foley, *Female Acts in Greek Tragedy*, 2001. J. Barrett, *Staged Narrative: Poetics and the Messenger in Greek Tragedy*, 2002. R. Rehm, *The Play of Space*:

*Spatial Transformation in Greek Tragedy* (2002). A. H. Sommerstein, *Greek Drama and Dramatists*, 2002 (original Italian edition of 2000): both Tragedy and Comedy briefly introduced, with an anthology of texts. C. Sourvinou-Inwood, *Tragedy and Athenian Religion*, 2003. R. Garland, *Surviving Greek Tragedy*, 2004 (on what has survived, and its reception). Gregory, *CGT* (2005): studies by various authors of all aspects of Tragedy and its reception, with a splendid bibliography. I. C. Storey and A. Allan, *A Guide to Ancient Greek Drama* (2005): a detailed basic introduction.

**6.1.** *General studies of Aeschylus.* M. Gagarin, *Aeschylean Drama*, 1976 (a useful general study). J. Herington, *Aeschylus*, 1981. Rosenmeyer, *AA*: the fullest dramatic and literary appreciation. R. P. Winnington-Ingram, *Studies in Aeschylus*, 1983 (see also his chapter in *CHGL* (1985), 281–95). Sommerstein, *AT* 1996: comprehensive handbook. Conacher (1996). A. J. Podlecki, *The Political Background of Aeschylean Tragedy*, 2nd edn., 1999. M. Lloyd, *Oxford Readings in Aeschylus* (2006).

**6.2.** *Language and Style in Aeschylus.* *W. B. Stanford, *Aeschylus in his Style*, 1942. *B. H. Fowler, 'Aeschylus' Imagery', *Classica et Mediaevalia*, 28 (1967), 1–74. *D. Sansone, *Aeschylean Metaphors for Intellectual Activity*, 1975. Cf. Rosenmeyer, *AA* 75–142, Garvie (§7.3 below, 1969[1] and 2006[2]), 64–72, and Conacher (1996), 119–45.

**6.3.** *Characterization in Aeschylus.* R. D. Dawe, 'Inconsistency of Plot and Character in Aeschylus', *Proceedings of the Cambridge Philological Society*, 9 (1963), 3–19. P. E. Easterling, 'Presentation of Character in Aeschylus', *Greece & Rome*, 20 (1973), 3–19 (= *G&R Studies 2; Greek Tragedy* (1995), 12–28). Rosenmeyer, *AA* 211–55. Essays by P. E. Easterling, 'Constructing Character in Greek Tragedy' and S. Goldhill, 'Character and Action', in Pelling (1990) in §5 above, 83–99 and 100–27.

**6.4.** *Aeschylus on the ancient stage.* A. D. Trendall and T. B. L. Webster, *Illustrations of Greek Theatre* (1970), 41–9. Taplin, *Stagecraft* (1977): documents, subsumes, and qualifies all previous studies (cf. Taplin (1978) in §5 above). Rosenmeyer, *AA* 45–74. J. R. Green and E. W. Handley, *Images of the Greek Theatre*, 1995. P. E. Easterling and E. Hall (eds.), *Greek and Roman Actors: Aspects of an Ancient Profession*, 2002. E. Hall, *The Theatrical Cast of Athens* (2006). Cf. also

Arnott (1989), Rehm (1992 and 2002), Green (1994), and Wiles (1997 and 2000), in §5 above.

7. *Studies of the individual plays in this volume.*

**7.1.** *Persians*: Monographs: A. N. Michelini, *Tradition and Dramatic Form in the* Persians *of Aeschylus*, 1982. P. Ghiron-Bastagne (ed.), *Les Perses d'Eschyle*, 1993 (wide-ranging collection of papers). T. Harrison, *The Emptiness of Asia: Aeschylus'* Persians *and the History of the Fifth Century*, 2000. H. T. Wallinga, *Xerxes' Greek Adventure*, 2005, esp. 47–52 and 114–48 on the Battle of Salamis. See also H. Bacon, *Barbarians in Greek Tragedy*, 1961; E. Hall, *Inventing the Barbarian: Greek Self-definition through Tragedy*, 1989; P. Georges, *Barbarian Asia and the Greek Experience: From the Archaic Period to the Age of Xenophon*, 1994. Articles: S. M. Adams, 'Salamis Symphony: the *Persae* of Aeschylus', in M. White (ed.), *Studies in Honor of Gilbert Norwood* (1952), 34–41 (reprinted in E. Segal (ed.), *Oxford Readings in Greek Tragedy* [1983], 34–41); G. Clifton, 'The mood of the *Persai* of Aeschylus', *American Journal of Philology*, 85 (1964), 173–84; H. C. Avery, 'Dramatic devices in Aeschylus' *Persians*', *Greece & Rome*, 10 (1963), 111–22; B. Alexandersson, 'Darius in the *Persians*', *Eranos*, 65 (1967), 1–11; M. Anderson, 'The imagery of the *Persians*', *Greece & Rome*, 19 (1972), 166–74 (reprinted in I. McAuslan, P. Walcot (eds.), *Greek Tragedy*. 'Greece and Rome' Studies, vol. II [1993], 29–37); S. Ireland, 'Dramatic structure in the *Persae* and *Prometheus* of Aeschylus', *Greece & Rome*, 20, (1973), 162–8 (reprinted in I. McAuslan, P. Walcot (eds.), *Greek Tragedy*: 'Greece and Rome' Studies, Vol. II [1993], 38–44); R. P. Winnington-Ingram, 'Zeus in the *Persae*', (1983) in §6.1 above, 1–15; S. Goldhill, 'Battle narrative and politics in Aeschylus' *Persae*', *Journal of Hellenic Studies*, 108 (1988), 189–93; M. McCall, 'Aeschylus in the *Persae*: a bold stratagem succeeds', in M. J. Cropp, etc. (eds.), *Greek Tragedy and its Legacy: Essays Presented to D. J. Conacher*, 1986, 43–9; J. F. Lazenby, 'Aischylos and Salamis', *Hermes*, 116 (1988), 168–85; S. Said, 'Tragédie et renversement: l'exemple des *Perses*', *Métis*, 3 (1988), 321–41; Conacher (1996), 3–35; J. Barrett, 'Narrative and the messenger in Aeschylus' *Persians*', *American Journal of Philology*, 116 (1995), 539–57 (revised in *Staged Narrative* [2002 in §5 above], 23–55, cf. 14–19); C. Pelling, 'Aeschylus' *Persians* and History', in Pelling (§5 above, 1997), 1–19. M. Griffith, 'The king and eye: the rule of the father in Greek tragedy', *Proceedings* *of the Cambridge Philological Society*, 44 (1998), 20–84, at 44–65 (on Darius and Xerxes); A. F. Garvie, 'Text and dramatic interpretation in "Persae" ', *Lexis*, 17 (1999), 21–40; M. Ebbott, 'The list of the war dead in Aeschylus' *Persians*', *Harvard Studies in Classical Philology*, 100 (2000), 83–96. L. McClure, 'Maternal authority and heroic disgrace in Aeschylus' *Persians*', *Transactions and Proceedings of the American Philological Association*, 136 (2006), 71–97.

7.2. *Seven against Thebes*. *Monographs*: H. D. Cameron, *Studies on the* Seven against Thebes *of Aeschylus*, 1971; W. G. Thalmann, *Dramatic Art in Aeschylus'* Seven against Thebes, 1978; F. I. Zeitlin, *Under the sign of the shield: semiotics and Aeschylus'* Seven against Thebes, 1982; A. Aloni, etc. (eds.), *I Sette a Tebe: del mito alla letteratura*, 2002 (papers from an international seminar; contains exhaustive bibliography). *Articles*: L. Golden, 'The character of Eteocles and the meaning of the *Septem*', *Classical Philology*, 59 (1964), 79–89; A. J. Podlecki, 'The character of Eteocles in Aeschylus' *Septem*', *Transactions and Proceedings of the American Philological Association*, 95 (1964), 283–99; O. L. Smith, 'The father's curse: some thoughts on the *Seven against Thebes*', *Classica et Mediaevalia*, 26 (1965), 27–43; A. L. Brown, 'Eteocles and the chorus in *Seven against Thebes*', *Phoenix*, 31 (1977), 300–18; P. Vidal-Naquet, 'The Shields of the Heroes', in J.-P. Vernant and P. Vidal-Naquet (1981 in §5 above), 120–49, at 128–41; R. P. Winnington-Ingram, '*Septem contra Thebas*', (1983) in §6.1 above, 16–54; A. A. Long, 'Pro and contra fratricide: Aeschylus, *Septem* 653–719', in J. H. Betts, etc. (eds.), *Studies in Honour of T. B. L. Webster*, I, 1986, 179–89; Conacher (1996), 36–74; H. M. Roisman, 'The messenger and Eteocles in the *Seven against Thebes*', *L'Antiquité Classique*, 59 (1990), 17–36; J. A. Johnson, 'Eteocles and the posting decisions', *Rheinisches Museum*, 135 (1992), 193–7; L. Edmunds, 'Sounds off stage and on stage in Aeschylus' "Seven against Thebes" ', in Aloni, *I Sette a Tebe* (2002 above), 105–15; D. W. Berman, ' "Seven-Gated" Thebes and Narrative Topography in Aeschylus' *Seven against Thebes*', *Quaderni Urbinati di Cultura Classica*, 71 (2002), 73–100; E. Stehle, 'Prayer and curse in Aeschylus' *Seven against Thebes*', *Classical Philology*, 100 (2005), 101–22.

7.3. *Suppliants*. *Monographs*: R. D. Murray, *The Motif of Io in Aeschylus'* Supplices, 1958; A. F. Garvie, *Aeschylus'* Supplices: *Play and Trilogy*, 1969[1], 2006[2] (the fundamental work). *Articles: (A) chiefly on the trilogy and its date*: H. Lloyd-Jones, 'The "Supplices" of Aeschylus: the new date and old problems', *L'Antiquité Classique*, 33 (1964), 356–74 (= *Academic Papers. Greek Epic, Lyric and Tragedy* [1990], 262–77; reprinted in E. Segal (ed.), *Oxford Readings in Greek Tragedy* [1983], 42–56); A. J. Podlecki, 'Reconstructing an Aeschylean trilogy', *Bulletin of the Institute of Classical Studies*, 22 (1975), 1–19; A.H. Sommerstein, 'The beginning and the end of Aeschylus' Danaid trilogy', *Drama*, 3 (1994), 111–34; S. Scullion, 'Tragic dates', *Classical Quarterly*, 52 (2002), 81–101, at 87–101. *(B) general*: P. Burian, 'Pelasgus and politics in Aeschylus' Danaid trilogy', *Wiener Studien*, 8 (1974), 5–14; S. Ireland, 'The problem of motivation in the *Supplices* of Aeschylus', *Rheinisches Museum*, 117 (1974), 14–29; J. K. Mackinnon, 'The reason for the Danaids' flight', *Classical Quarterly*, 28 (1978), 74–82; R. P. Winnington-Ingram, 'The Danaid trilogy of Aeschylus', (1983) in §5 above, 55–72; F. I. Zeitlin, 'La Politique d'Éros: féminin et masculin dans *Les Suppliantes* d'Eschyle', *Métis*, 3 (1988), 231–59; S. des Bouvrie, *Women in Greek Tragedy: An Anthropological Approach*, 1990, 147–66; Conacher (1996), 75–111 (with Appendix on the trilogy); G. W. Bakewell, 'Metoikia in the *Supplices* of Aeschylus', *Classical Antiquity*, 16 (1997), 209–28; A. H. Sommerstein, 'The Theatre Audience, the *Demos* the *Supplices* of Aeschylus', in Pelling (1997) in §5 above, 63–79; C. Turner, 'Perverted supplication and other inversions in Aeschylus' "Danaid" trilogy', *Classical Journal*, 97 (2001), 27–50; L. G. Mitchell, 'Greeks, Barbarians and Aeschylus' *Supplices*', *Greece & Rome*, 53 (2006), 205–23.

7.4. *Prometheus Bound. Authenticity*: C. J. Herington, *The Author of the* Prometheus Bound, 1970; \*M. Griffith, *The Authenticity of the Prometheus Bound*, 1977; M. L. West, 'The Prometheus trilogy', *Journal of Hellenic Studies*, 99 (1979), 130–48 and in his *Studies* (1990) in §2 above, 51–72; R. Bees, *Zur Datierung des Prometheus Desmotes*, 1993. *Monographs*: Conacher (1980); S. Said, *Sophiste et tyran ou le problème du Prométhée enchaîné*, 1985. *Articles*: B. H. Fowler, 'The imagery of the *Prometheus*', *American Journal of Philology*, 78 (1957), 173–84; M. Griffith, 'Aeschylus, Sicily and Prometheus', in R. D. Dawe, etc. (eds.), *Dionysiaca: Nine Studies... presented to Sir Denys Page*, 1978, 105–39; W. S. Scott, 'The development of the chorus in the *Prometheus Bound*', *Transactions of the American Philological Association*, 117 (1988), 85–96; K. De Vries, 'The Prometheis in vase-painting and on the stage', in R. M. Rosen, J. Farrell (eds.), *Nomodeiktes: Studies... Martin Ostwald* (1993), 517–23; J. Davidson, 'Prometheus *Vinctus* on the Athenian stage', *Greece & Rome*, 41 (1994), 33–40; J. Mossman, 'Chains of imagery in *Prometheus Bound*', *Classical Quarterly*, 46 (1996), 58–67; S. West, '*Prometheus Bound*, 420–4: Arabia in Caucasus', *Hermes*, 125 (1997), 374–9; M. Finkelberg, 'The geography of the *Prometheus Vinctus*', *Rheinisches Museum*, 141 (1998), 119–41; S. A. White, 'Io's world: intimations of theodicy in "Prometheus Bound"', *Journal of Hellenic Studies*, 121 (2001), 107–40; H. Lloyd-Jones, 'Zeus, Prometheus, and Greek ethics', *Harvard Studies in Classical Philology*, 101 (2003), 49–72 (= *Further Academic Papers*, 181–202).

8. 'Reception' of Aeschylus in later times (many of the following works deal chiefly with the *Oresteia*). J. T. Sheppard, *Aeschylus and Sophocles: Their Work and Influence*, 1927. J. D. Reid, *Oxford Guide to Classical Mythology in the Arts, 1300–1990s*, 1993. K. V. Hartigan, *Greek Tragedy on the American Stage: Ancient Drama in the Commercial Theater*, 1995. P. Burian, 'Tragedy Adapted for Stages and Screens: The Renaissance to the Present', *CCGT* (1997), 228–83 (extremely well documented). F. Macintosh, 'Tragedy in Performance: Nineteenth- and Twentieth-Century Productions', *CCGT* (1997), 284–323. Wiles (2000) in §5 above. L. Hardwick, *Reception Studies*. 'Greece & Rome' New Surveys in the Classics, 33 (2003). M. MacDonald, *The Living Art of Greek Tragedy*, 2003. R. Rehm, *Radical Theatre: Greek Tragedy in the Modern World*, 2003. Garland (2004) in §5 above, 147–85, 207–32. E. Hall and F. Macintosh, *Greek Tragedy in the British Theatre, 1660–1914*, 2004. E. Hall, F. Macintosh, A. Wrigley (eds.), *Dionysus since 1969: Greek Tragedy at the Dawn of the Third Millennium*, 2004. Gregory, *CGT* (2005) in §5 above, throughout 394–489 (various authors). F. Macintosh, P. Michelakis, E. Hall, O. Taplin, *Agamemnon in Performance, 458 BC–AD 2004*, 2005. L. Hardwick, 'Remodeling Reception: Greek Drama and Diaspora in Performance', in C. Martindale, R. F. Thomas (eds.), *Classics and the Use of Reception* (2006), 204–15.

# A Chronology of Aeschylus' Life and Times

| | |
|---|---|
| c.525 BC | Born into a prominent aristocratic family in Athens |
| 510 | Final expulsion from Athens of the sixth-century tyrants and the first movements towards democracy |
| c.500 | Begins his career as a dramatist |
| 490 | Fights at Marathon against the first Persian invasion (King Darius) |
| 484 | First victory in the dramatic competitions |
| 480–79 | Fights, or is present, at the battle of Salamis, and perhaps of Plataea, against the second Persian invasion (King Xerxes) |
| 470s | Athens heads an anti-Persian alliance of Greek city-states which eventually becomes regarded as her 'empire' Aeschylus visits Sicily, by invitation—an indication of his already established fame |
| 472 | Victorious with *Persians*, in a disconnected trilogy |
| 469–8 | Sophocles may have been victorious over Aeschylus in one of these years; his dramatic career had begun perhaps a year or two earlier |
| 467 | Victorious with *Seven*, in a connected trilogy on the Oedipus-myth |
| 460s | Further major democratic advances and reforms at Athens |
| c.463 | Victorious with *Suppliants*, in a connected trilogy on the Danaid-myth |
| 458 | Victorious with the *Oresteia* |
| 456 | Dies at Gela in Sicily |
| 455 | Euripides' dramatic career begins |

Only attested dates, or those reconstructed with some probability, and events relevant to the plays, are given. For discussion of the poet's life and biography see M. Lefkowitz, *Lives of the Greek Poets* (1981), 67–74 and 157–60; Rosenmeyer, *AA* 369–76 (with a 'Table'); and Sommerstein, *AT* 13–32.

# Maps

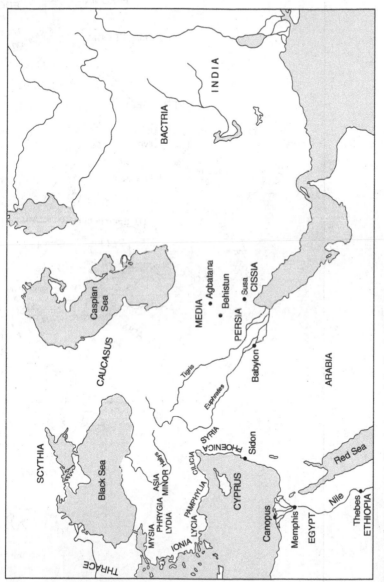

Map 1. The Eastern Mediterranean and the Persian Empire

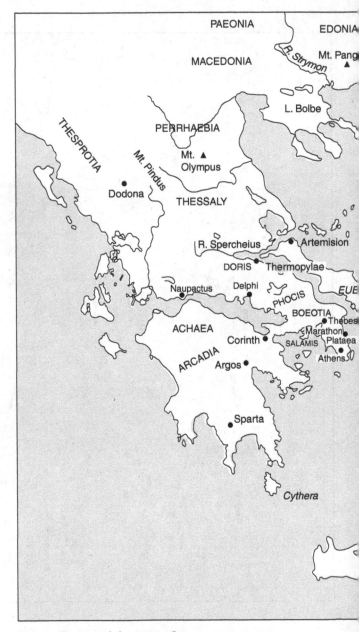

**Map 2.** Greece and the Aegean Sea

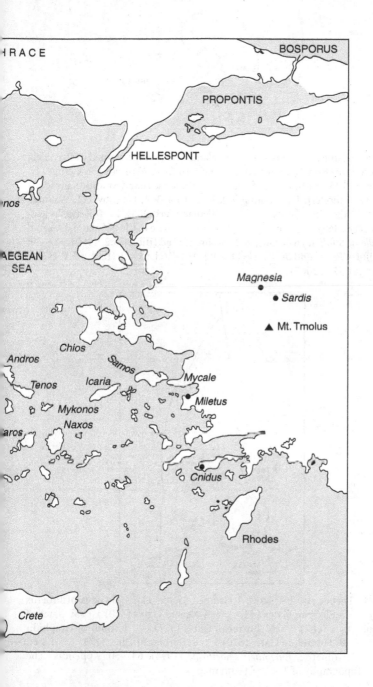

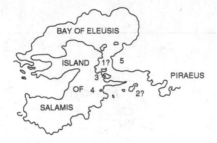

**Map 3.** Salamis. 1? 'the island near Salamis' (*Pers.* 447), named as Psyttaleia by Herodotus 8.76.1; identified with modern Ayios Yeoryios (St. George) by Hammond 33 and Broadhead 323    2? the same island, traditionally identified with modern Lipsokoutali (cf. R. Burn 473–4, Lazenby 171, Wallinga 51)    3 the city of Salamis    4 Sileniae (*Pers.* 303)    5 Xerxes' viewpoint (*Pers.* 465)    See: N. G. L. Hammond, 'The battle of Salamis', *Journal of Hellenic Studies*, 76 (1956), 332–54; Broadhead (Bibl. § 3.2, 1960), 322–39; R.A. Burn, *Persia and the Greeks* (1984²), 450–71; Lazenby (Bibl. § 7.1, 1988); Wallinga (§ 7.1, 2005)

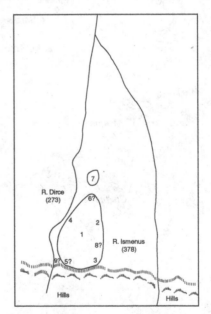

**Map 4.** Thebes and its Gates. 1 Cadmea (*Seven* 1)    2 Gates of Proetus (377)    3 Electran Gates (422)    4 Neistid Gates (460)    5? Gates of Athena Onca (487)    6? Borraean Gates (527)    7 Tomb of Amphion (532)    8? Homoloid Gates (570)    9? Springs of Dirce (273)    Based on D. Mastronarde, *Euripides. Phoenissae* (1994), 647–50: Appendix 'The Poetic Topography of Thebes' (with map)

**Map 5.** Io's Wanderings (*Prometheus Bound* and *Suppliants*): A Notional Map.

- - - - - - Io's course in *Prometheus* (676–7, 829–41, 707–35, 790–815, 844–7)
- -×- -×- - Io's course in *Suppliants* (in part only, 538–61, 307–11)

See: J. D. P. Bolton, *Aristeas of Proconnesus* (1962), 45–64 (discussion); Griffith (Bibl. §3.2, 1983), vi (map) and Commentary on 696–741 (discussion); West, *Studies* (Bibl. §2, 1990), 304–9 (discussion); Podlecki (Bibl. §3.2, 2005), 201–9 (discussion with map).

# Persians

# Persians

## CHARACTERS

CHORUS of elderly and noble counsellors at the Persian court
QUEEN, widow of King Darius
MESSENGER from King Xerxes' forces defeated in Greece
DARIUS (a ghost)
XERXES, son and successor of Darius

There are mute parts for the Queen's women attendants.

*Scene: near the royal council-chamber in the Persian capital of Sousa,
by which the tomb of King Darius stands. The* CHORUS *enters
the* orkhêstra *from one side, stepping and chanting to a regular
rhythm.*

CHORUS.    We here, from the Persians who are gone
   to the land of Greece, are called 'the faithful',
   and guardians of the palace with its great wealth in gold;
   in accord with our seniority, lord Xerxes himself,         5
   the king, the son of Darius,
   chose us to watch over the land.
   As to the king's return
   and his army's, with its many men,
   my heart is already flayed raw within me, all too prophetic of
      disaster;         10
   for the whole might of Asia's people
   is gone, noising anxiety for the young man;
   and no messenger or any horseman

comes to the Persians' capital.                                                      15
Those men who left Sousa and Agbatana
and Cissia's ancient bulwark behind them, and went,
some on horses, some on ships, and those on foot
making war's dense column as they marched—                          20
men such as Amistres and Artaphrenes
and Megabates and Astaspes,
the Persians' captains, kings subject to the great king,
hastened as overseers of the army's host:                               25
they were invincible archers, and mounted,
fearsome to see and terrible in battle
through their spirit's brave confidence;
Artembares too, the horse-knight, and Masistres,                   30
and noble Imaeus, invincible archer, and Pharandaces
and the cavalry-marshal Sosthanes.
Others were sent from the Nile, the great nourisher of many
    lives,
Sousiscanes, Pegastagon born in Egypt,                                  35
and great Arsames ruler of sacred Memphis;
and Ariomardus governor of ancient Thebes,
with marsh-dwellers as the ships' skilled oarsmen
and in masses beyond number.                                               40
Soft-living Lydians follow
in a multitude, those who hold subject all the mainland peoples,
whom Mitragathes
and brave Arcteus, kings and governors,
and Sardis with all its gold                                                    45
sent off riding in many chariots,
squadroned by four or six horses,
a fearsome sight to behold;
eager in their threats to throw slavery's yoke upon Greece
are those living near sacred Tmolus,                                       50
Mardon, Tharybis, anvils against the spear, and javelin-men
from Mysia; and Babylon with all its gold
sends a multitude all mixed in a long, sweeping column,
with marine soldiers and men confident of their archery.      55
The sword-bearing peoples of all Asia follow with them
at the king's dread summons.

Such is the flower of men that has gone from Persia's land,       60
for whom the whole region of Asia
which nurtured them sighs in fierce longing,
while parents and wives counting the days
tremble at the time's lengthening.

*The* CHORUS *cease pacing through the* orkhêstra *and begin a solemn,
sung dance.*

By now it has passed, the army of the king, city-sackers,       Str. 1
over the strait to the neighbour, facing land,       66
crossing the sea of Helle the daughter
of Athamas, on a raft-bridge roped with flax,       70
a roadway made with many nails,
a yoke thrown round the ocean's neck.

Furious for war, the ruler of Asia's many peoples       Ant. 1
drives his prodigious flock against every land       75
from two directions, trusting the command
by land and sea to stalwart, hard lieutenants—
descendant of a golden line,
a man born the equal of god!       80

There is a black gleam in his eyes,       Str. 2
the stare of a murderous snake.
With many troops and many sailors
he speeds his Syrian chariot on;
against men renowned with the spear he brings       85
the war of invincible bows.

No one has the tested prowess       Ant. 2
to withstand the great tide of men
and hold it back with sure defences—
one cannot fight an ocean-swell;       90
there is no resisting the Persian host,
a people stalwart in their hearts.       92

For Fate from god prevailed of old,       Str. 3
imposing on the Persians       104
the conduct of wars which splinter towers,

chariot-fighting with its tumult,
and overturning of cities.

They learned to cross the sea's domain,                    Ant. 3
the broad paths of the ocean                                        110
whitened by fierce gales; they put their trust
in thin-spun cables and devices
to carry their people across.                                          113

Cunningly planned deceit by a god, however—            Epode
which mortal man will escape it?                                    94
Who is there who commands an easy leap over it, swift with his
     feet?
Though friendly at first in fawning forward
Ruin decoys him into her nets;
over their top no mortal can flee in escape.                    100

Therefore my mind wears mourning black,                    Str. 4
lacerated by its fear—                                                 115
'O-ah! Cry it out
for the Persian host!'—
fear that the city, Sousa's great capital,
may hear this lament when emptied of men;

fear that the Cissian townsfolk too                            Ant. 4
will sing in thudding response                                       121
'O-ah! Cry it out!',
and that women there,
thronging in numbers with this cry as lament,
may fall to tearing their fine-linen dress.                       125

All the army, horsemen riding                                    Str. 5
and infantry marching,
has left and gone like bees in a swarm
with the commander of the host;
it has made its crossing over the headland               130
where the two lands are linked by a common sea.

Marriage-beds are filled with weeping                      Ant. 5
and longing for husbands;
Persian wives are softly lamenting,                             135

each in love's yearning for her man:
she sent off a husband furious for war,
and is now left alone in her marriage-bond.

*The* CHORUS *now chant.*

Come then, Persians!                                                    140
Let us seat ourselves in this ancient chamber
and offer sound, deeply considered thought:
the need has come.
How in fact does King Xerxes fare,
and our race named after Danaë's son?                                  145
Has victory come from drawing the bow,
or have the strong spear-shaft and its point the mastery?

*The* QUEEN *begins to enter from the side in a carriage; she is attended.*

But here, approaching with a light in her eyes like that of gods,      150
is the king's mother, our queen!
I prostrate myself before her;
and all must address her with words of greeting.

*The* CHORUS *make obeisance as the* QUEEN *dismounts, then rise to
speak excitedly, setting a tone for the whole episode.*

O our Queen, supreme among deep-girdled Persian women,    155
revered mother of Xerxes, wife of Darius, greetings! You were the
bedmate of a god among the Persians, and mother too of a god—
unless our army's ancient fortune has now changed.

QUEEN.   The very reason why I have come here and left the gold-
decked palace, and the bedchamber which I and Darius shared!—    160
and why anxiety tears my heart. I have a story to tell you in no way
my own; and I am not without fear, my friends, that great Wealth
may kick the ground into dust and overturn the prosperity which
Darius raised high, and with some god's aid. There is this twofold,
inexpressible concern in my mind: that massed riches should not    165
be held in respectful honour where there are no men, nor light
shine to its full strength upon those without riches. Wealth itself is

blameless, but there can be fear for its precious eye; for I consider the presence of a house's master to be its saving light.

This being so, please help counsel me, you Persians, faithful 170 elders, about what I have now to say; for it is on you that all our safe resolutions depend.

CHORUS. Be sure of this, queen of our land: you need mention nothing twice, either word or action, in which I may give a willing lead; you are inviting us to help counsel you when you have our goodwill in these matters. 175

QUEEN. Many night-time dreams have been my company ever since my son equipped a host and has been gone, in his wish to sack the Ionians' land; but I never yet saw any such dream so clear as that of last night. I will tell it you. 180

Two women in fine clothing, one attired in Persian dress and the other in Greek, seemed to come into my view, both of them far superior in stature to women now and faultless in beauty, and sisters of the same descent. Of the two, one lived in Greece as her 185 allotted fatherland, the other in the eastern world. These two, I thought I saw, were quarrelling with each other; and my son had learned of it and was trying to restrain and soothe them, putting the two of them to his chariot and placing the yoke-straps under 190 their necks. The first stood tall and proud in the traces and kept her mouth submissive to the reins; the other struggled and tore the chariot's harness apart with her hands, wrenching all away violently, getting free of the bridle, and smashing the yoke at its 195 middle; and my son was thrown. His father Darius stands by in pity for him; and when Xerxes sees him, he tears the robes on his body.

And that, I tell you, is what I saw in the night. After I had risen 200 and put my hands in fine spring-water, I stood at an altar, sacrifice in hand, in my wish to pour an offering to the powers that turn away harm, to whom these rites belong. I saw an eagle fleeing to Phoebus' altar-hearth—and I stood speechless in fear, my friends. 205 Later I saw a hawk flying to attack it in a rush of wings, tearing at its head with its claws; but the eagle only cowered and gave over its body.

Those are the frightening things I saw, and for you to hear; 210 for be certain of this: were my son to succeed well, he would be

admired, but were he to have bad success—he is not answerable to
the people, and if he is saved he is no less the ruler of this land.

CHORUS. We have no wish, our queen and mother, to alarm you
by what we say or to hearten you too much either; but when you   215
approach the gods in supplication, if you did see anything bad, ask
them to avert it, and for good to result for you and your children,
and for the city and all those dear to you. Next, you should have
libations poured to Earth and to the dead; ask their favour, that   220
your husband Darius, whom you say you saw in the night, may
send a happy outcome for you and your son, up from below the
earth into the light, and that the opposite may be kept in the earth
and extinguished in darkness. My heart is my prophet here, and I
encourage you out of kindness; our judgement of these things is
that they will turn out well for you in every way.   225

QUEEN. Goodwill indeed, and from the first to judge my dream,
with your firm interpretation for my son and house! May the
outcome indeed be good! We shall arrange all this, as you
urge, for the gods and our dear ones below the earth, when
we reach the palace. Yet I have this I wish to learn from
you, my friends: where do men say that Athens lies upon the   230
earth?

CHORUS. Far away, near where the Sun-lord goes down when he
fades.

QUEEN. And yet my son desired to capture this city?

CHORUS. Yes; for then all Greece would become subject to the
King.

QUEEN. Have the Athenians so much the fullest numbers in its
host, then?   235

CHORUS. Yes, and such a host as did the Medes great harm in fact.

QUEEN. And what else besides do they have? Sufficient wealth for
their houses?

CHORUS. They have a source of silver, a lode which is their land's
treasure.

QUEEN. Are bows and sharp arrows prominent in their hands?

CHORUS. Not at all: they use spears to stand and fight, and carry
shields in heavy armour.   240

QUEEN. And who is set over their people as shepherd and master?

CHORUS. They call themselves no man's slaves or subjects.

QUEEN.   So how would they withstand enemies who come against
them?

CHORUS.   Well enough to destroy Darius' great and splendid army!

QUEEN.   What you say is truly frightening, an anxiety for the parents of those who go against them.                                    245

CHORUS.   But I think you will soon know the whole truth from
a report: (*pointing off-stage to one side*) this man's running marks
him clearly as Persian, and he brings some definite outcome to hear
about, good or bad.

*A* MESSENGER *enters.*

MESSENGER.   O you cities of all Asia, O you land of Persia and great
harbour of wealth, one blow has destroyed your great prosperity,   250
and the flower of the Persians is fallen and gone! Ah me, it is bad to
be first with bad news! Still, I must unfold the whole disaster, men
of Persia: the East's entire host is lost.                            255

*The* CHORUS *break into song.*

CHORUS.   Harsh news, harsh,                                       Str. 1
both sudden and cruel:
weep, alas, you Persians, now you hear this woe.

MESSENGER (*who continues in speech*).   Our whole cause in Greece
is quite destroyed;—and I did not myself expect to live and see the 260
day of my return.

CHORUS.   Our years seem                                           Ant. 1
somehow too long-lived;
we are old, to hear this unexpected blow.                             265

MESSENGER.   I was there, men of Persia, I did not hear others'
accounts! I'll tell you the kinds of disaster that were brought on us.

CHORUS.   (*lamenting loudly*) Useless,                            Str. 2
all that great and varied weaponry
that went from Asia to attack                                         270
Zeus' land, the land of Hellas.

MESSENGER.   The corpses of our men destroyed in an evil fate fill
the shores of Salamis and all the nearby places.

CHORUS.   (*lamenting loudly*) Our friends'                     Ant. 2
 sea-buffeted bodies all awash                                    275
 in death, you say, carried adrift
 in their doubled-over mantles!

MESSENGER.   Yes, for our archery was not enough, and the whole
 host was destroyed, overcome by ramming ships.

CHORUS.   Lament, raise a cry of disaster                       Str. 3
 in deepest grief for Persian friends,                             281
 since the gods have dealt us total ruin
 all round. Our army destroyed!

MESSENGER.   Oh, the name of Salamis, most hateful to hear! Alas,
 how I groan in remembering Athens!                               285

CHORUS.   Yes, hateful she is, to her foemen!                  Ant. 3
 We may remember her indeed,
 since she has robbed many Persian mothers
 of sons, or made them widows.

QUEEN.   I have long been wretchedly silent, dismayed by our evil  290
 losses; for this disaster is extreme, its pain beyond telling or asking.
 Mankind must nevertheless bear calamities when the gods give
 them. (*turning to the Messenger*) Despite your grief at our losses,
 stay and unfold the whole of our pain; tell it us. Who has not been  295
 killed, and which of the people's leaders shall we be mourning? Any
 who was appointed to command and left his position unmanned
 when he was killed?

MESSENGER.   Xerxes himself is alive, and sees the light of day.

QUEEN.   Your words mean a great light of joy for my house, and  300
 brilliant day after storm-black night!

MESSENGER.   Artembares, however, the marshal of numberless
 cavalry, is being dashed along the hard shores of Sileniae; and
 Dadaces, commander of a thousand men, was struck by a spear
 and plunged from his ship in helpless fall; Tenagon, too, so brave,  305
 a true-born Bactrian, drifts along Ajax's sea-beaten island. Lilaeus,
 Arsames, and Argestes—all three of these were losing fight as they

buffeted against the rock-hard land by the islet which breeds doves;  310
so too Pharnuchus, neighbour to Egyptian Nile's streams, and
Arcteus, Adeues, and Pheresseues, all three thrown from one ship.
Matallus of Chrysa, commander of ten thousand, drenched his  314
great, full, black beard fiery red when killed, a bath of crimson  316
changing his face's colour; and Magus the Arab, like Artabes the
Bactrian, died there as an immigrant to a cruel land. Amistris
too from Amphistra, wielding a spear which dealt much harm,  320
and noble Ariomardus who has brought mourning to Sardis, and
Seisames the Mysian; and Tharybis the admiral of five times fifty
ships, a Lyrnaean by birth, a handsome man, lies miserably dead:
he had no very happy fortune. Syennesis too, first in courage, ruler  325
of the Cilicians, who singly dealt most harm to his enemies: he died
gloriously.

That much I recount about the commanders; but of our many
evil losses I report but few.                                     330

QUEEN.   Oh, sorrow! What I hear is the very height of evil disaster, both shame and shrill wailing for the Persians. Go back
again, however, and tell me this: just how large was the number
of Greek ships, to justify their engaging and attacking the Persian  335
fleet?
MESSENGER.   In mass you must know that the Persian ships would
have been superior; for the fact is, the Greeks' entire number came
to three hundred, and a tenth of these were select and separate.  340
Xerxes, on the other hand, massed a thousand (I know this as
a fact) under his command, while the faster ships came to two
hundred and seven; that was the count. We can't seem to you to
have been inferior in the battle, can we? Yet some divine power
destroyed our host, weighting the scale to unbalance fortune: the  345
gods have kept her city safe for Pallas its goddess.
QUEEN.   Then is the Athenians' city still not ransacked?
MESSENGER.   Yes, for while its men live, its wall is secure.
QUEEN.   Now tell what began the ships' engagement: who started  350
the battle—was it the Greeks, or my son exulting in his mass of
ships?
MESSENGER.   The beginning of the whole disaster, my queen, was
an avenging spirit or evil power which appeared from somewhere;

for a Greek man came from the Athenians' fleet and told your son 355
Xerxes this: 'if black night's darkness once arrives, the Greeks will
not stay, but leap on to their rowing-benches and scatter in unseen
flight to save their lives.' 360

Immediately he heard this, with no comprehension of the Greek
man's trickery or the gods' jealous anger, he made this proclamation to all his ship-commanders: as soon as the sun stopped burning the earth with its rays, and darkness occupied heaven's domain, 365
they were to position the mass of ships in three columns to guard
the outward passages and straits of the noisy sea, and other ships
in a circle round Ajax's island, since if the Greeks should escape an
evil death by secretly finding a run for their ships, it was decreed 370
for all commanders to lose their heads. His orders were that many,
and very much in a confident spirit, for he did not know what the
gods destined. With no indiscipline but obedient minds his men
began preparing their meal; crews looped their oars to the sturdy 375
rowing-pins.

When the sun's light died and night came on, every master of an
oar went to his ship, and every man-at-arms. Oar-bank encouraged
oar-bank on board the warships; and they sailed as each comman- 380
der had been positioned. All night long the masters of the ships
kept all their crews sailing to and fro.

Now the night was passing, and the Greek fleet made no attempt
at all to sail out secretly. When, however, day with its white steeds 385
filled the whole earth with light brilliant to the eye, first a cry rang
out from the Greeks in joyful affirmation like a song, and at once
its echo resounded piercingly from the island's cliff; and fear was 390
in all the Persians now their judgement had proved wrong, for
the Greeks were then singing a proud victory-hymn, not as if for
flight but in eager haste for battle, their courage high. The trumpet
set all on their side ablaze with its call; at once they pulled hard 395
together with a froth of oars, striking the salty deep in time with
the word; swiftly they all came on, clear to the view. First their
right wing led the way in good order and discipline, and next the
whole fleet came out for the attack. At the same moment a great 400
shout was to be heard, 'O sons of the Greeks, go on! Free your
fatherland, and free your children, your wives, and the shrines
of your paternal gods, and the tombs of your ancestors! Now the

struggle is for all!' And then!—from our side a clamour in the Per-    405
sian tongue rose up in answer, and it was the moment for no more
delay.

At once ship struck bronze ram against ship; the onslaught
began with a Greek ship which broke off a Phoenician ship's whole
ornate stern, and all drove their vessels everywhere against oppo-    410
nents. Now at first the Persian fleet's flowing advance held on; but
when a mass of ships had become packed in a narrow space, and no
help for one another was possible, they were hit by their own sides'
bronze-beaked rams; they began to shatter all the fleet's oars, while    415
the Greek ships circled round knowingly and struck them. Hulls of
ships were overturned, and the sea was no longer visible as it filled
with wreckage and slaughtered men. The shores and promontories    420
teemed with corpses.

Every ship of the Persian fleet began rowing in disorderly flight,
while the Greeks struck our men and broke their backs, like tunnies
or a catch of fish, with splintered oars and fragments of wreckage.    425
Groans and shrieking together took over the wide sea, till night's
black eye made an end. The full count of our losses, even if I had
ten days to tell them off in order, I could not completely give you;    430
for you must understand that never in one day has so great a count
of men been killed.

QUEEN.   (*lamenting loudly*) A great sea of disaster has indeed broken upon the Persians and their whole people.

MESSENGER.   Then know this too: the disaster was not yet at its
middle point; such catastrophe and loss came upon them as to    435
outweigh it in the scale twice over.

QUEEN.   But what misfortune could be still crueller than this? Tell
me, what was this further catastrophe you say came upon the host,
inclining the scale for our heavier loss?    440

MESSENGER.   All the Persians in their natural prime, those finest in
courage and eminent in nobility, and ever first in loyalty to the king
himself—all have been ignobly killed in a most inglorious fate.

QUEEN.   (*again lamenting*) Oh, how I suffer at this evil disaster!    445
How though did these men meet their death, do you say, and were
killed?

MESSENGER.   There is an island lying off this place on Salamis, tiny,
a bad mooring for ships, on its seaward shore a haunt of Pan who

loves the dance. Xerxes sent those men here so that, whenever the 450
enemy had ships wrecked and tried to reach safety on the island,
they should kill this body of Greeks when defenceless but save their
own side from the sea-ways—in this, Xerxes' study of the future
was badly wrong. For when the god gave glory in the ships' battle
to the Greeks, on the self-same day they clad their bodies in fine 455
bronze armour, leapt from their ships and ringed the whole island,
to put our men at a loss which way to turn, for they were much
battered by hand-thrown rocks; arrows shot from bows hit and 460
killed them; and at the last the Greeks rushed them in a single surge
and struck them down, butchering the poor wretches' limbs, until
they had destroyed the lives of all.

Xerxes groaned aloud on seeing the depth of the catastrophe; for 465
he had a clear view of the whole fleet, seated on a lofty hill near
the open sea. He tore his robes, keening and wailing; after passing
word at once to his foot-army he lets it go in disorderly flight. 470

There: such is the disaster, one truly to mourn in addition to the
one before.

QUEEN. Hateful deity, you cheated the Persians of their wits, it is
now clear! A bitter outcome my son found to his vengeance upon
famous Athens! The Persians whom Marathon killed before were
not enough: it was for them my son thought to exact penalty, but 475
he drew on himself so many painful losses. (*to the Messenger*) But
tell me: the ships which escaped destruction—where did you leave
them? Do you know a clear account to give me?

MESSENGER. The captains of the ships which were left took hastily 480
to flight in no good order, as the breeze carried them. The rest of
the army was destroyed in the Boeotians' land, some in distress
from thirst near fine spring-water, others (*text missing*); in exhaus-
tion we crossed into the Phocians' land, the territory of Doris and 485
the Melian gulf, where Spercheius waters the plain with kindly
stream. From there the soil of the Achaeans' land, and the Thessalians' cities, received us now very short of food, and there in fact
very many died of thirst and hunger; for both of these were present. 490
We reached the land of Magnesia and the Macedonians' country,
at the crossing over Axius; then Bolbe with its reedy marshes, and
Mount Pangaeus, and the Edonian land. In the night here a god
stirred winter into coming out of season, and froze holy Strymon's 495

entire stream. People who before had held the gods of no account then began to entreat them in prayer, falling to revere Earth and Heaven. When the army ceased from its many calls upon the gods, 500 it started crossing where ice had frozen hard. Then any of us who had set out before the sun-god's rays were shed around, got to safety; for the sun's brilliant orb gleamed and burned, and its fire warmed and melted the centre of the crossing; men fell on top of 505 one another; and the one who broke off life's breath the quickest was fortunate indeed.

All the rest who achieved safety, barely got across Thrace, and through great effort; they have escaped and are coming— but only some few!—to their homeland and hearths. So the 510 land of Persia is to mourn, in longing for the country's dearest youth.

This is the truth; and in the telling I leave out many of the evil blows which god has launched upon the Persians.

*The* MESSENGER *leaves by one side.*

CHORUS.   O you deity, so harsh in afflicting us! Too heavy your feet 515 in leaping on the whole Persian race!

QUEEN.   Oh, I suffer for our army's destruction! O you vision in my dreams at night, so clear, how very surely you revealed disaster to me! (*to the* CHORUS) You judged it too lightly, however. Still, 520 since your advice was firm on this point, I am willing to pray first to the gods; then, as gifts to Earth and to the dead, I shall come from my house to pour an offering—over what is past and done, I know it will be, but in case something better may happen for the 525 future.

Over all these events, you must add faithful counsel to your faithfulness before; and as to my son, if he comes here before me, console him and escort him to the palace, so that he adds no further 530 woe to the woes we have.

*The* QUEEN *leaves for the palace in her carriage. The* CHORUS *chant.*

CHORUS     O Zeus the king! Now (*a word missing*) you have destroyed the Persians' host

in its great pride and numbers of men;
the city of Sousa and Agbatana                                          535
you have hidden in mourning's gloom.
Many are the women tearing their veils apart
with delicate hands;
wet tears soak the folds on their breast
as they share their pain.                                              540
Softly weeping the Persian wives
miss husbands newly wed;
marriage-beds soft with coverings,
the joy of sensual youth, they have put away;
they mourn in quite insatiable grief.                                  545
I too take up the fate of those who are gone;
it is truly one for much mourning.

*The* CHORUS *change to dancing and singing.*

So now Asia's entire land                                 Str. 1
mourns aloud, emptied of men.
Xerxes took them (*a cry of bitter grief*),                            550
Xerxes destroyed them (*a cry of despair*),
Xerxes directed all things unwisely
for the vessels at sea.
Why then was Darius so unharmed when he held the command,
his people's archer-lord,                                          555
Sousa's dear leader?

Our foot-soldiers, our sea-crews,                          Ant. 2
oars and dark hulls all alike—
vessels took them (*a cry of bitter grief*),                           560
vessels destroyed them (*a cry of despair*),
vessels were rammed in total destruction,
at Ionian hands.
Our lord and king himself barely made his escape, so we hear,
across the Thracian plains,                                         565
their ways all wintry.

Now these men were overtaken (*a cry of sorrow*)          Str. 2
by their fate of dying first (*a cry of extreme distress*)

around the Cychrean headlands (*a wailing cry*) 570
[in shattered vessels]. Begin your grief
and let the hurt bite: cry deep-voiced sorrow
high to heaven (*a wailing cry*);
prolong your harsh-sounding
tones, loud with wretchedness. 575

Rock-torn dreadfully in the sea (*a cry of sorrow*)     Ant. 2
they are gnawed by the voiceless (*a cry of extreme distress*)
children of the undefiled sea. (*a wailing cry*)
A house mourns when bereft of its man;
and childless fathers, wailing their sorrow 580
sent by heaven (*a wailing cry*),
become old on hearing
their now absolute loss.

But the people throughout Asia's land     Str. 3
a while since are no longer 585
ruled by Persia, no longer pay tribute
at a master's compulsion,
nor will they prostrate themselves
under rule; the power of our king
has been quite destroyed. 590

And no longer are the tongues of men     Ant. 3
under guard; for the people
have been released, so that their speech is free,
with the release of might's yoke.
Bloodshed staining its ploughland, 595
the wave-dashed island of Ajax
holds what Persia was.

*The* QUEEN *returns from the palace on foot, carrying items of sacrifice;
she may be attended.*

QUEEN.  My friends, anyone with real experience of trouble knows
how, when a surge of it comes upon them, they are apt to fear
everything; but when fortune's tide is good, they trust that the 600
same breeze will blow favourably for ever. And so it is with me:

everything now is full of fear; the gods' hostility is evident, and
there is a cry shouting in my ears which means no healing. Such  605
shock from our trouble terrifies my mind.

Therefore I made my way back here from the palace without
the carriage and finery I had before, bringing libations to win the
favour of my son's father, the things which appease the dead: from  610
a sacred cow, milk white and sweet, and from the bee at work amid
flowers its distillation of pure-bright honey, with water trickled
from a virgin spring; and here an unpolluted drink from a country-
mother, delight from an ancient vine; and from the pale olive, its  615
leaves ever-flourishing with life, the fragrant yield is here to hand,
and woven flowers, children of Earth the mother of all.

Come my friends, speak and sing good words over these libations to the dead, and call up the god Darius; while I shall offer  620
these honours to the gods below, for the earth to drink.

*As the* CHORUS *pray for Darius to appear, they begin circling the altar
at the centre of the orkhêstra, chanting.*

CHORUS.    Royal Lady! Persian Majesty!
  Send your libations down to earth's mansions,
  while we will entreat the escorts of the dead with hymns          625
  to be kindly below the earth.
  You holy underworld powers!
  Earth, and Hermes, and King of those below,
  send up Darius' spirit from below into the light!                 630
  For if he knows any further cure for our troubles,
  he alone of mortals might tell their end.

*The* CHORUS *now begin a solemn sung dance.*

  Does our dear departed king, equal to god, hear me,      Str. 1
  my Persian words clear,                                          635
  uttered in changing, doleful lament?
  My absolute grief and sorrow
  I shall cry aloud
  on all sides. Is he hearing me from below?

  I entreat you, Earth and other rulers of the dead:       Ant. 1
  approve the coming
                                                                   641

of his proud spirit up from your house,
the Persians' god born at Sousa;
escort him upward,
one whose like Persian soil never yet covered.                    645

Dear friend indeed was the man, dear is his tomb;      Str. 2
for dear was the nature it hides.
Aïdoneus, sender-up to earth, Aïdoneus, send us up            650
our godlike lord, Darian—(*a cry of grief*)

for neither would he ever lose men to death          Ant. 2
in war's mad and killing ruin,
but the Persians called his mind godlike, and of godlike mind he
    was,                                                         655
since he led his armies well. (*a cry of grief*)

My shah, my shah of old, come to us, draw near;     Str. 3
mount to your tomb's high summit,
stepping up with your foot's saffron-dyed slipper;           660
display your royal tiara's crest.
Come, our father in safety, Darian (*a cry*)

...so you may hear of fresh and sudden sorrows.     Ant. 3
Master! O master, appear!                                        666
For a Stygian murk wings over us now,
and our whole youth has been destroyed.                      670
Come, our father in safety, Darian! (*a cry*)

Sorrow, sorrow!                                        Epode
Your death so much lamented by your friends,
why, [why,] my master, my master,                               675
these double, grievous failures for your land?
All its three-banked ships are lost in ruin,
are ships no more, ships no more.                              680

*The* GHOST OF DARIUS *comes into view.*

DARIUS.    Faithful among the faithful! Companions of my youth!
    Persian elders, what labour lies upon this land? Its soil groans, it
    has been stricken, and it is furrowed. I see my wife near my tomb,
    and I am afraid, but I received her libations with favour; and you  685

stand close by the tomb lamenting, wailing high to summon up
my spirit and calling on me piteously. Yet there is no easy way from
below the earth, above all since the gods there are better at taking
than releasing. Still, I used my authority among them, and I have 690
come. Hurry then, so that I may not be blamed for delay.
    What is the Persians' unexpected and heavy disaster?

CHORUS.    (*chanting*) I am in awe to see you,                              Str.
    I am in awe to speak to your face,                                        695
    from my ancient dread of you.

DARIUS.    But since I have come from below at your lament's persuasion, make no speech at length, but be concise; tell everything
to its end, and leave aside your reverence for me.

CHORUS.    I am in fear to please you,                                       Ant.
    I am in fear to say to your face                                          700
    what is hard for friends to tell.

DARIUS.    But since your mind's ancient fear stands in your way,
(*turning to the Queen*) you, aged partner of my bed, noble wife,
leave off these tears and lamentations, and speak to me quite
clearly. Human suffering befalls mankind, of course; much woe 705
comes to mortal men from the sea, and much from dry land, if
a life already long is extended further.
QUEEN.    O you who surpassed all mankind in prosperity through a
fortunate destiny! How you were envied while you saw the rays of
the sun and lived out like a god a life of years happy for the Persians! 710
So now too I envy you your death before you saw the depth of our
troubles.
    You shall hear the whole story, Darius, in a brief space: total ruin
for Persian fortunes, nearly total.
DARIUS.    In what way? Did some plague come to strike the city, or
    feuding?                                                                  715
QUEEN.    Not that at all. Our whole host has been destroyed near
    Athens.
DARIUS.    Which of my sons was leading the host there? Tell me.
QUEEN.    Xerxes, furious for war; he emptied the continent's whole
    expanse of its men.

DARIUS.   Was it on land or by sea that he made this foolish attempt, poor wretch?

QUEEN.   Both; two forces made a double front.                        720

DARIUS.   But how did so great a host on foot actually succeed in crossing?

QUEEN.   He devised a yoke for Helle's strait, to have a way across.

DARIUS.   And he achieved that—he closed the great Bosporus?

QUEEN.   Indeed so; but one of the gods must have joined in his resolve.

DARIUS.   It was some great god who came, alas, to make his mind unsound.                                                            725

QUEEN.   Yes, since the disastrous outcome of his actions is to be seen.

DARIUS.   And what actually did the men do, that you lament them so?

QUEEN.   Defeat for the forces at sea destroyed the forces on land.

DARIUS.   Have all the people perished so completely in war?

QUEEN.   Enough for Sousa's whole city to groan for its emptiness of men ...                                                        730

DARIUS.   Oh, grieve, I grieve for our host, and its fine power of support!

QUEEN.   ...and the Bactrians too are lost, their people all destroyed; none survives.

DARIUS.   Wretched man, to have lost such allies in their prime!

QUEEN.   Lonely and desolate, they say, with few companions, Xerxes ...

DARIUS.   What is the end of it for him, and where? Is he safe at all?   735

QUEEN.   ...was glad to reach the bridge yoking the two lands.

DARIUS.   And has he come safely to our continent? Is this true?

QUEEN.   Yes, in this at least the report is firm and clear; there is no contradiction in it.

DARIUS.   (*sighing*) Swiftly indeed came the oracles' accomplishment, and Zeus launched the prophecies' fulfilment upon my son.   740 I was confident myself, I suppose, that the gods would fulfil them after a lengthy time; but when a man shows haste himself, the god joins in. Here and now a fountainhead of woe, it seems, has been discovered for all those dear to me. My son achieved this in the ignorance of rash youth, in his hope to contain the flow of sacred

Hellespont with bonds like a slave, Bosporus the divine stream. He 745
tried to alter the crossing, and by throwing hammered fetters over
it, he achieved a great pathway for a great army. A mortal man, he
thought to master all the gods—it was folly!—and Poseidon with
them. A sickness of the mind possessed my son—what else? I fear, 750
my huge and hard-won wealth may soon be plunder for the first
men who come.

QUEEN.   The company of evil men has been Xerxes' teacher here,
in his fury for war; they told him that you got great wealth for
your children with your spear, but that he was unmanly and did
his spear-fighting indoors, and made no increase in his father's 755
prosperity. When he heard such reproaches frequently from evil
men he planned this campaign's path against Greece.

DARIUS.   Therefore the action he carried out has been extreme, to
be remembered always, such as never yet befell this city of Sousa 760
and emptied it of men, from the time when lord Zeus bestowed
this honour, for one man to rule all of Asia rich in flocks, and to
hold the sceptre of government.

Medus was the first leader of the people, and next to discharge 765
this task was his son, for good sense steered his heart. Third after
Medus was Cyrus, a man blessed by god, whose rule brought peace
to all his kin; he acquired the Lydian and the Phrygian peoples, 770
and ravaged all Ionia by force; the god was not his enemy, for he
had good sense. Cyrus' son was fourth to govern the people. Fifth
to rule was Mardus, a disgrace to his fatherland and ancient throne;
but he was killed at home in a plot by the noble Artaphrenes, with 775
the help of friendly men for whom it was an act of duty. Sixth was
Maraphis; seventh, Artaphrenes; and myself—but the lots fell out
for me exactly as I wanted.

I too made many campaigns with a great host; but I did not bring 780
so large a disaster on the city. Xerxes my son is young and has a
young man's rash thinking; he does not remember my instructions.
For be very sure of this, my old companions: of all of us who
have held this power, none could be shown to have done so much 785
harm.

CHORUS.   So then, lord Darius, what consequence turns upon your
words? How in the light of this should our Persian people still act
for the best?

DARIUS.  ...provided you do not campaign into the Greeks' space,  790
   not even if the Median army may be greater. Their land itself is
   their ally.
CHORUS.   How do you mean? In what way, their ally?
DARIUS.   Because it kills those who are too numerous, through
   famine.
CHORUS.   But it will be a well-equipped and chosen force we shall
   send out, you may be sure.                                       795
DARIUS.   But the army which has now remained in parts of Greece
   will meet with no safe return, either.
CHORUS.   How do you mean? Is not the whole Persian army to
   cross the strait of Helle from Europe?
DARIUS.   A few only, out of the many, if one is to have any trust  800
   in divine prophecies when looking at what has now been done;
   for they are coming true—not some, but all of them. And even
   though they are, Xerxes has been persuaded by empty hopes to
   leave behind a chosen number of his army; they remain where
   Asopus waters the plain with its streams, precious enrichment of  805
   the Boeotians' land. The worst of disasters are waiting there for
   them to suffer, atonement for their aggressive and godless thinking,
   men who went to the land of Greece and had no scruple in plundering gods' statues or burning temples; altars have disappeared,  810
   and holy shrines been uprooted from their foundations in scattered
   ruin. For their evil actions, therefore, they suffer no less and are
   destined for more; no solid floor yet lies beneath their woes, they
   well up still. So great will be the clotting blood from slaughter by  815
   Dorian spears in the Plataeans' land; heaps of corpses will declare
   voicelessly to the eyes of men, even to the third generation, that
   one who is mortal must not set his thoughts too high. Arrogance  820
   in full bloom bears a crop of ruinous folly from which it reaps
   a harvest all of tears. (*to the Chorus*) Such is its reward here; see
   it, and remember Athens and Greece, and let no one despise his
   present fortune and pour away his great prosperity from desiring  825
   that of others. I tell you, Zeus stands over thoughts which are
   too boastful as their punisher; he is a severe auditor. Accordingly,
   if you desire Xerxes to be moderate, correct him through reasoned advice to stop offending the gods through rash and excessive  830
   boasting.

And now you, Xerxes' aged and loving mother, go into the house.
Fetch suitable fine clothing and go to meet your son; tatters of his
embroidered garments hang in torn shreds round his body, wholly 835
from grief at his disaster. Yet soothe him kindly with your words,
for he will bear to listen, I know, to you alone.

And I myself will go away, down into earth's darkness; but I wish
you elders well, despite the disaster: give your spirits pleasure day 840
by day, since wealth is of no use to the dead.

*The* GHOST OF DARIUS *disappears.*

CHORUS.   It was truly painful for me to hear of the many evil blows
the Persians have already, and those still destined.
QUEEN.   O you deity, how much pain comes over me at our troubles! Yet this disaster most bites home now I have heard of the 845
indignity which surrounds my son, from the garments on his body.
I will go and fetch fine clothing from the house, and try to meet
my son at his approach; for I will not betray my dearest amid 850
troubles.

*The* QUEEN *leaves for the palace. The* CHORUS *sing and dance.*

CHORUS.   Oh our pain now! In truth we had enjoyed          Str. 1
a fine and good life in well-ordered cities,
when our king of old,
all-sufficient, safe in his cause, safe from defeat,                          855
godlike Darius, ruled in the land.

In the first place, the armies we displayed            Ant. 1
were famous, strong as towers in their formations
for every venture;                                                                  860
return from war brought them without toil, without harm,
[back home to] houses prospering well.

How many cities he took without crossing         Str. 2
the river Halys,                                                                   866
or leaving his hearth!—
like those neighbouring Strymon and its seaway,
in the Thracians' Acheloïd settlements,                                    870

and, away from the sea, those in dry places                    Ant. 2
with walls driven round
which obeyed this lord,                                              875
and those proud in their sites round Helle's broad strait,
with the inward Propontis, and Pontus' mouth,

and the wave-dashed islands near the sea-cape              Str. 3
which sit closely by our continent,                                  882
such as Lesbos and Samos rich in olives,
Chios and Paros, Naxos, Mykonos,                                885
and Tenos adjoining Andros its neighbour;

and he ruled those islands near the mid-coast,              Ant. 3
Lemnos and the seat of Icarus,                                       891
Rhodes and Cnidus, and Cyprus with its cities—
Paphos and Soli, also Salamis,                                       895
whose mother-city now causes this sorrow;

and the populous rich cities of the Greeks                      Epode
throughout the Ionian territory
he ruled in his wisdom.                                                   900
Untiring strength was to hand
in his armed men, and his allies mingling all nations.
Yet now we in our turn endure
in our wars this reverse willed indisputably by heaven,      905
our great defeat through the blows at sea.

XERXES *enters from one side, alone. His robes are tattered; he car-*
*ries only an arrow-quiver. He intones his grief, which the* CHORUS
*briefly echo before changing to a full lyric lament in antiphony with*
*him.*

XERXES.    Oh, it is my misery to have met
this hateful destiny, beyond comprehension!                    910
How ruthlessly the god has come down upon the Persian race!
What am I to do, poor wretch?
The strength in my limbs is undone
when I look at my aged countrymen here.
If only death as my fate had cloaked me too, Zeus,            915
together with the men who are gone!

CHORUS.    Alas for our brave army,
   the high glory of Persian rule, and the splendid men      920
   whom the god has now culled.

   The land bewails its native youth                 Prelude
   slain for Xerxes, who crammed Hades with Persians;
   for many heroes are gone to Hades,              925
   the flower of the land, archers supreme,
   a densely massed company of men; they have perished.
   Oh, grieve, grieve for their fine strength!
   King of our country! Asia's land
   has been bent terribly, terribly, to its knees.        930

XERXES.    Here I am, alas!, to be wept for;        Str. 1
   poor wretch, I became an evil thing,
   I now know, for house and fatherland.
CHORUS.    As greeting on your return, I shall utter,    935
   utter the cry of ill omen, the voice
   which makes disaster its concern,
   a Mariandynian's, a dirge-singer's voice,
   with many tears.                          940

XERXES.    Pour out your lament, all of sorrow,     Ant. 1
   grief's voice; for my fortune in this thing
   has turned itself round and against me.
CHORUS.    I shall pour out grief indeed, quite certainly,
   paying tribute to our army's defeat           945
   and the land's heavy blow at sea;
   the house's. I shall wail a grief-singer's cry,
   all heavy tears.

[XERXES.]    The Ionians' warfare robbed us of lives,    Str. 2
   the Ionians' armoured ships turned the battle their way,   952
   culling the death-dark sea
   and the unlucky shore.
CHORUS.    Cry out our loud grief, and learn all we may!    955
   Where are the others, your multitude of friends?
   Where are your close defenders,
   such as Pharandakes was,
   Sousas, Pelagon, and Datamas,

also Psammis and Sousiscanes,                                960
when they left Agbatana?

XERXES.   I left them behind me dead on the shores          Ant. 2
of Salamis, lost overboard from a Tyrian ship,
many of them striking
on the hard rocky shore.                                    965
CHORUS.   [Cry out] our loud grief! Where, if you know it,
are Pharnuchus, and the brave Ariomardus?
Where is the lord Senalces,
or the high-born Lilaeus,                                   970
Memphis, Tharybis, and Masistras,
Hystaichmas too, and Artembares?
I put such questions again.

XERXES.   Oh, they have my grief:                          Str. 3
after seeing that hated, ancient Athens,                   975
they all of them through one stroke, poor wretches, on the dry land
have gasped their lives away. I sob, I sob!
CHORUS.   You mean, the choicest flower of the Persians—
your always-faithful watching eye,
who put numbers to men beyond count, beyond count—         980
(*a name missing*), favourite child
of Batanochus
son of Seisames Megabates' son?
Parthus too, and great Oibares—
you left them—left them? Oh, the poor men!                 985
You tell of woe, total woe for our noble Persians.

XERXES.   I yearn, I do yearn                               Ant. 3
for my fine companions; you stir that up,
when you speak of [lasting,] lasting, hateful, utter evil. 990
My heart deep within me cries out, cries out!
CHORUS.   And there are others too whom we long for,
Xanthes who captained Mardian men
beyond all count; also Arian Anchares,
and Diaixis and Arsaces                                    995
the lords of horsemen;
also Dadacas, and Lythimnas too,

and Tolmus unsated in war.
I am amazement, all amazement,                                    1000
  they are not following behind your tented carriage.

XERXES.    Yes, those who were leading our host are gone.        Str. 4
CHORUS.    Gone, alas, leaving no fame.
XERXES.    I grieve and lament, I grieve and lament.
CHORUS.    Alas, you powers! You brought disaster               1005
  we did not expect, and so very clearly:
  such was the look we had from Ruin.

XERXES.    Struck down, alas, from our life long fortune ...     Ant. 4
CHORUS.    Struck indeed; this is quite clear ...
XERXES.    ... in sudden torment, in sudden torment ...         1010
CHORUS.    ... after our ill success in meeting
  the Ionian ships and their on-board fighters.
  War has been hard on Persia's people.

XERXES.    For sure! And my host was so great                   Str. 5
  it is cruel that I was struck down!                           1015
CHORUS.    But what is not lost, you great victim in our ruin?
XERXES.    You see this remnant of my clothing?
CHORUS.    I see it, I see it.
XERXES.    ... and this arrow-holder ...                        1020
CHORUS.    What is this you say has been saved?
XERXES.    ... my treasure-store of weapons?
CHORUS.    Few things, though, from so many!
XERXES.    And I lack men to support me!
CHORUS.    The Ionian folk do not flee battle!                  1025

XERXES.    They are too warlike! I have seen                    Ant. 5
  a harsh blow I could not expect.
CHORUS.    The rout of our fleet, you mean, our strongly armoured
  ships?
XERXES.    I tore my robes as the evil fell.                    1030
CHORUS.    Oh alas, oh alas!
XERXES.    No, much more than Alas!
CHORUS.    Yes, for us twofold and threefold ...
XERXES.    ... grief—but delight for our foes.

CHORUS.    Yes, our strength was shorn away... 103

XERXES.    And I am stripped of attendants.

CHORUS.    ...in ruinous defeat of our friends at sea.

XERXES.    Weep, weep at the blow; but go to the palace.    Str. 6

CHORUS.    Alas, alas! The torment, the torment!

XERXES.    Cry out then in loud response to me.    104

CHORUS.    It is woe's gift of woe to woe.

XERXES.    Wail, and join your tones to mine!

CHORUS.    (*a wail of extreme grief*)
  Heavy indeed, this disaster!
  Alas, I do grieve for this, very much.    104

XERXES.    Beat, beat at your breast and lament for my sake!    Ant. 6

CHORUS.    My eyes are wet, I am tears and sorrow.

XERXES.    Cry out then in loud response to me.

CHORUS.    Master, my care for this is here!

XERXES.    Raise your voice high then, in tears.    105

CHORUS.    (*a wail of extreme grief*)
  Sorrow's blackness will be mingled,
  alas, in the beating of our lament.

XERXES.    Strike your breast and cry out the Mysian way.    Str. 7

CHORUS.    Oh, our deep pain, our pain!    105

XERXES.    And ravage, I ask, the white hair of your beard.

CHORUS.    Ceaselessly, ceaselessly, wholly in sorrow!

XERXES.    And wail out high and loud.

CHORUS.    This too I shall do!

XERXES.    Tear the folds of your robe with fingers and hands.

  Ant. 7

CHORUS.    Oh, our deep pain, our pain!    106

XERXES.    And pluck out your hair in pity for our host.

CHORUS.    Ceaselessly, ceaselessly, wholly in sorrow!

XERXES.    And wet your eyes with tears.

CHORUS.    Look, they are streaming!    106

XERXES.    Cry out then in loud response to me.    Epode

CHORUS.    Oh, I grieve, I grieve!

XERXES.    Wail aloud as you enter the palace.

CHORUS.  O-oh, o-oh!
XERXES.  Cry 'O-o-h!' through the city.                                    1070
CHORUS.  Cry 'O-o-h!' indeed; yes, yes!
XERXES.  Lament as you go with soft tread.
CHORUS.  O-oh! Persia's soil is sad to tread.
  (*two lines missing*)

XERXES.  (*a new pitch of lament*) Oh! the pain, the loss—our three-
  banked . . .

CHORUS.  Oh! the pain, the loss . . . ships and their dead!          1075
XERXES.  Escort me then into the palace.
CHORUS.  I shall indeed escort you, my voice loud in harsh grief.

  XERXES *escorted by the* CHORUS *in procession leaves by one side.*

# Seven against Thebes

# Seven against Thebes

## CHARACTERS

ETEOCLES, son of the dead Oedipus, ruling Thebes
SCOUT, reporting from outside Thebes
CHORUS of young, unmarried women of Thebes

There are mute parts for Theban citizens, for attendants upon Eteocles, and for bearers of the dead Eteocles and his brother Polynices. (Two late and inauthentic scenes have parts for a HERALD and for ANTIGONE, sister of Eteocles, and a mute part for Ismene, a second sister.)

*The play is set inside Thebes; the city is under imminent attack from forces led by the 'Seven' including Eteocles' brother Polynices. Some Theban citizens have already gathered; ETEOCLES enters from one side to make them a ruler's proclamation.*

ETEOCLES. Citizens of Cadmus, the duty to say what meets the moment is the man's who keeps guard upon affairs, taking the tiller at the city's stern, with no lulling of his eyes in sleep. For were we to prosper, a god gets the thanks; if, however—may it not happen!— disaster were to occur, Eteocles would be the one man much on the 5 city-people's lips, in constant murmurings and lamentations. May Zeus avert these from the Cadmeans' city and so prove true to his name!
  You too have a duty now—the man still short of youthful prime 10 as well as the man past youth but greatly increasing his bodily strength—each concerned in any fitting way to aid our city and our native gods' altars, so that their due honours may never be

obliterated, and to aid our children, and Mother Earth, our dearest   15
nurse. For she it is who accepted the whole labour of your upbringing, when you came to her as new children, and on her kindly soil
she bred you to found homes and to bear weapons faithfully for
our present need.                                                     20

And now up to this day the god has inclined the scale favourably;
already during the time we have been besieged inside the walls,
our success in fighting has come for the most part from the gods;
but now, as the seer states, the husbander of birds who hears and
ponders their prophetic omens in his mind without help of fire,
his art unerring—this master of such divination speaks of a very   25
great Achaean attack being planned against the city and debated
last night.

Quickly now, all of you, to the battlements and our walls' gates!
Hurry with all your weapons, man the breastworks, and take your   30
stand on the tower platforms; stay by the gates' outlets in good
heart, and do not fear the throng of outside attackers too much:
the god will end things well!                                       35

*(The Theban citizens leave by one side.)*

For my part, I sent scouts and spies upon their army, who I trust
were not slow on their way. When I have heard from them, it is
impossible I shall be caught by any trickery.

*The* SCOUT *enters from the other side with news.*

SCOUT.   Eteocles, most mighty lord of the Cadmeans, I come with
sure reports of the army outside; for I have spied upon its actions   40
myself.

Seven men, captains furious for war, were cutting a bull's throat
into a black shield; they touched their hands to the bull's blood
while they swore oaths by Ares, Enyo, and blood-thirsty Terror that   45
they would either sack the Cadmeans' town by force and raze their
city, or die and mix their blood with this soil. They hung memorial tokens of themselves on Adrastus' chariot, for their parents at   50
home, while weeping tears; but there was no pity at all on their
lips, for a spirit of iron determination breathed in them, like lions
with war in their eyes.

My news of this is not delayed by sloth, for I left them drawing
lots how each was to lead a company against the gates which fell  55
to him. Therefore marshal the city's best and choicest men at the
gates' outlets, speedily: the Argives' host is already nearing in full
armour, stirring up the dust; and white lather dripping from their  60
horses' lungs flecks the ground. And you now, like a ship's good
helmsman, must make the city safe, before the blasts of War shatter
it; their army is a wave roaring on dry land. Seize the soonest
moment for this! Myself, I'll keep my eye on trusty look-out, for  65
what's left of the day; and through my clear report you'll know what
happens outside, and be unharmed.

(*The* SCOUT *leaves*; ETEOCLES *is again alone.*)

ETEOCLES.   O Zeus, and Earth, and you gods who hold the city, and
you Curse, my father's powerful Fury, do not, I beg you, raze the  70
city root and branch in total destruction, a captive of Greek foes.  72
The land and city of Cadmus are free: never hold them in the bonds  74
of slavery, but be our defence! I speak of our common interest, I  75
hope; for when a city prospers, it honours its gods.

ETEOCLES *leaves by the side, to go to the walls. The* CHORUS *of young
unmarried women enters from the other side, moving and singing to
an irregular rhythm indicative of panic.*

CHORUS   [*text missing*] I cry out in a great agony of fear.
Their army is let loose, it has left its camp;
a great host is streaming here, horsemen running at its front;  80
dust high as heaven, plain to see, convinces me,
a messenger without voice, but clear and true;  82
the plains beaten by hooves bring their noise to my ear;  84
it flies in the air, it roars like irresistible water  85
striking a mountain.

O you gods and goddesses,
avert the rising evil!
[*a word missing*] shouts over the walls;
the host with bright shields sets out,  90
clear to see in its swift march [*a word missing*] on the city.
Who then will save it, who then protect it,

among gods or goddesses?
And myself: should I fall in supplication                                95
at our gods' [ancestral] images?
You blessed ones in your fine temples:
the hour has come to cling to your images; why do we delay and
      lament so much?
Do you hear, or do you not hear, the clash of shields?                  100
[When,] when if not now shall we have [need
to throw] prayerful offerings of robes and garlands round you?
I have seen the clashing; there is the rattle of many spears.
What will you do, Ares ancient in the land—
will you betray your own city?                                          105
God of the golden helmet, have an eye, have an eye for the city
you once counted well worthy of your love.

           *The* CHORUS *now turn to set dancing and singing.*

You gods of city and land, come to us, all of you together;    Str. 1
see this band of maidens
in supplication against enslavement.                                   110
A wave of men round the city, helmet-crests slanting,
rises and seethes with the War-god's blast.                            115
Now, O Zeus our father, with whom lies the outcome of all,
do all you can to ward off capture by our foes!
The Argives have the citadel of Cadmus                                 120
encircled; we fear the war of their weapons;
the bits which are bound through the mouth
of their horses pipe tones of death.
Seven leaders of men, conspicuous                                      125
amid their host in spearmen's panoply, take stand each
at the seven gates, as their lot fell.

And you, daughter of Zeus, in your might, in your love          Ant. 1
      of battle,
be our city's rescue,                                                  130
Pallas! And you lord of horses too, ruler
of ocean, (*words missing*) with your wrought fish-spear,
give us release from our fears, release!                               135
And you, Ares progenitor, protect our citadel

named for Cadmus, and manifest your care for it!
And Cypris, you are the race's foremother:                         140
keep danger away; we are your descendants
by blood; with prayers invoking god
we approach you calling aloud.                                     145
And you, Lycean lord, prove Lycean
toward the host of our foes, while you, O maiden child
of Leto, have your bow well prepared!

(*sobbing their fear*)
I hear the chariots' clatter round the city—            Str. 2
O mistress Hera!—                                                 152
laden axles squealing at the hubs.
Beloved Artemis!
The spears as they are brandished are driving the air mad!        155
How is it with our city? What is to happen?
Where has god yet to lead the outcome?

(*sobbing their fear*)
Stones hail upon our battlements from slingers.         Ant. 1
O dear Apollo!—                                                   160
shields of bronze are clashing at the gates!
You son of Zeus who have
the sacred power to ordain war's outcome in battle,
and you, blessed Queen Onca Outside the City,
save our abode and its seven gates!                               165

O you all-sufficient gods,                              Str. 3
O you gods and goddesses with power
to guard our land and walls,
do not betray them in the toil of war
to an army with a foreign tongue.                                 170
Hear these maidens' entreaties, hear them very well,
as they stretch our their hands.

O beloved deities,                                      Ant. 3
stand over and deliver our land;                                  175
show that you hold it dear!
Let the people's offerings concern you,
and protect them out of that concern.

This too: our city's rites are fond of sacrifice;                    180
be mindful, we beg you!

ETEOCLES *re-enters angrily from the side; he has heard the* CHORUS'
*panic.*

ETEOCLES.   You intolerable creatures! I ask you: is this best for
the city and its safety, and does it give heart to its people here
under siege, that you go falling before the images of gods who
hold the city, and howling, keening—things hateful to sensible   185
minds? May I share my house with women and their sex neither
amid bad times nor in precious prosperity: when they have sway,
there's no living with their audacity, and once they are afraid,
they are more trouble for house and city. And so now, with your  190
running around to escape, your noise has spread an evil lack
of heart among our citizens, while you give the enemies' cause
outside the best possible support; and our ruin is coming from
within ourselves. This is what you will get when you live among
women!                                                            195

So, if any person will not obey my rule—man, woman, and anything between—sentence will be determined for their execution;
and there will be no escape from death by public stoning. What lies
outside the house is a man's concern—let a woman give no advice:  200
you are to stay indoors and cause no harm. (*pausing for the Chorus
to respond*) Do you hear me, or not hear me? Or am I speaking to
the deaf?

*The* CHORUS' *unabated fear moves them to further song and dance;
Eteocles interposes further calming speech.*

CHORUS.   O beloved son of Oedipus, I became afraid          Str. 1
after I heard the chariots' clatter sounding, sounding
as hubs screeched with the turning wheels                         205
and the horses' harness gave out a voice
from the parts through their mouth, bits born in the fire.
ETEOCLES.   Well, does a sailor who flees from the stern to the prow
find a means of safety when his ship labours in the ocean-wave?    210

CHORUS.   But it was the ancient images I ran to approach,   Ant. 1
putting my trust in their deities, when the blizzard
of death roared in storm at the gates;

it was then that my fear roused me to pray
for the blessed gods' strength to shelter us here. 215

ETEOCLES. Do you pray that the walls keep out the enemy's war?
Then this will be to the gods' advantage; yet, men say, the gods of a
captured city forsake it.

CHORUS. May these our assembled gods never leave it Str. 2
while life is mine; nor may I see this city 220
overrun street by street and consumed
by flame from an army of foes!

ETEOCLES. Do not be ill-advised, I beg you, when you invoke the
gods; for there is Obedience, mother of Well-being, wife of the
Saver—so goes the saying.

CHORUS. There is; but god has a strength far superior: Ant. 2
often it sets the man helpless in trouble
upright, and even free of hardship
when the clouds hang over his eyes.

ETEOCLES. Men's part is this, to offer the gods victims in sacrifice
and for divination when testing their enemy; your part, however, is 230
to be silent, and to stay inside the house.

CHORUS. Thanks to the gods the city we live in is still unvan-
quished; Str. 3
its wall keeps off the mass of foes.
How can you be angry with us, how detest us? 235

ETEOCLES. I do not take amiss your honouring the family of gods,
but, so that you do not make cowards of our citizens, stay calm and
do not be too fearful.

CHORUS. When I had heard the clatter and the shouts flying
towards me, Ant. 3
I came in fear and great dread 240
here to the citadel, the gods' seat of honour.

ETEOCLES. Should you hear, then, of men killed or wounded, do
not seize on that for shrill lament; for this is Ares' nourishment, the
blood of men.

*The* CHORUS *are at last calmer, and change to speech.*

CHORUS.   But there! I hear horses neighing!                                    245
ETEOCLES.   If you do hear them, do not hear them too clearly.
CHORUS.   The citadel is groaning from the earth, as men encircle
   it.
ETEOCLES.   So? It is enough if I deliberate about that.
CHORUS.   I am afraid: the crashing at the gates increases.
ETEOCLES.   Will you not be silent? Say nothing of this through the
   city!                                                                        250
CHORUS.   O you gods our partners, do not betray the walls!
ETEOCLES.   Damnation take you—can you not bear to be silent?
CHORUS.   Gods of our city, grant I do not meet with slavery!
ETEOCLES.   You're making your own slavery, and mine, and the
   whole city's.
CHORUS.   Almighty Zeus, turn your bolt upon our foes!                          255
ETEOCLES.   O Zeus, what you have bestowed on us in women, as a
   kind!
CHORUS.   One to endure misery—just like men whose city is taken.
ETEOCLES.   Words of ill omen again, while you are touching the
   images?
CHORUS.   It is lack of courage; fear ran away with my tongue.
ETEOCLES.   I beg you: grant me if you will a small favour.                     260
CHORUS.   Name it quickly, please, and I'll quickly know.
ETEOCLES.   Be silent, you wretch: don't frighten your friends!
CHORUS.   I'm silent; with others I'll suffer what is fated.
ETEOCLES.   I prefer your last words to those earlier. And, furthermore: go away from the images; make this better prayer, for the   265
   gods to be our allies, and when you have heard my prayers too,
   then raise the sacred chant for victory, with good heart, and follow
   the Greek custom of crying out over sacrifice, an encouragement
   for friends, releasing them from war's fear. (*the* CHORUS *begin to*   270
   *move to the* orkhêstra)
   I say to the gods who hold land and city, those who both inhabit
   our plains and watch over our marketplace, and to Dirce's springs
   and the water of Ismenus, that if good success attends us and
   the city is saved, we will bloody the gods' hearths with sheep,   275
   and set up trophies over the enemy, and dedicate our foes' spear-   277
   struck armour as spoil in their holy temples. Make vows like these
   to the gods, not with the lamentations you love, and not amid

useless and wild sobbing; you'll have no greater escape from what is  280
fated.

As for me, I will go and post six men, with myself as seventh, to
oppose our enemies in proud style at the walls' seven gates, before
words come as hurried messengers, noisy in their haste, and set all  285
ablaze from urgency.

ETEOCLES *again leaves by the side. The* CHORUS *are now in the*
    *orkhêstra to sing and dance.*

CHORUS.    I do care, but my heart is sleepless                    Str. 1
    with fear; anxieties which are my heart's neighbours
    inflame my dread of this host
    surrounding our wall,                                             290
    just as snakes, grimmest of bedmates,
    are feared by a trembling dove, in dread
    for its nestling young.
    Some of that host are approaching our walls                       295
    in all their force, in all their mass—
    and what is to happen to me?—
    while others are slinging
    jagged stones, a hailstorm
    against our townsmen assaulted on all sides.                       300
    In every way that you can,
    gods born of Zeus, protect our city,
    and its people born of Cadmus!

    What country and soil better than this                          Ant. 1
    will you take in exchange, once you have forsaken                  305
    this land of deep earth to foes,
    and Dirce's river,
    the most enriching of waters
    let flow by Poseidon, lord of land,                                310
    and Tethys' daughters?
    O you gods holding our city, visit
    therefore on those outside the walls
    the cowardice fatal to men,
    their weapons thrown away                                          315
    as blind ruin takes them.

Ensure battle's glory for our townsmen,
and [be] this city's saviours;
stay firmly where you have noble shrines;
hear our tearful, shrill entreaties.                                    320

A cause for pity's tears it is, to hurl a city                    Str. 2
so age-old down headlong to Hades,
enslaved as the prey of war, in dust and ash
if an Achaean man sacks it
with god's will, in dishonour,                                          325
its women overpowered and led away (*a sobbing wail*),
both young and old,
by their hair like horses, their garments
torn apart on them. A city
being emptied cries out,                                                330
its women lost as pillage, their shrieking all mingled.
Heavy indeed is the fate I dread.

A cause for weeping tears it is that girls just of age            Ant. 2
should be plucked unripe before marriage
to travel a hateful road, their homes destroyed;                        335
in truth, I declare a dead man
to fare better then they do.
For whenever some city is overcome (*a sobbing wail*),
its fate is harsh:
man leads man away, another kills,                                      340
others carry fire; the city
is all smoke and foul stain.
Ares the slayer of people blasts madly against it,
polluting all piety's restraint.

Uproar through the city; against it a net                         Str. 3
encircling the walls; and man killing                                   346
man (*a word missing*) with spear;
new-born infants
suckling at the breast
are wailing and screaming in their own blood.                          350
Plundering too, the kin of rampage:
looter joins with looter,

and empty-handed calls to empty-handed
from wishing to gain a companion,
though he desires neither less nor equal; 355
to picture what follows, words are to hand.

All manner of produce is thrown on the ground, Ant. 3
offending the eye, once it falls in
with vindictive storemen.
Earth's great bounty, 360
all randomly mixed,
is carried along by the surge and spoiled.
New women-slaves encounter fresh hurt,
wretchedly enduring
the bed of a man who has fortune's success, 365
since from their enemy's supremacy
they must expect nocturnal rites to come
where all is a surge of weeping and pain.

*The* CHORUS *turn to speech as the* SCOUT *returns, followed very
quickly from the other side by* ETEOCLES, *who has attendants.*

CHORUS. (*first voice*)  See, my friends, our spy on their army brings
us, I think, important new information; haste wheels his steps 370
along on their errand.
CHORUS. (*second voice*)  And look, here is the king himself, Oedipus' son, exactly in time to learn the messenger's report; haste 375
disorders his steps too.
SCOUT.  I'll speak, by your leave; I've good knowledge of the enemy
and how each of them has drawn his lot at the gates.
　　Tydeus is already at the Gates of Proetus, roaring; but the seer
does not let him ford the crossing of the Ismenus, for the sacrificial
victims give no good omen. Tydeus in his frenzied lust for battle 380
is loud as a snake with its midday hissing; he strikes at the seer,
the wise son of Oicles, with abuse that he slinks fawningly before
death and battle, out of cowardice. While he bawls out like this,
he shakes the three overshadowing plumes which crest his helmet, 385
and under his shield of hammered bronze bells ring out terror. On
the shield he has this arrogant device, the heaven wrought blazing
with stars; brilliant and conspicuous in mid-shield is the full moon,

most reverend of stars, the eye of night. Raving like this in his 390
vainglorious armour he bawls out beside the river-banks, longing
for battle, like a horse snorting fiercely against its bridle, eager to
go while awaiting the trumpet's cry.

Whom will you post against him? Who can be relied upon to
stand defending the Gates of Proetus when the bars are undone?    395
ETEOCLES.   No fine array on a man would frighten me! Nor do
devices cause wounds; plumes and bells do not bite home without a
spear. This night you speak of, too, set upon his shield and glitter-  400
ing with the heaven's stars—its folly might perhaps be prophetic
for someone; for were night to fall upon his eyes in death, this
vainglorious device would indeed prove right and true in meaning
for its bearer, and its arrogance will be his own prophecy against   405
him. For my part, I shall post as defender of these gates against
Tydeus the trusty son of Astacus, a man of very noble birth who
honours the throne of Modesty and abhors over-proud words. He   410
has no part in shameful acts, and his habit is to be no coward. His
roots spring from the Sown Men whom Ares spared, and he is truly
a native of the land: Melanippus. Ares will decide the action with
his dice; but the Justice of blood-kin very much sends him forward  415
to keep enemy spears from the motherland which bore him.

*The* CHORUS *sing and dance briefly.*

CHORUS.   Now may the gods grant success for our champion,

                                              Str. 1

justly setting out to fight for our city;
but I do tremble for our friends,                                   420
in fear to see their bloody death
if it comes to killing.

SCOUT.   May the gods grant him this success!
Capaneus has drawn the lot at the Electran Gates. This next man
is a giant, taller than the one I spoke of before, and his boastful
thinking is not a mortal man's: for he will sack the city, he says,   425
both if god be willing and if not willing, and Zeus' opposition with  426
a blast that strikes to the earth is not to stop him—he likened Zeus'
flashing bolts of lightning to the warmth of midday. As his device   430

he has a naked man bearing fire, a torch blazing in his hands as his weapon; in letters of gold he is crying out 'I shall burn the city!'

Against such a man, send...who will stand against him? Who 435 will stay there without fear of the man's boasting?

ETEOCLES. Here too one gain gives birth to another. Men's tongues, I tell you, are the true accusing evidence of their wild thoughts. Capaneus is threatening those prepared to act; in his 440 contempt for the gods and wild delight in his well-practised mouth, although he is a mortal man, he sends Zeus in heaven loud and swelling words. I trust, however, that the lightning-bolt of fire will come to him, not any likeness of it. A man has 445 been posted against him whose mouth may be too ready but who 447 burns with courage, mighty Polyphontes, a protection to be relied upon, with the goodwill of Artemis the defender, and the other gods' aid. 450

Speak of another man who has drawn the lot at another gate.

CHORUS. Death to the man for his proud imprecations    Ant. 1
on our city! May the lightning-bolt check him
before he bursts into my home
and drags me from the maidens' rooms
in war's brutal ransack.    456

SCOUT. Speak I shall: third was Eteoclus, with the third lot leaping 458 from the upturned bronze helmet for him to pitch his company against the Neisteïd Gates. He keeps his horses circling; they snort 460 in their headbands, in their wish to fall upon the gates; the muzzle-pipes whistle in barbaric fashion as they fill with their nostrils' proud breath. His shield's device is formed in no modest fashion: 465 a man in armour climbs the steps of a ladder against his enemies' wall, in his wish to storm it; and he too cries out in lettered syllables, that not even Ares would throw him from the battlements.

For this man too send one who can be relied upon to keep 470 slavery's yoke from our city. 471

ETEOCLES. He is already sent, in fact; and his boast consists in his two hands: Megareus, offspring of Creon of the Sown Men's race. 473 With no fear at all of the horses' whinnying and din he will go out 475 from the gates, and either repay the land fully for his upbringing

by his death, or take the two men, and the city on the shield, and
glorify his father's house with these spoils.
　　Go on with the boasts of a further man; and don't grudge me the
telling.                                                                    480

CHORUS.　And I here pray that you may have good success,　Str. 2
　you champion of my house!—but that ill success befalls the other
　　side;
and just as they speak against our city
too boastfully in their minds' madness,
so may Zeus the punisher look upon them in wrath.                           485

SCOUT.　Fourth and next, his place the gates which neighbour
　Athena Onca, Hippomedon stands shouting, huge in form and
　stature. The great orb he holds—I mean the round of his shield—
　I trembled as he flourished it; I will not deny it. It was no cheap  490
　maker of devices, seemingly, who bestowed this work upon his
　shield, Typhon issuing through his fire-breathing mouth the black
　smoke which is fire's changeful sister; and coiling snakes are riv-
　eted at the lip running round his hollow-bellied shield. Hippome-  495
　don himself cried out triumphantly; possessed by Ares he rushes
　towards battle like a frenzied maenad, looking terror.
　　Such a man's attack must be well defended: Terror is already
　boasting at the gates.                                                    500
ETEOCLES.　First, Pallas Onca the city-gates' close neighbour will
　keep the man off in hatred of his arrogance, like a fierce serpent
　kept from nestlings; and Hyperbius, the trusty son of Oenops, is
　chosen to fight him man to man: he wishes to seek out his destiny  505
　in the stress of fortune. In neither form nor heart nor bearing of
　arms is he to be faulted. Hermes has brought them together with
　good reason, for the man is enemy to the man he will stand against,
　and in the gods upon their shields the two will be bringing enemies
　together: the first has fire-breathing Typhon, while for Hyperbius  510
　father Zeus is set standing upright on his shield, thunderbolt blaz-
　ing in hand. That is the nature of these gods' friendship; and we  513 5
　are on the victorious side, and they on the vanquished, at least if
　Zeus is mightier in battle than Typhon; and it is probable, the men  517
　will fare like this as opponents; and for Hyperbius, in accord with  519

his device's meaning, Zeus there upon his shield should prove the 518
saviour.                                                          520

CHORUS.    Indeed I trust that he who has on his shield        Ant. 2
the inimical figure of Zeus' antagonist, the evil power
now under the earth, a semblance hateful
to both mortals and the long-lived gods—
I trust that in front of the gates he'll smash his head down.       525

SCOUT.    I wish it may be so! The fifth man is the next I speak of,
and the fifth gates are his post, the Borraean, by the very tomb of
Zeus' son Amphion. He swears by the spear he holds—he reveres
it with his trust more than a god and higher than his eyes —he    530
swears he will sack the Cadmeans' city by force. So declares Ares'
son of the handsome face, his mother the frequenter of mountains,
a man both boy and man; the beard is just coming across his
cheeks in youth's prime growth, its hair springing up thickly. Cruel  535
in spirit, in no way girlish like his name, but with a fierce eye,
he takes his stand. Not that he stands against the gate without a
boast: on his shield of hammered bronze, his body's rounded protection, he was brandishing that reproach to our city, the Sphinx  540
who ate men raw, artfully worked on with rivets, her embossed
figure gleaming; she carries beneath her a single Cadmean, for
the most missiles to strike upon this man. Now he has come, it
seems, to do no petty trafficking in battle, and not to disgrace his  545
long road's journey. He is Parthenopaeus the Arcadian. Such is this
man, an immigrant to Argos who repays it for his fine upbringing by threatening these walls with what I wish the god may not
fulfil.

ETEOCLES.    If only they get from the gods what they intend with  550
those unholy boastings! They would be destroyed, for sure, all in
ruin and in all misery. This Arcadian you speak of—for him too
there is a man, one who does not boast but whose hand sees to
the deed, Actor, brother of the last I named. He will not allow talk  555
without deeds to stream inside our gates and make disaster grow,
nor that hateful monster the Sphinx to pass in from outside. She  558
will blame her bearer when she gets constant battering under the  560
city's wall.

    If the gods will it, I should prove right!

CHORUS.   His words go through my breast;                          Str. 3
and my hair in its locks is standing on end
as I hear great boasting from boastful, impious men;              565
If gods are gods,
I wish they may destroy them in our land!

SCOUT.   The sixth I would speak of is a man most prudent, a seer
excellent in valour, mighty Amphiaraus. By the Homoloid Gates
he has his post, and he is shouting much abuse at mighty Tydeus,  570
with 'Slayer of men! Confounder of cities! Supreme teacher of
evil to Argos! Fury's Summoner! Servant of Slaughter! Counsellor
of Adrastus in this wrong!' Next he addresses and calls to your  575
brother, mighty Polynices, his eyes turned up in contempt, at the
end dwelling twice on his name. These words pass his lips in
speech: 'Can such a deed be welcome also to the gods, and good for 580
future generations to hear and tell, the sack of your father's city and
native gods after pitching against them an army of outsiders? What
lawful cause will quench the life-source of a mother, any more than
your fatherland will become your ally if your eager purpose is to  585
capture it in war? I myself, on the contrary, shall enrich this land,
a seer covered by an enemy's soil. To battle, then! I expect a death
of no dishonour.' So the seer declared, untroubled as he bore his
shield all of bronze. No device was on its round, however; his wish 590
is not the appearance of prowess but its reality, for he crops the
deep furrow from which good counsel grows. Against this man I
urge sending wise and brave opponents: the man who honours god 595
is dangerous.

ETEOCLES.   Ominous, alas, to ally a righteous man with those too
impious! In every undertaking there is nothing worse than evil
company; it is a crop not to be taken in. Either a pious man, who  600
joins on board a ship sailors hot upon some villainy, is lost together 602
with a breed of men the gods abhor, or a righteous man, among
fellow-citizens who are hostile to guests and unmindful of the gods, 605
is caught unjustly in the same net and beaten down by the god's
impartial scourge. In this same way the seer, the son of Oicles, I
mean, a prudent, upright, valorous, reverent man, a great prophet, 610
mixed despite his judgement with unholy, bold-mouthed men who
stretch their mission too far to return; Zeus willing, he shall be
dragged down with them. Yet I think he will not even attack the   615

gates, not from lack of heart or cowardice of spirit, but he knows
that he must die in the battle if Apollo's oracles are to have their
fruit; for the god's habit is to be silent or to say what hits the mark.
Nevertheless we shall put a good man against him to guard the   620
gate, mighty Lasthenes, an enemy to outsiders. Nature gives him
an old man's wisdom in a body prime with youthful growth; his
eye runs swift; he is not slow of hand to seize with his spear on
what a shield leaves exposed at its side. Yet men's success is the gift
of god.                                                          625

CHORUS.   You gods, hear and fulfil                      Ant. 3
   our just prayer, so our city may have success;
   turn evil war's harm away onto its attackers.
   Outside our walls
   may Zeus with his lightning strike and kill them!        630

SCOUT.   Here now is the seventh man I shall speak of, at the seventh
   gates, your very own brother, and here is the kind of fortune he
   invokes with curses for the city, crying out joyously a victory-hymn   633
   for its capture: for yourself to be his opponent and for himself to   635
   kill you and to die close by, or to punish you with living exile in the
   very same way as you dishonoured him with expulsion. Those are
   the things he is bawling, and he calls upon the gods of his birth and
   fatherland to keep absolute watch over his prayers—the mighty   640
   Polynices. He has a newly finished shield, a perfect round, and a
   double device worked on to it: a man of beaten gold seen in full
   armour, and a woman modestly leading him as guide; in fact, she   645
   says she is Justice, as the letters state: 'I shall bring this man back
   home, and he will possess his father's city and the freedom of his
   house.'
      Those have been the devices these men invented; and you your-
   self must now decide, whom you think to send against Polynices.   650
   You can be sure, you will never fault me for my reports here; but
   you yourself must decide how to steer the city's course.

(*The* SCOUT *leaves.*)

ETEOCLES.   Oh, the family of Oedipus, and mine, maddened by
   the gods, and their great detestation, and all the tears to shed for it!

Oh, alas for me, now my father's curses are brought to fulfilment! 655
Yet neither tears nor sorrow is fitting, in case they give birth to
grief even harder to bear. This man so well named, Polynices I
mean—we shall soon know where his device will have its fulfilment, whether letters wrought in gold, the wittering of wandering 660
wits, are to bring him back home. If Justice the maiden daughter
of Zeus had attended his actions and thoughts, this might perhaps
now be so; but neither when he escaped from the darkness of his
mother's womb, nor during his upbringing, nor since his youth, 665
nor when the hair gathered in his beard, did Justice look on him
and find him worthy; nor yet, I swear, does she stand at his side to
support him now while he injures his fatherland. In truth, Justice
would be wholly false in name if she kept company with a man 670
minded for every audacity. Of this I am confident, and I will stand
against him myself; who else can do so more justly? Leader against
leader and brother against brother, enemy against enemy, I will take
my stand.

    (*to his attendants*) Bring my greaves at once, protection against 675
spear and arrow! (*One or two attendants leave.*)

CHORUS.   No! Dearest of men, Oedipus' son, do not be like that
ill-named one in nature! It is enough that Cadmeans fight hand to
hand with Argives; their bloodshed can be cleansed, but the death 680
of two men who are blood-kin killing each other like this—there is
no old age for this pollution.

ETEOCLES.   If someone really were to bring this evil on, let it be
without disgrace: it is the only profit among the dead; you'll not
speak of any glory from cowardice and shame.                                      685

CHORUS.   (*singing and dancing*) Why this raging desire, my son?
    Let no mad ruin bear you away,                                    Str. 1
filling your heart with war's frenzy; cast out
this evil love at its start.

ETEOCLES.   Since a god very much hurries the business on, let the
whole line of Laius detested by Apollo go along with the wind now 690
that Cocytus' wave is its lot.

CHORUS.   Desire all too raw with its bite is urging you forward to
    perform                                                            Ant. 1

a man's killing in unlawful bloodshed
which will bear its bitter fruit.

ETEOCLES.   It is because my own father's black curse is my enemy; 695
it sits nearby with dry, unweeping eyes, speaking of earlier death as
profit over later.

CHORUS.   But do not yourself press on! You will not be called

Str. 2

ignoble if you secure your life well;
the Fury cloaked in black storm will go out of the house        700
once the gods get your hands' sacrifice.

ETEOCLES.   The gods are already past caring for me, it would seem,
and the favour they prize from me is my death. Why then should I
still fawn to avoid my fated death?

CHORUS.   Wait while it stands at your side, since in a late veer

Ant. 2

of its mood the divine power might perhaps        706
be changeable and come on more gently with its breath;
but the storm is still boiling now.

ETEOCLES.   It boiled up, yes, in Oedipus' curse. The sights I imagined asleep in my dreams were all too true, in their division of my 710
father's wealth.

CHORUS.   Let women persuade you, although you have no love for
them.

ETEOCLES.   You may speak, where it is to effect; but it must not be
at length.

CHORUS.   Don't take this road to the seventh gates—not you!

ETEOCLES.   I am whetted now, you can see, and you will not blunt
me by any argument.        715

CHORUS.   Yet victory has the god's honour, even if ignobly won.

ETEOCLES.   No man of arms should love that saying.

CHORUS.   But is it your wish to reap a crop from your own brother's
blood?

ETEOCLES.   If the gods give it, you can't escape evil.

ETEOCLES *leaves by the side for the gates, his attendants following.*
*The* CHORUS *dance and sing.*

CHORUS.    I shudder that the goddess                    Str. 1
    unlike gods, the destroyer of houses,                    721
    the wholly true prophet of evil
    invoked by a father, the Fury,
    may fulfil the impassioned curses
    of the demented Oedipus;                    725
    this strife destroying sons drives her.

    A stranger is assigning                    Ant. 1
    the portions, Chalybian emigrant
    from Scythia, bitter divider
    of wealth and possessions, cruel Iron,                    730
    granting land enough to inhabit
    for just the dead to occupy,
    without a share in these great plains.

    Once they have killed each other,                    Str. 2
    have hewn each other to death, and dusty earth                    735
    has drunk the bloody gore down, hard and black,
    who is to give expiation? who provide them with release?
    Oh, how the harsh new sufferings
    of this house mingle closely with its ancient woe!                    740

    Of the ancient transgression                    Ant. 2
    I speak, its penalty swift; and it remains
    to the third generation, ever since,                    745
    despite Pythian Apollo in his seat of oracles,
    the world's navel, thrice telling him
    to save his city by dying without issue,

    Laius was conquered by pleasing folly                    Str. 3
    and got for a son his own death,                    751
    the father-killing Oedipus,
    who sowed his seed in his mother's
    sacred tilth where he had grown,
    a root yielding bloodshed—                    755

foolhardy! Insanity from wits destroyed
coupled them in marriage;

like the sea it drives on waves of trouble: Ant. 3
one falls but another rises
of triple greatness, crashing too 760
around the city's stern. Between,
here is our wall extending
defence of narrow width;
but I fear the city may be overwhelmed
together with its kings. 765

When curses spoken long ago are fulfilled, Str. 4
the settlement is harsh;
their destructiveness does not slip away.
The prosperity of mortal men
when fattened to excess 770
must jettison all from the stern.

For who of men had such esteem from the gods Ant. 4
that share the altars here,
and from men frequent in their gatherings,
as the honour they gave Oedipus 775
who removed from the land
that bane, the snatcher of our men?

But when the wretch was fully conscious Str. 5
of his dreadful marriage,
distraught with grief and rage past bearing, 780
and madness in his heart,
at the two evil acts he had performed
with hands that slew his father, he went
astray from better judgement:

against his sons, in vengeful anger Ant. 5
they had not sustained him, 786
he launched, alas, embittered curses,
they should one day divide
his possessions with swords of iron in hand;

and now I fear this may be fulfilled                                    790
by the swift-running Fury.

*The* SCOUT *arrives from the battle at the gates.*

SCOUT.   Take heart, you daughters of noble parentage! Our city has
escaped slavery's yoke: the boastings of high and mighty men are
overthrown; amid both calm and the storm's mighty blows the city   795
has let in no water. The wall holds firm, and we secured our gates
with reliable single champions. Mostly, things go well, at six of
the gates; the seventh was chosen by that holy leader of all sevens   800
the lord Apollo, fulfilling for Oedipus' sons the ancient folly of
Laius.

CHORUS.   What further unwelcome trouble is there for the city?     803

MESSENGER.   The men are dead, slain by their own hands.            805

CHORUS   Who? What do you mean? Fear at your words puts me
out of my senses.

MESSENGER.   Come to your senses then, and listen: Oedipus'
sons . . .

CHORUS.   Oh, this is misery for me: I am our disaster's prophet.

MESSENGER.   . . . yes, there is no doubt: felled to the ground . . .

CHORUS.   . . . they both lie there? Heavy news, but tell it all the same.   810

MESSENGER.   They went to kill themselves this way with hands too
closely kin in blood; both together had the demon in common—
indeed it is this which has consumed the ill-fated family. Such
things as these are for joy and tears, with the city faring well but
those at the head, the two commanders, dividing their whole prop-   815
erty and possessions with a hammered, Scythian sword; they will
have what land they may get at their burial, borne along in a cruel
fate according to their father's prayers.                               819

*The* SCOUT *leaves.*

CHORUS.   (*chanting*) O great Zeus and you deities                 822
guarding our city, you whose [concern it was]
to protect these walls of Cadmus,
am I to rejoice and cry victory                                         825
at the city's safety unscathed,
or weep for the cruelly fated sufferers,

the commanders in war who leave no children,
who were indeed rightly named
['of true glory'] and 'of much contention'                    830
and killed in their impious purpose?

(*The* CHORUS *now sing and dance.*)

Oh, the black curse of Oedipus upon his line,            Str. 1
now complete in fulfilment!
Chill misery has fallen round
my heart; I begin a chant for the tomb,                       835
possessed by grief on hearing they are killed, bodies
dripping with blood, an evil death their fate;
an evil omen,
truly, two spears piping music as one!

There has been exaction in full, with no failing,       Ant. 1
by the father's spoken curse;                                    841
Laius' disobedient resolve
had lasting effect; around the city
there is despair; the oracles are unblunted.
Oh, we lament you men greatly; your act                   845
was beyond belief;
the blow is here to mourn, and no mere tale.

*The* CHORUS *see bearers approaching with the bodies of Eteocles and
Polynices, which are put down in the* orkhêstra.

Here things are, they make themselves plain; the messenger's report
    was very clear.                                           Mesode 1
Double, grievous blows bring double sorrows.
These are disasters fulfilled in two deaths, mutual slaughter! What
    am I to say?                                               850
What else is there but agony upon agony at the hearth?
Come though, my friends, go along with the wind of grief,
and with hands around your head                              855
beat out its escorting rhythm which passes ever across Acheron,
steering the mission
of no return, its canvas black,

to the dry shore which Healer Apollo may not tread,
sunless, where all are received into dark invisibility.                    860

(*The following brief scene is inauthentic.*)

{{But here are Antigone and Ismene
for a bitterly painful task:
without disputing, I think,
they will lament their two brothers from their lovely bosoms,
dressed in deep folds; the event well merits sorrow.                    865
It is right that before their voices start
we cry the ill-sounding hymn
of the Fury and intone
the hateful paean to Hades.

Oh, sorrow! They have suffered the worst in their brothers                    870
of all who pass a breast-band round their dress!
I weep, I lament, and there is no deceit:
I truly wail from the heart.}}

*The* CHORUS *now divide, to dance and sing.*

SEMI-CHORUS A.    Oh, sorrow! Oh, you men were senseless,
                                                                        Str. 2
disobeying friends, unwearying in wrong,                    875
destroying your father's house, you wretches, with your fight!
SEMI-CHORUS B.    Wretches indeed, and they found a wretched
        death
in working the house's violent ruin.

A.    Oh, sorrow! Oh, you men who smashed down                    Ant. 2
the walls of your house, who saw the bitter cost                    882
of single rule! Now you have been reconciled through the sword.                    885
B.    Only too well was that outcome brought about
by Oedipus their father's potent Fury.

A.    Through their left sides they were struck,                    Str. 3
struck, I tell you—the sides
of brothers from one womb                    890
(*a line missing*)
Oh, lament their curse sent by god,
oh, lament their deaths by mutual killing!

B.   A piercing blow, you say, they were struck                    895
    to house and bodies,
    through their unspeaking anger,
    fated by their father's curse
    to unity of purpose.

A.   Lament goes through the city;                    Ant. 3
    the walls lament, the soil                                   901
    laments for men it loved.
    The property remains for successors,
    through which came their terrible fate,
    through which came their quarrel and death as its end.       905
B.   They split the possessions, tempers keen
    to get equal parts;
    but the arbiter they had
    was not blameless to their friends,
    nor Ares to their pleasure.                                  910

A.   Struck by iron, they are here like this,        Str. 4
    and struck by iron are certain shares—
    one might say—awaiting them
    in the tombs of their fathers.
B.   Loud-sounding lament escorts them                             915
    from the house, rending
    in its own grief, in its own pain,
    rending the senses, no friend of joy,
    truly streaming tears
    from a heart which wastes                                    920
    away as I weep for these two princes.

A.   One may say of these two wretched men            Ant. 4
    that they inflicted much on our folk
    and much on the foreign ranks,
    with many slain in the fray.                                 925
B.   Their poor mother was ill-fated
    beyond all women
    who bear the name of a parent.
    She made her own son her own husband
    and then gave them birth;                                    930

and they died like this,
from brothers' hands killing each other.

A.   Brothers indeed, and now wholly destroyed                    Str. 5
in a parting without friendship,
their duel a madness                                                                  935
at the end of their quarrel.
B.   Their enmity has stopped;
their life is now mixed
in the earth running with bloodshed; truly they share one blood!   940
Harsh the resolver of their quarrel,
the sea-borne foreigner, who leapt from fire,
whetted Iron; harsh too the evil
divider of their property,
Ares, bringing true the curse of their father!                              945

A.   They got and keep their portion—oh, poor men!—        Ant. 5
[by] agonies the gods gave them;
beneath earth's body
they will have bottomless wealth.                                               950
B.   Oh, they have crowned their line
with many sorrows;
over the ending these Curses here have cried out in joy
victory's shrill chant, now that the house                                    955
and line have been routed in total flight;
Ruin's trophy stands now in the gates
at which they struck each other down;
with both overcome, the demon has ceased.                              960

A.   You were struck; and struck back.                           Mesode 2
B.   And you slew; and you died.
A.   You slew with the spear.   B.   You died by the spear.
A.   Hurt done!   B.   Hurt borne!
A.   Let lament come!   B.   Let weeping come!
A.   You lie in death.   B.   And you dealt death.                          965

A.   Cry sorrow!   B.   Cry sorrow!                                        Str. 6
A.   My heart is mad with lamenting.
B.   My heart within me is groaning.

A.   Oh, oh! You shall have all our tears!
B.   You too, your wretchedness complete!                              970
A.   By your kin you died.
B.   And your kin you slew.
A.   Two to tell of...   B.   ...and two to see...
A.   ...these miseries are near at hand...
B.   ...the fall of brother with brother.

CHORUS (*refrain*)   Oh, alas! O Fate, heavy in what you give to
        endure,                                                        975
    and you potent shade of Oedipus,
    black Fury, you are indeed a mighty power!

A.   Cry sorrow!   B.   Cry sorrow!                          Ant. 6
A.   Disasters dreadful to look on...
B.   ...he brought from exile and showed me...
A.   ...but failed in his goal when he slew.                           980
B    City safe, but he lost life's breath!
A.   He lost it, indeed!
B.   But took away *his*!                                              982
A.   Deaths to tell of...   B.   ...and deaths to see...               993
A.   ...shared blood to lament, heavy grief!                           984
B.   We weep the pain of triple blows!                                 985
CHORUS   (*refrain*)   Oh, alas! O Fate, heavy in what you give to
        endure,
    and you potent shade of Oedipus,
    black Fury, you are indeed a mighty power!

A.   (*of Polynices*) You knew her, at the end of your march...   Epod.
B.   (*of Eteocles*) You too, no later in learning...                  990
A    ...when you came back to your city...
B.   ...and as antagonist to your spear.                               992
A.   Oh, the agony...   B.   Oh, the tragedy...                        994
A.   ...for the house!   B.   ...and the land!                         995
A.   (*of Eteocles*) Oh, alas! Your lamentable tragedy, my lord!       998
B.   (*of Polynices*) (*a line missing*)
A.   Oh, alas! Their wrongdoing, their whole disaster!                 1000
B.   Oh, alas! Their possession by ruinous folly!
A    Oh, alas! Where in the land shall we lay their bodies?

B.   Oh, alas! Where the honour will be greatest for them!
A.   Oh, alas! Hurtful for the father they lie beside!                    100
(B. *A line missing*)

*After 1004 the original ending of Aeschylus' play, perhaps only a few*
*lines of farewell from the* CHORUS *as they accompany the solemn exit*
*of the bodies, has been displaced by the following inauthentic scene.*

{{A HERALD *from the new authorities in Thebes enters; a few citizens*
*may now gather too, joining* ANTIGONE *and* ISMENE.

HERALD.   It is my duty to announce present and past decisions   100
    of the people's counsellors in this city of Cadmus: it is decided
    that Eteocles here, in virtue of his goodwill towards the land,
    should have funeral through loving burial in the earth; for he
    chose death within the city in keeping out the enemy; pure and
    blameless towards its ancestral temples, he died exactly where it is   101
    honourable for the young to die. About Eteocles, such words are
    my instruction; but his brother, the dead Polynices here, is to be
    thrown outside without funeral, for dogs to seize upon, since he
    was to overturn the Cadmeans' land had not some god stood in   101
    his way with Eteocles' spear; and even in death he shall keep the
    guilt of polluting his ancestral gods: he dishonoured them when
    he brought an outside army and tried to take the city. So it is
    decided that he should have a dishonourable funeral from the birds   102
    of the air, and this be honour's reward that he gets; no hands to
    work at heaping a tomb are to accompany him, no holy attention
    with shrill laments, no honour of being carried out from home
    by kin.
        Such is the decision of the Cadmean authorities here.        102
ANTIGONE.   And I for my part say to your Cadmean leaders: if
    no one else is willing to share giving him funeral, I will give him
    funeral myself and risk the danger for having given it to my own
    brother; and I feel no shame in this disobedience, in defying the
    city's rule. To be born as we were from a common womb, from a   103
    wretched mother and a hapless father—this is a powerful thing:
    therefore, my soul, share willingly in his unwilling misery, the
    living with the dead, kin in spirit with kin. His flesh (*a line missing*)   103
    nor hollow-bellied wolves shall rend: let no one think of that! His

funeral and burial I will myself find means for, although I am a woman, carrying things in the fold of my linen dress; and I myself will cover him. Let no one think the contrary: a means to act will come with courage. 1040

HERALD. I tell you not to do this violence against the city.
ANTIGONE. And I tell you not to make superfluous proclamations against me.
HERALD. A people which has escaped disaster is harsh, however.
ANTIGONE. Be harsh! But Polynices here shall not go without funeral. 1045
HERALD. But will you honour with funeral one whom the city hates?
ANTIGONE. Certainly, if he has not had full honour by the gods.
HERALD. No, he has not, at least not before he threw this land into danger.
ANTIGONE. He suffered wrongly, and answered that with wrong.
HERALD. But this was a deed against all, instead of a single man. 1050
ANTIGONE. Strife is the last of the gods to end an argument; but I will give him funeral myself. Make no long speeches!
HERALD. Follow your own will, then; but I forbid you.

*The* HERALD *leaves. The* CHORUS *and the bearers divide into two groups; one with the body of Eteocles is joined by* ISMENE, *and the other with that of Polynices is joined by* ANTIGONE. *The* CHORUS *chant.*

CHORUS A. Oh, our sorrow! O you proudly triumphant Spirits of Death,
    you Furies, you annihilators of family, 1055
    who have destroyed the family of Oedipus root and branch like this!
    What is to become of me? and what am I to do? and what plan for myself?
    How am I to bear neither weeping for you, Polynices,
    nor escorting you to the tomb?
CHORUS B. But I am afraid, and I wish to avert the citizens' anger. 1060
    Eteocles, you will have many honours, however,
    while he, poor wretch, will go his way without lamentation,

and have only the tears of a sister's dirge.
Now, who could believe this?                              106

A.  Let the city act or not act
    against those who weep for Polynices.
    We here will go and help his funeral as escorts.
    For this is a blow we share with the family;          107
    and any city approves what is right differently at times.

B.  And we shall go with Eteocles, exactly as the city
    and what is right together approve;
    for after the blessed gods and mighty Zeus
    he, most of all, saved the Cadmeans' city             107
    from overturn and swamping
    by a wave of foreign men.

*The two groups with the bodies leave by opposite sides.*}}

# Suppliants

# Suppliants

## CHARACTERS

CHORUS of the daughters of Danaus
DANAUS, brother of Aegyptus king of Egypt
PELASGUS, king of Argos
EGYPTIANS forming a second chorus
HERALD from the Sons of Aegyptus
MEN OF ARGOS forming a third chorus

There are mute parts for women servants attending the CHO-
RUS, and for armed men of Argos attending PELASGUS and later
DANAUS.

*The play is set on the shore near Argos, by a sacred mound which has
an altar, and images, of all the city's gods. The CHORUS enter the
orkhêstra in procession from one side, chanting in rhythm with their
steps. They carry the wool-wreathed branches which identify suppliants,
and have women attendants. DANAUS follows them.*

CHORUS.   May Zeus the god of suppliants watch favourably over
      our company
    which set out by ship from the Nile's outer mouth
    where the sand runs fine! We are in flight
    from Zeus' land whose pastures neighbour Syria—                    5
    not condemned by a city's vote
    to public exile for bloodshed,
    but by our own action in flight from men:
    we abominate union with Aegyptus' sons
    and their impious [intention].                                     10

Danaus our father, both the leader of our counsels and the leader
    of our group,
determined this as the best of the painful moves to hand,
to flee in haste across the ocean's wave,
and to land our ship at Argos, where actually our line          15
was brought into being, proudly claiming descent
from Zeus' touch upon the gadfly-maddened heifer and from his
    breath upon her.
What more kindly disposed land, then,
could we come to than this                                      20
with suppliants' emblems here in hand,
branches wreathed with wool?
(*a line missing, probably including the words* [ancestral deities])
to whom the city belongs, and its land and bright water;        23
and you gods on high; and you heroes heavy with honour
who have tombs in its earth;                                     25
and Zeus the saviour and third, guardian of their house for pious
    men:
receive this company of women suppliants
in the reverent spirit breathed by your land;
and the swarm of violent men, the sons of Aegyptus—             30
before they set foot on this sandy shore,
send them swiftly in their vessels
out to sea; and there in tempest and battering storm,
in thunder and lightning and rain-bearing winds,                35
may they meet the sea's rage and be destroyed,
before ever they subject us, their uncle's daughters,
to themselves, and make us mount
the unwilling marriage-bed which Right denies them.

*The* CHORUS *now dance and sing.*

And now I call upon                                    Str. 1
the calf who was Zeus' child                                    41
as my helper beyond the sea, the son of my ancestress
the flower-grazing heifer through the breath of Zeus,
her son by his touch;
suitably for his name                                           45
her fated term was duly fulfilled,
and she bore Epaphus;

in calling on him now                                         Ant. 1
amid the grassy pastures                                   50
of his mother an age ago, recalling her past ordeals,
these are the marks of proof I shall now present;
they will be made plain
to dwellers in this land
though unexpected; in my long tale                                55
men will come to knowledge.

If some bird-augur nearby,                                  Str. 2
a native of this land, happens to hear my lament,
he will imagine he listens to the voice                             60
of Tereus' scheming wife crying her sorrow,
the hawk-driven nightingale,

who beside leafy rivers,                                      Ant. 2
excluded from her haunts, grieves for her unheard-of fate,
composing the story of her son's death:                             65
how he was killed, his blood shed by her own hands,
meeting a mother's cruel wrath.

I myself too love weeping like that; to Ionian modes and strains
                                                  Str. 3
I am gashing my tender cheek, warm with summer,                     70
and my heart unacquainted with tears;
I am picking flowers of lamentation
in fearful hope, there is someone to care
for us in our friendless flight                                      75
from Egypt the land of mists.

Now, you gods of our ancestral line, hear well, and see what is right;
                                                  Ant. 3
grant no undue consummation to lustful youth,                         80
but truly detest arrogant force:
you would be upholding rightful marriage.
An altar also protects against harm
those fleeing hard-pressed from war;
it is holy to the gods.                                         85

May all be made well at Zeus' desire,                               Str. 4
if Zeus' it really is. This is not easy to hunt down;                   87
for the paths of his thought                                    93

extend in much shadow, dim and obscure,
beyond the eye's mark.                                    95

The outcome is sure—no throw on the back!—        Ant. 4
if ever the nod of Zeus ordains that a thing be fulfilled.   92
Everywhere it blazes out,                                 88
even in darkness when fortune is black
for mortal peoples.                                       90

He hurls men down from their hopes high as towers    Str. 5
into absolute destruction,                               97
but makes no armed array of force.
Among gods all is effortless;                            100
although seated, Zeus still somehow achieves his purpose
right there from his holy throne.

So let him look at such outrage as that              Ant. 5
with which the young stock of Belus                      105
grows luxuriantly, men bent on
marrying me—perverse resolve,
a maddened intent the spur they cannot escape,
minds changed by ruin's deceit.                          110

Such piteous suffering I have                         Str. 6
to tell and wail, shrill, heavy, all falling tears!
Cry grief!
Openly here I cry out in my grief;                       115
my laments honour myself—while living!

I beseech Apis' country of hills and cattle—    Ephymnion 1
you are a land that knows foreign speech well.
Again and again I fall on my Sidonian veil               120
to tear and destroy its linen.

Irreligious rites, if they succeed,                   Ant. 6
incur the gods' onslaught where death keeps away.
Oh, oh!                                                  125
Oh misery beyond determining!
Where is this wave now swelling to take me?

I beseech Apis' country of hills and cattle—    Ephymnion 1
you are a land that knows foreign speech well.

Again and again I fall on my Sidonian veil                    130
to tear and destroy its linen.

Yet a ship with oars and a deckhouse                    Str. 7
stitched with flax, shielding from the sea,                    135
brought me here on the winds, without storm, and I do not com-
    plain;
but as to the outcome, may the all-seeing father
in full time make it favour me.                    140

May he grant the offspring of so very august a mother
                                   Ephymnion 2
escape from the beds of men—my horror!—
unwed, unbroken.

In turn, let the chaste daughter of Zeus                    Ant. 7
look willingly on my own will,                    145
her august countenance kept steadfast; and so with all her strength,
aggrieved I am pursued, let her be my saviour,
unwed rescuing unwed.                    150

May she grant the offspring of so very august a mother
                                   Ephymnion 2
escape from the beds of men—my horror!—
unwed, unbroken.

But otherwise we,                    Str. 8
a race dark-complexioned, sun-beaten,                    155
will approach with our suppliant boughs
that Zeus below the earth, that one
who most welcomes the dead,
once we die in hung nooses                    160
should we meet with no favour from the gods on Olympus.

Ah, Zeus! Oh, Io, poor Io, and the divine anger        Ephymnion 3
which hunted her! I know it too well,
that of [Zeus'] wife triumphant in heaven;                    165
for after a hard gale will come a further storm.

And then will not Zeus                    Ant. 8
be held liable to just censure
for dishonouring the heifer's son—                    170

that child he himself once fathered—
and now keeping his eyes
turned well away amid pleas?
But now that we call on him, may he listen well on high!          175

[Ah, Zeus! Oh, Io, poor Io, and the divine anger          Ephymnion 3
which hunted her! I know it too well,                              175]
that of [Zeus'] wife triumphant in heaven;                        175◀
for after a hard gale will come a further storm.]                 175◀

DANAUS.   My children, good sense is needed: and good sense has
come with you in your faithful old father here, the captain of your
ship. Now I have taken forethought for matters on dry land too,
and I urge you to keep my words safe; inscribe them in your mind.
(*pointing off-stage*) I can see dust, the voiceless messenger of an
army; wheel-hubs driven round their axles are not silent; and I  180
see men in a mass, armed with shields and spears, together with
horses and round-fronted chariots. They will perhaps be this land's
rulers come to watch us, after messengers informed them. Whether  185
they have set out on this mission intending no harm, or with anger
fiercely whetted, it is better for every reason, my daughters, to go
and sit at the altar-mound of these assembled gods: an altar is
stronger than a towering wall, it is an unbreakable shield. Come—  190
and at once! Hold the white-wreathed suppliant boughs reverently
in your left hands, emblems for Zeus who ensures respect for
them; answer the strangers with tearful words deserving respect,
and showing great need, as befits newcomers; tell clearly of your  195
flight here, and that it is untainted by bloodshed. First, have no
boldness accompany your voices; then, let no wildness show from
faces sensibly composed, and with a calm gaze. Do not be forward
in your speech, any of you, nor yet laggard: the people here are very  200
prone to take offence. Remember also to defer: you are in need, a
stranger, a fugitive. Bold words do not suit weaker persons.

DANAUS *begins to move towards the altar-mound.*

CHORUS.   Father, you speak with good sense to those who have
good sense. I shall keep these excellent instructions safe in my
memory. And may Zeus our ancestor look on us!                      205

DANAUS.   Look on us indeed, and with a favouring eye!   210

CHORUS.   Please, I would like a seat close by you now.   208

DANAUS.   Don't delay, then; and may our plan succeed!   207

CHORUS.   O Zeus, take pity on us for the blows we suffer, before we are lost!   209

DANAUS.   If Zeus wishes, the outcome here will be well. And now   211
call upon this son of Zeus.

CHORUS.   We call upon the saving rays of the Sun.

DANAUS.   Holy Apollo, the god who was an exile from heaven!

CHORUS.   With his knowledge of this fate, may he sympathize with
mortals!   215

DANAUS.   Sympathize indeed, and stand by us with his favour!

CHORUS.   So which others of these deities am I to call upon?

DANAUS.   I see a trident here, emblem of the god.

CHORUS.   Well, just as he gave me a good voyage, let him give me a
good welcome on land!

DANAUS.   This next one is the herald, in Greek belief.   220

CHORUS.   Well, let him herald good things for our freedom!

DANAUS.   Revere the altar shared by all these kingly gods; and
within its pure sanctity sit down like doves flocking in fear of
hawks, their fellow birds but enemies of common blood who defile
their kinship. How could bird eating bird be pure? And how could   225
a man who marries the unwilling daughter of an unwilling father
be pure? If he has done this he will not escape blame for wild folly
even in Hades' house after death. There too, it is said, another Zeus   230
makes the last judgements among the dead upon offences.

See that you answer in the manner I have said, so that you win
well in your action here.

PELASGUS *the king of Argos enters from the side; he carries a staff, and
is attended by armed men.*

PELASGUS.   Where is this company from, which we now address?
It is not Greek in clothing, but luxuriates in barbarian robes and
headbands; this is no women's dress from the Argolid or places   235
in Greece. Your bravery in coming to our land without guides,
unannounced by heralds, and with no sponsors, unafraid, is a thing
for wonder. Yet you have laid branches like suppliants near these   240
assembled gods; only this will suit conjecture that Greece is your

homeland. About the rest too it would be right to make many
further guesses, were there not voices here to inform us.　　　　245
CHORUS.　What you have said about our dress is quite correct; but
　　am I speaking to you as a plain citizen, or a warden with a sacred
　　staff, or a city's leader?
PELASGUS.　Answer accordingly, and speak confidently, for I am
　　Pelasgus, this land's ruler and the son of Palaechthon who was born
　　from it. The Pelasgian people, named suitably for myself as their　250
　　lord, harvest the land's crops. All the territory too through which
　　the holy Strymon goes, I rule on the western side; my boundaries　255
　　are the land of the Perrhaebians and the parts beyond Pindus, near
　　the Paeonians, and the mountains of Dodona; there the waters of
　　the sea define the boundary; these parts this side of it are under
　　my rule. The territory here of the Apian land itself has long been　260
　　named for a great physician: for Apis, the doctor-seer son of Apollo,
　　came across from Naupactus and purged this land of creatures
　　lethal to men, those evil things which the earth sent up in anger
　　when fouled by ancient, polluting bloodshed, thronging snakes　265
　　hostile to live with. Remedies to be rid of these Apis cut and made
　　for Argos' land without recrimination, and found remembrance
　　then in prayers as his reward.　　　　270

　　　　Now you have these clear identifications from my side, please
　　claim your own family descent and speak further; our city,
　　however, has no liking for a long speech.
CHORUS.　My story is brief and clear: we are Argive women, claim-
　　ing our descent and parentage from the heifer and her splendid
　　son; and that this is true, I shall graft proof on to my account.　275
PELASGUS.　What I hear you say, women strangers, is incredible
　　to me—how your descent is from Argos here; for you very much
　　more resemble women of Libya, and not in any way those native
　　to our land here. The Nile might nourish a race such as yours; and　280
　　your male ancestors have struck the likeness of Cyprian character
　　on your female forms. The Indians, I hear, have nomadic women
　　who ride side-saddle over the land on camels fast as horses, and　285
　　who live as neighbours to the Ethiopians; and if you had bows I
　　should certainly have imagined you to be those Amazons who have
　　no men and live on meat. But if I were told, I might have more
　　knowledge how it is that your descent and parentage are Argive.　290

CHORUS. Men say that Io was once a temple-priestess of Hera in this land of Argos.

PELASGUS. She was, quite certainly; the tradition is very strong. 293

CHORUS. Is there not also a story that Zeus lay with her, a mortal? 295

PELASGUS. Yes, and that his struggle with her was not to be hidden from Hera.

(CHORUS. *A line missing.*)

PELASGUS. Then how did this quarrel end for the two sovereign gods?

CHORUS. Argos' goddess made the woman into a cow.

PELASGUS. So did Zeus no longer go with the fine-horned cow? 300

CHORUS. Men say he did, in a body resembling a bull's when mounting a cow.

PELASGUS. And what did Zeus' powerful wife do in consequence?

CHORUS. She set that all-seeing guard over the cow.

PELASGUS. What all-seeing cowherd do you mean, set over her alone?

CHORUS. Argos, Earth's son, that Hermes killed. 305

PELASGUS. Well, and what else did Hera devise for the ill-fated cow?

CHORUS. A cattle-driving fly to goad her forward.

(PELASGUS. *A line missing.*)

CHORUS. The people by the Nile call it the gadfly. 308

PELASGUS. All that you have said coheres too with what I know. 310

CHORUS. Yes, and I must tell you that Io came to Canopus and as far as Memphis. 311

PELASGUS. Why, did the fly drive her there from Greece on a long course? 309

CHORUS. Yes, and Zeus got a son on her with his hand's touch. 313

PELASGUS. So who made claim to being Zeus' calf from the cow?

CHORUS. Epaphus, truly named for this act of rescue. 315

(PELASGUS. *A line missing.*)

CHORUS. Libya, who reaps the largest [harvest] on earth.

PELASGUS. Well, and what further progeny of hers can you tell of?

CHORUS. Belus of the two sons, the father of my father here.

PELASGUS. Now tell me his name, all-wise that he is. 320

CHORUS. Danaus; and his brother with fifty sons is ...

PELASGUS.  Disclose his name too; do not grudge telling me.

CHORUS.  ... Aegyptus. Now that you know my ancient descent, please act as you would in supporting a company of Argives.

PELASGUS.  You do seem to me to be part of this land from long   325
ago. Yet how could you brave leaving the home of your fathers? What misfortune struck down on you?

CHORUS.  Lord of the Pelasgians, mankind's troubles flicker about, and you'll nowhere see misery fly on the same wings. For who was expecting that kin from a previous generation would land at Argos   330
in this unexpected escape, put to trembling flight in their hatred of a marriage bed?

PELASGUS.  What is your supplication, do you say, from these assembled gods, with your newly cut, white-wreathed boughs?

CHORUS.  Not to become a slave to Aegyptus.                      335

PELASGUS.  Is this out of hatred, or do you speak of what right forbids?

CHORUS.  What woman would blame her lord and master if she loved him?

PELASGUS.  Well, this is the way men increase their power.

CHORUS.  Yes, and the way they are quite easily rid of the unfortunate.

PELASGUS.  So how am I to act reverently towards you myself?      340

CHORUS.  By not surrendering me to Aegyptus' sons when they ask you.

PELASGUS.  It's a very heavy thing you say, to take upon oneself an unwelcome war.

CHORUS.  Justice makes a stand, though, for her allies.

PELASGUS.  Yes, if she is a partner in matters from the start.

CHORUS.  Respect your ship of state when wreathed like this by suppliants!                                                        345

PELASGUS.  I tremble at seeing this abode of gods in the shadow of wreaths; but the wrath of Zeus who protects suppliants is heavy indeed.

*The* CHORUS *dance and sing, alternating with* PELASGUS *who continues in speech.*

CHORUS.  Please hear me, son of Palaechthon,                   Str. 1
with a heart offering goodwill, you Pelasgian lord and king!

and see me, your suppliant here, and in flight,                    350
running about like a heifer pursued by wolves,
high up amid steepling crags, where trustful of his aid
she lows to tell the herdsman of her plight.

PELASGUS.   I see the company of these assembled gods, shadowed
over with newly cut boughs, nodding their assent. May this matter   355
of our citizens from abroad cause us no harm; and may no feuding
come to the city from things unexpected and unprovided for; the
city has no need of them.

CHORUS.   Yes, may Right, god of suppliants,                    Ant. 1
aiding Zeus who protects men's hearths, see no harm come from
   our flight!                                                    360
And you, though old in wisdom, yet learn from one
later in birth: if you respect a suppliant
[you will not be poor in life]: the gods' tempers incline
to accepting a pure man's offerings.

PELASGUS.   You are not suppliants of any hearth of mine, I tell you!   365
If the city is polluted as a community, let the people make it their
united concern to work out remedies. I will not myself guarantee
a promise in advance, but only after sharing these things with all
citizens.

CHORUS.   *You* are the city, and *you* the people's voice:        Str. 2
since you preside, you are immune from judgement,
and you govern the altar, the land's hearth,
through your single nod of assent;
enthroned in your single rule you execute
every matter—so guard yourself against pollution!                375

PELASGUS.   Let pollution be for my enemies; but I cannot help you
without harm! But again, it is not sensible to dishonour these pleas
of yours. I am at a loss, and fear has hold of my mind, of action as
well as inaction and taking a chance.                            380

CHORUS.   Keep up a watch for the watcher high above,             Ant. 2
the guardian of poor suffering mankind
who sit as suppliants of those nearby

but get no justice under law.
Look, the wrath of Zeus Suppliant lies in wait,                    385
implacable towards an offender's cry for pity.

PELASGUS.   Look: if the sons of Aegyptus have power over you in
your city's law, claiming they are the closest of kin, who would be
willing to oppose them? You must defend your case under your
laws at home, I tell you, on the ground that the sons have no  390
authority over you.

CHORUS.   No! May I never be subject at all                    Str. 3
to the power of men; and I am marking out my remedy
against an ill-meant marriage by flight beneath the stars above.
But now choose Justice as ally and give                    395
a judgement holy to the gods!

PELASGUS.   The judgement is not easy; do not choose me as judge!
I said earlier, too, I would not do this, not even though I have
the power, so that the people may never say, should anything not
for the better happen, 'By honouring outsiders you destroyed the  400
city.'

CHORUS.   The Zeus of blood-kin watches both parties        Ant. 3
in this, ready to incline either way, fairly crediting
unrightful acts to bad men, and righteous to law-abiding.
Why, when these things are weighed impartially,                    405
do you grudge doing what is just?

PELASGUS.   It needs deep thought for safety, I tell you, to reach
the depths like a sponge-diver with eyes that see and are not too
clouded by wine, so that these matters may end, first, without harm
to the city, and then well for our own selves; and so that Battle  410
may not seize us as plunder, nor we surrender you who are seated
so firmly in the gods' shrines, and make that all-destructive god a
heavy housemate, the demon Revenge, who does not let the dead  415
go free even in Hades. Surely you realize there is need for thought
of safety?

CHORUS.   Think, and become our sponsor                    Str. 4
in total right and reverence;

do not betray your fugitive here,                                    420
driven far away from home
into exile offensive to god;

nor see me seized as plunder                             Ant. 4
from an abode of many gods—
you with the full power over the land!—                  425
but learn of the men's arrogance,
and guard yourself against the gods' wrath.

Do not bear to see me,                                   Str. 5
your suppliant, led from sacred images                   430
with my rights abused, and seized by my fine-woven dress
like a horse by its headband.

And know this: for your sons                             Ant. 5
and house, whichever of these two things you do,
this waits: returning an equal due. Consider that!       435
Justice does prevail through Zeus.

PELASGUS.   I have indeed thought; and this is where I come to land:
taking on a great war against either the one or the other side is
wholly inevitable; the nails have been driven home as in a ship's
hull brought into dock by twisted cables; and there is nowhere a  440
conclusion without pain. Now for goods plundered from a house  443
there may come, as a grace from Zeus the god of possessions, others  445
even greater than the loss, to replace the cargo fully; so too, when  444
a tongue at the wrong moment shoots off sharp-pointed words  446
to rouse and hurt the spirit, speech may well soothe speech—yet  448 447
to prevent bloodshed among kin, there is certainly need to offer  449
sacrifice, and for many victims to fall to many gods for divination,  450
as remedies against disaster. Most certainly I am trying to draw
aside from this quarrel myself; I wish to be ignorant of trouble
rather than wise in it. May all be well, however, and show my
judgement wrong.
CHORUS.   Hear the end of my many words deserving your respect.  455
PELASGUS.   I hear you, so please speak them; they will not escape
me.
CHORUS.   I wear breast-bands and a sash, to hold my dress round
me.

PELASGUS.   These would be suitable for a woman, perhaps.

CHORUS.   Well, from these, I tell you, comes an excellent device.

PELASGUS.   Speak out with what you are going to say, and your
meaning.                                                          460

CHORUS.   Unless you promise our company here something we can
trust...

PELASGUS.   What is a device from bands to achieve for you?

CHORUS.   ...to deck these images with unwelcome tablets....

PELASGUS.   Riddling words! Come: speak simply!

CHORUS.   ...to hang ourselves instantly from these gods.        465

PELASGUS.   I hear words to lash at my heart!

CHORUS.   You understand: I have opened your eyes quite clearly.

PELASGUS.   Yes, (*words missing*) and issues that in many ways are
hard to wrestle with! A multitude of troubles comes on like a river;
I have embarked here on an ocean of bottomless ruin; it is far from
easily crossed, and there is nowhere a harbour from trouble. If I do   470
not meet this need of yours, you spoke there of a pollution beyond
my range of overcoming; but in turn, if I take my stand before the
walls and go to battle's outcome with your kin the sons of Aegyptus,
how can the cost not be bitter, for men to bloody the ground for      475
women's sake? All the same, I must respect the wrath of Zeus the
god of suppliants; it is the supreme fear among men.

   (*turning to Danaus*) And you now, these maidens' old father: (*a*  480
*line missing*) and quickly take these boughs in your arms and go
and place them against other altars of the land's gods, so all the
citizens may see evidence of this supplication, and no talk be flung
out against me; for a people loves to blame its rulers. In fact anyone  485
who sees all this and takes pity may well hate this company of men
and their arrogance, and our people be better disposed towards
yourselves; for everyone bears goodwill towards weaker persons.

DANAUS.   This is worth much to us, to have found and got a spon-   490
sor who shows us respect. Send companions and guides with me
from among the inhabitants, so that I may find the altars fronting
the temples of the gods which hold the city, and their shrines
with many wreaths, and have safety as we go through the city. My    495
physical appearance differs: the Nile breeds a race unlike that of
Inachus. Be on your guard in case boldness generates fear; men
have even killed a friend out of ignorance!

PELASGUS. (*to some of his attendants*) Go with him, men, if you
please; the stranger speaks well. Lead him to the altars and shrines 500
of the city's gods; and you must not talk much to those you meet
as you bring this man from overseas to supplicate at our gods'
hearths.

*Some of* PELASGUS' *attendants leave with* DANAUS *to escort him
towards Argos.*

CHORUS. (*gesturing towards* DANAUS *as he leaves*) You had words
to give *him*, and I pray that he reaches there as instructed; but
how am I to act myself? Where can you find confidence to give
me? 505
PELASGUS. Leave your boughs where they are, the token of your
troubles.
CHORUS. See, I leave them; I submit to your words (*they step away
from the sacred mound*).
PELASGUS. Now turn down into this broad grove.
CHORUS. And how will a grove protect me when it is open to entry?
PELASGUS. We shall not surrender you, be sure, for winged things
to seize. 510
CHORUS. But what if they should be worse than evil serpents?
PELASGUS. Use words of good omen, please, just as you heard
good words from me!
CHORUS. Distress is not surprising, surely, in a mind afraid?
PELASGUS. Fear is always immoderate in the defenceless.
CHORUS. Then you must gladden my heart with deeds as well as
words. 515
PELASGUS. Yes, but your father will not abandon you for any
length of time. (*turning to depart*) I go to call the land's inhabitants
together, to make the community feel kindly towards you; and I
shall teach your father the kind of things he should say. So wait here
and entreat the native gods with prayers to gain what you desire. I 520
shall go myself to win this for you; and may persuasion and good
fortune attend me to effect!

PELASGUS *leaves by one side, together with his remaining attendants.
The* CHORUS *have now moved clear of the mound and begin singing
and dancing.*

CHORUS.   King of kings, most blest                          Str. 1
   among the blest, power most perfect                    525
   of the perfect, in your bliss, Zeus,
   be persuaded, and defend
   your line from outrage by the men; feel proper loathing!
   Strike down in a sea purpled with storm
   the black-built vessel of ruin.                           530

   Watch the women's cause!                             Ant. 1
   Renew the tale of your kindness
   to a woman, the one long told,
   dear ancestress of our line:
   remember full well, you who gave your touch to Io!        535
   From Zeus we proudly claim our descent,
   by her who lived here in this land.

   I have moved to her ancient tracks,                  Str. 2
   our mother's when she grazed flowers under watch,
   to the fodder-rich meadow, from where Io,                 540
   goaded by the fly,
   went fleeing, her wits all lost,
   passing through many tribes of men;
   cleaving the strait and its waves,
   she marked the edge                                       545
   of the land opposite, in her cruel torment.

   Then she hurls across Asia's land,                   Ant. 2
   her path right through Phrygia where sheep are reared,
   beyond the Mysian city of Teuthras
   and Lydia's vales,                                        550
   and through Cilicia's mountains,
   quickly past the Pamphylians' land
   with its ever-flowing streams
   and deep rich earth,
   and Aphrodite's land of abundant grain.                   555

   She comes, her winged cowherd still coming           Str. 3
   upon her with its sting,
   to Zeus' plain that nourishes all,

the meadow fed by snow, which Typhon
in his might traverses, and the Nile                              560
with waters safe from disease.
Frenzied by her shameful ordeal
and the sting's harsh agony,
she is Hera's maenad.

The people then living in that land                    Ant. 3
were shaken to the heart                                          566
by fear, paling before the strange sight,
beholding the repellent creature,
human hybrid, part cow, part woman;
the portent astounded them.                                      570
And at that time, who was it healed
the wretched, much-wandering,
gadfly-harried Io?

Ruling throughout unending life                        Str. 4
(*a line missing*);                                              575
by the unharming power of Zeus
and breath divine
she has an end; and she lets
drip tears of shame and sorrow.
Taking Zeus' freight in her womb—the tale is true—              580
she bore him a son without fault,

whose life of great length was all bliss;              Ant. 4
whence the whole land cries out,
'Truly this is the child of Zeus,
who makes life grow!'                                            585
For who else would have ended
Hera's vengeful afflictions?
This was Zeus' work. And in telling of our line
from Epaphus, you would be right.

Which god's deeds give me juster claim                 Str. 5
in reason to call on him?—                                       591
[our] father [himself], his own hand planting his seed,
our lord, our line's great architect, anciently wise,
all-devising, favouring Zeus!

He sits under no one's command,                                          Ant. 5
no less powerful than the strong;                                             596
revering the power of no one seated above,
his deed can be swift as his word. What of things here
does Zeus' mind not bring about?

*DANAUS returns from the assembly at Argos.*

DANAUS.   Have confidence, my children! There is good from this
land's countrymen; the people have resolved on it, voting with full   600
authority.

CHORUS.   Welcome, sir, with this most grateful news! Tell us what
the final decision has been, and how the people's sovereign hands
voted in majority.

DANAUS.   The Argive people resolved, with no division, but in a   605
way to make me young again in my old heart—why, the air bristled
with right hands as the people all together ratified this proposal: we
are to reside as immigrants in this land, free and not subject to legal
seizure, and inviolable by others; and neither resident nor foreigner   610
is to carry us off; but if one brings force against us, that man among
the inhabitants who does not come to our defence is to lose his
citizen-rights, with exile enforced by the people. The Pelasgians'
king persuaded this in his speech on our behalf; he proclaimed   615
the anger of Zeus who protects suppliants to be great, fearing that
Zeus might let it grow full at some later time; and he said that if a
double pollution of strangers and citizens together shows through
the city's action, it becomes nourishment for disaster beyond remedy. When they heard such arguments the Argive people ratified by   620
their hands, without a herald's call, that all should be as proposed.
The assembled people of the Pelasgians heard good and persuasive
turns in their popular debate; but it was Zeus who ratified the
outcome.

*The CHORUS chant; DANAUS remains silent.*

CHORUS.   Come! To honour the people of Argos let us say                625
prayers for their good, repayment for their good to us;
and may Zeus who protects strangers watch over this blessing
from the lips of strangers, so that it proves true
and reaches every goal without fault.

*The* CHORUS *now sing and dance.*

| | |
|---|---|
| Now may these gods, Zeus-born, | Str. 1 |
| listen to my voice | 631 |
| as I pour out prayers for my race, | |
| that Ares, insatiably crying war and lustful, | |
| never destroys this land of Pelasgus here by fire, | 635 |
| Ares who harvests men as crop in others' fields; | |

because the people pitied us,
and cast their vote to show favour:         640
they respect Zeus' suppliants,
our flock in its misery;

nor did they cast their vote         Ant. 1
on the side of men,
slighting our women's argument;         645
for they had in view Zeus' exactor, the constant watcher,
hard to fight, whom no house would be cheered to have
upon its roof; he weighs down hard once seated there.         650
For they show respect for their kin
now supplicating holy Zeus;
therefore they will placate the gods
with their altars' purity.         655

Therefore let our prayer,         Str. 2
eager to bring them these blessings, go winging
from lips in wreaths' shadow:
may no pestilence ever empty         660
this city of its men,
nor [faction] bloody its heartland,
as native son kills native son.

Let the bloom of its youth
go unculled; and may Ares too,
Aphrodite's bedmate, havoc to men,         665
not shear away its flower.

For those dignified         Ant. 2
by age and office let welcoming altars
be laden and blazing;

may the city thus be well governed 670
in honouring great Zeus,
and Zeus of strangers supremely,
who by age-old law directs fate.

We pray that fresh wardens
of the land may always be born, 675
and far-shooting Artemis watch over
its women in childbirth.

And let no havoc killing                                                  Str. 3
its men come upon this city
and tear it apart, 680
arming for war which has no dancing, has no lyre,
but begets tears, and for civil strife's clamour.

May diseases, an unlovely swarm,
settle away from citizens' heads; 685
and may the Lycean one show favour
to each generation of youth.

And let Zeus indeed ensure                                              Ant. 3
full yielding for the land's produce
in each due season; 690
and may their beasts outside the walls bear many young;
may the gods' gifts bring them to thrive completely.

May singers too perform their music
propitiously over the altars; 695
and may the voice in friendship with the lyre
be offered from lips that are pure.

May the body public, which rules the land,                              Str. 4
safeguard the citizens' rights, governing
with prudent counsel for the common good; 700
and may they grant strangers,
before arming for war, well-agreed rights
to justice, to plead cases unharmed.

May the people honour the native gods                                   Ant. 4
who hold their land with ancestral honours, 705

bearing bays and sacrificing oxen.
Respect for parents too—
this is written third among the statutes
of Justice, whose honour is greatest.

DANAUS.  I approve these wise prayers, my dear ones; but now 710
don't be afraid on hearing from your father some unexpected and
unwelcome news: for from this watch-point which received us as
suppliants I can see the ship—it is easily known, the set of the sail
does not escape me, or the side screens on the ship and the prow 715
with its eyes at the fore to see the way, obeying too well the tiller at
the vessel's rear which steers it straight—such a ship could not be
friendly! The men on board stand out to the eye with their dark-
skinned limbs against white clothing. The other ships and all their 720
support stand out clearly too; the leader itself has furled its sail and
is being rowed to land with all oars splashing. Yet you must look
calmly and collectedly at the matter, and not neglect these gods
here; and I will return with aid, and advocates to aid your case. For 725
perhaps a herald or embassy may come, in their wish to carry you
off, and make seizures to prevent reprisal. (*the* CHORUS *show their
alarm*) But nothing of this will happen; don't be afraid of them!
Still, it is better, in case I should be slow in fetching help, never for 730
a moment to forget the protection here (*he points to the shrine*).
Have confidence! In time, I tell you, and on the day appointed, any
mortal man who dishonours the gods will pay the penalty.

*The* CHORUS *now sing in their anxiety, while* DANAUS *continues in
speech.*

CHORUS.    Father, I am afraid, because the ships have come on swift
        wings;                                                    Str. 1
    there has been no long interval of time.                       735
    Fear and great dread now possess me,
    whether my far-run flight truly helps at all;
    I am quite lost, father, to fright.
DANAUS.    The Argive's vote had full authority, my children, so have
        confidence! They will fight on your behalf, I know for certain.   740

CHORUS.    Quite accursed, the lust-mad race of Aegyptus,
        insatiable                                                  Ant. 1

with fighting; and I speak to one who knows.
In timber-built, dark-eyed vessels
they have sailed their way here in such splashing haste,
with dark-skinned men in a great host.                                745

DANAUS.    And they will find themselves facing many men well-
    toughened by midday heat!

CHORUS.    Don't leave me all alone, I beg you, father;        Str. 2
a woman left on her own is nothing; no war is in her.
Killing is in their hearts, and guile in their designs;               750
with impure minds they are like ravens
unconcerned for any altars.

DANAUS.    This might well be to our advantage, my children, if your
    hatred for them is shared by the gods.

CHORUS.    No fear of these tridents and sacred emblems      Ant. 2
of the gods will ever keep their hands away from us, father.     755
They are too arrogant; in unholy fury
they are maddened by lust, bold as dogs;
to the gods they do not listen.

DANAUS.    There is a saying, however, that wolves are stronger than
    dogs; and papyrus as a harvest-crop does not beat ears of corn.    760

CHORUS.    Since they do have the passions of lewd and unholy
    beasts, we must protect ourselves speedily.

DANAUS.    Neither dispatching nor mooring a ship-borne force is
    speedy; and ships' commanders are not confident of taking safety-    765
    cables ashore or of anchoring immediately, above all when they
    come to a harbourless land towards nightfall, with the sun's depar-
    ture: night usually gives birth to anxiety for a wise captain. So    770
    disembarking a force wouldn't be good either, before a ship had
    confidence in its mooring.

    Take thought, then, because of your dread, not to neglect the
    gods! [And I] (*a line missing*) after securing help. The city will not
    fault a messenger who may be old but has youth's vigour to speak
    his mind clearly.                                                   775

DANAUS *leaves by the side, to go to Argos.*
The CHORUS *sing and dance.*

CHORUS.    O country of hills and cattle, revered and righteous,

Str. 1

what shall we suffer? Where should we flee to
in Apia's land, if there somewhere exists a dark hiding-place?
May I become black smoke,
a neighbour for Zeus' clouds,                                            780
and disappear completely, flying upward to vanish,
unseen like dust, without wings, and die!

Disaster may be avoided no longer; my heart          Ant. 1
is greatly shaken, taking on darkness.                                  785
That sighting by my father holds me captive; I am lost to fear.
I wish I meet my fate
in a noose of hanging rope,
before any detested man comes close to my body.                         790
Sooner my death, with Hades my lord!

Oh, if only I could find a seat in the sky,          Str. 2
one near which the water-clouds become snow,
or some bare hanging cliff
too sheer for goats, too distant
to point out, mind-lonely,                                              795
a haunt of vultures, to witness my deep fall
before my heart is forcibly torn in two
by meeting with marriage!

And then—I do not decline to become the prey          Ant. 2
and food for the dogs and birds of this land;                           801
for death does liberate
from the evils loved by grief.
Let death come, and I wish
it happens before any bed of marriage!                                  805
What path towards escape am I yet to cut,
to free me from marriage?

Wail out, in strains heaven-high,          Str. 3
prayers to supplicate the gods and [goddesses],
to reach fulfilment for me somehow                                      810
in a release from marriage, with no storm.
Watch over me, father Zeus; see violence with no friendly eye;

secure my rights; respect your suppliants,
you protector of this land, in all your might, Zeus!　　　　　815

Aegyptus' line, in its men,　　　　　　　　　　　　　Ant. 3
(*a word missing*) an outrage which is unendurable.
They have run quickly and pursued me
in my escape, clamouring their lewdness.　　　　　　　820
They are seeking to take me by violence. In your hands, O Zeus,
however, are the balance and its beam:
without you, what is fulfilled for mortal beings?

*A band of* EGYPTIANS *burst in from the side, urgent with crude
menace.*

EGYPTIANS.　(*making raucous cries*)　　　　　　　　825
　Here I am to rob (*words missing*)
　on shipboard (*words missing*)　　　　　　　　　　826a
　on land (*words and at least one further line missing*).　　826b
CHORUS.　(*crying out in panic*)
　Before that, you robber, I wish you death and disaster—how I hate
　　you!—
　and to go back again (*words missing*).
　Now I see you I cry aloud (*words missing*)!
　I see here a prelude to violent struggle for my sponsor.　　830
　(*crying out in panic*)
　Go, fly to safe protection!
　(*words missing*) minds fierce with arrogance,
　unendurable on shipboard and on land.
　Lord of this country, stand and defend us!　　　　　　835
EGYPTIANS.　Hurry, hurry to the bark! Run with your best speed!
　You want hair pulled out? You want hair pulled out, and branding,
　the blood and gore of heads hacked off?　　　　　　840
　Hurry, hurry, you accursed women, to the cutter!

*The* CHORUS *begin dancing and singing their hate and alarm.*

CHORUS.　I wish that when you were crossing　　　　Str. 1
　the salty ocean's mighty flow,
　you had been lost
　with your close-nailed ship and violent masters!　　　845

EGYPTIANS. All blood you'll be when the cutter has you aboard!
So, quiet now! Let go what must be lost.
Leave off the shouting, I order you (*word missing*)
Longing (*text corrupt and missing*)                           850
Leave those seats, go to the ships;
you get no honour in a city of pious men!

CHORUS. I wish you never see again                    Ant. 1
those waters that make cattle thrive,                    855
and give men's blood
its increase, and vigour for procreation.
EGYPTIANS. Warfare's man am I, of ancient and noble ilk
(*text hopelessly corrupt*)                              860
Soon you'll be going on shipboard, shipboard,
willy-nilly.
Force enforces much! (*words missing*) are gone.
Go, you accursed women
(*text hopelessly corrupt*)!                             865

CHORUS. (*wailing*)                                  Str. 2
I wish you helpless destruction,
wandering over the plain
of the flowing sea, with Syrian winds to blow you        870
on to Sarpedon's great bank of sand.

A HERALD *from Aegyptus' Sons on their ship enters abruptly from the side.*

HERALD. (*speaking*) On board our speedy bark at once, I order
you, and let no one be slow about it! Dragging along has no 882
respect at all for hair in braids, I tell you!             884

CHORUS. (*shrieking*)                                Ant. 2
This outrage (*text                                       877
hopelessly corrupt*) you swell with it!
(*text corrupt*) may mighty Fate crush you
in your arrogance, quite lost to sight!                   881
HERALD. Do howl and shriek and call upon the gods—for you'll 872
not be jumping out of any Egyptian bark! Your wailing will be
harsher than the pain itself!                             875

CHORUS.   No! Father, help from the statue is useless!            Str. 3
    I'm being dragged seaward [by force];                              886
    it's like a spider walking,
    a nightmare, a black nightmare!
    (*drawn-out wailing*)
    Mother Earth, Mother Earth!                                        890
    Turn the fearsome monster away!
    O father Zeus, Earth's child!

HERALD.   I don't fear the gods of this place, I tell you! I was not in
    their care at my rearing; and I'll not grow old in their caring!

CHORUS.   Look! Raging near me, a snake with two feet!      Ant. 3
    It's like a viper (*word missing*) me!                             896
    Whatever is it (*word missing*),
    a monster (*words missing*)?
    (*drawn-out wailing*)
    Mother Earth, Mother Earth!                                        900
    Turn the fearsome monster away!
    O father Zeus, Earth's child!

HERALD.   Unless someone consents and goes on shipboard, her
    clothes will be ripped with no pity for their making!

CHORUS.    Oh! Help, you city-captains, leaders! I am overcome!    905
                                                                 Str. 4

HERALD.    I'll be seizing you by the hair to drag you, so it seems,   909
    since you're not sharp enough to obey what I'm saying.             910

CHORUS.    It is the end for us! We suffer beyond words, my lord!   908
                                                                 Ant. 4

HERALD.    Many enough will be the lords, the sons of Aegyptus,    906
    you'll see! Have confidence: you'll not speak of no rulers!

As the EGYPTIANS *move to seize the* CHORUS, PELASGUS *returns
abruptly from Argos, from the side; he again has armed attendants.*

PELASGUS.   (*shouting*) You there! What are you doing? What kind
    of mentality makes you insult this land of men, of Pelasgians?   911
    Do you imagine you've come to a city of women? You must be a
    barbarian with your excessive contempt for Greeks; and with your
    many mistakes you've done nothing correct.                        915

HERALD. But what have I done wrong among these things, without a good right?

PELASGUS. First, you don't know how strangers should behave.

HERALD. Do I not? How so? I'm finding and taking away what is mine and was lost.

PELASGUS. Which sponsors in our land did you speak to?

HERALD. To Hermes, the greatest of sponsors, the god of lucky searches. 920

PELASGUS. You spoke to gods, but you have no reverence for those gods.

HERALD. The gods by the Nile have my reverence.

PELASGUS. And ours here are nothing, I hear you tell me.

HERALD. I will carry these women off, unless someone removes them from me.

PELASGUS. You'd pay for it, if you touched them, and before very long! 925

HERALD. I hear you; those words are not at all hospitable to strangers.

PELASGUS. It's because I'm not hospitable to those who despoil the gods.

HERALD. I'll go and tell this to Aegyptus' Sons!

PELASGUS. That's no concern of mine; I'll not brood upon it.

HERALD. Well, so I may know and speak more definitely—for a 930 herald properly reports everything clearly—how, and at whose hands, should I say when I return that I have had the company of their own women-cousins taken from me? There's no judging here with the help of witnesses, I tell you—not by Ares! And he does not resolve a quarrel by accepting silver—before that many men fall in 935 battle and their spasms kick life away.

PELASGUS. Why should I tell you my name? In time you'll learn and know it well enough—yourself and your fellow-traders. As to these women: if they were willing and their minds well-disposed, 940 you might take them away, were some reverent words to persuade us (*a line missing*). The unanimous vote of my city, given full authority by its people, is this: never to surrender this company of women to violence. This is final, nailed right through and driven home, to remain fixed. This is not inscribed on tablets, nor sealed 945 up in folded sheets of writing, but you hear it clearly, from a tongue free to speak. Take yourself out of our sight at once!

HERALD.   We already seem about to begin an unwelcome war; but   950
may victory and full power go to the men!

*The* HERALD *and the* EGYPTIANS *leave by the side.*

PELASGUS.   (*speaking to their backs*) Well, you'll find this land's inhabitants are real men, not drinkers of barley-beer!

(*to the* CHORUS) Now, all of you, with your dear servants, take confidence and go to the city; it has good defences, and towers   955
contrived for height bar entry. Houses too there are, many of them public lodgings, while I myself have built with no mean hand either, where you may dwell in well-made homes with many others; but if it will please you more, you may live in houses by   960
yourselves. Out of these choices pick the best and most agreeable to yourselves—you may do so. I am your champion, as are all the citizens whose vote is here enacted. Why wait for greater authority than theirs?                                             965

*The* CHORUS *begin chanting.*

CHORUS.   Then may you abound in good things, in return for your
        goodness, you most glorious of Pelasgians.
Be kind, however, and have our father sent here,
Danaus the confident, the prudent, the leader of our counsels.   970
His advice comes first, where our houses to live in should be.
(*words missing*) and a friendly place.
Every person is ready to pronounce blame upon foreigners;
may it be for the best!

(PELASGUS *leaves.*)

(*lines missing*)
and with good repute and no anger                                 975
in the talk of the native people.
(*turning to their attendant women*) Place yourselves, dear maids,
just as Danaus allocated you to each of us
as our dowry of servants.

DANAUS *suddenly returns from the city; he has an armed escort of* MEN OF ARGOS, *who form a further chorus.*

DANAUS.   My children, we must vow thanks to the people of Argos, 980
and do sacrifice and pour libations as if to Olympian gods, since
they are undividedly our saviours. They heard from me what had
been done to their own dear kin, and showed bitterness towards
your cousins; and they appointed these escorts and soldiers for me,
so that I may have honour and privilege, and neither be surprised 985
and killed unseen by a spear's fatal blow, thus becoming an everlasting burden for the land, [nor] (*text missing*). In meeting with
such goodness we must pay respectful thanks and honour from the
bottom of our hearts.                                                         990
  And write this in your minds together with the many other
wise precepts from your father you have written there: when a
company is unknown, it faces the test of time; and in the matter
of an immigrant every man has his tongue ready for abuse, and is
somehow easily prone to speaking his distaste. I urge you not to 995
disgrace me, with your young beauty here that turns men's eyes.
Tender ripeness is in no way easy to preserve; animals and men
ruin it—what else? Creatures too that fly and walk the ground—
Cypris proclaims their ripe readiness, at the same time half-heating 1000
the unripe too, to madden them with desire; also with virgin
girls, delicate and shapely—every passing man shoots a glance
to charm them, as longing overcomes him. And so let us not 1005
suffer what we made great effort to avoid, and why our ship
ploughed the great sea, and not create disgrace for ourselves but
pleasure for my enemies. As to dwellings, two kinds are open
to us too: one is Pelasgus' gift, and the other is the city's; liv- 1010
ing is to be free from payment; this falls out easy for us. Only
observe these instructions of your father, valuing modesty more
than life.
CHORUS.   In everything else I wish us good fortune, in the name
of the Olympian gods; but about my ripe youth, father, be
quite confident: unless the gods have formed some new and 1015
unwelcome design, I will not turn aside from my heart's former
track.

*The* CHORUS *dance and sing.*

CHORUS.   Now go and celebrate                Str. 1
   the blessed gods, the city's lords,
   both those who hold the city                     102
   and those who dwell by Erasinus' ancient flow.
   Take up our song, you escorts,
   and let praise possess this city
   of the Pelasgians; and let us no longer
   worship the streams of the Nile,              102

   but the rivers that pour                      Ant. 1
   their tranquil draught across the land
   and multiply its children,
   gentle to this soil here with their enriching flow.
   May holy Artemis too                    103
   watch over our band in pity,
   and no Cytherean rite come to compel us—
   may this be a prize for Styx!

*The* MEN OF ARGOS *form a further dancing chorus.*

MEN OF ARGOS   Cypris is not for neglect; this is a sensible law,
                                      Str. 2
   for she with Hera has the power closest to Zeus;    103
   she is a goddess honoured for her varied wiles
   in her holy rites.
   Sharing in these with their dear mother
   are Desire and [she to whose] charm
   no fulfilment is denied, Persuasion.             10-
   A part in Harmony is given to Aphrodite,
   and the whispering paths of love.

   But for those fleeing her breath on them, I fear in advance
                                   Ant. 2
   the evil of grief, and wars in their bloodiness.
   Why, why did those men achieve a good voyage, sped   10-
   on a swift pursuit?
   Truly, what is fated will happen;
   there can be no circumventing

Zeus' great mind, it is beyond escape.
In company with many women of earlier times                          1050
may marriage be your outcome here!

CHORUS.   May great Zeus protect me                                 Str. 3
  against marrying the sons of Aegyptus!
MEN.   This indeed would be for the best.
CHORUS.   You'd try charming where none can be charmed!             1055
MEN.   And you do not know what the future will be.

CHORUS.   Why am I to look down                                     Ant. 3
  into Zeus' mind, a view beyond fathom?
MEN.   Then utter a moderate prayer!
CHORUS.   What right measure are you teaching me?                   1060
MEN.   Concerning the gods, do nothing in excess.

CHORUS.   I wish lord Zeus may withhold from me                     Str. 4
  marriage to an evil man,
  an enemy—the very Zeus who rightly
  set Io free from torment,                                         1065
  checking her with healing hand,
  its force transformed to kindness;

and may he grant women victory!                                     Ant. 4
  Evil's better part I can
  be content with, and with two parts out of three,                1070
  and for justice to follow
  justice, as is now my prayer,
  in release devised by god.

*The* MEN OF ARGOS, DANAUS, *and the* CHORUS *with their women*
*servants leave in procession by the side.*

# Prometheus Bound

# Prometheus Bound

## CHARACTERS

POWER; his companion FORCE has a mute part
HEPHAESTUS, god of fire and metal-working
PROMETHEUS, a Titan
CHORUS, the daughters of Oceanus whose river surrounds the earth
OCEANUS
IO, daughter of Inachus king of Argos
HERMES, messenger of Zeus

*The play is set beneath a remote and towering ravine in the mountains
of the Caucasus, near the sea. POWER and FORCE, accompanying
HEPHAESTUS, enter from one side; at ZEUS' order they are bringing
PROMETHEUS, who may already be pinioned, to be fettered to the
cliff-face.*

POWER.  We have come to a far region of the earth, to a tract of
Scythia, to a wasteland without human life. Your duty, Hephaestus,
is to these instructions which father Zeus laid on you, to harness
this malefactor to high, rocky cliffs in the unbreakable fetters of 5
adamantine bonds; for it was the flower of your skill, gleaming
fire and all its arts, that he stole and bestowed upon men; and
for such a crime he must surely pay penalty to the gods, to be
taught acceptance of Zeus' rule, and to stop his habit of favouring 10
mankind.
HEPHAESTUS.  Power and Force, for both of you Zeus' order is an
end, and there is no further obstacle. I myself lack the hardness,
however, to put a god who is my kin forcibly in bonds, in a ravine

beaten by storms; yet it is absolutely necessary for me to be this 15
hard, because it is a heavy matter to disregard the word of father
Zeus.

(*addressing Prometheus*) Son of Themis right in her counsel, you
are over-lofty in your designs! Against your will, and my will too,
I shall nail you to this mountain uninhabited by men, in forged
bronze fetters that cannot be undone; here you will know neither 20
the voice nor the form of any mortal, and be scorched by the sun's
brilliant flame until you lose your skin's fine colour. You will be
glad when night's starry cloak hides the light, and when the sun
scatters the dawn frost again. The burden of your ever-present 25
agony will wear you down, for the one who is to alleviate it is not
yet born. Such is your reward for your habit of favouring mankind;
for as a god you did not cower before the wrath of gods when you
bestowed privileges upon men beyond what was just. In return for 30
this you shall keep guard of this unlovely cliff, standing upright and
unsleeping, with no flexing of your legs; many will be the wails and
laments you voice, uselessly, for the mind of Zeus is inexorable;
every ruler new to power is harsh. 35

POWER. (*to Hephaestus*) Now then, why your delay, and pity? They
are in vain. Why do you not loathe the god who is the gods' worst
enemy, who betrayed your prerogative to men?

HEPHAESTUS. Kinship is strangely powerful, I tell you, as is comradeship.

POWER. I agree; but how can father Zeus' word be disobeyed? Do 40
you not fear this more?

HEPHAESTUS. Yes, but you are always ruthless and overbearing.

POWER. This is because there's no remedy in weeping for
Prometheus here; and you are not to waste effort on what is useless.

HEPHAESTUS. O the worth of my hands! How much I hate you! 45

POWER. Why detest it? I am simply saying, your skill has nothing
to do with your present task.

HEPHAESTUS. Even so, I wish it had fallen to someone else.

POWER. Everything is a burden except ruling over gods; no one is
free except Zeus. 50

HEPHAESTUS. I know it by these things here (*pointing to the fetters*); and I cannot deny it.

POWER.  Then hurry to put bonds round Prometheus, so that
father Zeus does not see you dawdling.
HEPHAESTUS.   Look, the fetters are here to see, ready to hand.
POWER.   Throw them round his arms then, and hammer them   55
home, striking with powerful might; nail him to the rocks!
   (*Hephaestus begins fettering Prometheus to the cliff.*)
HEPHAESTUS.   The work is under way, you can see, and there's no
idling.
POWER.   Smash down harder! Tighten them up! Leave no slack at
all! He's clever at finding a way out even from impossibilities!
HEPHAESTUS.   This arm at least is fixed beyond getting free.        60
POWER.   Fasten this one home as well, then, securely, so he learns
he's slower than Zeus for all his cleverness.
HEPHAESTUS.   No one will rightly find fault with me—except
Prometheus!
POWER.   Now nail an adamantine wedge's remorseless point right
through his chest—strongly, now!                                    65
HEPHAESTUS.   Poor Prometheus, I lament for your ordeal.
POWER.   Here you are hesitating again, and lamenting over Zeus'
enemies; watch you don't end up pitying yourself!
HEPHAESTUS.   Are you seeing a sight hard for eyes to watch?
POWER.   I see Prometheus getting what he deserves. Now throw   70
bands round his ribs!
HEPHAESTUS.   I do this under compulsion; don't give me too
many orders!
POWER.   On my oath, I'll give you orders, and urge you on loudly
too! Move downward, and force bonds round his legs.
HEPHAESTUS.   Look, the work is done: no lengthy labour.          75
POWER.   Strike the cross-fetters home—use your strength! Our
work has an overseer, and a heavy one!
HEPHAESTUS.   Your voice's tone matches your appearance!
POWER.   Grow soft if you will, but don't throw it back at me that
my temper's harsh and obdurate.                                      80
HEPHAESTUS.   Let us go: he has bonds round his limbs. (*he begins
to leave*)
POWER.   (*addressing Prometheus*) Now do your outrages here, and
plunder the gods' prerogatives and attach them to ephemeral

mankind! What part of this ordeal can mortal men make lighter
for you? The gods call you Prometheus, but the name is false; for 85
you yourself need foresight to find a way to roll free of skilled
handiwork like this!

POWER *and* FORCE *follow* HEPHAESTUS *out by the side;*
PROMETHEUS *is now immobile for the rest of the play.*

PROMETHEUS. (*voicing his despair, alternately speaking and
chanting*)
    O sky divine, and winds swift-winged, and river-springs, and
ocean waves' bright laughter beyond counting, and earth the
mother of all, and the sun's circle which sees all—I call on you: 90
look upon the kind of suffering I have, a god at the hands of gods!
See the kind of torments which are to wear me away,
to be my ordeal for the time of numberless years:                    95
such is the shameful bondage
which the blessed gods' new captain has invented against me!
(*in despair*) Oh, I groan with the pain, both present and to come!
Where is a limit for my agonies ever to be set?                      100
    And yet what am I saying? I have accurate foreknowledge of all
that is to be, and no pain will come to me unexpectedly. I must
bear my destined lot as easily as I can, knowing that the power
of fate cannot be fought. Yet I can neither keep silent about my 105
misfortunes nor break my silence; it was for giving prerogatives to
men that I am yoked in these harsh constraints, a miserable wretch:
I hunted down fire from its source, to steal it in a filled fennel-stalk,
and it has proved mankind's teacher in every craft, and their great 110
resource. Such are the wrongdoings for which I pay penalty under
the open sky: in bonds; nailed fast!

*He senses an imminent arrival; he voices his alarm and astonishment.
The* CHORUS *of the daughters of Oceanus begin to enter in winged
carriages, still out of his sight.*

What? What's this?
What sound, what scent has winged towards me, invisibly?           115
Is it sped here by god, or come from men, or does it mix these?
Has [someone] come to this mountain at the world's end

to view my misery—or with what wish, then?
See me in bonds, a god ill-fated,
the enemy of Zeus, the one who came                                              120
to be hated by all the gods
that frequent the courts of Zeus,
all because of his too great friendship for men!
(*in renewed alarm*) Oh, whatever is the fluttering I hear again
close by me of birds?
The air is whirring with the light beat of wings.                                125
All that approaches is fearsome for me.

### *The* CHORUS *sing.*

CHORUS.   Have no fear! We come in formation as friends     Str. 1
  to this crag, our wings swift in rivalry,
  after barely persuading our father's mind;                                      130
  rapid winds bore me here as my escort.
  Echoes from hammered iron had pierced our inmost cave;
  it struck and shocked me out of my shy reserve;
  I came unshod; I sped in this wing-borne carriage.                              135

PROMETHEUS.   (*intoning his despair*) Oh, lament for me!
  You offspring of Tethys of the many children
  and daughters of father Oceanus
  who coils round all the earth with his unsleeping stream,                       140
  look! See in what kind of bond
  I am fastened in the high crags of this ravine,
  and must endure as its unenviable guard.

CHORUS.   I do see, Prometheus, but a mist of fear     Ant. 1
  rushed over my eyes, filling them with tears                                    145
  when I saw your body put to wither here
  on rock, tortured by adamantine bonds.
  New masters are ruling and guide Olympus' helm;
  fresh laws too without due base are Zeus' power;                                150
  what was mighty before, he now obliterates.

PROMETHEUS.   If only he had sent me below the earth,
  and down where Hades receives the dead
  into boundless Tartarus,

and savagely confined me in unbreakable bonds,                    155
so that no god or any other would be rejoicing over me here!
Now, high up in the air, a thing shaken and battered,
a miserable wretch, I suffer for my enemies' delight.

CHORUS.    Who among gods is so hard of heart          Str. 2
    as to find delight in this?                                   161
    Who does not share resentment
    at your misery, except of course Zeus?
    Always rancorous and unbending
    in purpose he subdues the race
    of Ouranos, and will not cease                               165
    before either he sates his heart or someone
    by some ruse gains the rule that is hard to attain.

PROMETHEUS.    I swear: the blessed ones' president will yet have
        need of me,
    tortured though I am in strong fetters round my limbs,
    to reveal the new plan through which                          170
    he is to be despoiled of his sceptre and prerogatives.
    He will not charm me at all with honey-tongued spells
    of persuasion, anymore than I will ever cower
    beneath harsh threats and give this information away,
    before he looses me from cruel bonds                          175
    and is willing to pay penalty for this torture.

CHORUS.    You are too headstrong and yield not at all     Ant. 2
    in your bitter agonies;
    your mouth is too free in speech.                            180
    My mind, however, is pierced by sharp fear;
    my dread is for you and what happens—
    wherever it will be your fate
    to come ashore and see the end
    of this pain; for Cronus' son has a nature
    beyond reach, and a quite inexorable heart.                  185

PROMETHEUS.    I know that he is harsh and keeps justice to him-
        self.
    Still, I think he will one day soften in temper,

when he is smashed in this way.
Once he has calmed his obdurate anger                                    190
he will one day enter a bond of friendship with me,
eager joining with eager.

CHORUS.  (*speaking*) Reveal the whole story, and tell us on what
kind of charge Zeus has taken and tortures you so ignominiously
and harshly. Inform us, unless you are hurt in some way by speak-  195
ing.

PROMETHEUS.  Yes, even to speak of these things is painful, but
silence too gives me pain; in every way they are a cruel fate.

   As soon as the divine powers became angry, and faction stirred
between them all, with some wishing to throw Cronus from his seat  200
so that Zeus, of course, might be lord, while others were eager for
the opposite, that Zeus should never rule the gods—then despite
my best advice I was unable to dissuade the Titans, children of
Heaven and Earth: scorning crafty means, they thought in their     205
arrogant might that they would effortlessly become the masters by
violence; but I had been given prophecy, and more than once, by
my mother Themis and Earth, one form with many names, how the  210
future would be fulfilled: that those who came out superior must
prevail not by strength or violence, but by cunning. Although I
told them this and set it out fully, they did not deign even to glance
at it. Quite the best of the courses then to hand seemed to be to    215
join my mother to me in a willing stand to aid a willing Zeus; and
through my counsels the hidden black depths of Tartarus conceal
the ancient-born Cronus and all his allies. Although the tyrant of  220
the gods received such help from me, he has answered me with this
evil reward. In tyranny there is somehow this vice, not to trust one's
friends.                                                                                225

   Well, as to your question, then, on what charge he tortures me,
this I shall make clear. So soon as he was seated on his father's
throne, he at once assigned various prerogatives to deities and dis-
tributed command; but of wretched mortals he took no account,    230
instead he desired to obliterate their whole race and to generate
another from new. In this he had no opposition except mine; but I
was daring: I set men free from being smashed into destruction and  235
going to Hades. That is why, I tell you, I am bent in these agonies,

as painful to suffer as they are pitiable to see. After being readier
with pity for mortals I was not myself held worthy of getting it,
but have been brought ruthlessly into line like this, a sight to bring 240
Zeus infamy.

CHORUS.  Anyone who does not share resentment at your ordeals,
Prometheus, has a heart of iron indeed, and is made of stone. I
would not have wished to look upon this myself, and now that I
have looked, I am hurt to the core. 245

PROMETHEUS.  Yes, I truly am pitiable for friends to look at.

CHORUS.  You didn't perhaps go even further than you said?

PROMETHEUS.  I did; I stopped men from foreseeing their death.

CHORUS.  What sort of remedy did you find for this affliction?

PROMETHEUS.  I gave blind hopes a home within them. 250

CHORUS.  This was a great benefit you gave men!

PROMETHEUS.  In addition, however, I bestowed fire on them.

CHORUS.  And now ephemeral men possess fire's bright flame?

PROMETHEUS.  They do, and from it they will learn many crafts.

CHORUS.  Those were the charges against you, I suppose, upon
which Zeus... 255

PROMETHEUS.  ... tortures me, yes, and in no way relents from the
evil he does me.

CHORUS.  And is no end set for your ordeal?

PROMETHEUS.  No, none, except when Zeus himself decides.

CHORUS.  And he will decide—how? What hope is there? Do you
not see that you did wrong? But that you did do wrong, I have
no pleasure myself in saying, while you have the pain. Let us drop 260
this, however; and you seek some means to be freed from your
ordeal!

PROMETHEUS.  A light thing for someone with his feet out of
harm's way, to urge and advise the one in trouble! Everything of
this I knew: I did wrong willingly, willingly, I will not deny; and 265
in helping mortals I found misery myself. I swear, I did not think
at all that punishments like these would have me withering away
on lofty crags, and getting this desolate, lonely mountain. Please, 270
do not weep for the sufferings I have here, but step down and
hear what things are on their way to happening, so you learn the
whole tale through to its end. Let me persuade you, please, let me
persuade you: share the troubles of one now struggling to endure

this, for misery wanders around and settles now upon one person,     275
now upon another.

*The* CHORUS *dismount from their winged carriages, chanting.*

CHORUS.   We were not unwilling to have you urge this on us,
 Prometheus;
and now with light step I shall leave
the seat in which I sped rapidly,
and the sacred heaven, passage-way of birds,     280
and set foot on this jagged land.
I desire to hear your miseries all through.

*There is a sudden entry:* OCEANUS *appears, riding upon a griffin; he is chanting.*

OCEANUS.   I come to you, Prometheus,
and reach a long journey's end,     285
directing this swift-winged bird
by thought, without bridle;
know that I share the pain of your misfortunes!
Kinship, I think, compels me forward in this way,     290
and apart from kin there is no one
I should give greater due than you.
You will learn that this is true; and it is not in me
to speak empty compliments.
So, come: indicate what I should do to help you;     295
you shall never say, you have a friend
more sure than Oceanus!

PROMETHEUS.   What? What's this? You too have come, of course,
to view my miseries? How did you brave leaving the stream named
for you and its rock-roofed, natural caverns to come to the land     300
that mothers iron? Have you come to observe my misfortunes and
share resentment at my troubles? Look at the sight: here is the
friend of Zeus, the one who helped establish his rule—see what     305
pains I am bent in by him!
OCEANUS.   I do see, Prometheus; and, yes, I do wish to give you the
best advice, however ingenious you are. Learn to know yourself!
Modify your ways for new ones: there is also a new ruler among

the gods. If you go on in this way hurling out harsh words sharp   310
with anger, Zeus might perhaps hear you, though he is seated far
off and higher; and then the mass of your present ordeals would
seem child's play. No, you poor wretch: let go of the angry passions
you have, and seek release from this disaster. Perhaps I seem to you   315
old-fashioned in what I say; but the truth is, your state like this,
Prometheus, is the wages of a tongue too lofty in its speech. Aren't
you humble yet, and don't you yet yield to your troubles?—and do   320
you wish to add others to your present ones? Use me as teacher,
and you won't kick against the pricks, when you see a monarch in
power who is harsh and not answerable.

   And now I will go and try if I can to free you from this ordeal;   325
and you stay quiet, and don't speak too violently! Or don't you
know definitely, with your extreme intelligence, that punishment
is inflicted upon a wild tongue?

PROMETHEUS.   I envy you for escaping blame when you have   330
shared everything courageously with me. And now let be, and don't
concern yourself: you will absolutely not persuade Zeus; he is not
easily persuaded. Rather, keep looking out for yourself, so that you
don't get hurt through your journey.

OCEANUS.   You are much better at advising those close to you than   335
your own self! Facts, not words, are my evidence. Now I am eager,
don't pull me back; I am confident, yes, confident, that Zeus will
give me this gift, your release from this ordeal.

PROMETHEUS.   In part I commend you, and will never stop doing
so, for you're not lacking in eager concern. Make no effort, how-   340
ever: your efforts for me will be wasted, and no help, even though
you wish to make some effort. No, stay quiet, and keep yourself
out of the way; for even in my misfortune, I would wish it to harm   345
as few as possible. Very much that, since what happened to my
brother Atlas oppresses me: he stands in western parts supporting
on his shoulders earth's and heaven's pillar, a burden not easy
for the arms. That child of earth too, the inhabitant of Cilician   350
caves, hostile, monstrous, with a hundred heads—I saw and pitied
him as he was violently overcome—Typhon furious for war, who
stood against all the gods, hissing terror with dreadful jaws, and   355
who flashed a fierce gleam from his eyes, intent on the violent
ruin of tyranny. Zeus' unsleeping bolt came to him, however, the

lightning which descends in a blast of flame; it hit him out of
his lofty boastings; he was struck to the very soul of his being,  360
blazing like a coal, and his strength blasted from him in thunder.
Useless now and sprawled flat, his body lies near the sea-narrows,
crushed beneath the roots of Etna; and seated on its topmost peak  365
Hephaestus has his glowing smithy, from which rivers of fire will
one day erupt to devour the broad fields of fertile Sicily with savage
jaws: such is the anger Typhon will send boiling upward in red-hot  370
bolts of blasting fire, a storm none may approach, although he is
burnt to embers by Zeus' lightning.

But you are not without experience, nor do you need me as
teacher: save yourself as you know how, while I shall endure my
present fortune to the dregs, until Zeus' mind relents from anger.  375

OCEANUS.   Surely you know, Prometheus, that words are doctors
for a sick temper?

PROMETHEUS.   Yes, if one softens a heart at the right moment and
does not forcibly reduce swollen passions.                         380

OCEANUS.   But what loss do you see in eager intention and boldness? Tell me.

PROMETHEUS.   Wasted effort and simple-minded foolishness.

OCEANUS.   Allow me to be sick with this weakness, for most profit
lies in a man of good sense seeming not to be sensible.            385

PROMETHEUS.   This fault will seem to be mine.

OCEANUS.   Your words are for sending me back home again,
clearly.

PROMETHEUS.   Yes, in case your laments for me bring you enmity.

OCEANUS.   You mean from the one newly seated on the all-
powerful throne?

PROMETHEUS.   Guard against his heart ever becoming aggrieved.  390

OCEANUS.   Your disaster is my teacher, Prometheus!

PROMETHEUS.   Be on your way, take yourself off, keep to your
present mind!

OCEANUS.   Your words urge me on when I am already starting: my bird-like steed is brushing heaven's wide path with its
wings. It would clearly be glad to rest its limbs in its home  395
stable.

OCEANUS *leaves on his griffin. The* CHORUS *sing and dance.*

CHORUS.  I lament you, Prometheus, in your evil fate;    Str. 1
 tears are dripping from my tender eyes;
 I let them pour out, streaming and soaking    400
 my cheek in their wet flow.
 This is how Zeus rules unsparingly,
 with private laws,
 and displaying the arrogant power of his spear
 to those former gods.    405

The whole earth has already cried out its lament.    Ant. 1
 Men lament for your magnificence
 and rank, ancient in splendour (*text missing*),
 and that of your blood-kin;    410
 and all mortal men inhabiting
 homes settled here
 in sacred Asia, share the hurt and pain you bear,
 to their great lament;

the inhabitants of Colchis as well,    Str. 2
 those maidens fearless in battle;    416
 and Scythia's hordes
 who occupy the furthest place
 on earth around Maeotis' lake;

and Arabia's flower, its warriors,    Ant. 2
 those who inhabit a city    421
 on high sheer cliffs
 near Caucasus, a fighting host
 who roar amid sharp-pointed spears.

Only one other Titan before did I see    Str. 3
 in such ordeals, subdued by the outrage    426
 of untiring bonds—a god!—
 Atlas, pre-eminent in the power of his strength,
 [who] supports [earth] and heaven with its sky
 on his back like a covering roof.    430

(*a line missing*)    Ant. 3
 and ocean's wave cries out (*words missing*)
 as it falls, its depths lament,

while Hades' black recess in the earth is roaring
below, and river-springs in sacred flow
are lamenting your piteous pain.                                                435

PROMETHEUS. Don't think—no, don't!—that I keep silent
through pride or obduracy; but painful awareness gnaws my heart
when I see myself treated so contemptuously. Yet who else but
myself completely determined their prerogatives for these new
gods? I keep silent on that, however, for I would be telling you  440
when you already know. Hear rather the miseries of mortal men—
how I made them intelligent when before they were silly, and gave
them wits to use. I will tell you without any blame for mankind,  445
but explain the goodwill in what I have given them. At first they
had sight but saw to no effect, had hearing but did not hear,
confusing everything randomly like dream-shapes for the length
of their life; and they knew neither brick-built houses catching the  450
sun, nor carpentry, but dug out underground homes like scurrying
ants in sunless, tunnelled caves. They had no sure mark for either
winter's coming, or that of flowery spring and fruitful summer,  455
but did everything without design until, that is, I showed them
the risings and settings of the stars, so hard to determine. Number too, supreme among skills, I invented for them, and letters
in combination, the record of all things, the mother and crafter  460
of poetry. I was first too in yoking and harnessing beasts, to be
subservient to yoke-loops and saddles, and to take over from men
their greatest exertions; and I brought horses to accept the reins
beneath a chariot, that ornament of extreme wealth's luxury. Next,  465
no one else but myself invented ships to carry sailors, roaming the
sea on wings of linen-cloth. Although I had invented, wretch that I
am, such clever means for men, I have myself no stratagem to free  470
me from the torment I have now.
CHORUS. You have suffered a shameful outrage; your wits have
been taken away, and you wander, and like some bad doctor you
have fallen ill and lost your spirit, and you cannot discover the
kinds of medicine to cure yourself.                                          475
PROMETHEUS. When you hear the rest from me you will be more
amazed at what skills and means I devised. The greatest of them:
if any man fell ill, there was nothing in defence, either to eat

or rub in, or yet to drink, but men were wasting away for lack
of medicines until the time I showed them the mixing of gen-    480
tle remedies with which they drive away all sickness. Also, I set
out in order many ways of divination. I was the first to judge
from dreams what must be reality; I explained for them difficult    485
omens from people's remarks, and signs met on their journeys;
I precisely defined the flight of birds of prey both favourable
and sinister in nature, the habits of life they each have, and the    490
enmities and affections between one another, and their perch-
ings together; the smoothness of entrails too, and what colour
the gall-bladder would have when marking the gods' pleasure,
and the mottling of a well-shaped liver; I had men burn the    495
thigh-bones and long spine wrapped in fat, and I put them on
their way into the difficult skill of marking the signs, and gave
them clear sight from flames of indications which were previously
obscure.

So much for things of that kind; but the benefits for men hidden    500
below the earth, from bronze, iron, silver and gold—who will say
he discovered them before myself? No one, I am sure, unless he
wishes to talk empty nonsense.

To put everything briefly together: you should understand that    505
men have all their skills from Prometheus!

CHORUS.   Don't then help men unduly but neglect yourself in your
misfortune; for I have good hopes that you will yet be freed from
these bonds and be no less strong than Zeus.    510

PROMETHEUS.   Fate who brings all to fulfilment is not yet destined
to accomplish that this way; but I am to escape my bonds while
bent like this by countless agonies and pains. Skill is weaker by far
than the inevitable!

CHORUS.   So who is at the helm of the inevitable?    515

PROMETHEUS.   The Fates and the ever-mindful Furies, three in
form.

CHORUS.   Is Zeus then weaker than they?

PROMETHEUS.   He'll not escape what is destined, certainly!

CHORUS.   Why, what is destined for Zeus except to rule for
ever?

PROMETHEUS.   You'll learn nothing further of this; and don't
entreat me.    520

CHORUS. It must be some holy secret you are keeping close, I
suppose.

PROMETHEUS. Mention another subject; it is not at all the
moment to speak of this one, rather it must be concealed as much
as possible; for it is by keeping it safe that I am to escape my
shameful bonds and torments.                                    525

The CHORUS *sing and dance.*

CHORUS.   May he who directs all things, Zeus,          Str. 1
    never set his power to oppose my thinking,
    nor I ever cease to approach
    the gods at the sacred feasts                           530
    where oxen are killed near my father Oceanus' unquenchable
        stream,
    nor I ever sin in the words I say;
    and I wish this remains firm for me,
    and never melts away.                                   535

    It is sweet to draw out one's life                      Ant. 1
    to its length in confident hopes, and nourish
    one's spirit in bright cheerfulness;
    but I shudder to see you                                540
    worn away and reduced by agonies without number (*words miss-
        ing*).
    With no fear of Zeus in your own thinking,
    the regard you have for mortal men,
    Prometheus, is too high.

    Come, my friend, say: how can they return your favour   Str. 2
    with favour? Where is there help to save you?           546
    What aid can there be from ephemeral men?
    And did you not see the feeble weakness to act,
    dream-like, with which the race of men
    has been hampered in their blindness? Never (*word missing*)  550
    will the plans of men
    elude the ordered government of Zeus.

    I came to this understanding when my eyes saw            Ant. 2
    the evil of your fate here, Prometheus.
    This song that wings to me is quite different           555

from that when I raised the wedding-hymn beside bath
and bed to honour your marriage,
when you led in our half-sister Hesione
with the wedding-gifts,
persuading her to share your bed as wife.                              560

IO *enters abruptly from one side, in a headlong rush; her head is horned
like a cow. She chants and sings excitedly.*

IO.   What land? What people? Whom do I see, should I say,
storm-beaten here in bonds of stone?
For what crime are you put to death as punishment?
Tell me where on the earth I have come to in the wandering I
    endure.

(*suddenly crying out in frenzied pain*)                               565

I am stung again, in this misery, by some gadfly—
keep it away! Oh, away!—
as I see that cowherd with the countless eyes:
he moves with cunning in his look;
even in death the earth does not cover him,                            570
but in hunting me down in this misery,
he has passed from the dead below, and he has sent me wandering
in hunger over the sand by the sea,

while his wax-bound reed-pipe noisily drones          Str.
its music, to destroy my sleep.                                        575
Oh, how I suffer! Where are my far wanderings
leading me to, [these] wanderings?
What, O son of Cronus, whatever did you find
that I had done wrong, to yoke me under these torments,
(*crying out in distress*)
and exhaust and derange me so,                                         580
abject from the gadfly's driving terror?
Burn me with fire, or bury me in earth, or give me
to sea-creatures to devour; do not grudge me
my prayers to you, my lord.
I am well-wearied enough by my many, many wanderings,                  585
nor can I learn in what way I am to escape

my torment. Do you hear
the voice of this maiden who is horned like a cow?

PROMETHEUS.  (*speaking*) This must be Inachus' daughter that I
hear, the maiden harried along by the gadfly—who kindled Zeus'
heart with love, and now through Hera's loathing is forced past  590
weariness on her overlong course!

IO.  How can you know to speak my father's name?            Ant.
Tell me in my agony here!
Who are you, who then, you poor wretch, to address me          595
so surely in my wretchedness,
and name the affliction launched upon me by god
which wastes me away, and goads me to wander madly?
(*crying out in distress*)
In the tortures of wild bucking
and hunger, I have come with headlong speed;                   600
I am victim of a rancorous scheme [of Hera].
Some unfortunates there are, who—Oh, alas!—
endure a fate like mine.
But now tell me clearly, please, what suffering still remains for me!  605
What means to a cure is there for my affliction?
Reveal it, if you know!
Do speak; tell this maiden put to cruel wandering!

PROMETHEUS.  I shall tell you clearly all you wish to learn, without
riddles woven in, but with plain words, as is right when open-  610
ing one's lips to friends. You see the giver of fire to mankind—
Prometheus.
IO.  O you who appeared as mankind's common benefactor! O
wretched Prometheus, why are you suffering this punishment?
PROMETHEUS.  I have only just stopped mourning my troubles.    615
IO.  So will you not make me this gift?
PROMETHEUS.  Say what gift you seek; you may learn everything
from me.
IO.  Tell me who harnessed you fast in the ravine.
PROMETHEUS.  The plan was that of Zeus, and the hand that of
Hephaestus.
IO.  And the penalty you pay—what was your crime?             620

PROMETHEUS.   I do enough in making only this much plain to you.

IO.   Well, also reveal the end of my wandering to me, and how long the time of my misery will be.

PROMETHEUS.   It is better for you not to learn than to learn this.

IO.   Don't, please, hide from me what I am about to suffer.                          625

PROMETHEUS.   Well, I don't begrudge you this gift.

IO.   Then why delay telling me everything?

PROMETHEUS.   I've no grudge, but I hesitate to put your mind in turmoil.

IO.   Have no further worry for me. This will please me.

PROMETHEUS.   Since you are eager, I should speak. Listen, then.   630

CHORUS.   (*breaking in*) No, not yet! Let me share in the pleasure too! Let us inquire first into her affliction, with herself telling of her long, cruel misfortunes. As to what remains of her ordeal, let her learn that from you.

PROMETHEUS.   It's your job, Io, to gratify them, above all as your  636 father's sisters; it's worth taking time to weep and grieve fully for misfortunes, here in this place, where one is bound to earn tears from one's listeners.

IO.   I do not know how to refuse you all; and with a clear tale you  640 will find out all you desire—and yet I weep even to speak about the storm launched upon me by god, and the reason why the ruin which I now endure swept suddenly over my form.

Visions in the night came constantly into my maiden's chambers  645 and kept blandishing me with smooth words: 'Girl, you are greatly blessed by heaven! Why so long a maiden, when you may have the greatest of unions? Zeus has been inflamed by a shaft of desire, and wishes to make love with you. Child, it is not for you to spurn Zeus'  650 bed! No, go out into Lerna's deep meadow, to your father's herds and ox-stalls, and relieve Zeus' eyes of their desire.' Such dreams held me fast in misery every night, until, that is, I had the courage  655 to tell my father of these dreams which appeared in the night; and he sent frequent sacred envoys to Pytho and as far as Dodona, to learn what he should do or say to please the gods. They kept coming  660 to report oracles that had shifting voices, spoke obscurely, and were hard to determine; but finally a clear response came to Inachus with definite instructions in its wording, to thrust me outside my

home and fatherland, to be let loose to wander over earth's furthest 665
boundaries; and should he not be willing, fiery lightning would
come from Zeus to obliterate his whole line. Persuaded by such
prophecies from Loxias he drove and shut me out of the house, 670
against my will, and his will too; but Zeus' curb compelled him to
do this forcibly. Straightaway my form and wits were sent awry;
I was given horns, as you see; and I was stung by the fly's sharp
bite and rushed maddened and bucking to Cerchne's flow of good 675
water and Lerna's spring. A cowherd born from the earth, all raw
anger, accompanied me along my tracks, Argos, watching me from
his clustered eyes. Unexpectedly a sudden death deprived him of 680
life, but stung by the gadfly I have been driven by a god's scourge
from land to land.

    You hear what was done to me. If you can say what remains of
my ordeal, tell me; but don't warm my heart with false words out
of pity; for I say that made-up tales are the most shameful vice. 685

CHORUS.   (*singing their extreme alarm*) No! Stop!
  Never, never did I expect
  such strange tales to come to my hearing,
  nor such violent, fearful outrages, 690
  so hard to watch and hard to bear,
  to strike and pierce my heart with doubled sharpness.
  Oh, what a fate, what a fate!
  I shudder to see what has been done to Io. 695

PROMETHEUS.  (*to the* CHORUS) You are too early with your
  lament, and with the fear which fills you. Hold back until you learn
  the rest as well.
CHORUS.   Say, tell it all; it pleases those afflicted to have clear foreknowledge of their future pain!
PROMETHEUS.  (*to the* CHORUS) Your first request you gained
  from me easily; for your first desire was to learn Io's own account 700
  of her ordeal. Now hear what further suffering this young woman
  must endure at Hera's hands. (*to* IO) And you, Inachus' child, take
  my words to heart, to learn the end of your road. 705

    First: turn yourself from here towards the sun's rising and make
  your way to unploughed lands: you will come to the nomadic

Scythians, who live in woven shelters raised high on easy-wheeling
carts, and are armed with far-shooting bows: do not approach 710
them, but cross their land and as you go keep close to the rocky
shores loud with the sea. On your left hand live the Chalybes,
workers with iron: you should guard against them, for they are 715
uncivilized and not for strangers to approach. You will come to the
river Hybristes—not falsely named! Do not go over it, for it has no
good way across, before you reach the Caucasus itself, looking for
its highest point, where the river bursts out in force from the very 720
peaks; you must pass over these summits that neighbour the stars,
and go a southerly way, where you will come to the Amazons' host
with their loathing for men, who will one day inhabit Themiscyra
near Thermodon, where Salmydessus makes a rugged jaw into 725
the sea, inhospitable to sailors, a stepmother evil to ships. These
Amazons will guide your way, and very gladly. You will come to
the Cimmerian isthmus, at the very gates where the lake makes a
narrow passage; you must leave it and cross the Maeotic basin bold- 730
heartedly; and there will be a great tale for ever among mankind
of your journey, and the Bosporus will be called after your name.
After leaving Europe's soil you will come to mainland Asia. 735

    (*to the* CHORUS) Do you not think the tyrant of the gods is
equally violent in everything? Although he was a god who desired
union with this mortal woman he weighed these wanderings down
on her! (*to* IO) A cruel suitor you found for your bed, young
maiden! For you must think of the account you have just heard 740
as not yet even a prelude.

IO. (*suddenly terrified*) Oh! Why me, me? No!

PROMETHEUS. Here you are crying out and moaning loudly: what
in the world will you do when you learn the rest of your troubles?

CHORUS. Why, is there something left of her miseries that you will
tell her? 745

PROMETHEUS. Yes, a cruel and stormy sea of consuming torment.

IO. What use for me to live then?—and why not quickly throw
myself from this hard cliff, to plunge to the ground and be rid of
my whole ordeal? It is better to die once and for all than to suffer 750
miserably every day.

PROMETHEUS. You'd not easily bear what I endure, when it is not
my destiny to die! That would rid me of my torments; but now

there is no end set for my agonies until Zeus is thrown from his 755
tyranny.

IO. Why—is it possible for Zeus to be thrown from his rule?

PROMETHEUS. You'd be pleased, I think, to see this disaster for
him.

IO. Of course I would, as one who suffers miserably through Zeus!

PROMETHEUS. Well, since these are the facts, you may rejoice.  760

IO. What will rob him of his tyrant's sceptre?

PROMETHEUS. His very own empty-headed designs.

IO. In what way? Tell me, if there's no harm in it.

PROMETHEUS. He will make such a marriage as he'll one day
regret.

IO. One among gods, or to a mortal? If it may be spoken, say.  765

PROMETHEUS. Why ask which? This may not be spoken aloud.

IO. Is he to be deposed from his throne by the wife?

PROMETHEUS. Yes, one who will bear a son mightier than his
father.

IO. And is there no averting this outcome for him?

PROMETHEUS. Indeed not, unless it should be through my own
release from bonds.  770

IO. So who is to release you if Zeus is unwilling?

PROMETHEUS. It is fated to be one of your descendants.

IO. How do you mean? Will a son of mine deliver you from this evil?

PROMETHEUS. Yes, one born from the third generation after ten
others.

IO. This prophecy is becoming hard for me to understand.  775

PROMETHEUS. Then do not seek to learn your own ordeal either.

IO. Do not offer me an advantage and then deprive me of it!

PROMETHEUS. I will reward you with one or other of two
accounts.

IO. Two? What kind are they? Reveal them first, and give the choice
to me.

PROMETHEUS. I give it you, so choose: I shall tell you clearly either
your remaining miseries, or who is to set me free.  780

CHORUS. (*again intervening*) Please agree to favour her with one
of those, and myself with the other; and don't think me unworthy
to be told. Tell the rest of her wanderings to her, and tell *me*, who
is to set you free.  785

PROMETHEUS.  Since you are both eager, I shall not resist telling
you all you desire. You first, Io: I shall tell you your wanderings,
and your constant harrying; write them in your mind's tablets of
memory.

　　Once you cross the flow bounding the continents, make your        790
way beside the roaring sea towards the sun's fiery rising until you
reach the Gorgon plains of Cisthene where the Phorcides dwell,
three long-lived maidens with hair white as swans, possessing one
shared eye and a single tooth; neither sun nor moon by night ever      795
looks on them with its rays. Nearby are their three winged sisters,
the snake-haired Gorgons hated by men; no one who sees them will
keep hold of life's breath. Such is the garrison of this place, I tell   800
you! Now hear of a further barely tolerable sight: be on your guard
against the sharp-beaked, unbarking hounds of Zeus, the griffins,
and the host of one-eyed Arimaspian horse-riders who live around      805
the stream and golden flow of Pluto's river: do not approach these!
You will come to a distant land, a black race which dwells near the
sunlight's source; the river Ethiops is here. Make your way along
its banks until you come to the cataract where the Nile discharges    810
its revered, pure flow from the Bybline mountains; the river will
guide you to the three-cornered Nilotic land—and this is where it
is your destiny, Io, and your children's, to establish your far-distant
colony.                                                                815

　　If any of this is said indistinctly and is hard to comprehend, go
doubling back again and ask for clearer knowledge; I have more
leisure than I wish.

CHORUS.  If you have anything left to tell her, or that has been
omitted, of her long, cruel wandering, say it; but if you have said    820
everything, then grant us in our turn that favour we were asking;
you remember it, of course.

PROMETHEUS.  She has heard the end of her journey, all of it; but
so she knows that she has not been listening to me in vain, I shall
tell what she has endured before she came here, giving this in itself  825
as proof of my words.

　　(*to* IO) I shall leave out the great mass of the account, and go
to the very end of your wanderings. Now, when you came to the
Molossian regions and Dodona on its steep ridge, where the oracles   830
and seat of Thesprotian Zeus are, and a marvel beyond belief, the
speaking oak-trees, by which you were told in full clarity, and with

no riddling, that you were to be the glorious partner of Zeus—does
anything in this win me your belief? Next in your gadfly-frenzy you   835
rushed along the coastal path to the great gulf of Rhea, from which
you have wandered back again on your stormy course; in future
time this sea's deep inlet—know this clearly!—will be called Ionian,   840
a memorial for all men of your journey. These are proofs for you,
of how my mind sees rather more than has appeared openly.

The rest I shall tell you and Io jointly, and return to the same
track as my earlier words. There is a city Canopus, the earth's   845
most distant, by the Nile's very mouth and banked-up silt. Here
it is that Zeus will restore your senses merely with the touch of
a calming hand; you will bear dark-skinned Epaphus, named for   850
this begetting by Zeus, who will harvest all the land which the
Nile waters with its broad flow. The fifth generation from him,
one of fifty children, will come back to Argos unwillingly: they
will be women, in flight from kindred marriage to their cousins.   855
These, their minds excited by passion, hawks closely in pursuit of
doves, will come hunting marriages not for hunting; but the god
will deny them possession of the women bodily. Pelasgus' land will
accept (*words missing*) when (*words missing*) are killed in a war of   860
murderous women boldly alert in the night; for each wife will take
the life of her husband, dipping a two-edged sword in slaughtered
blood. I wish Aphrodite might come against my enemies like that!
Yet one of the daughters will be bewitched by desire against killing   865
her husband; instead she will have her resolve blunted: of the two
choices, she will prefer to be called a coward rather than a mur-
derer. It is she who will bear a royal line in Argos. It needs a long   870
account to relate this clearly, but from this seedbed will be born
one bold and famous with his bow; it is he who will set me free
from these miseries. Such was the oracle my ancient-born mother
recounted to me, the Titan Themis; but how, and by what means—
to tell this needs a lengthy account, and you will gain nothing from   875
learning it.

IO *bursts suddenly into frenzy again; she starts to leave.*

IO.   (*chanting*) Onward! Onward!
Spasms and madness battering my senses inflame me again,
and the gadfly's fiery spear-point pierces me.                        880

My heart is kicking inside me with fear,
my eyes roll and spin dizzily,
and I am carried off-course by a furious blast of frenzy.
I am powerless over my tongue; my words strike randomly in thick
    confusion                                                                 885
against the waves of a hateful ruin.

     IO *rushes away; the* CHORUS *sing and dance.*

CHORUS.  Wise indeed, yes, wise, was he                               Str.
    who first pondered the thought in his mind,
    and whose tongue said it in words,
    that marriage within one's own kind is far superior;              890
    and no poor artisan should desire
    union with those either made effete by wealth
    or vaunting themselves greatly on their descent.

    Never, never, O you Fates,                                        Ant.
    (*text missing*) may you see me                                  895
    as bedmate of Zeus' couch,
    nor may I come as bride near any groom from Heaven;
    for I begin to fear now I see
    the maiden Io hating her husband, consumed
    in cruel wandering, her ordeal from Hera.                        900

    For me, when marriage is with an equal, it has no terror,      Epode
    and I do not fear; but I wish the inescapable eye
    of the mighty gods may not look towards me.
    That is war beyond warring with, what it deals beyond dealing
      with!
    I cannot know what would become of me,                           905
    for I do not see how I might escape Zeus' design.

PROMETHEUS.  Zeus shall yet be humble, I swear, for all his stub-
    born thinking, such is the marriage he is preparing, which will
    throw him from his tyrant's throne into oblivion; and then the
    curse of his father Cronus will at once be totally fulfilled, his  910
    imprecation when expelled from his ancient seat. No god but I
    could show Zeus clearly how to avert such struggles: I know all
    this, and the means. So, now let him sit there in high confidence,  915

trusting to his battering thunder high in the sky and brandishing
in hand his bolt of blasting fire—for these will avail him nothing
against an ignominious fall into a collapse past bearing: so strong
a rival in the ring is he now making ready against his own self, 920
portentous and quite invincible, one who will invent a flame more
powerful than lightning, and a mighty crash surpassing thunder,
and a disturbance in the sea to make the earth shudder, one to
splinter Poseidon's three-tined spear. When he dashes on this evil 925
reef he will learn how far apart ruling and slavery are!

CHORUS.   You are of course reviling Zeus with what you desire for
him!

PROMETHEUS.   With exactly what will be fulfilled—but I am saying too what I wish.

CHORUS.   And should we expect that someone will master Zeus?   930

PROMETHEUS.   Yes, and Zeus will have struggles even more crip-
pling than these!

CHORUS.   How can you throw out such words without fear?

PROMETHEUS.   Why on earth should I be afraid? I am not fated to
die!

CHORUS.   But Zeus might contrive an ordeal for you still more
painful than this!

PROMETHEUS.   Well, let him do that, then! I expect everything.   935

CHORUS.   Those who humble themselves before Nemesis are wise.

PROMETHEUS.   Go on, pay your honours, make your prayers, give
your flattery to one whose power is for the moment! I care less than
nothing for Zeus. Let him act, let him use his power for this short
time as he wants: he will not rule the gods for long.   940

But now I see Zeus' runner here, the new tyrant's servant; he has
doubtless come to announce some fresh unpleasantness.

HERMES, *Zeus' messenger, enters from the side.*

HERMES.   You, the clever one!—the one so extreme, too extreme for
his own good!—the one who wrongs the gods by giving ephemeral
men privileges!—the thief of fire—I mean you! Father Zeus com- 945
mands you to declare what marriage you are vaunting, by which he
is to be thrown from power. You are to tell this, moreover, with no
riddling, but each detail as it is, and not, Prometheus, to impose

a double journey on myself. You see that Zeus does not grow soft  950
before such threats as these.

PROMETHEUS. This speech is pompous talk, and full of arrogance, as suits a gods' servant! You are all new, new to power,
and you think of course that you live in a citadel free of sorrow!  955
Did I not see two tyrants expelled from it? The third I shall watch
expelled is the one ruling now; it will happen most shamefully and
most speedily. I don't seem to you, do I, to be at all afraid and
cowering before the new gods? No, I'm far from that—altogether  960
far from it! Now, you hurry back again on the road you came; for
you'll learn nothing of what you're asking me.

HERMES. You were also obstinate like this before, and it brought
you to anchor in these torments!  965

PROMETHEUS. I wouldn't change my poor success for your servitude, be quite certain!

HERMES. Better, I suppose, to be in servitude to this rock than to
be father Zeus' trusty messenger!

PROMETHEUS. (*a line missing*)...it is a duty to return insult for
insult like this.  970

HERMES. You seem to luxuriate in your present state!

PROMETHEUS. I luxuriate? I wish I might see my enemies in such
luxury!—and I count you among them.

HERMES. Why—do you blame me too in some way for your disaster?

PROMETHEUS. In one simple word: I hate all the gods who came  975
off well but maltreat me unjustly.

HERMES. I can hear the madness in you—it's no small illness!

PROMETHEUS. I'd happily be ill, if loathing one's enemies is being
ill.

HERMES. You'd be intolerable, if you enjoyed success!

PROMETHEUS. Alas for me!

HERMES. That is a word Zeus does not know.  980

PROMETHEUS. Yet time as it ages teaches everything.

HERMES. And yet you still don't know how to be sensible yourself.

PROMETHEUS. No, for I would not be talking to you, servant that
you are.

HERMES. It seems, you'll say no word of what father Zeus desires.

PROMETHEUS.   And yet if I owed him gratitude, I'd pay it.          985
HERMES.   Now there you're mocking me like a child.
PROMETHEUS.   Why, aren't you a child, and even more silly than
   that, if you expect to learn anything from me? There is no torment
   or device by which Zeus will induce me to tell these things openly   990
   until these torturing bonds are released. Therefore let him hurl his
   blazing flame, and embroil and confound everything in a feathery
   white snowstorm, and in thunderings in the earth: none of these
   will bend me into saying who is fated to throw him from his          995
   tyranny.
HERMES.   Now see if this proves helpful to you!
PROMETHEUS.   I've seen very long ago, and resolved on it.
HERMES.   You rash fool! Bring yourself, at last bring yourself to
   right thinking in the face of your agonies here.                     1000
PROMETHEUS.   You're bothering me uselessly; it's like advising a
   sea-wave! Never let it enter your head that my mind will weaken in
   womanly fear of Zeus' intention, and that I shall implore this Zeus
   I greatly loathe to free me from these bonds with palms upturned
   like a woman: I'm far from all of that!                              1005
HERMES.   If I speak I shall be saying much to no purpose, it seems;
   for you don't soften or relent at all under my entreaties, but like
   a colt new to harness you gnash the bit and fight violently against
   the reins. You are too headstrong, however, when your stratagem is   1010
   weak. Obduracy in one whose thinking is unsound has less than
   no strength on its own. Consider, though, if you are not to be
   persuaded by words of mine, the kind of storm and huge wave
   of disaster which will inescapably overtake you. First, father Zeus  1015
   will tear this jagged ravine apart with thunder and fiery lightning,
   and bury you bodily, and arms of rock will embrace you. When
   you have completed a long duration of time, you will come back       1020
   again into the light; and Zeus' winged hound, I tell you, a tawny
   eagle, will tear greedily at the great rag of your body, an uninvited
   banqueter approaching every day, and will feast from your liver
   blackened with its gnawing. Do not expect any end to such an         1025
   ordeal until some god appears to succeed to your miseries, and
   is willing to enter Hades where there is no ray of light, and to go
   among Tartarus' gloomy depths.

Deliberate accordingly, because what I assert is no fabrication    103
but spoken all too surely; Zeus' lips do not know untruthful speech,
and their every word is fulfilled. Look about you, and ponder, and
do not think obduracy better at any time than sound deliberation.    103
CHORUS.   To us, Hermes seems to speak not wide of the mark, for
he orders you to abandon your obduracy and to search for good
and wise counsel. Be persuaded! It is shameful for one who is wise
to go badly wrong.

*All three voices now turn to chanting.*

PROMETHEUS.   I knew, of course, this message he urged on me;    104
but there is nothing unseemly in an enemy suffering badly from
enemies.
And so let the double fiery flare be hurled against me,
and the heaven be convulsed by thunder and wild winds' fury;    104
and may their blast shake the earth
from its foundations, roots and all,
and an ocean-wave's surging tumult
block the orbits of the heavenly stars.
May Zeus hurl me down bodily sheer into dark Tartarus    105
in cruel spirals of compulsion—
killing me will be wholly beyond him.
HERMES.   (*to the* CHORUS) Exactly the kinds of resolve and
speech
one may hear from those with stricken minds!    105
Where does his prayer fail to hit
the wrong note? Where ease back from madness?
Well, as for yourselves,
who sympathize with his agonies,
at least go quickly away somewhere from this place,    106
so that the thunder's merciless bellowing
does not stupefy your senses.
CHORUS.   Make some other speech, and exhort me
only with what will actually persuade me:
the word you slipped in there is quite intolerable.    106
How can you order me to practise cowardice?
With Prometheus here I am willing to suffer what must be;

I have learned to hate traitors,
and there is no plague I abominate more.                                    1070

HERMES.   (*beginning to leave*) Well, at least remember what I do
    predict,
and don't blame fortune when you are hunted down by ruin;
nor ever say that Zeus threw you
into unforeseen disaster—                                                  1075
no, do not say that, for you have thrown your own selves;
knowingly, and not suddenly or unawares,
you have entangled yourselves
in ruin's inescapable net through folly.

HERMES *leaves; the* CHORUS *remain as the cataclysm noisily begins.*

PROMETHEUS.   Look now! Here is the reality, no longer mere
    words: the earth is shaking;                                        1080
its depths echo the bellowing
of thunder; branches of lightning flash out pure fire;
whirlwinds spiral with dust;
blasts from all the winds leap wildly about,                               1085
mutual discord displayed as they blow in opposition;
and the heaven is confounded with the ocean.
Such a storm hurled against me by Zeus
creates terror as it comes—too clearly!                                    1090
O my most holy mother,
O heaven revolving the light common to all,
do you see how unjustly I suffer?

*The play is over. The* CHORUS *remain immobile round*
PROMETHEUS. *The noise of the cataclysm ends.*

# Explanatory Notes

## PERSIANS

THE medieval manuscripts preserve an ancient *hypothesis* ('introduction') to the play going back to Aristophanes of Byzantium who edited Aeschylus at Alexandria in the third century BC. It was expanded by later scholars but the Aristophanic core can be identified confidently; this summarizes the action with extreme brevity, and ends with an extract from the official performance-records kept at Athens: 'the scene of the play is at the tomb of Darius. The plot is this: after Xerxes had campaigned against Greece and been defeated on land at Plataea and on sea at Salamis, he fled through Thessaly to Asia. In [the archonship of] Menon (i.e. 473/2 BC) Aeschylus won the prize for tragedy, with *Phineus, Persians, Glaucus of Potniae, Prometheus*' (not the *Prometheus* in this volume: see Introd. 2.4 Appendix p. li). There follows a list of the play-characters which includes the Queen's historical name, Atossa; but Aeschylus does not use it.

*s.d.*: for *Sousa* see n. on 16–17. The council-chamber (its presence is inferred from 141) and the royal palace from which the Queen comes by carriage (see 150 n.), and to which Xerxes and Chorus go at play end (1068), are therefore notionally off-stage; for Darius' tomb see 623 n.

1–154 This long opening passage, the entry-song (*parodos*) of the Chorus, is similar to that of the probably later *Suppliants*. It begins with 'marching anapaests', regular in rhythm, 1–64, cf. *Supp.* 1–39; it gives the play's background. Then five 'responding' pairs of stanzas in freer, danced lyric (65–139) enlarge on the present anxious predicament with moral and religious analysis (cf. *Supp.* 40–175, eight pairs of stanzas which are more emotional because the Chorus' involvement is intensely personal). The first three pairs and the epode (65–100) employ predominantly ionic metre, one of the most regular of sung rhythms and characteristic of solemnity and ritual (it occurs sporadically again in 633–80, cf. *Supp.* 1018–61); it is used here to convey the unrelenting majesty of Persian war. In the epode (93–100) anxiety nevertheless appears, leading to more irregular rhythms for the remainder of the parodos (114–39). In 140–54 this sequence is extended by a return to 'regular' anapaests, as the Chorus seem about to leave again for the council-chamber (141), only to be interrupted by the Queen's approach.

1 *who are gone*: cf. 13 and 252, sinister in prospect, for the verb's sense is often 'departed in death' (252, when the fact is made known, and 546, 915; the same verb in 60 and 178 seems to register only their having gone away). The expanded ancient *hypothesis* (see above) says that Aeschylus modelled this opening line on that of the *Phoenician Women* of his earlier contemporary tragedian Phrynichus (Introd. 2.1 p. xxi and n. 7), which began 'From the Persians who are gone we are . . .', where the verb has the same ambiguity.

2 *'the faithful'*: their official title; the Queen alludes to it at 171, 528. As such, Darius vouchsafes them explanation of Xerxes' disaster, 681.

9 [*with its many men*: a likely correction of MSS 'with its great wealth in gold', avoiding a weak repetition from 3.]

10 *flayed raw*: a rare and remarkable metaphor, lit. 'with backside flayed', an image from a pursuer cutting at a fleeing foeman's rear. Desire 'bites raw' at *Seven* 692; fear 'lacerates' at 115 below.

12 *noising anxiety for the young man*: for Xerxes. The translation is uncertain, and *noising anxiety* represents a Greek metaphor from a dog's rough snarling; it recurs in 574 of 'harsh-sounding' sorrow. At *Ag.* 449 it appears to be 'snarl hostility', but translation here as 'snarling "The man is (too) young!"' gives impossibly overt criticism of Xerxes before his defeat is reported (744); after it, and Darius' own condemnation, the Chorus do voice misgiving about his youthful rashness (782, 831) [some editors nevertheless suppose corruption or loss of text].

14 *no messenger or any horseman*: the mounted Persian couriers were uniquely fast: Herodotus 8.98.1; cf. n. on 247.

16–17 *Sousa*: the supreme Persian capital, regularly coupled with the northerly and older Medic capital *Agbatana* (e.g. 535). *Cissia*: a province.

19–59 The Chorus parade the overwhelming numbers and wide origins of the forces which attacked Greece: 19–32 Persians, 33–40 Egyptians, 41–52 Lydians and Mysians from Asia Minor, 52–9 Babylonians and peoples from all Asia. Cf. the fleet-numbers at 341–3 (n.). See Map 1.

21–2 *Amistres . . . Astaspes*: the first four of about forty individual Persians named in the play, very many of them otherwise unrecorded and perhaps invented by Aeschylus (see Introd. 2.1 p. xxii n. 9). The names are concentrated in this initial anxious roll-call, 19–59, in the Messenger's opening list of casualties, 302–31, and in the closing lament over their disaster, 955–1001;

some of them occur more than once. Their abundance and sonority lend impressiveness to the size of the eventual Greek victory.

34–40 *Nile*: Persia overcame Egypt and made it pay tribute in the sixth century: Herodotus 3.1–15; *the great nourisher*: cf. *Supp*. 855–7 and n. *Memphis*: sacred principally through the worship of Apis, the bull-god. Egyptian *Thebes* is given the adjective *ancient* which characterizes also the very old Greek city in Boeotia, *Seven* 321. *marsh-dwellers*: of the Nile-Delta, not only skilled shipmen but known to Thucydides (1.110.2) as the most warlike of the Egyptians.

41–8 *Lydians*: in W. Asia Minor. To Greeks their rich capital *Sardis* and their *soft-living* ways were bywords for effeminate luxury; their king Croesus advised his conqueror the Persian Cyrus (mid-sixth century) to make them 'women in place of men' (Herodotus 1.155.4). *chariots . . . four or six horses*: these large teams were Persian practice, as imposing signs of power, but of little use in hard warfare.

49–52 *sacred Tmolus*: this mountain, associated with the beginnings of the cult of the god Dionysus (Euripides, *Bacchae* 64), was near Sardis. *anvils against the spear*: a strong metaphor for warriors unflinching in the face of spears.

53–64 *Babylon*: the catalogue suddenly returns from W. Asia Minor to the inland Middle East; but the place name perhaps suggests the gathering-point for all the anonymous contingents from Asia, 54–61. Babylon was overrun by the Persians in 538 BC. *sword-bearing*: lit. 'short-sword-bearing', for stabbing not hacking; but probably no more than 'warlike' is meant, swords being common to all troops.

60 *flower*: a very common metaphor, 252, 926, *PV* 420, etc.

65 *s.d.*: *a solemn, sung dance*: see n. on 1–154.

65–73 *It has passed . . . city-sackers*: this line was parodied in fr. 207 of Eupolis' comedy *Maricas* of the 420s—fifty years later than *Persians*. *Helle*: in magical flight to escape her vindictive step-mother, Helle, daughter of *Athamas*, fell into the strait named after her, the Hellespont; cf. 876. *raft-bridge*: Herodotus 7.36. It is admired here but later condemned by Darius as folly, a disastrous offence to god, 725, 745–51.

74 *furious for war*: also 135; see n. on 718.

75–80 *prodigious* (lit. 'divine', i.e. 'superhuman') *flock . . . man . . . equal of god*: echoes of Homeric language, esp. of commanders as 'shepherds of the people', cf. 241 'shepherd and master', *Supp.* 767. *descendant of a golden line*: ultimately from the mythical Perseus, son of Zeus by Danae, whom he impregnated in a shower of gold. The Chorus claim Persian royal supremacy through relationship to Zeus the king, in the regular Greek manner (cf. Darius at 532 and n.)—even though the same Zeus justly punished Persian excess (827). The Persian claim is attested also by Herodotus 7.61.3, 150.2 (cf. n. on 185 below).

81–2 *black*: lit. 'blue-black'; the Greek word gives us 'cyanide (blue)'. Here, the adjective may be transferred from *snake* [some editors have altered the Greek accordingly]; but the implication is perhaps 'ominous and merciless'.

84 *Syrian*: the usual Greek name for 'Assyrian', in loose reference to the East.

87–92 *tide of men … ocean-swell*: a Homeric image, cf. *Seven* 64, 112; *people* too is a Homerism, and frequent, e.g. 127, 729.

102–113 Editors generally move these lines here so that the Chorus' pride in Persian might by both land and sea may precede, rather than follow, 93–100, where there is fresh anxiety for the outcome (cf. 8 15, 61 4). In 105–7 the images are again Homeric.

109–113 I follow most editors in thinking that these lines first restate Persian mastery of the sea (39, 76–8) but then allude to the bridge of boats (69–72); a hint of doubt in *they put their trust* becomes effective when it directly precedes 93. [*to cross* is a conjecture for the impossible MSS 'to behold', which West leaves obelized.]

93–4 *deceit by a god*: very much an Aeschylean idea, e.g. *Supp.* 110–11, *Ag.* 273, 478.

95–100 *friendly at first in fawning forward*: the Greek too alliterates on 'p(h)'. *Ruin*: working a man's destruction by first deluding him, 1007, cf. 822; *Seven* 957: see the *Oresteia*, esp. *Ag.* 386, 771, 1192, *LB* 1076. *nets*: similarly a constant image of inescapable destruction in the *Oresteia*, e.g. *Ag.* 359–60, 1375–6. [Editors agree that there has been considerable damage to the text; West too adopts a number of conjectures. The translation of *Who is there … his feet?* is insecure. The ancient commentary appears to relate this question not to a man (although masculine in the Greek) but to (female) *Ruin*, whose feet are nimble already in Homer, *Iliad* 9.505 f. The question is best taken as emphasizing 94 by repetition, and the idea is itself repeated in 100.]

116–17, 122 *'O-ah!'*: this exotic cry of grief recurs at 570, 573 = 580, 581, when the defeat is reported.

118–19 *fear that the city ... emptied of men*: text and translation insecure. In 118 *lament* expands bare *this* in the Greek, a pronoun which some editors read as part of the cry, as 'O-ah for this Persian host!'. Another difficulty is the apparent emphasis in the Greek word-order on the adjective *emptied of men*, i.e. implicitly after their death (cf. 730); to avoid this emphasis some translate 'now emptied of men', i.e. emptied of men gone to war: see n. on. l. 1, 'gone'.

120–5 *Cissian ... thudding response ... tearing their fine-linen dress*: a word-picture of demonstrative grief, in the 'kommos' or 'beating' of head, breast, and body which was accompanied by antiphonal wailing (see 908–1077 n. and Introd. 3.3. p. lxii; *LB* 24–31, 423–8), cf. *Supp.* 120–1. Both Greeks and orientals practised it, but see 135 and n.

130–1 *headland ... common sea*: elaborate wording, not satisfactorily explained, because this description of the Hellespont (69–70) names the waterway itself as linking the two sides, rather than the bridge of boats which did join them (66–72).

135–9 *wives ... softly lamenting*: 541. Greek distaste for oriental excess, perceived as effeminate, is often registered; cf. nn. on 41–8, 1072.

141 *this ancient chamber*: just off-stage (see n. on 1, *s.d.*), not the more distant 'gold-decked palace' (159, cf. 1 and 3–4) from which the Queen arrives by carriage. Some editors take the noun translated 'chamber' to refer to Darius' tomb itself, but this becomes the action's focus only at 619 ff.; also see 1 n.

145 *Danae's son*: Perseus: see on 75–80. [The text here depends upon West's own conjectures.]

149 *strong spear-shaft*: the Greek line too has marked assonance, but on 'k(h)'.

150 *s.d.: in a carriage*: 'The reader does not discover till ll. 607 ff. that the first entry of the Queen was made ceremoniously in a vehicle', Taplin, *Stagecraft* 75. *she is attended*: an inference, but safe, since she is royal; the play text is silent. *light in her eyes like that of gods*: a Homeric picture, e.g. *Iliad* 1.200 the goddess Athena's brilliant gaze upon Achilles; alternatively, her eyes shine like the heavenly bodies, sun and moon.

155 *s.d.: speak excitedly*: for the dialogue metre here see next n., at start.

155–531 A very long episode, almost entirely in speech (matched for length in Aeschylus by *Seven* 369–685). The Queen reports her dream foreboding the defeat (176–214); seeks and receives advice from the Chorus to entreat the aid of her dead husband Darius to protect herself and her son; and gets worrying answers to questions about Athens as Persia's foe, 155–248 (cf. 231–45 n.). Beginning (155–75) and end (215–48) of this first 'scene' are cast in trochaic tetrameters, the more pacy spoken verse (Introd. 3.2 p. lxi; cf. 697–758): the Queen's alarm, and anxious interrogation of the Chorus, surround her account of the dream, which is in the iambic trimeters normal for dialogue (176–214). Then in the second 'scene' the Messenger describes the naval defeat at Salamis and the equally disastrous retreat of the army overland, 246–514 (but the land-defeat at Plataea is not itself mentioned: that is left to Darius' Ghost, 800–31: see n. on 681–851 and Introd. 2.1. p. xxii n. 9). Once there has been an initial exchange between the Chorus in highly emotional lyric and the Messenger in brief statements (256–89 n.) his long narratives are carefully paced (290–514 n.) interrupted by promptings from the Queen. The episode within its own span both confirms the Queen's dream and at its end makes the Chorus' advice even more urgent: that she should placate and pray to the gods and to the dead, 515–31 (cf. 215–30).

155 *deep-girdled*: a Homeric adjective for a lady of high standing, whose clothing fell in rich folds; at *LB* 169 it registers elegance in a rich young girl.

157 *bedmate…and mother…of a god*: the Persians regarded their kings as (semi-)divine: see 80 and 631–2 and nn.

158 *unless our army's ancient fortune, etc.*: the long divine ancestry of Persian kings will bring further victory unless…; and the Queen may fear the loss of that divinity if Xerxes is heavily defeated. At 236 and 244 the Chorus make a guarded reference to Darius' disaster at Marathon (490 BC), at 475 the Queen names it outright; cf. also n. on 287–9, 652.

161–4 *a story…overturn the prosperity*: translation insecure [text and punctuation are disputed]: the 'story' is a reference to the Queen's dream which she will narrate in 176–200 (its message is certainly *in no way [her] own*); others translate as 'saying', a reference to the traditional axioms in 165–9 about wealth and its safeguarding through circumspection (cf. *Ag.* 750–62, also introduced as a 'saying'). *Wealth* is personified here and so has the divine adjective *great*: 725, used of Zeus at e.g. *Supp.* 593; without personification e.g. 755. The imagery of *kick the ground into dust* is not clear: is wealth (168) made into dust like that raised by a crashing chariot (Xerxes' chariot in the dream, 190–7, and therefore his wealth's destruction)? Cf. Shelley's 'Ozymandias'.

166–7 *massed riches…nor light shine*: an awkward pair of clauses, and opaque. The Queen seems to follow concern for wealth's self-destruction (163–4) with anxiety first that it should not be regarded as in itself a guarantee of victory when the men who possess it are no longer present (as the

Persians are away on campaign, and among them the king, 169); and second that the poor (she may mean the Greeks, despite a reference to Athenian riches at 231–8) should not enjoy success, for in her dream the Persian woman is overthrown by the Greek, 181–97. Some, however, take both clauses as general moralizing, and the second clause as typical 'automatic' contrast with the second.

168 *precious eye... saving light*: the English adjectives fill out the bare but regular Greek imagery. Orestes, like Xerxes here, is the 'light' (lit. 'eye') of his house at *LB* 934. See also 211–14 and n.

176–200 The Queen's dream is laden with symbolism and like all dreams in Tragedy forebodes a fulfilment impossible to thwart, despite all human effort (see Introd. 2.1 p. xxvi n. 14); 518–19 confirm the Queen's failure to avert it.

178 *Ionians*: comprehending all the Greeks, of the mainland and the W. Aegean seaboard: so again at 563, 949, etc., but at 771 only the latter.

185 *sisters of the same descent*: apparently an allusion to the mythical Asia and Europa, daughters of Oceanus; but Herodotus records a tradition of close Persian and Greek relationship, 6.54, 7.61–2. Countries are (grammatically) feminine, and depicted in art as women.

187 *the eastern world*: lit. 'barbarian', i.e. non-Greek, 'foreign'. The Persians in the play regularly describe themselves with this word, e.g. 255, 391, 423.

188 *quarrelling*: alluding to the hostilities preceding Darius' unsuccessful invasion in 490. Xerxes tries to compose both Greece and Persia under one rule.

198–9 *Darius... in pity*: his Ghost voices it at 733 and esp. 832–8. *Xerxes... tears the robes*: as he does in the misery of defeat, 847–8 (n.), cf. 468, 835–6, 1030; cf. Introd. 2.1 p. xxv.

201–4 *spring-water*: to purify herself from the dream and its menace. *pour an offering*: in Greek practice, a viscous mash of cereals or fruit with oil, milk, honey, wine, etc., ingredients described in 611–17; used to propitiate the dead; cf. n. on 220.

205–10 *eagle... hawk*: the Queen is again made to follow primarily Greek notions: the eagle was Zeus' bird, symbolic of his granting victory (famously at *Ag.* 111–20, 134–8), but was also an emblem of Persian kingship; its flight in face of the *hawk*, the smaller bird (i.e. the Greeks), here forebodes Xerxes' defeat despite his greater power, and suggests his seeking sanctuary with the Sun-god so prominent in Persian religion (cf. 232).

*fleeing...Phoebus...fear...friends*: the Greek alliterates here upon 'p(h)' very markedly; the intention may be to emphasize the paradox of an eagle's flight.

210–14 *Those are the frightening things I saw, etc.*: the Queen repeats but varies her fears of 161–9; her chief concern is for the continued prosperity of Persia (163–4), now vested in her son Xerxes as its master, its 'eye' (168–9); there she feared that the physical separation of wealth from its absent master might endanger it (166–7), but now she reasserts that even defeat will not imperil her son's throne: 213–14 (on these issues see Introd. 2.1 p. xxv). So her *succeed well, etc.* evades the omen of general defeat and appears selfish in asserting that only Xerxes' personal safety matters to the royal family; this is her main relief when news of the defeat comes, 299–301. Note the Chorus' careful response in 215 (n.), 218–19, 222. *answerable*: a term very familiar to Athenians, for their elected magistrates were subject to scrutiny on leaving office; also 828, *PB* 324 (and n.), cf. *Supp.* 371.

215–48 After the Queen's long speech in iambic trimeters, the metre reverts to the more emotional trochaic tetrameters: see 155–531 n.

215 *our queen and mother*: like the British 'Queen Mother'. The Chorus tactfully recognize that the Queen's principal anxiety is for her son.

220 *libations...to Earth and to the dead*: as e.g. Electra prays, seeking help from the underworld gods and from her murdered father, *LB* 125 ff. and throughout 308–475.

225 *Goodwill...from the first to judge*: such immediate confirmation is the best comfort.

231–45 The earliest surviving example of stichomythia (Introd. 3.2 p. lx). This form of exchange appears here in one of its commonest and most natural functions, the closely progressive eliciting and giving of information (cf. 715–38). No less typically, the stichomythia notches a gradually rising emotional temperature: the Queen's sudden question about Athens (230–1) leads only to answers which increase her already extreme anxiety, 242–5; and this is at once justified by the Messenger's news.

235 *so much the fullest numbers*: if Athens is overcome, the rest of Greece will hardly resist.

236 *the Medes*: see n. on 765–79.

238 *source...a lode*: a single Greek word, 'spring' metaphorically. The silver-mines of Laurium and Thoricus in Attica itself are meant. Aeschylus

alludes to the expenditure in 483 BC, three years before Xerxes' attack, of unexpectedly large income from the mines upon a reserve of ships, for use in an emergency; and so the major Athenian contribution to victory at Salamis became possible.

240 *spears . . . heavy armour*: Athenian hoplites, heavy infantry. [Some editors put 239–40 after 236, to avoid questions about the army interrupting those about wealth. West himself suspects loss of two lines after 238, and thinks of moving 239–40 after 244.]

241 *shepherd*: see 75 n.

247 *running . . . Persian*: in the theatre the man's dress as much as his haste would identify him (cf. Pelasgus and the non-Greek dress of the Egyptian Danaids at *Supp.* 234–7).

250–2 *harbour of wealth*: i.e. safety for its riches. *flower*: 60 n.

256–89 The earliest surviving 'epirrhematic' structure, in which speech from a second voice (here the Messenger) answers a first lyric voice (here, as usual, the chorus); cf. e.g. *Seven* 203–44, and see Introd. 3.3. p. lxii. These structures occur at moments of tension or stress.

270–1 *Zeus' land, the land of Hellas*: possibly a reflection of the myth which told of Hellen, after whom the Hellenes were called, as son of Zeus; possibly a suggestion that Greece was favoured by Zeus in the war (cf. Darius' Ghost at 739 ff.); possibly a mere reference to a land through the supreme god of its religion (cf. *Supp.* 5, Zeus' Egypt; 347 below Pallas Athena's Athens).

273 *Salamis*: the first mention of the great sea-battle, offered as if the Persians already know its location; in 284 the Messenger abominates its name.

275–7 *doubled-over mantles*: rich robes worn by the nobility (cf. n. on 155 'deep-girdled women'); a fatal impediment for men thrown into the sea. [*bodies all awash*: good sense, but the Greek is metrically at fault; no convincing correction has been found.]

280–9 [Text extremely insecure throughout, especially in metre, and much altered by editors. I follow West throughout, except in 281 where I accept his conjecture *friends* for MSS 'enemies' which he leaves obelized, and in 288 where I keep mainly to the MSS.]

287–9 *We may remember, etc.*: the Chorus remember Persia's defeat at Marathon: cf. nn. on 158 and 652.

290–514 The Messenger's long and vivid narratives are carefully stage-managed for variety but also for logical and climactic order (see Introd. 2.1 p. xxviii). The first (302–30) is a roll-call of the principal Persian dead, evocative merely through the multiple sonority of their names (cf. n. on 21–2), and through just a few colourful personal details. The Messenger's brief exchange with the Queen (331–52) gives a broad introduction to his detailed account of Salamis (353–470); it is briefly interrupted by the Queen (433–46) and concluded by her bleak moral commentary (473–9). Last comes the destructive land-retreat (480–514). The narration is vivid and always active, but at times slows for close-ups, esp. of the bloodshed (408–21, 454–64) and the disastrous crossing of the river-ice (500–7); the Greeks' battle-cries are heard in direct speech (402–5); Xerxes' despair and headlong flight are pictured (465–70).

299 *Xerxes himself is alive*: Aeschylus gives the Messenger the same tactful priority with the life of the Queen's son, as had the Chorus (215).

300–1 *a great light of joy*: the return of Agamemnon from Troy means such light, *Ag.* 522 (there is no deliberate play here upon 'light' in 299). *brilliant day after storm-black night*: when it brings relief to sailors, *Ag.* 900.

302–30 Many individual Persian names occur in this first description of the battle at Salamis; all are of the dead, in contrast (302 *however*) with Xerxes the survivor. The Messenger's Greek regularly mixes narrative past tenses with vivid presents, a common device; but close translation makes for awkward English, and some presents have been changed.

304 *Sileniae*: part of the landward shore of Salamis, near the place, so the ancient commentator says, where the Greeks raised their victory trophy. The name suggests an association with Dionysus: Silenus was the leader of the god's attendant satyrs (on satyr-drama see Introd. 2.5 p. liv).

307 *Ajax's ... island*: also 368. The mythical hero is meant; his father Telamon ruled Salamis. There was a report in early 2006 that the site of their palace had been identified.

309–10 *the islet which breeds doves*: ancient sources are not clear whether this description is of Salamis itself, or of the smaller island of 447, Psyttaleia. *losing fight as they buffeted*: rather weak sense, and seemingly a metaphor from fighting animals which gradually weary till they are overcome, or used here of helpless men dashed against hard rocks (965–6); for the three Persians may have been dead before the sea claimed them (cf. 305 'plunged', 313 'thrown', 964) [but the text is suspect: for 'losing fight' some MSS have 'being pounded together', and e.g. 'groaning' has been conjectured].

[315 This line, 'the leader of thirty thousand black horse', is omitted because it clashes with 314; to keep it here, loss of text must be assumed before it; some editors move the line to follow 'Artabes the Bactrian' in 318.]

319 *immigrant to a cruel land*: only to be killed and buried there; the same black irony as at *LB* 684. For the local Athenian implication of 'immigrant', see n. on *Seven* 548.

320–5 The places named in these lines are located all in W. Asia Minor; they are conquered or willing allies of the Persians, therefore. *Sardis*: 45 n. [The name *Ariomardus*, also in 38 and 967, creates a metrical anomaly in spoken verse; some editors alter it or suppose loss of text directly after it.]

340 *tenth*: because Herodotus 8.82.2 gives a larger Greek count of 380 ships, some interpret these *select* ones as additional, i.e. 'a tenth of that number' forming a separate squadron, to make a slightly more compatible total of 330.

341–3 *a thousand...two hundred and seven*: similarly Herodotus 7.89.1, 184.1; later authors round the figure down to 1,200 or 1,000 (as Aeschylus rounded Homer's 1,186 for the Greek ships attacking Troy down to 1,000, *Ag.* 45), and the number seems improbably high.

345 *some divine power* (...354 'an evil power'): Aeschylus has the Messenger begin to emphasize the divine as the true cause of Persian defeat: see Introd. 2.1 p. xxv.

348–9 *the Athenians' city still not ransacked?—Yes*: factually untrue, since Athens had been pillaged early in the attack and the news taken back to Persia, Herodotus 8.53–4. Aeschylus is probably sparing his countrymen's feelings, since the ravaged acropolis was left unrestored until long after this play's production. The idea 'a city is its men and not its wall' was a commonplace, used most famously of Athens again at Thucydides 7.77.7; cf. Sophocles, *Oedipus the King* 56.

353–471 The battle of Salamis: Aeschylus seems, from comparison of Herodotus' more complete if still difficult account (8.40–97), to have included (and perhaps enhanced) only incidents which tended to glorify the tactical supremacy of the Greeks, and especially the role of the hoplites who landed on the island of Psyttaleia (447–64). There has been repeated and detailed reconstruction of the battle, with dispute over the location of this island (447 and n.): see the Bibliography §7.1 and Map 3.

354 *avenging spirit*: to punish both Darius' earlier attack and Xerxes' defiance of god in his own attack. For such a 'spirit' see n. on *Supp.* 415, and cf. personified Ruin 99 above (95–100 n.), 1007.

355 *for a Greek man, etc.*: the Messenger implies that to deceive Xerxes, the *spirit* or *power* took living Greek form; cf. the Chorus at 93 ff. Herodotus 8.75.1 names the man as Sicinnus, in the service of the Athenian commander Themistocles.

356–7 *if black night's, etc.*: the false message (361) suggested that when dark came (as was inevitable), the Greeks would use it (inevitably) to cover the flight they were already planning.

364–5 *the sun... heaven's domain*: Aeschylus is colouring Xerxes' proclamation with a solemn dignity; cf. 369, 386, 397, and nn., and Introd. 2.1 p. xxviii.

366 ff. *position the mass of ships, etc.*: the scheme described by Herodotus 8.76.1.

369 *an evil death*: a Homeric phrase.

371 *lose their heads*: decapitation was common in the East; ordered for individuals by Xerxes at e.g. Herodotus 8.90.3, 118.4. Egyptians threaten it at *Supp.* 840.

380 *Oar-bank, etc.*: alternative, more difficult translation: 'Squadron of warships encouraged squadron.'

386 *day with its white steeds*: the Sun traversed the heaven in chariot and four (Aeschylus fr. 346), with horses white like the light (301) they carried; conversely night's chariot has black horses, *LB* 660, fr. 69.5; cf. also 428 n.

397 *striking the salty deep*: another Homeric echo, as is 402 *sons of the Greeks*.

406 *from our side a clamour*: an uncoordinated surge of noise; Aeschylus suggests to his Athenian spectators that it was inferior to the Greeks' determined and unified singing.

424 *struck our men... like tunnies*: such fish were caught in nets and hauled ashore, where they were speared or clubbed to death. Here, the Greeks from their boats kill the Persians in the water this way.

428 *night's black eye*: an expression like Euripides, *Phoenician Women* 543 'night's unlit eye'; Aeschylus appears to mean just 'night' [the most authoritative MS, however, has 'black night's eye', i.e. the moon, like *Seven* 390].

433 *sea of disaster*: possibly an ironic play upon 426–7 'groans and shrieking together took over the wide sea', but the metaphor is common enough to be almost inert, e.g. *Seven* 758, *Supp.* 470.

435–40 *middle point… outweigh it in the scale… inclining the scale*: the whole passage strongly recalls 345–6 'some power… weighting the scale to unbalance fortune'. The effect is emphasized by the repetition of *catastrophe* at the same point of the Greek verses 436 and 439.

447–9 *an island… tiny*: named Psyttaleia in antiquity (Herodotus 8.76.1); most recent historians identify it with St George, not Lipsokoutali: see Map 3. *Pan who loves the dance*: a powerful rural deity, evoked in his Salaminian haunt by Sophocles, *Ajax* 694–9; he may be named here for his association with 'panic', because more chaotic destruction soon fell upon the Persians, 457 ff. (at *Ag.* 55 he is named as a deity aiding the punishment of Troy). It is more likely that Aeschylus reflects the Athenian legend that Pan met Phidippides as he ran to Athens with the news of Marathon (490 BC, l. 475; cf. 158 n.) and told him he would help the city in the future (Herodotus 6.105.2): as here. Certainly the Athenians established a cult of Pan soon after Marathon: Herodotus 6.105.

456 ff. *(the Greeks armed)… leapt, etc.*: according to Herodotus 8.95 these Greeks were from Salamis and had been ferried over.

470 *lets it go*: some translate as 'rushes away'. Aeschylus stresses Persian disorder after the battle; Herodotus 8.97.1 records that Xerxes' flight was more deliberate, and delayed for a few days.

472 *deity… cheated the Persians of their wits*: cf. Darius at 725; also 345–54 n.

474 *famous Athens*: a commonplace of poets.

475 *Marathon*: see n. on 158.

480–1 *the ships… took hastily to flight, etc.*: this is all we hear in the play about the remnants of the Persian fleet, except for a few names in Xerxes' own tearful account, e.g. 955–1001. The Messenger now speaks only of the ruinous retreat by land, like Darius' Ghost later, 805 ff.

482–509 For the Persians' return-route by land, see Map 2.

483 *in distress from thirst near fine spring-water*: meaning disputed; explained by the ancient commentator with the idea that the thirsty Persians drank too deeply and so died, and by modern scholars that they died from being crushed in their desperate need to drink.

488 *Achaeans' land*: S. of Thessaly (Herodotus 7.196), perhaps the origin of those who later inhabited the larger and more famous Achaea of the N. Peloponnese (*Seven* 28).

492–5 *Magnesia*: a mountainous coastal land E. of Thessaly. *Axius*: the principal river of Macedon. *Bolbe*: a lake joined to the sea by a small river, and lying S. E. of *Pangaeus*. *Edonian*: a tribal name in Thessaly. For Aeschylus' liking for colourful geographical description (not always accurate, as here), see the wanderings of Io at *Supp.* 547–73, and cf. the even longer account of them in *PB* 707–35, 790–815, 827–52.

495 *a god*: Zeus, probably, is meant as god of the 'weather', not the anonymous 'power' of 354. The N. Aegean winter is cold enough 'to kill birds', *Ag.* 563.

497 *Strymon*: the major river of Thrace, 867, *Supp.* 255, *Ag.* 193; it is *holy* like all great waters, as again at *Supp.* 254; cf. the Hellespont at 745.

501 *it started ... frozen hard*: Aeschylus' Greek line lacks the usual midway word division, metrical irregularity perhaps expressing the irregular crossing; but so do e.g. 489 'and the Thessalians ... very short', where no similar intention can be imagined, and 519 'how very surely ... disaster to me'.

505 *melted*: translation uncertain, if apt, since the Greek verb too is uncertainly identified and may mean 'was pervading'.

515–6 *Too heavy your feet, etc.*: a common image for a god's punishment; cf. 911 and the Furies at *Eum.* 372–6.

518 *my dreams at night*: 176–200 and n.

520 *You judged ... too lightly* and 528 *faithful counsel ... before*: see 215–25.

523 *to Earth and to the dead*: 220; the *gifts* are solemnly enumerated, 610–18.

526 *something better ... for the future*: but Darius will reveal the further defeat already at Plataea, 816–17.

527–31 [Because the Queen does in fact return before Xerxes comes, some editors move these lines to follow 851, where the Queen faces the future after hearing from Darius why Xerxes was defeated, but when he also has not yet come (see n. on 852); but there she does not return at all. In their place here, the lines at least mark the end of the episode definitively. The text and interpretation of 528 *to your faithfulness before* were uncertain in antiquity itself.]

531 *adds...woe to the woes we have*: does the Queen fear more rash acts from Xerxes, such as retaliation at home?

532–97 This ode, like the next (623–80 and n.), begins with chanted sorrow which anticipates its general lyric character; here it is extreme grief for the dead, there it is extravagant invocation of the great and dead Darius. This formal sequence is essentially that of the *parodos* 1–154 (n.), of the *parodos* and first great ode of *Agamemnon* (40–257, 355–487), and of e.g. *Eum.* 308–96. The ode has an emotional style which intensifies as the sorrow mounts: there are many repetitions of wording, and of word- and sound-patterns within stanzas, sometimes in 'responsion' (e.g. in 550–3 = 560–3); these are typical of ritual grief (see Introd. 3.3 p. lxii). The metre is very varied, but much of the final two pairs of stanzas is cast in the 'high' lyric rhythm favoured by Pindar for his impressively evocative odes.

532 *O Zeus the king*: cf. 762–4 and n., *Eum.* 626; Homer, *Iliad* 1.175, Hesiod, *Theogony* 96, etc.

535 *Sousa and Agbatana*: 16 n.

537–40 [Regarded by some editors as out of place, since women's general grief precedes that of the war-widows; so they move the lines to follow 545.]

539–40 *wet tears soak the folds on their breast*: a frequent poetic picture, but cf. the evocation of extravagant Oriental mourning by men in 1038, 1047, 1054 ff.; women also *LB* 22–31, 423–8. Alliteration in the Greek of 537–43 helps the effect.

542 *husbands newly wed*: 135–9 n.

555 *Darius so unharmed*: the Chorus ask why Darius succeeded, when he had campaigned with the same ambitions, and used some of the same methods, as Xerxes; the idea recurs in 663 = 671, 781, 786, 855. If the Persian defeat at Marathon is meant, Darius himself had not been there: cf. 652, 865–7 and nn.

558–9 The Greek metre is faulty and the text therefore uncertain in the words translated as *oars and dark hulls all alike*; but they may echo Homer's regular description of 'well-balanced' ships, and *dark* translates 'dark-eyed', possibly a reference to the eyes often painted on prows and visible in archaic vase-paintings: see n. on *Supp.* 716.

567 *their ways all wintry*: 501–5.

568–71 *these men, etc.*: the Chorus revert to those killed in the sea-battle. *dying first*: in the sea (420–2), before those killed on the land-march of retreat, 482–507. *Cychrean*: Cychreus was a mythical hero-king of Salamis, who according to Pausanias 2.36 appeared as a snake to defend his home-island against the Persians. [*in shattered vessels*: slightly expansive translation of a verb 'have been shattered' supplied here by conjecture when the original word seems to have been copied erroneously after 'childless father' in the metrically corresponding l. 580.]

573 = 582: *sorrow high to heaven* and *sorrow sent by heaven*: these words occupy the same positions in the Greek stanzas.

577–8 *voiceless children of the undefiled sea*: 'dumb' fish; Aeschylus may mean that the fish can tell no tale of the hideous injuries to the dead. For the 'kenning' cf. e.g. 'dust, the voiceless messenger' at *Seven* 82, *Supp.* 180, *Ag.* 496; cf. the heaps of dead at 819 below. *undefiled*: naturally pure, the sea as common purifier of pollution but unaffected by it (e.g. Homer, *Iliad* 1.344, Euripides, *Iphigenia in Tauris* 1039, 1193, etc.).

582–3 *become old on hearing their now absolute loss*: translation most insecure [I follow only in part West's own suggestion 'become old men completely on hearing their loss'; he compares 262–5].

584–94 *But the people . . . with the release of might's yoke*: regarded by editors as 'Greeks' wishful thinking', since Persian control of W. Asia Minor was only gradually and not fully dismantled during the fifth century. Aeschylus may be alluding to the anti-Persian defensive confederacy formed soon after Persia's defeat, the 'Delian League' (Thucydides 1.96); see Introd. 2.1 p. xxiii. *Bloodshed staining, etc.*: distorting the truer picture of 450–64, most Persians being killed at sea or drowned before coming ashore on Salamis.

598–622 The Queen returns with her offerings to Darius and the dead, 609–18. So she is ready to make them in silence while the Chorus summon up Darius: see 619–22, followed by the ode 623–80 (n.). Her single speech is one of the shortest 'episodes' in Tragedy; cf. *Supp.* 600–24, Introd. 3.1 p. lviii.

598 *s.d.*: *she may be attended*: see n. on 607–8.

598–606 *trouble*: deliberately repeated and recalled (cf. also 600), in mild ring-composition, to prepare for ritual efforts to ameliorate it, through summoning the dead Darius for comfort and explanation, 607–22.

599–602 *surge... tide... breeze... blow*: the elements of water and air are natural metaphors for fortune's turns; cf. e.g. *Seven* 708, 758, 795.

607–8 *without the carriage and finery I had before*: Taplin, *Stagecraft* 99–100 infers that the Queen now wears black dress appropriate to the occasion, and that she is carrying the offerings herself, unattended; while the play-text says nothing on these last two points, the lack of attendants seems contrary to the Queen's royal dignity: see n. on 150.

609–10 *libations to... appease the dead*: notably at *LB* 15, 44 ff., 85 ff., Clytemnestra appeasing Agamemnon. The Queen is enacting the Chorus' advice of 216–23 given after her dream, but now in the horror of its fulfilment, 517–26; for the latter, cf. *Seven* 710–11.

611–18 *milk... honey... water... vine*: see n. on 204. The poetically allusive list stresses the natural purity of the offerings, and impresses the audience like the awed invocation of Darius which follows (and ends when his Ghost appears) 623–80. Details: *sacred cow*: 'pure' because unspoiled by working. *its (distillation)*: 'her' in the Greek: bees are invariably female in antiquity, except for the 'king'. *ancient vine*: perhaps literally, mature vines yielding the best grapes, but 'ancient' may be transferred to vine from wine, just as *pale* appears transferred from oil to the *leaves* of the *olive*, naturally and in poetry often 'grey-green'; wine is included here, but absent from offerings to the underworld Furies at *Eum.* 107, 860. *flowers*: probably for ritual wreaths, laid on a tomb to accompany offerings at *LB* 95. *Earth the mother of all*: cf. *Seven* 18, *PB* 90.

619–22 *good words over these libations, etc.*: similarly, Electra invites the chorus of women-slaves to 'crown' the libations to her father with ritual song, *LB* 149–51.

621 *the god Darius*: 157 n.

623 *s.d.*: Perhaps the central altar 'becomes' for this scene notionally Darius' tomb, as object of the Queen's offerings and as centre of the Chorus' dance; similar problems arise for Agamemnon's tomb in *Libation Bearers*, which is alluded to vaguely at the play's start but focuses the action ever more strongly, esp. at 306 and 584. Since this altar was not large enough to conceal the actor playing Darius until he 'ascends' at 681 (see 659), making realism impossible, scholars have speculated how any theatrical effect was managed. Opinions vary between entry from one side, from behind a rocky outcrop still standing to one side of the *orkhêstra* at this date, or a temporary structure there, and up and over the terrace-wall backing the

performance-area; either of the last would achieve more impact than by the actor's merely walking into view. Cf. Introd. 2.5 p. liv.

623–80 The Chorus passionately invoke Darius. Nostalgic praise of him pervades 634–64, renewing the note of contrast with Xerxes' headstrong defeat struck first by the Chorus in their previous ode at 548 ff.; it is a theme of Darius' own message to the Queen and Chorus (see esp. 739–52, 780–6, 818–31), and it recurs in greatly changed proportions, emphasizing Darius' greatness, in the following ode, 852–907 (n.). For the general character of this ode 623–80, see n. on 532–97; here too repetitions and elevated style are common: see nn. on 635, 664, 672–80, 679–80. The metre is again very mixed; a marked infusion of the 'hieratic' ionic rhythms found in 65–100 suits the Chorus' awe here: see 1–154 n.

625 *the escorts of the dead*: see 629 n.

629 *Earth* is entreated as the god of the dead's resting-place (cf. 640), *Hermes* as the divine escort of the newly dead (*LB* 165 and 124 5) and of their spirits when temporarily released (630 below), *Hades* as god-*King of those below* (*Supp.* 791, cf. 650 n. below). Aeschylus allows the Persians to appropriate Hermes as a Greek god, as they do Zeus (532, etc.); for Hermes as 'Greek', see *Supp.* 220.

631–2 *any further cure*: beyond what may be got by the Queen's prayers to the gods both heavenly (522) and infernal (523–6, 621–2); the wording recurs in Agamemnon's famous quandary at Aulis, *Ag.* 199–200. *he alone of mortals*: Darius has been a 'man' (647, 650) and died (634, 645–6), but is now a divinity (620, 634, 642), just as he was called 'god' in life (157, 655, 711), cf. his son Xerxes 'born the equal of god', 80.

635 *my Persian words clear*: the detail seems artificial and redundant, but the wording as far as *lament* registers Greek perception of Asiatic grief as extreme in manner and sound, 541 and n. The lament is self-referential, like 939 (n.) and esp. 1038–77 (cf. *LB* 423–8); its *changing* rhythm is expressed through music and metre, which is very fluid here. Invocations needed explicit clarity if they were to be effective: *Supp.* 117, *LB* 315–17, 418.

640 *Earth and other rulers of the dead*: cf. the appeals to 'send up' Agamemnon at *LB* 405, 489–90, cf. 399.

643 *born at Sousa*: the royal capital (16 n.); but Darius' father was a provincial, 765–79 n.

647 *Dear friend, etc.*: cf. 557 'dear ruler', 743 (Darius) 'my friends'. Strabo 15.730.8 records an inscription on Darius' tomb: 'he was a friend to his friends'; but this is a cliché of all cultures, and the dead Agamemnon is similarly praised at *LB* 355; *dear is his tomb*; cf. *LB* 106 'I respect your father's tomb like an altar'.

650 *Aïdoneus*: a variant poetic or ritual name of Hades (or Aïdas), retaining its supposed etymology <u>a-id-</u> 'not seen', i.e. 'The Unseen One' or 'The One Not To Be Seen'.

651 *Darian*: possibly a dialect-influenced form of the name, possibly a popular form (the -<u>i</u>- is a short vowel, against the long one in 'Darius'); also in 662 = 671. The Greek form of the Eastern word 'shah' in 658 (n.) also ends unusually in -<u>n</u>.

652 *neither would he ever lose men*: Aeschylus contrasts wise father and rash son as kings, by presenting Darius as bringing no harm in war (555 f. and n.); he ignores his campaign losses in Thrace (Herodotus 6.44–5) and above all at Marathon (6.113.2, 7.1.1: see n. on 158).

655–6 *his mind godlike*: Homer's description of Priam of Troy, *Iliad* 7.366; but the adjective here merely follows the general Persian view of their royalty: 157 n., 621 n. [656 *led his armies well*: MSS corrupt; this is the likely sense only.]

658–60 An exotic word-picture of opulent Persian royalty, *saffron* being its emblematic colour (as of many Oriental potentates); Darius is invoked to appear in the majesty of life, to advise with the same authority. *shah*: translates an Oriental, perhaps Phrygian, title. *tomb's high summit*: the term used in 411 of a ship's ornate stern. *tiara's crest*: all noble Persians wore a tall headdress, and the King's was uniquely pointed.

664 *father in safety*: of Darius again, at 855 (n.). The line is repeated in refrain at 671, marking the climax of the invocation (similar effects at e.g. *Ag.* 121 = 139 = 159, cf. 694–5 = 700–1 below).

667 *Stygian*: the Styx was a river which led through Hades and its perpetual gloom of death. For such *murk*, cf. *Eum.* 379; *LB* 52 has 'blackness covers the house through the death of its master'.

672–80 The Chorus end with bleak despair and incomprehension which only a voice beyond the living world can ease; Aeschylus tries to convey this crisis through extreme metrical effects [which led to hopeless corruption in the MSS at 675–8; the general meaning is, however, clear].

676–8 *double...failures*: the naval defeat at Salamis and the death-strewn land-march back home, known to the Chorus from the Messenger; Darius himself will reveal the third catastrophe for Xerxes, the land-defeat at Plataea (816–17).

679–80 *three-banked*: banks of oars, again at 1074. *ships no more*: the rhetoric of grief accommodates a poetic trope first attested here, lit. 'ships non-ships', a plangent oxymoron; so e.g. *Eum.* 1033 'children (who are) non-children', i.e. ageless (the Furies).

681 *s.d.*: The staging of Darius' appearance is much discussed: see 623 n.

681–851 Darius' Ghost: effective drama. The other ghost in Aeschylus' surviving plays, that of Clytemnestra in *Eum.* 94–139, is more briefly on stage but powerful in a different way, because she appears suddenly of her own accord to wake the sleeping Furies into avenging her. Aeschylus may have liked ghosts on stage, for he wrote a *Ghost-Raisers* (frs. 273–8), probably a satyr-play, a burlesque upon Odysseus' summoning up of the dead in Homer, *Odyssey* 11. The ghost of Trojan Priam's murdered son Polydorus appeared in Sophocles' fragmentary *Polyxena* and Euripides' surviving *Hecuba*: in both the ghost was prophetic, one function of Darius here, for he confirms Xerxes' ragged return (833–6: 1019), as the Queen dreamed it (198–200). Aeschylus' main purpose with Darius is deeper: he interprets Persia's present and future from its past. In his long speeches 739–52, 759–86, and 800–839 he explains and links them, by contrasting the attitudes and conduct of himself and Xerxes; more importantly still, he gives the fullest explanation yet of the disasters as the work of the gods, a causation already advanced briefly by the Chorus (282–3, 515–16, 532 ff.), the Queen (294, 472, 598–606), and the Messenger (345–7, 354). See Introd. 2.1 p. xxv.

Darius needs to enquire about the fact of the defeat at Salamis and the retreat by land (693, 715–39), but is able to recount the land-defeat at Plataea himself (803–18). Although it is possible to read these last lines as an extrapolation of the oracles Darius knew while living (800–2), Aeschylus' dramaturgical need overcomes logic (for another example see n. on *Seven* 720–91): he is emphasizing for the spectators the significance of Darius' historical and moral analysis, as well as encouraging their continued vigilance against Persian ambitions: see the Introd. 2.1 p. xxii, and the n. on 852–907. For Darius' account of his predecessors as kings of Persia, and his own succession, see 765–79 n.

681–2 *Faithful among the faithful*: the Chorus used this title themselves (2); the Queen alluded to it in her appeal to them at 528. In 681–2 the Greek has striking assonances, which the translation cannot reflect, but except in *labour lies upon this land* they seem not to emphasize the meaning; cf. 751, 1041 and nn.

683 *groans...stricken...furrowed*: the last two words apply metaphorically to a battered country, all three allude to the battered bodies of its mourners (635 n.). Darius has heard the mourning through the earth.

687–8 *no easy way, etc.*: at Euripides, *Hecuba* 49 the Ghost of Polydorus appears only after persuading the infernal gods to release him.

690 *better at taking than releasing*: a grim euphemism like *Eum.* 339–40 'each comes down below the earth; and after death he is not too free'.

691 *my authority among them*: similarly the dead Agamemnon is pictured as powerful at *LB* 335 ff., and the dead Achilles by Homer at *Od.* 11.485.

694–6 = 700–2 The correspondences in sense, word division and sound (cf. 623–80 n.) here express the awed formality of address to a king, above all one returning from the dead; the words suggest Persian obeisance, 147. For a subject's fear to under- or over-please a king, cf. the chorus at *Ag.* 785–6.

697–9 Darius answers the first stanza of the Chorus with trochaic tetrameters (for this verse see n. on 155–531), and this metre continues during his exchange with the Queen.

706–8 *Human suffering, etc.*: the anticipatory consolation is directed at those whose old age (Chorus 682, Queen 704) has outlived Darius' prosperity.

713 *in a brief space*: Darius is anxious for no delay, 692.

715–38 A second 'interrogative' stichomythia, which like the earlier 231–45 (n.) slowly darkens in mood.

715–17 *feuding... Which of my sons*: Darius had three children by a first wife, and four, including Xerxes, by his second, the Queen here. Herodotus 7.3.4 implies that she helped Xerxes be named by Darius as his successor.

718 *furious for war*: of Xerxes also 74, 754 (cf. Introd. 2.1 p. xxv); it is a variant of Homer's frequent adjective for Ares the war-god.

722–5 *Helle's strait*: the Hellespont (n. on 70 for the name). *Bosporus*: at the opposite end of the Sea of Marmara, and used here and 746 as a synonym for the Hellespont, to stess the enormity of what Xerxes did. *some great god, etc.*: 681–851 n., end of first paragraph; Introd. 2.1. p. xxv. All crossings of water risked some offence to its deity. The unnatural bridging must have presumed upon divine acquiescence at least, but here the Queen says that a god encouraged the human offence. Aeschylus makes Darius criticize as folly against god (750–1) a mode of crossing which the historical king had himself used to reach Thrace in 513 BC (Herodotus 4.83.2), and against which he had himself been advised by one of his nobles (according to Herodotus 7.10.b.1, c.1).

728 *Defeat... at sea destroyed the forces on land*: the fleet's remnants fled, abandoning the army to its disastrous march home, 480–511.

730 *emptiness of men*: 118 (n.), 718, 761.

731 *fine power of support*: a war-host described through its function, like *Supp.* 721, *Ag.* 47, 73.

732 *none survives*: heavy duplication of *all destroyed* for full emphasis, like the redundancy in 734 [but the phrase is conjectural, the MSS having the grotesque error 'and no old man', which West leaves obelized].

736 *the bridge*: Herodotus 8.117.1 says that storms had destroyed it before the return.

739–52 Darius' explanation begins with his awareness while living of oracles prophesying disaster (739–42): see Introd. 2.1. p. xxvi. Herodotus records various such oracles, 8.77.1, 96.2; 9.43.2. The Queen's dream (176 ff.) has been a subsequent warning.

742 *When a man shows haste, etc.*: so also the Queen at 724. The idea and phrasing are proverbial, cf. Aeschylus fr. 395 'God usually shares a victim's haste' and Euripides fr. 432.2 'God too cooperates with a sufferer'.

745–8 *Hellespont... Bosporus*: 722–5 n. *sacred*: epithet of any extraordinary natural feature, e.g. 494 and *Supp.* 254 the major river Strymon. *bonds... hammered fetters*: the bridge of boats (69–72) was held in place by iron anchors according to Herodotus 7.36.

751 *huge and hard-won wealth*: an attempt, with two English alliterations, to reproduce a single one across three Greek words, which apparently emphasizes yet again the importance to Persian royalty of wealth and its retention: cf. 163, 168, 250, 755–6—and contrast 842 (Introd. 2.1. p. xxiv).

753 *The company of evil men*: Persians, like the ambitious Mardonius (Herodotus 7.5–6), as well as Greeks, like the vindictive Pisistratid tyrants exiled from Athens, who hoped that the Persians might restore them (7.6.2). For the moral idea of tainted associates, cf. *Seven* 599–608.

755 *unmanly... spear-fighting indoors*: implying that he preferred women's company (a reproach levelled at Aegisthus, the cowardly paramour of

Clytemnestra, *Ag.* 1224, 1671). At 299–301 the Queen's doting love for Xerxes has been made plain; cf. 846–51 below.

**759–851** The Greek dialogue metre reverts from emotional trochaic tetrameters to the usual iambic trimeters, as Darius sets out the history of the Persian throne (759–86) and then, in response to the Chorus' questioning, foretells and explains the Persians' disastrous retreat from Greece (787–831). Then he makes his farewells (832–51).

**762–4** *Zeus bestowed this honour, etc.*: Aeschylus gives Persian Darius the Greek attribution of all mortal kingship to Zeus as himself king of gods: 532 n.

**765–79** *Medus, etc.*: the following account of the Persian royal succession is not far from that of historians today; in just one or two important details it matches the celebrated cliff-face inscription at Behistun ordered after his succession by the historical Darius and intermittently continued (alluded to by Herodotus 3.88; illustrated and cited in part in *Omnibus* 25 (1993), 15–19). Aeschylus knows that power passed from Medic (765–7) to Achaemenid Persians (clan-names), to Cyrus first (768 n.); he gets right Darius' succession to a murdered usurper (775 f.: n.); but he omits Darius' own parentage, from Hystaspes, a provincial governor (Behistun, Herodotus 1.209–10). *Medus* may be not a personal but a clan-name, a king as anonymous as his son in 766 [some editors think that Cyaxares is meant, and that 'next' in 766 refers to Astyages]. Praise of the son's undefined wisdom in 767 is nevertheless remarkable [some editors move the line to follow 'friends' in 769 or 'duty' in 777].

The purpose of this catalogue of kings is made plain in 759–64 and 780–6: Xerxes' foolish disaster ends a long sequence of wise Persian conquest and expansion.

**763** *Asia rich in flocks*: the ornamental phrase appears to originate from the Greeks in W. Asia Minor themselves.

**767** *steered his heart*: for this nautical metaphor of the mind, cf. *Ag.* 802; of government, cf. *Seven* 2–3, 62, etc.

**768–72** *Cyrus*: he deposed his grandfather Astyages (possibly the implication of *whose rule brought peace to all his kin*), conquered the Medes, 'acquired the Lydian and the Phrygian peoples and ravaged all Ionia' (cf. Herodotus 1.28) and 'ruled all Asia' (1.130.3). *the god was not his enemy*: the conquered Lydian king Croesus says to Cyrus at Herodotus 1.124.1: 'the gods watch over you, else you would never have attained so much good fortune.'

773–7 *Cyrus' son*: Cambyses, whose violent conduct (Herodotus 3.80.2) Darius does not mention, despite criticizing his brother *Mardus'* behaviour—but the Behistun inscription says that Cambyses killed Mardus, and Darius here thinks that Mardus was rightly assassinated. A usurper impersonated the dead Mardus and took the throne (he is named as Smerdis both in the Behistun text and at Herodotus 3.61, etc.); but see the next n.

776–9 *Artaphrenes*: the man apparently called Intaphrenes by Herodotus 3.70, etc., who like the great Behistun inscription names neither him nor *Maraphis* as Persian kings. [778 was therefore doubted as genuine by ancient scholars and some modern editors.] Indeed, the text of 778–9 is uncertain, but that of West translated here conforms with Herodotus 3.84–7, where the assassins of Smerdis (774 n.) determined the succession by recourse to lots. Aeschylus associates Artaphrenes, as leader in the plot (775–6), with Darius in the immediate succession, before he fell victim to Darius' own trickery; in 779 Darius no more than alludes to his apparent 'fixing' of the outcome (he contrived that his horse should neigh and this be taken as an omen, according to Herodotus 3.85–7).

781 *I did not bring so large a disaster*: see 652 n.

782 *rash thinking*: 'rash' is not expressed, but implicit in the Greek idiom; cf. 744. There are two dialect oddities in the Greek, which suggest that Aeschylus may be echoing a widespread Greek saying about youth.

783 *my instructions*: perhaps an invention of Aeschylus, to maximize the contrast between the grave's wisdom and youth's arrogance (Darius at 827; cf. also his 830–1).

794 *kills... through famine*: as it did the starving Persians in retreat, 489 f., Herodotus 8.115.2. Xerxes was warned of this danger before the campaign, 7.49.5.

796–9 *the army which has now remained*: that under Mardonius, in Boeotia, 805–6, Herodotus 9.15. Darius appears to mean a chosen force, 803; the Messenger spoke of them loosely as the army left behind, 482. *Is not the whole Persian army to cross*: but the Chorus were told by the Messenger that almost all had already perished, 508–10.

800–1 *if one is to have any trust*: a formula of precautionary understatement; of oracles also *LB* 297–8. *prophecies*: presumably those he named in 740–1.

809–12 *plundering gods' statues*: of their rich decoration. Persian sacrilege in Greece: Herodotus 5.102.1 (in return for Greek sacrilege at Sardis), 8.109.3.

813–15 *For their evil actions... they suffer no less*: almost the philosophy of the *Oresteia, Ag.* 176–8, *LB* 314, etc.; cf. Introd. 1 p. xviii. *no solid floor... well up still*: text insecure, partly conjectural, and mixing metaphors; 'no floor' implies no visible origin and therefore no end to troubles which are still flooding out [some editors write 'the fountain of their troubles is not yet quenched, they well up...'].

817 *in the Plataeans' land*: the first precise location of the defeat (Herodotus 9.16 ff.), inflicted chiefly by Peloponnesian, esp. Spartan, infantry (*Dorian*); at 482 the Messenger named just 'the Boeotians' land', like Darius at 806.

818 *to the third generation*: a solemn formula, *Seven* 744 (n.).

819 *declare voicelessly*: for this conceit, cf. also 577–8 and n.

822 *folly... reaps... tears*: image as in the spurious verse *Seven* 601 'the ploughland of ruinous folly reaps death as its crop'.

823–5 *reward*: sardonic: 'penalty' is meant (cf. 827 'punisher'), as when at *Seven* 1021 Polynices goes unburied for his treachery. *remember Athens*: Darius after his defeat at Marathon ordered a slave to say three times at every meal 'Master, remember the Athenians': Herodotus 5.105.2.

827–8 *Zeus... punisher*: cf. *Seven* 485 and e.g. Euripides, *Children of Heracles* 387 'Zeus punishes thoughts which are too proud', a commonplace. *auditor*: 213 n. Persian Darius arrogates Greek Zeus as the supreme god: 532 and n.

829–31 *excessive boasting*: heavily repeating 827, that too recalling 808, 820, 825; cf. Introd. 2.1. p. xxiii. [In 829 *if you desire* text and translation are very insecure.]

832–4 *Xerxes'... mother... go to meet your son*: see on 846–51.

837 *soothe him*: Darius' command to the Elders at 530.

841–2 *give your spirits pleasure day by day*: 'Eat, drink, and be merry' is a common enough sentiment throughout antiquity, but here seems dissonant on the lips of Darius, as if the poet in 842 has him cynically give advice he did not himself follow. Aeschylus, however, sometimes uses trite maxims to emphasize important moments or ideas (e.g. *Seven* 719, Eteocles' farewell to life). Darius' last words here match his advice to Persia to learn from his mistakes, to recover its happiness, 787–91; furthermore, the words are an ironic headline for the lamentation which now takes over the play: see nn. on 852–907, 908–1077.

849–51 *fine clothing, etc.*: the Queen's concern for the immediate outward restoration of royal finery seems trivial to us, but it was Darius' own command, 833–6, and an element both literal and symbolic of her dream, 199–200; cf. Introd. 2.1. p. xxvii. Her anxiety serves to remove her plausibly from the stage, and in fact she neither reappears nor is even mentioned again; her presence would mar the concentration now on Persia's greatness and fall, in the actions of Darius and Xerxes: so Taplin, *Stagecraft* 120. Xerxes enters after the Chorus' ode at 907, still in rags, and the emotional emphasis returns wholly to his personal humiliation from the Persian defeat. [The Greek text of 850 is corrupt and so far without cure, even if the sense is good; West entertains also the loss of a whole line. Some editors 'explain' the disappearance of the Queen by moving ll. 527–31 after 851, so leaving the work of soothing him entirely to the Chorus, 530.]

852–907 The Chorus mark Darius' departure with further evocation of his greatness, at first in general terms, 852–64, then with details of his conquests, 865–902. The few lines spared at the end, 903–7, for the contrast with Xerxes' defeat (623–80 n.), now stand out more strongly; but this ending picks up precisely a point with which the ode begins: Darius ruled without defeat like a god (854–7); the defeat is now equally a god's doing (904: a major emphasis in Darius' own analysis, 681–851 n.)—and it immediately precedes the defeated son's sudden entry at 908. While the ode lists Darius' many conquests in the E. Greek world (some of the names coincide with Darius' list in the Behistun inscription), it does not mention his defeats in Thrace (see 652 n., 781). This emphasis on the Greeks perhaps comforted the play's contemporary Greek audience, esp. the Athenians; for many of the places named, the islands above all, were already free of Persian control and now federated to oppose it (585–94 n.).

The ode has a certain amount of topographical colour, like the Messenger's reports of Salamis and the land-retreat, but much of it is notional (870–5 n., 880–97 n.). The metre is heavily dactylic, 'epic' in feel (cf. e.g. *Ag.* 104–59, the preliminaries of the Trojan War), and again suggestively solemn: this is eulogy of the dead.

855–6 *safe in his cause, safe from defeat*: recalling the praise of Darius at 555 ( n.), etc.

859–60 *strong as towers … venture*: a suitably Homeric tone (*Iliad* 13.152, cf. our 873, *Supp.* 956) for this stress upon Persian arms [plausibly created by West's text, in which he prints his conjecture *for every venture* but keeps his *in their formations* to the apparatus, obelizing the MSS; they have (approximately, and unmetrically) 'laws strong as towers directed everything'].

863 [*back home to* is an editor's supplement; the MSS are again unmetrical.]

865–7 *he took without crossing... or leaving his hearth*: taking the credit from his commanders, Herodotus 8.102.2–3. *Halys*: the river historically separated Medic Persia from Lydia in S. Asia Minor, Herodotus 1.72.2, etc.; see Map 1.

870–5 *the Thracians' Acheloïd settlements*: Aeschylus' geography is unclear, perhaps founded on loose reports and deliberately colourful, like the account of the land-retreat in 482–511 (*Strymon* was named at 497). *Acheloïd*: the place name is allusive, apparently connoting any fine, freshwater river; only one major historical river Acheloûs is known, but it was in W. Greece (Herodotus 2.10.3), not Thrace.

876–9 *those proud in their sites round Helle ... Pontus*: long-established places, important for trade, around the Hellespont and the Propontic gulf (the Sea of Marmara), and northwards on the E. shore as far as the Bosporus near the Black Sea (*Pontus*).

880–97 Aeschylus takes us from N. to S. through the islands of the Aegean round into the E. Mediterranean, with a certain freedom in their relative positions; see Map 2. (In the translation I have tended to keep the modern Greek names.) 891–4 *the seat of Icarus*: the island Icaria in the S. E. Aegean, named from the boy's mythic fall into the sea when his wings failed.

895 *Salamis, whose mother-city, etc.*: a colony on Cyprus of the Athenian Salamis; for the latter's 'hateful name' see 284–5.

898–900 *the Ionian territory*: the W. and S. W. seaboard of Asia Minor, colonized by mainland Greeks and rich through trade in natural products. [The Greek text in 900 is badly damaged and left obelized by West; *he ruled* has almost certainly invaded from 890; if *in his wisdom* is sound, the Chorus are repeating their compliment to Darius at 867.]

907 *the blows at sea*: the comprehensive defeat at Salamis stays with the Chorus more than the land-defeat at Plataea. The Greek word 'blows' evokes too the blows dealt by god, e.g. *Ag.* 367.

908–1077 Xerxes' return and extreme grief. The play's end is unbroken lyric lament, after a brief, chanted exchange with the Chorus, 908–21; similarly, *Seven* 822–1004 (see nn. there); though comparable in form, the ending *Eum.* 916–1046 is, however, celebratory, with one short interruption by the goddess Athena, 1021–31. Our long lyric sequence is still more remarkable directly after the ode of 852–907, even if that is eulogy (see n.); it is wholly antiphonal from 923 on, whole stanzas, part-stanzas, single lines, and even shared lines being exchanged, always in exact responsion.

It is a *kommos*, a strongly rhythmic lament. It moves from the invitation to extreme grief in the first stanzaic pair, 931–49, through naming of many of the dead in the second two pairs, 950–1001, to the *kommos* proper in 1002–77; there an almost total breakdown into single-line voice parts simulates the rhythmic 'beating' and tearing of head, hair, body, and clothes, which gives the *kommos* its name, and is called for by the mourners from 1038 (1040 = 1047 = 1066, 1046, 1054, 1060, 1062), as is copious weeping (1038, 1047, 1065) and wailing (1040, 1050, 1058, etc., cf. 988). The frenzied ending abandons stanzaic form altogether, 1066–77. All is full of the wild ejaculations of grief, many 'outside the metre', remarked in 532–97 (n.). Such *kommoi* are an essential and seemingly original part of tragic drama, persisting into late Euripides at the end of the fifth century. In Aeschylus, cf. *Seven* 870–1004 noted above, and, best known, the tripartite *kommos* between Orestes and Electra, and their supporters the Chorus, both mourning and invoking their dead father whom they intend to avenge, *LB* 306–475. See also Introd. 3.3 p. liii.

908 *s.d.* Xerxes enters in ragged robes (1030; Darius had warned of these, 833–6), but he still carries a quiver (1020–3) if not, it seems, also the bow which is the chief emblem of Persians kings in war (556, cf. 85, 145, 926, etc.). The text gives no indication that he is attended, and he may well be on foot. All these effects signal his complete humiliation; they would be destroyed if he entered in a chariot (a popular inference from 1000–1: see n.): so Taplin, *Stagecraft* 121–3. This scene in its simple power anticipates many final moments of broken royalty in later tragedy, such as that of Oedipus in Sophocles (*Oedipus the King*) and Hecuba in Euripides, *Trojan Women*. See also Introd. 2.1 p. xxvii.

915 *death... cloaked me*: a Homerism ( e.g. *Iliad* 12.116); of covering earth 646.

921 *culled*: again at 953, cf. *Supp.* 666 'shear away (youth's) flower'.

924–5 *slain for Xerxes, who crammed Hades with Persians*: remarkably forthright language, not least in the hearing of Xerxes himself; but the Chorus make him only a perfunctory greeting (929: n.) and voice sympathy only from 1031 when caught up in his violent grief. [The forthrightness, and an ancient paraphrase of this line explaining *who crammed Hades* as Ares, the war-god (cf. 952), has caused some editors in fact to replace Xerxes' name with 'Ares'. *are gone to Hades* is a conjectural replacement for an unexplained word or name qualifying *heroes*, which West nevertheless retains as sound, noting an ancient gloss 'a Persian tribe'; '(many heroes) of Agbatana' (961, cf. 16 n.) is also conjectured.]

929 *King of our country*: a very flat address [sometimes emended or deleted, therefore].

935–49 *Mariandynian*: a people of N. Asia Minor known for their ritual dirges. At *LB* 423–8 the Chorus of women-slaves captured from Troy describe their extremely demonstrative grief with remarkable vocabulary which includes the names of two other Oriental peoples; cf. also on 1054 below. 942 *turned itself round*: for such 'change' in Persian fortunes cf. 158. 946 *the house's*: the Persian royal house, as in 933. [Much of the Greek text in 944–6 is most insecure, but the general sense is clear enough; in 944–5 West has made and printed particularly bold conjectures in trying to rescue the sequence of sorrows.]

951–4 *Ionians*: the Athenians in their fleet are meant, to which some islands in Ionia or the E. Aegean, not overrun by the Persians, sent ships. *warfare*: the name of the war-god Ares is here depersonalized, but retains an adjective appropriate to the god (translated as *turned the battle their way*). The *sea* and the *shore* are again those of Salamis, where so many Persians died (273, 310, 413, etc.; cf. 965–6); *death-dark*: this is the implication of a Greek adjective meaning lit. 'by night', here uniquely applied to the sea.

958–99 Aeschylus again parades the names of prominent Persians, historical, otherwise unrecorded, and invented: see nn. on 21–2, 302–30.

964–5 *Tyrian ship*: i.e. 'Eastern', as vague in reference as 'Phoenician' (a synonym) at 410. *Salamis*: a colony on Cyprus (895 n.): Xerxes was returning by sea to Tyre, the quickest route for Persia.

967 [In [*Cry out*]... *Where* the MSS are metrically unsound, and left obelized by West; I adopt a conjectural supplement corresponding with 955.]

978 *choicest flower*: for the metaphor see 60 n. [restored by conjecture here. Indeed the text of 978–86 is full of uncertainties in the form, or even presence, of the proper names, and in metre].

979 *your... watching eye*: at Herodotus 1.114.2 a child, elected 'king' by his playmates and destined to be the Persian king Cyrus, appoints one of them 'the eye of the king'; but Xenophon, *Education of Cyrus* 8.2.11 corrects a belief alluded to by Aristophanes, *Acharnians* 92 that the Persian king had a court-officer with this title (a head of the 'secret police').

985 *you left them—left them?*: this sounds like a rebuke for abandonment, but may mean no more than 'you left them behind you after they were killed', as in 963.

990 [The supplement [*lasting*] is for metrical reasons.]

993–7 *Mardian men*: a nomadic Persian tribe, Herodotus 1.125.4. *Arian*: a Medic people (*LB* 423), Herodotus 7.62.1. [*Dadacas*: the name is restored by conjecture here, because it has occurred at 304.]

1001 *tented carriage*: canvas-covered to protect it from the weather (like the ship's 'deck-house' at *Supp.* 134–5: n.), the travelling vehicle of Persian royalty and notables. Herodotus 7.41.1 records that Xerxes' carriage was immediately followed by a large bodyguard of nobles. The lines seem to have a double point: Xerxes no longer has his carriage, nor therefore its usual retinue, which he has left 'offstage': see n. on 908.

1002 ff *Yes, those who were leading, etc.*: the lament becomes unrestrained and general, with strong demands for ever more demonstrative grief.; see also on 1038 ff. below. *gone*: to their death: cf. 2 n. [1002. (*those*) *who*: here I revert to the generally accepted reading of the MSS, a relative pronoun; West prints his own conjecture, a relative adverb 'to the same place as (those who)'; but the dead just listed were actually among 'those who were leading'.]

1006 *disaster we did not expect*: also 1027; cf. 265.

1007 *the look we had from Ruin*: for the idea of a god's 'look' cf. (unfavourable) *Seven* 485, (favourable) *Supp.* 1, 145, 210, etc. *Ruin*: personified as at *Seven* 957; see above on 95–100.

1008 [*alas, from our lifelong fortune*: West's replacement for dubious Greek meaning approximately 'by such fortune from a deity'.]

1022 *treasure-store*: not a rare metaphor for valued things or persons.

1030 *I tore my robes as the evil fell*: 198–9 and n.

1038–77 Yet freer metres mark a further increase in unrestrained grief, as Xerxes invites the Chorus to answer his every gesture and lament in the traditional *kommos*: 908–1077 n. [1069–end: the Greek wording and the arrangement of voice-parts become ever more insecure.] A 'procession' of Chorus and Xerxes presumably forms after 1065, when he repeats his order to enter the palace (1068, from 1038); the wholly irregular lyric epode would accompany their exit.

1041 *woe's gift of woe to woe*: such verbal redundancies evoke extreme suffering, e.g. 682 (also with alliteration), *Seven* 851.

1045 *Alas...very much*: language awkward to us but not untypical of repetitive lament [the text is nevertheless suspect].

1046 *Beat, beat*: lit. 'row (with oars)', a metaphor of rhythmic regularity, familiar to Athenians who had rowed a warship to a bellowed or beaten 'in-out, in-out'; of grief also at *Seven* 855.

1049 *my care for this*: cf. *Seven* 287 and n., a similar context.

1052 *Sorrow's blackness, etc.*: metaphorical of utter despair, not of bruises left by the beating; 'black fortune' at *Supp*. 89.

1054 *the Mysian way*: the ancient commentator says that the Mysians (from N. Asia Minor) were known for their lamentations; cf. n. on 'Mariandynian' at 937.

1057 = 1064 *ceaselessly*: a rare word, used also of such laceration at *LB* 425.

1072 *soft tread*: Aeschylus uses yet again the description registering barbarian luxury or effeminacy (41, 135–9 and nn., 543); but here there may be no contempt.

1074–5 *our three-banked...ships and their dead*: it is noteworthy that the naval defeat recurs so emphatically at the play's very end, perhaps reminding the Athenian audience of their city's major part in it: cf. Introd. 2.1 p. xxiii.

1077 *s.d.*: processional exits of the chorus end also *Seven* (grieving), *Suppliants* (relieved but apprehensive), and *Eumenides* (rejoicing).

## SEVEN AGAINST THEBES

THE principal medieval MS preserves most of an ancient *hypothesis* ('introduction') to the play (see on that to *Persians*, p. 130); it has been corrected with help from a fragmentary papyrus text of about 200 BC first published in 1952: 'The scene of the play is laid in Thebes, and the chorus is composed of Theban maidens. The plot is the army of Argives besieging the Thebans, who in fact are victorious, and the death of Eteocles and Polynices. It was performed during the archonship of Theagorides in the first year of the seventy-eighth Olympiad (i.e. 467 BC); Aeschylus was victorious with *Laius*, *Oedipus*, *Seven against Thebes*, and the satyric *Sphinx*.'

Most MSS have a list of play characters, naming a single 'Messenger-Scout' who makes a first entry at 39 and re-enters at 375 and 792 (for his function as a scout, see 36, 41, 66, 369). Some editors suppose that the report in 792–819 is given by a separate messenger, because of its brevity and difference in verbal style from the long speeches of the Scout earlier in the play; these editors ask also whether the brevity, untypical of Aeschylus' messengers at *Pers.* 249–514 and *Ag.* 502–82, indicates, loss of a fuller report in 792–819. In favour of the single character are the certainty that only one actor was involved, and a gain in dramatic and visual continuity if he returned in the same function and costume.

*S.d.*: The play, like *Persians*, was almost certainly produced while the theatre lacked a backcloth (see Introd. 2.5 p. lv). The scene is set inside the city, and perhaps to be imagined as a public space, probably near the royal palace and the city's temples (see Introd. 2.5. p. lv n. 54). All entrances and exits are made by the side passages one leads towards the city's gates, and therefore the imminent battle, the other to the temples and perhaps also the palace.

The opening scene would lack impact if there were no Theban citizens (mute extras) to respond visibly to Eteocles' speech and his final command at 30 'Quickly now...to the walls!'; some scholars nevertheless argue that this scene plays as well if Eteocles simply addresses the theatre audience, their imagination supplying his own on stage: on this question see Taplin, *Stagecraft* 123 ff.

1–77 This prologue scene is bound into the coming drama in a way rare in Greek Tragedy. Not only does it introduce the play's single character of consequence, Eteocles, in two monologues (1–38, 69–77), but between these it shows him interacting briefly with the only secondary figure of consequence, the Scout. Eteocles has been expecting the Scout (36–8), who leaves before the scene ends to gather more definite news of the attackers (66–8). Their scene here prepares for their second, much longer interaction, the 'Shield Scene' which fills the whole centre of the play (369–676: n.) and leads to a climax which is also the climax of the trilogy: Eteocles decides to duel with his brother Polynices, so fulfilling his father Oedipus' curse (677–719).

Eteocles is depicted in his sole responsibility for Thebes' safety (1–9); he is the steersman of the state (2–3, 62–4); he must manage its whole defence (10–20, 30–8, 76–7; cf. the Scout at 57–8, 62–5; Introd. 2.2. p. xxx). He knows through a seer of the imminent attack upon the gates (24–9), which the Scout then confirms with news of the principal attackers, the Seven (42, 55–6). The attackers have sacrificed in hope of victory (43–53—unsuccessfully, their own seer tells them, we later learn, 379): so a note of dependence upon the gods is struck at the outset which dominates the play (cf. Introd. 2.2

p. xxxi). Eteocles' strong concern here for the city and its people prepares for the Chorus who are their stage voice (78–181: n.).

Eteocles' second monologue, however, begins with two lines (69–70) weighted heavily with premonition: he appeals to the gods and to his father's curse to spare the city (71–6). Because we lack the two preceding plays, *Laius* and *Oedipus*, we cannot know what impact Aeschylus may have intended on the spectators with these lines, and why he formulated them as he did: see 720–91 n., and Introd. 2.2. p. xxix.

Eteocles then leaves to consolidate the defence (76, cf. 63).

1 *Cadmus*: 137–40 n.

2–3 *taking the tiller at the city's stern*: the ship of state, a frequent metaphor throughout antiquity: Eteocles again at 32 (n.), 62 and 652; cf. 208–10, 758–61.

8–9 *Zeus avert… true to his name*: as 'Zeus Averter' (of ill, etc.); the Greek wording reflects this variable title. There was a belief that to call on a god by a cult name appropriate to one's situation gave the best chance of success: see e.g. 116–19, *Supp.* 26–7, *Ag.* 160–6.

11–13 *the man still short… bodily strength*: the translation smooths out Greek expressions very difficult in their phrasing; the text is much disputed. West's text (translated) keeps two kinds of men, the underage and the mature, the latter still putting on strength [but many editors favour the reversal of ll. 12 and 13, giving roughly 'and the man past his youth, and every man taking care and as may befit him increasing the growth of his body's strength': this gives three categories, the first two separate, the third inclusive of these and others].

16–20 *Mother Earth*: 416. *accepted the whole labour*: the Greek verb connotes the wide hospitality of an innkeeper; similarly at 860 (n.).

24–9 *the seer… birds*: the blind Tiresias, not named, but famous for his unique understanding of birds' cries, and of their flight as reported to him (he 'husbanded' them for observation); cf. Sophocles, *Antigone* 999 ff., *Oedipus Tyrannus* 484; bird-augury in general *PB* 488–92. *without help of fire*: observing the combustion of sacrifices was a dominant mode of prognostication, *PB* 496–9. *Achaean*: a loose synonym for Greeks from the Peloponnese; here Argives are meant, from Argos the city of Adrastus (50, 575), to whom Polynices appealed for help against Thebes.

32 *breastworks… tower-platforms*: terminology for both land-fortifications and warships.

34–5 *the throng of outside attackers*: slightly contemptuous and attempting reassurance. *the god will end things well!*: see on 77.

42 *captains furious for war*: later found to include the seer Amphiaraus, who foresaw his own death and so fights reluctantly (587–8), but is a great warrior (569, 593, 616). For 'furious for war' see n. on *Pers*. 73.

43–8 *a bull's throat, etc.*: swearing over a sacrificial victim's blood was usual; touching it gave the oath heavy solemnity through the symbolic joining of blood from actual slaughter and of blood vowed (48), and here adds awful prophetic significance; a similar rite solemnizes an alliance at Xenophon, *Anabasis* 2.2.8–9. Aeschylus' description here was famous, cited e.g. at Aristophanes, *Lysistrata* 187–9 and (the whole passage 42–56) by later literary critics, orators, and anthologists. *black*: literally 'black-bound', but '-bound' as in 160 'bronze(-bound)' may mean 'cross-banded' for strength, with leather or metal, perhaps painted black. *Ares*: god of War, 63, 115. *Enyo*: (goddess of) Havoc, Homer, *Iliad* 5.592. *Terror*: (personified) *Iliad* 13.299. Three divinities are named, as in 224–5, the number being ritual: *Supp*. 26, *LB* 244, *Eum*. 759, etc.; cf. n. on 'thrice' at 745–6. *sack...by force*: l. 47 is repeated almost word for word at 531, in the attacker Hippomedon's individual oath.

49–53 *memorial tokens*: locks of hair, probably, sent home in case the dead body itself does not return, Euripides, *Iphigenia in Tauris* 821; these were also common tributes of the living to the dead (see esp. *LB* 168, 172, etc.). *Adrastus*: they presume that their leader (575) will return safely to Argos (as myth indeed told; he figures in Euripides' *Suppliants*, in which the bodies of the Seven are recovered for burial by Athens under its king Theseus). *lions*: nature's prime comparison for ferocity, and Epic's: in war at e.g. Homer, *Iliad* 15.592.

55 *lots*: for their apparent importance in the play see Introd. 2.2 p. xxxiv.

64 *a wave on...land*: the image again at 111, also 'noisy', 112–15.

66 *look-out, for what's left of the day*: an artifice in translation, the Greek being 'for the future a watcher-by-day'. The Scout saw in the previous night the attackers' preparation of which Tiresias had warned Eteocles (29), and will soon return with news of their actual positions, 375–6.

68 *through my clear report you'll...be unharmed*: cf. Eteocles in 36–8.

69–77 A passionate prayer for his city's survival by its responsible but endangered leader closes the prologue-scene with credible force; but the implicit appeal for his own safety (70) strikes a grimly prophetic note: see the n. on 1–77, at end.

71–2 *raze...root and branch*: a Homeric image, of 'clearing woodland', *Iliad* 12.148; it complements the image of destruction by sea storm, 63–4. [After 72, editors generally delete the awkward and anticlimactic l. 73 'as it (the city) pours out its voice, and (do not raze) its hearths and homes'.]

77 *when a city prospers, it honours its gods*: 'ring-composition' closes the prologue scene; cf. 4, 35. The converse idea, conquest and the gods' desertion, comes at 217–18.

78–181 Entry-song (*parodos*) of the Chorus. They are women, and young unmarried women at that (109, 171): in a time of extreme crisis, Aeschylus chooses not male citizens (contrast the counsellors of *Persians*) but terrified females as foil to the determined leader Eteocles. Their vivid imagination of a noisy attack (78–91) leads to appeals to the gods (92–181), interrupted by renewed imaginings (111–27, 155, 161) and by fear of a woman's fate if captured, slavery and rape (110: a fear which returns violently at 326–8, 351, 363–9, 454–6). The Chorus' chief anxiety, however, is that of Eteocles himself, for the city, its people, and its gods (87–8, 104–5, 108–21, 130, 139–45, 156–7, 164–81). In this way Aeschylus maintains common safety as the theme dominating the play's first half (Introd. 2.2. p. xxx); in it he gives the Chorus no awareness of Oedipus' curse, or concern for Eteocles' individual destiny.

The *parodos* does not begin with the chorus chanting to the regular 'marching' rhythm with which they begin *Persians* and *Suppliants*; instead, there is free lyric (78–107), in the excited dochmiac metre; then come three pairs of responding stanzas (108–81) in which dochmiacs also dominate (as later in 686–711). Sung dance is here at its most free and emotionally expressive. [The extent of the textual loss at 78 is not determinable.]

81–2 *dust...messenger without voice*: this conceit also at *Supp.* 180, in a similar image of a moving army.

84 [The line is corrupt in the MSS, but an ancient paraphrase allows confident reconstruction of the sense; 83 is wholly unintelligible.]

85–6 *flies in the air*: of sound, *PB* 115, of words *Supp.* 657. *irresistible water*: *Persians* 87–90, also of an army. *striking a mountain*: mountain torrents after heavy rain?

89 [*a word missing*]: either 'evil' (88) or a new noun like 'warfare' (cf. 90–1) *shouts over the walls*.

90 *bright shields*: glittering armour is often described, but 'bright' here is Greek 'white' and the shields of Argos (etymologically interpretable as 'White City') are white elsewhere. It is hard not to hear in *shields* a pre-echo of the play's central 'Shield-Scene', 369–676; even more so in 125–7.

95 and 99 *gods'... images*: receiving ritual supplication, 211 ff., cf. *Supp.* 189–92, 241–2, etc. [For the supplement *ancestral*, cf. *Pers.* 404.]

102–3 *robes and garlands*: regularly dedicated for gods' images to wear, in high festivals no less than in crises. At Homer, *Iliad.* 6.90 ff. Hecuba of Troy offers a robe for (the image of) Athena protectress of cities (cf. our 129 ff.). [West's *When* and *need to throw* supply defective sense and metre.]

108–49 [West judges that these lyric lines make up two responding stanzas; most editors reject this because the excited metre of 87–100 continues in them, hardly alleviated by the more regular rhythms which dominate the two certain stanza-pairs of 150–81. West's text in 108–49 therefore has many conjectures and some deletions, to achieve 'responsion'.]

113 *helmet-crests slanting*: either transverse, as depicted in some older vase-paintings (rather than from back to front); or nodding with a head's movement or in the wind?

115 *seethes*: (also 761) makes the metaphor in *wave of men* (cf. 64) concrete.

116 *with whom lies the outcome of all*: a variant of Zeus 'the fulfiller' and the like, e.g. *Ag.* 973, 1486; Zeus all-powerful 255 below, *Supp.* 815.

122 [The Greek text is defective metrically; there is no major loss of sense.]

124 *bits... pipe tones of death*: see 463–4 and n.

125–7 *conspicuous amid their host*: not least for their ornamented shields, 385 ff. etc. *as their lot fell*: 55–6 (n.), 376, etc.

129–31 *daughter of Zeus... in your love of battle... Pallas*: similarly evoked at e.g. *Eum.* 292–6.

131–4 *lord of horses... ruler of ocean*: Poseidon, potent by land as well as sea (310 n.). He was credited variously with the creation, or first breeding or taming, of horses, and depicted himself as a horseman. *wrought fish-spear*: lit. 'fish-spearing contrivance', elevated language for the trident, emblem of Poseidon's power, *Supp.* 218, *PB* 924–5; the Chorus imply that he should use it against the attackers of Thebes. [*words missing*: —but not sense; e.g. 'wielding power' has been supplemented.]

137–40 *Ares progenitor*: the Theban founding hero Cadmus was the god Ares' relative in some way (mythical details are vague) and gave his name to the citadel he built, the Cadmea (l. 1); in most accounts he married Harmonia, Ares' daughter by *Cypris... the race's foremother* (Aphrodite). *your care*: the Greek word connotes duty to family. [The Greek is corrupt in these lines, but the general sense clear enough; West leaves some words obelized as incurable, amid which 'alas! alas!' are here replaced by the conjecture *progenitor*.]

146–9 *Lycean lord*: Apollo; this cult-title, also e.g. *Supp*. 686, is not convincingly explained; it may reflect an ancient association with his defence of men against wolves ('wolf' is *lyk*-in Greek), rather than with a cult in Lycia in Asia Minor (cf. also *Ag*. 1257 and my n. in Collard, 2002). Thus the point of *prove Lycean* is unclear, unless the linking of the god with his sister Artemis in 149, invoked here for her huntress's bow, is to invite also Apollo's archery (*Ag*. 510) against the attackers. [West makes deletions to achieve metrical responsion; the MSS end 149 with an express vocative 'beloved Artemis' (cf. 154).]

151 *Hera*: Zeus' wife. Her temples were very ancient throughout Greece, and frequently at the heart of cities. She was in particular the patroness of Argos (*Supp*. 299), by which Thebes is now attacked.

153 *laden axles squealing*: also at 205.

157 *god... lead the outcome*: 35, cf. *Eum*. 544 'An end is appointed and waits', where 'end' is the word often translated as 'outcome' or 'fulfilment', see e.g. 116 and n.

159 *Stones hail, etc.*: the sense is appropriate rather than got confidently from the text [but a papyrus fragment of 155–64 gives some support to the MSS].

162–3 *the sacred power*: normally part of Zeus' supreme authority, but apparently deputed here to Apollo [but the text is badly corrupt, the papyrus defective, and *son of Zeus* is a conjecture. Some editors make everything refer to Athena as 'daughter of Zeus' in 162, for at *Eum*. 826–8 she has her father's power in war].

164 *Onca Outside the City*: also 487, 501: Athena's local title and temple very near Thebes in an outlying settlement named Oncae.

170 *an army with a foreign tongue*: the Argives, as attackers from another country (34, 583 and n.); together with their Peloponnesian allies they spoke chiefly the Doric or Arcadian dialects, and the Thebans themselves Boeotian (*Persians* 805–6). [There is a metrical problem in the Greek line, but the sense seems sound.]

175 *stand over*: as over a man wounded in battle, a Homeric expression.

178–9, 180–1 *Our city's rites, etc.*: the native gods are invited to save the rituals from which they themselves benefit through sacrifice; for comparable prayers, cf. *LB* 483–5 (to the dead Agamemnon), 789–92 (to Zeus himself); cf. also 304–5 and n.

182–286 First episode: Eteocles returns and calms the Chorus' panic. His first angry speech condemns such panic as demoralizing; and women should not range abroad when action belongs only to men (182–202: n.). There follows a mixed lyric and spoken exchange of extreme tension (203–44: the so-called 'epirrhematic' structure found first in *Persians* 255–89 (n.) and recurring at e.g. 686–711 below; cf. Introd. 3.3 p. lxii); while the Chorus again sing of their fear, Eteocles argues them into a proper quiet; but he achieves this only through a wholly spoken dialogue (245–63: n.). His final speech (264–86) accepts the women's need to invoke the gods (264–70, 279–80), while he himself will sacrifice for their favour, as men may and must (271–8; cf. his earlier 230–2). Before he leaves to post Theban opponents of the Seven (282–6: n.), he is given one line, 281 'you'll have no greater escape from what is fated', which takes up the Chorus' 263 'I'll suffer what is fated' and suggests that he is in fate's grip, and is strongly recalled in 719, his final words before fate indeed takes him; see also n. on 281.

182–202 Eteocles' violent attack upon the female Chorus shows many traditional male antipathies, the earliest in Hesiod, *Theogony* 690 ff., cf. Semonides 7.72 ff.; in drama cf. the (female) chorus' attack upon unnaturally assertive women at *LB* 594–630, and generally Eur. *Hippolytus* 616 ff., *Medea* 412 ff., Aristophanes, *Women at the Thesmophoria* 786 ff.

195 *what you will get, etc.*: 'Second Person' in a half-colloquial generalization, as at 281, 685, 719. [The line is written separately at the bottom of a page in the principal MS, so that some editors move it to follow 186 or 190; in both places it weakens context and sequence. It is the important bridge from Eteocles' generalizations to his immediate concern.]

197 *anything between*: illogical, an automatic extension under stress to a completed antithesis; similarly at *PB* 116. Eteocles means 'all besides', groups rather than individuals.

198–9 *determined*: by Eteocles as sole ruler (196, cf. 2–8); cf. Creon's sentence of stoning proposed for Antigone at Soph. *Antigone* 36, 60. *public stoning*: the people share 'anonymously' the punishment of the people's enemy; so a regicide deserves this fate, *Ag.* 1118, 1616.

200–1 *What lies outside the house, etc.*: cf. 232. The ultimate ancestor of this axiom is Hector's instruction to Andromache in Homer, *Iliad* 6.490 ff. 'go into the house and see to your own work … the war is to be all men's concern, and especially mine'.

203 *son of Oedipus*: also 372, 677; cf. Introd. 2.2. p. xxix n. 24; a not uncommon form of address to a person of high lineage, or of reference to one, e.g. at 407, 504, 609.

206–7 *a voice from the parts through their mouth*: for these 'pipes', see 463–4 and n. [The Greek text here is badly damaged but convincingly restored on the model of those lines.]

208–10 *a sailor who flees from the stern*: the helmsman, usually the captain, useless on *the prow*; Aeschylus has Eteocles repeat the imagery of 'the ship of state' (2, 62–4, etc.). With *flees* Eteocles rebukes the Chorus precisely: their terror has caused general flight (191).

212–13 *the blizzard of death, etc.*: the metaphor is powerful through its abruptness, unlike the milder image in 159 [some editors therefore replace *blizzard* with 'hail of stones' from there].

217–18 *Then this will be, etc.*: the implication seems to be 'your terrified prayers will only bring on the city's capture and the gods' desertion' [if the text is sound; some editors write 'Do they not say, the gods, etc.', a clearer implication of danger].

221–2 [*consumed by flame from an army of foes*: text partly conjectural (West leaves it obelized), but the general sense is sure.]

223 *Do not be ill-advised, etc.*: Eteocles wants calm, not signs of panic, when the Chorus pray: 237–8.

224–5 *Obedience… Well-being… the Saver*: printed as personifications by West, because of the explicit *mother* and *wife*; for such abstractions, see e.g. 45, 535, *Supp.* 1039–41. [The text is doubtful, however; 'wife' as a relationship between abstractions is most insecure; *the Saver* is usually a title of Zeus himself, e.g. 520, *Supp.* 26. No convincing emendations have been found.]

230–1 *victims in sacrifice and for divination*: regular before battle, 42 ff., 378–9; in any crisis e.g. *Supp.* 449–51. The nature of the flames and the appearance of the entrails were consulted (see n. on *PB* 493–9). Eteocles, however, seems to have no time for such consultation now, instead promising the gods rich offerings should he win, 271–7.

232 *stay inside the house*: see n. on 200–1.

235 *How can you be angry with us, etc.?*: as Eteocles was in 182–95.

236 *honouring*: prayers as 'honour', 77, *Supp.* 625–9; cf. sacrifices at 15.

239 *shouts flying*: the image of 85 [but *and the shouts* is West's bold conjecture for an adverb '(clatter) in confusion' which many editors keep].

243 *Ares' nourishment, the blood of men*: a Homeric picture, *Iliad* 5.289 'another man falls and sates Ares with blood'.

246 *do not hear them too clearly*: a folk maxim, usually including also 'see and don't see them'.

247 *groaning*: both literally and metaphorically, 901; cf. *Pers.* 683.

251 *partners*: an appeal to common interest, like 253, 271, etc.; cf. also 220 'our assembled gods'; 178–9 n.

252 *Damnation take you*: a brusque colloquialism, occasional in tragedy, e.g. *Ag.* 1267; Soph. *Oedipus Tyrannus* 1146 'Damnation take you! Will you be quiet?'

253–4 *slavery*: the prime fear of women captives, 110, 326–31, *LB* 77; cf. Eteocles at 75, the Scout at 471, 793.

255 *Zeus...your bolt*: his lightning, 453, 513, etc.

256 *women*: Eteocles loses patience again, after his earlier anger on this subject, 182–202 n.

258 *Words of ill omen again...?*: a similar rebuke in the exchange at *Supp.* 512.

260 *I beg you*: the Chorus' admission in 259 makes Eteocles suddenly gentler. His wording in this line is close to that of a prayer to a god, but Aeschylus seems to intend exasperated irony.

264–86 Eteocles' masterful speech matches that beginning the episode, 182–202. The Chorus are to be silent (264–70) while he makes his own prayers to the gods (271–8), and then to join in with their own ritual invocations (279–81): thus the content and mood of the following choral ode are prepared (287–368). Aeschylus has Eteocles recall the Scout's appeal to post seven defenders at the seven gates (57–8) and so anticipate more urgent calls to act (282–6: but see n.): these last lines pre-echo the 'Shield-Scene' (369–676).

265 *away from the images*: 'motivating' the Chorus' move into the *orkhês-tra* for their ode at 287; a similar dramatist's manoeuvre at *Supp.* 506–8.

266 *make this better prayer, for the gods to be our allies*: the Chorus have prayed before to the gods to save the city (130–81), but not as 'allies', for which idea cf. *LB* 2. [266 is deleted by some editors who judge it a damaging anticipation of Eteocles' instruction at 279.]

268–9 *raise the sacred chant…sacrifice*: richly intermingled terms for women's ritual cries (825, *Ag.* 28, 595), and men's battlefield cries, for victory (497 below). *the Greek custom*: implicitly warning the Chorus not to go to the noisy excesses associated with 'barbarians' (cf. 280; *Pers.* 635–6, 939 and nn.).

270 *encouragement for friends*: the reverse of 237; *releasing…from war's fear*: cf. 135.

271–2 *gods who hold land…city…plains…marketplace*: a similarly comprehensive list in prayers at *Ag.* 88–90.

273 *Dirce…Ismenus*: Thebes' two rivers, worshipped as gods; cf. 308.

275–8 *set up trophies*: the idea returns at 958, in ironic reversal, after Eteocles has been killed. [The MSS have suffered interpolation of glosses subsequently expanded, it seems, into whole lines (276, 278a) or displacing original text (277). After 275 *we will bloody…with sheep* is found 276 'slaughtering bulls I thus vow to the gods', possibly constructed from 43, and after 278 *holy temples* comes the nonsensical 278a 'I shall garland in front of the temples and garments of the enemy'. The last phrase is duplicated in the MSS from 277, where West has boldly replaced it with *and dedicate*.]

281 *you'll have no greater, etc.*: on this line, see 182–286, n., at end. Similarly worded axioms occur at *Ag.* 902, *PB* 518.

282–6 These lines pose a dramaturgical question not certainly answered. Eteocles announces that he *will…post* (284) the seven defenders, including himself, before further reports come (285–6), and he leaves to do this at 286; but the future tense here seems to pre-empt and conflict with his response when he does later hear the Scout's detailed report of the seven attackers, and with his need and undertaking at that time still to post some of the defenders. See also n. on 369–719 (1) below. Many scholars find no inconsistency or weakening of the later scene, but Taplin's full discussion (*Stagecraft* 142 ff.) leads him to diagnose interpolation of 282–6 (perhaps by the fabricators of the inauthentic passages 861–74,

1005–77), or possibly displacement from elsewhere in the play, rather than simple carelessness in Aeschylus. *in proud style*: evoking the Homeric ideal of heroes duelling; the expression is varied at 465, in a different context.

287–368 First ode; alone again, the Chorus return to their fears, and again imagine the onslaught and the dreadful outcome for Thebes and its women if it succeeds (cf. 78–181 n.). These horrors are unrelieved throughout the closing two pairs of stanzas (321–68); but the first pair (287–320) ends with further impassioned appeals to Thebes' gods not to leave a city where they are so long established amid its natural fertility, the riches which, the Chorus imply, they enjoy from sacrifices (304–12).

The ode is shot through with Homeric colouring: see nn. on 291–4, 298–300, 321–2, 326–9, 343–4. The Greek metres are extraordinarily various, and so enhance the images of chaos.

287–9 *I do care*: that is, to 'make vows like these', 279; for the expression in this context cf. *Pers.* 1049. *heart…sleepless with fear*: it can dance with fear, *LB* 167, 1025. *anxieties…neighbours*: a similar metaphor of disease at *Ag.* 1004.

291–4 *snakes…feared…for…young*: cf. 501–3, *LB* 247–9, an image originating in Homer, *Iliad* 2.308–14; vultures losing their young react angrily, *Ag.* 50–4. *grimmest of bedmates*: perhaps echoed in the pictures of rape, 333–5, 363–8.

298–300 *others are slinging, etc.*: slingers assailing defenders on walls are at odds with the generality of siege-descriptions: after Homer, *Iliad* 12.159–60 defenders hurl down stones on attackers, and defending slingers use smooth stones [so editors conjecture 'our townsmen hurl jagged stones in a hail against those who besiege them']. *jagged stones*: a Homeric phrase, *Iliad* 4.518.

302 *gods born of Zeus*: not all were, despite the catalogue 129–54, headed by Athena his daughter, 129; e.g. Poseidon 310, his brother.

304–5 *What…soil better than this*: an appeal to a god's own interest, like 327: see 178–81 and n.

308 *Dirce*: 273 n. *most enriching of waters*: at *Supp.* 1024–9 the immigrants to Argos learn to praise its fertile rivers more than their native Nile.

310 *Poseidon*: god of the world's whole surface, controlling its waters by sea and land: 131–4. *Tethys*: wife to Oceanus, the supreme river bounding the earth, *PB* 139–40.

319 *noble shrines*: cf. 166–8, 241, of the Theban acropolis.

320–68 These details of a ransacked city recur throughout Tragedy, and are vividly dwelt upon by Clytemnestra at *Ag*. 321–9 and by choruses of captive women at Eur. *Hecuba* 901–42 and *Trojan Women* 551–67.

321–2 *hurl...to Hades*: Aeschylus appropriates a Homeric phrase used of human slaughter, e.g. *Iliad* 1.3, 5.190. Throughout 321–32 a 'city' is variously both the buildings and the inhabitants; cf. the anxieties of 220–2.

324 *an Achaean man*: the singular seems deliberate, as if to evoke Adrastus the leader of the attackers (50 and n.).

326–9 *led away...by their hair*: the victims at Troy were thus imagined, Homer, *Iliad* 22.62 ff. *like horses*: the simile also *Supp*. 430–1.

331 *its women lost as pillage*: this is the implication of Aeschylus' allusive wording, lit. 'its booty lost amid mingled shrieking' [but the text is insecure]. This whole stanza is about the cruel seizure of women; later comes their rape, explicitly in 333–5, their concubinage in 363–8 (nn.).

333–5 *plucked unripe before marriage... their homes destroyed*: rape: pathetic reversal of a bride's happy journey to the groom's house. [The text and translation are insecure; but cf. the captured women at *LB* 75–7.]

340–1 *leads...away...kills...carry fire*: vivid compression, evoking chaotic haste, an effect continued in 345–55.

343–4 *Ares...restraint*: Aeschylus at his most densely allusive (the imagery and vocabulary of Ares the war-god is Homeric)—but also paradoxical: the god's insatiable war-frenzy (*Supp*. 635–6) destroys all conduct tempered by respect for heaven (fr. 281a.33); at *Ag*. 338–42 the Greek's lust for booty at Troy causes carnage. *blasts*: war, 63–4, 115.

345–68 [While the general sense of these lines can be established, many corruptions in the MSS make detailed restoration of the text uncertain, esp. in 345–7, 356, 363–8.]

345–7 *a net encircling the walls*: the besiegers visualized as such, a metaphor. Some translate 'a net of siege-towers', although these are not attested in Aeschylus' day; but ladders are, 466 and n. Zeus' and Night's 'net' is thrown over Troy's walls, *Ag*. 357.

348–9 *infants...screaming in their own blood*: extreme exaggeration; the Greeks seldom killed infants (Astyanax, Hector's son at Troy, was an infamous exception, e.g. Eur. *Trojan Women* 725, 1173–9), but took them into slavery with their mothers.

355 *he desires neither less nor equal*: all want more than both successful looters (352) and unsuccessful (354).

356 *what follows*: the pillage described in 357–62.

357–62 *produce... Earth's... bounty*: grain, fruit or oil, ruined when storage-vessels are smashed as looters run amok (351, 359–61). *vindictive storemen*: cruel irony: plunderers are meant, not the previous stewards.

363–8 [The translation approximates to West's conjectural restoration of these lines, but he leaves 364–5 obelized in his text]. *bed* is consistent with *nocturnal rites* (for the latter see Cassandra serving her captors at *Ag.* 1438–43, 1446–7); *rites* here are grimly ironic, the term being used properly of marriage, not rape: see n. on *Supp.* 123–4.

369–719 Second episode: in 369–676 the Scout reports and describes successively the Seven attackers, ending with Eteocles' brother Polynices; Eteocles names his opposing defenders, ending with himself (he had named himself among them at 282)—and recognizes how his father's curse has worked their confrontation (653–5, 672–5). In 677–719 the Chorus in horror try to dissuade him from the duel, but Eteocles is inflexible. The episode is remarkable in its power, part of which comes from its unique structure (cf. n. on 1–77, Introd. 2.2 p. xxxii). See also Map 4.

(1). 369–676: the 'Shield-Scene' (Introd. 2.2 ibid.). The seven 'pairs' of speeches, each a Scout's description and Eteocles' response, are set off from one another by three pairs of responding lyric stanzas in which the Chorus renew their fears and prayers, but appropriately to the descriptions they have just heard. This variation between extended speeches and brief lyric has a secondary benefit: it avoids possible visual monotony in the theatre, however mobile or demonstrative the actors playing Scout and Eteocles; for such alternation of brief choral lyric with dialogue, see Introd. 3.3 p. lxii. The formal sequence of itself increases the tension for an audience, well though they know the inevitable conclusion. There are other important ways in which Aeschylus orchestrates the climax. The first five of the Seven are described as boastful and aggressive, in their shield-devices as in their persons, for they are bad men; but the sixth is the tragic Amphiaraus, a seer long aware of his coming death at Thebes (587–9, 609–18); he has been accused of cowardice in its face (382–3) but is calmly acceptant (590), a good and pious man caught up with bad (598–614); he even denounces both Tydeus and Polynices on his own side (571–86), deploring the latter's attack on his native land (for Amphiaraus see Introd. 2.2 p. xxxii). This comes immediately before Polynices is revealed as the seventh and last attacker, and as Eteocles' inevitable opponent. Simultaneously, Eteocles matches each attacker with a defender whose qualities are in moral contrast—except for Amphiaraus, whose opponent is a man of uncomplicated prowess, and for Polynices, whom Eteocles denounces for betrayal in the same terms as Amphiaraus had done (664–71), and whom he opposes confident in a true justice where Polynices claimed a false one (659–73, cf. 645–8); but he confronts Polynices chiefly as brother against enemy brother, both of them accursed (674–5, cf. 653–7; subsequently, 695–7, 709–11). Lastly, there is the brilliance of the attackers' character-portraits and shield-descriptions, always vivid and forceful, sometimes dramatized with direct speech; and of Eteocles' calculated, apt, and cogent responses, sometimes equally colourful: his collected behaviour and command of language have been carefully antici-pated in his prologue-scene. The whole sequence reveals Aeschylus' complete mastery of dramatic poetry; it is a tour de force comparable with the greatest scenes of the *Oresteia*. [The variations in Eteocles' verb-tenses for his acts of posting worry editors: present at 553, futures at 408, 621, 672, simple past at 505, perfects at 448, 472, especially because they seem to conflict with Eteocles' earlier statement that he would leave immediately to post the defenders (282–4: see n.). The variations are in themselves not problematic, however: Eteocles may be imagined to name defenders he has already chosen in his mind, or already posted, or now decides upon; see also n. on 378–9. Nor is there a dramaturgical difficulty: Aeschylus simply subordinates reality or plausibility to impact; a similar issue is discussed in the n. on 720–91.]

(2). 677–719: Eteocles rejects the Chorus' dissuasion (677–85); the antiphonal section which follows, mixing choral lyric and actor's speech (686–711; cf. 182–286 and n.), shows him inflexible before his fate, for the gods are fulfilling his father's curse. The Chorus' alarm is passionate, using again the irregular dochmiac metre (78–181 n., at end); they describe Eteo-cles' determination as a mad lust to shed unlawful blood, the ruinous work of the house's Fury (700); this becomes the preoccupation of their following ode (720–91: n.). Eteocles' resigned farewell is cold (702–4, cf. 713, 715) but honourable (683–5, cf. 717). In a final, intense exchange (stichomythia, 711–19 and n.) he goes off to his death, for the will of heaven is inescapable (719): Introd. 2.2. p. xxxi.

369 *s.d.*: Eteocles' use of demonstrative pronouns for some of his nominated defenders does not mean that they were visible; such pronouns regularly refer to persons or things 'offstage', nearby or far off (e.g. *Pers.* 141 and n.).

Furthermore, if six defenders were visible, it would become even more heavily predictable that Eteocles is to be the seventh.

369–74 The two part-voices of the Chorus are made deliberately similar in wording to emphasize the equal haste of Scout and Eteocles; although spoken, they 'correspond' like lyric stanzas.

370 *important new information*: cf. 40.

371 *haste… errand*: a sort of 'concealed stage-direction'; cf. *Pers.* 247–8, of the approaching Messenger. The Greek contains a metaphor from chariots, lit. 'in haste driving the hubs of his feet on their errand': leg-joints move as easily as wheels on their axles.

373–4 [*exactly in time… disorders*: the Greek text is disputed, but no emendation is fully satisfactory.]

375 *I'll speak, etc.*: the Scout begins abruptly, without greeting the king; this suits their common haste, 371 – 374.

378–9 *Tydeus*: father of the *Iliad*'s Diomedes, 14.113 ff.; see 571–5 n. *Proetus*: a remote ancestor of the founding king of Thebes; for the Gates see Map 4. *The seer*: Amphiaraus, 382 (n.); unnamed like the seer Tiresias at 24. He restrains the violent Tydeus, whom he detests (571). This delay in the attack also 'explains' why Eteocles has had time to choose his defenders deliberately (n. on 369–719 (1), at end). *victims*: those slaughtered at 43, in the hope of victory.

381 *a snake… midday hissing*: its most active time, held to be the most dangerous.

382–3 *son of Oicles*: the patronymic suffices to identify Amphiaraus; the office of seer was hereditary in his family. With *wise* Aeschylus is either himself anticipating the attack's disastrous outcome through Amphiaraus' foresight (587–9, 615–19) or infusing the Scout's words with ironic allusion to it. *slinks fawningly before*: like a cowering dog; Eteocles rejects such fawning at 704. *death and battle*: possibly hendiadys for 'fatal fight' (the Greek has alliteration). *cowardice*: the Scout later absolves Amphiaraus of this, 569.

384–6 Tydeus' nodding plumes and ringing bells mean to warn eye and ear of his terrible advance; cf. Eteocles at 398–9; such bells on shields evoke a barbaric warrior also at Sophocles fr. 859 and in the fourth-century tragedy *Rhesus* 384 (ascribed to Euripides). The passage is used by Aristophanes, *Acharnians* 964–5 in paratragedy to evoke the exaggerated and loud soldier-figure Lamachus, a contemporary; cf. 581–4 there.

387–90 *arrogant device*: Tydeus through his shield arrogates pre-eminence among his fellow Argives (and the Thebans) just as the brilliant full moon dominates the stars of heaven. *wrought*: the word is Homeric, for fine metalwork, e.g. *Iliad* 23.741. *moon... the eye of night*: so too in Pindar, e.g. *Olympian* 3.19–20; a different 'eye of night' at *Pers.* 428 (n.); the sun is day's eye, e.g. Sophocles, *Antigone* 103–4.

393–4 *horse snorting, etc.*: cf. the pictures of 122–3, 206–7.

395–6 *relied upon.*: the full meaning is 'guaranteed', metaphorical from pledges placed in the palm of the hand when bargaining; the image recurs in 449, 470, 797.

399 *plumes and bells, etc.*: variations on this folk-maxim are found in all cultures; for Tragedy, cf. e.g. Eur. *Children of Heracles* 684.

402 *prophetic for someone*: i.e. for Tydeus himself, disastrously, as 403–6 show. Some identify the 'someone' as his yet to be named opponent, i.e. favourably prophetic. This use of the indefinite pronoun for an enemy is semi-colloquial and contemptuous; cf. *Supp.* 683, 883, 903.

403–5 *prove right and true in meaning*: the Greeks invested names with meaning, often finding them a guide to a person's nature or destiny (often grim: Latin *nomen omen*). This play on names begins in Homer and is very common in Tragedy; Aeschylus delights in it, e.g. 440–5, 526–8, 576–8 (and nn.); it often includes terms like *right* and *true* (for these see esp. Plato, *Cratylus* 385b–c, a dialogue devoted to the significance of names and words). The most famous example is at *Ag.* 690, Helen 'hellish' to ships, etc.: see any commentary there. Tydeus' arrogation of heaven's *night* for his device (388–90 n.) implies that death's 'night' is inevitable for himself.

407–13 *son of Astacus...from the Sown Men...Melanippus*: a descendant of the founding Cadmeans (137–40 and n.) of Thebes, who grew from the teeth of Ares' dragon sown in the earth by Cadmus; mythic accounts vary, and it is not clear here whether *whom Ares spared* refers to the generating teeth or to just a few of those generated. With *truly a native of the land* Aeschylus makes a heavy play upon *Sown Men*. Melanippus' name ('Black Horse') is not exploited by Eteocles, despite an opportunity of linking 'black' with the fatal night of Tydeus' device, and the simile comparing him with an eager horse (393). In Euripides' fragmentary *Meleager* (fr. 537) Tydeus is said to have eaten Melanippus' brains after killing him: cf. n. on 571.

414–15 *Ares...with his dice*: Eteocles, like a Homeric hero, sees fighting as determined by the gods, often capriciously, but is confident that *Justice* will triumph for the Theban motherland's soil when it sends its son, *blood-kin*, to defend it; for *Justice* see Polynices' device, 646–8, and Eteocles' riposte, 667. [*of blood-kin*, a minority reading among the MSS, is superior to the majority reading 'divine (Justice)': the Greek words differ by only one letter.]

417–21: the first strophe of three responding pairs which piece out the description of the first six of the Seven and their opponents; the first anti-strophe is at 451–6. See 369–719 n.

422 *may the gods grant, etc.*: the Scout echoes the Chorus' prayer of 417–18.

423 *Electran Gates*: named after Electra, a sister of Thebes' founder Cadmus (1).

425 *a giant, taller, etc.*: Tydeus (*the one... before*) is said at Homes, *Iliad* 5.801 to be a small man. Here, 'giant' associates Capaneus with the true giants or Titans, rebellious and defeated opponents of Zeus, such as Typhon (493 and n.). [After 425 the line 426 'he makes terrible threats against our walls, which I pray fortune may not fulfil' is deleted as an interpolation weakly keeping apart 425 and 427, and duplicating 427; it was adapted from the very similar 549.]

428–9 *and Zeus'... stop him*: text and translation insecure. *opposition with a blast* in the translation expands and gives the connotation of a single Greek noun meaning 'strife, contention'. Capaneus' defiance is extreme.

430–1 *likened... to the warmth of midday*: this absurd belittlement of Zeus' lightning in itself suggests Capaneus' inevitable destruction by it, as Eteocles picks up, 444–5.

432 *naked*: as normally in heroic art; there is no implication that Capaneus is himself going 'naked' into war with Zeus. *letters of gold*: figures are often named in vase-paintings, less often given 'speech' in letters near or round their heads. Cf. Eteoclus 468, Polynices 646–8.

435 *send...*: the imperative construction breaks off into two interrogatives [if the text is sound. The imperative 'send' is printed as a parenthesis by some editors, as '—do the sending!—who will take his stand?'; so too West, who entertains but does not print a conjectural substitute 'tell us!'].

437 *Here too one gain gives birth to another*: an adapted proverb, it seems, but translation is insecure; Eteocles may mean that Capaneus' doomed boasting

(425: 438–40) is one gain and his scorn of the gods (427–8) another because it will draw Zeus' punishment (443–5).

438–9 *tongues are...accusing evidence*: Aeschylus neatly uses an apt metaphor, from forensic language.

440 *those prepared to act*: allusive plural, for Zeus alone is meant.

441 *well-practised mouth*: alternative but less good translation: 'in laying bare his word'.

444–50 *lightning-bolt of fire will come to him, not any likeness*: a sardonic riposte echoing Capaneus' 'likening' Zeus' lightning to midday warmth, 432–3. Aeschylus plays here on Capaneus' name as 'Man of Smoke'; cf. Eur. *Suppliants* 495–6 'Has not Capaneus's body rightly been made into smoke by the lightning?' There may be an echo of this play when his opponent Polyphontes is named in 448 as one 'who burns with courage'. *Artemis the defender*: this is the implied meaning here of the literal adjective 'who stands before (houses)': Artemis' image, like that of her brother Apollo (e.g. *Ag.* 1081), stood before houses, to protect those who set out, as Polyphontes soon will, and Megareus at 476. [After 445 editors delete 446 '(likeness of it) to the sun's midday warmth', weakly interpolated on the model of 431.]

454–6 *drags me, etc.*: into captive slavery and concubinage: 363–8, n. on 331.

458–60 *Eteoclus*: rarely named in myth among the Seven, probably because his name is a doublet of Eteocles; both mean 'True Glory' or the like; but he appears at e.g. Eur. *Suppliants* 872, where his civic, not martial, virtues are given. *helmet*: used for drawing lots in Homer, e.g. *Iliad* 3.316 (a 'leaping' lot at 7.182). *Neistid*: the name appears to mean 'lowest' [but the MSS have also 'Neteid', which would suggest naming after a hero Neteus, otherwise unrecorded. Before 458 editors delete a line clumsily fabricated to amplify the terse *Speak I shall*, 'Next, now: of the man who next drew his lot at the gates'; but *Speak* adequately picks up 451 'Speak...'].

461–4 The eager and noisy chafing of Eteoclus' horses recalls the general descriptions of 123–4 and 206–7. It appears that *headbands* incorporated *muzzle-pipes* to magnify snorting, perhaps converting it into a roaring *whistle* (cf. 124, 206), with the object of creating terror, 476–7 (like Tydeus' shield-bells, 384–6: n.); similarly Aeschylus fr. 326 'colts with pipe-shaped mouth-pieces'. No representation of such a device has been found in art, however. *in barbaric fashion*: i.e. exotic in Greek eyes, again like Tydeus' bells [*fashion* in 463 is suspect to editors, as an invader from 465; so 'measure, strain' is conjectured, viz. 'sound a barbaric strain', or 'din', the word which appears in Eteocles' answer at 476].

466–8 *man in armour*: no doubt using his shield for protection against missiles. Scaling ladders are described at this same attack upon Thebes in Euripides, *Suppliants* 497 and *Phoenician Women* 180–1 and 488–9; and also in the fifth century in historians, e.g. Thucydides 3.23.1. *lettered syllables*: traditionally the invention of the mythical Palamedes (as in Euripides' fragmentary play of that name), but probably from his patron the demi-god Prometheus, who claims them too, *PB* 460. Cf. 'letters of gold', 434.

473–4 *his boast consists in his two hands*: he will not boast with words, his actions will show his proud worth; the same idea at 554. *Megareus*: although of prime Theban descent (*the Sown Men*, 412 and n.), his name is recorded elsewhere only at Soph. *Antigone* 1303, and incidentally. *Creon*: regent at Thebes after Oedipus' exposure as parricide, and king again after the deaths of Eteocles and Polynices (the inauthentic ending to our play has 'the people' as the sole authority, 1005–6, 1025; but cf. Soph. *Oedipus Tyrannus* and *Antigone*). [The line omitted after 471 is obviously interpolated, roughly, 'I would send this man at once, and with some good fortune'. Some editors delete also 473.]

475–6 *whinnying and din*: 163–4 and n. *he will go out from the gates*: meeting his opponent, not waiting for him (but cf. the Scout at 436).

477 *repay...for his upbringing*: all felt this obligation to their parents, but here and at 548 to their country as well—unlike Polynices, 584–6, 668. Eteocles stressed this duty at 16–20.

478–9 *the two men*: another sardonic joke (cf. 445 and n.): Megareus will *take*, that is, 'kill', the shield's bearer, and 'take' the armed man and the city fashioned on it (466) as spoil. *glorify...his father's house*: an Epic idea, the son's heroism replicating and enhancing the father's; failure in this is feared at Soph. *Ajax* 464–5.

485 *Zeus the punisher*: similarly at *Supp.* 401–4 Zeus watches over both bad and good men, punishing appropriately.

486–8 *Athena Onca*: 164 and n. *Hippomedon*: either brother or nephew of Adrastus (50 n.), and a native of Lerna near Argos where he became an ancestor-hero with cult. His huge size is noted also in Eur. *Phoenicians* 127–30.

489–90 *orb*: a rather grand word, used of the circumference of sun or moon; since Aeschylus half-apologizes for it (*I mean*: cf. 609), he must want it to imply a shield suiting its large bearer. *I trembled... I will not deny it*: the only explicit personal reaction in all the Scout's reports.

493–4 *Typhon*: a Titan, a monstrous but unsuccessful challenger of Zeus' supremacy, brought low by his lightning (425 n.), 517, *PB* 351–72 (n.); incarcerated fittingly under the volcanic Mt. Etna, *PB* 363–5 (one of several back-aetiologies for its swirling fires: Greek *-typho* means 'storm', whence our 'typhoon'); so he is 'the power under the earth', 522 below. *smoke... fire's changeful sister*: flame flickers amid smoke; for the 'kenning' cf. *Ag.* 494 'dust, mud's thirsty sister and neighbour'. *cried out triumphantly*: see 268–9 n.

495–6 *coiling snakes... shield*: art showed Typhon with snakes round his waist; presumably therefore Typhon filled the shield's centre, and snakes at least the lower part of its convex face, if not the whole rim as the wording seems to imply.

497–500 *maenad*: Hippomedon's loud onrush is like that of a bacchant, a frenzied female devotee of Dionysus ranging open land; 'maenad' in less forceful metaphor 836, *Supp.* 564. *looking terror*: cf. 500; similarly Typhon himself at *PB* 355–6. *Terror*: the personification (45 and n.) is very striking after the plain noun in 498.

501–3 *like a fierce serpent kept from nestlings*: the image also at 291–4 (n.); 'serpent' exploits Hippomedon's snake-device (495); cf. Tydeus' snake, 381.

504–8 *Hyperbius*: known in mythology only from this play, like the next Theban defender Actor (555); his name may mean 'Superior Force', as Actor's means 'Leader'. *trusty son*: wording as in 407. *in the stress of fortune*: he will fight to discover his fate, but ultimately fortune will decide the hard battle; cf. Melanippus' fate subject to the dicing of Ares the war-god, 414 (n.), Lasthenes' fate as god's gift, 625, and Eteocles' fatalism about himself, 699, 702, 719. *Hermes... with good reason*: the god guides all encounters, fortunate or unfortunate (*Supp.* 920); here both men and devices are esp. suited in their opposition (509–13), but the devices point clearly to victory for one (515–20).

512–13 *Zeus... set standing upright*: poised to hurl his bolt, which he cannot do while 'seated firmly' (an alternative translation). [A majority of MSS read 'bearing thunderbolt in hand'. After 513 the verse-lines seem disordered and duplicated. 514 is generally ejected, 'And no one yet of course saw Zeus defeated', but sometimes transferred to follow 517, where it is lame; 519

cannot stand before 520; it is variously placed, or deleted, by both MSS and editors. There is no certainty about the order adopted by West (translated), and some editors argue that 'it is probable' in 519 should be translated 'it is fitting' if 518 precedes it.]

515 *That is the nature, etc.*: matter-of-fact, or sardonic?

518 *at least if Zeus is mightier*: 'is' looks forward to the conflict of the shield-gods; the verb is lacking in the Greek (idiomatically) but implied by the context. Eteocles knows that in the mythical conflict Zeus 'was' mightier.

521–5 *evil power now under the earth*: Typhon, 493–4 n. *semblance*: both living men and gods detest any representation of the now invisible monster. *he'll smash his head down*: in death. The expression is anomalous, heads being smashed usually by opponents, e.g. *LB* 396.

526–8 The fifth attacker goes unnamed until 547, but the audience would quickly guess his name (Parthenopaeus: 'Maiden-boy') from the reference to his parents and his good-looking, boyish appearance in 532–6; see also 547–9 n. *Borraean (gates)*: i.e. 'Northern' (from 'Boreas'); but the name may be Aeschylus' invention. *Amphion*: builder of the Theban citadel together with his twin Zethus; they were sons of Zeus. One or both had a tomb outside the walls; its existence and location were disputed in antiquity: see Map 4.

529–52 [Vestiges of these lines stand in a second century AD papyrus.]

532–5 *Ares*: Parthenopaeus' father is jointly the war-god and the mortal Melanion (a famous hunter, like Atlanta *his mother the frequenter of mountains*); such double parentage is not unique, Heracles, for example, being son to both Zeus and Amphitryon. Aeschylus names Ares here, prominently, to verify the son's prowess in war, 545–9 [*Ares*' is a conjecture. The MSS are confused: most have 'of Zeus', but the papyrus and a few manuscripts have 'of the spear'.]

536 *in no way girlish like his name*: etymological play yet again; cf. 526–8 n., and e.g. 403–5 and n.

541–4 *the Sphinx*: this monster, winged, with a lion's body (but scaly) and a girl's face, tormented Thebes after king Laius disregarded Apollo's oracle and got a son, Oedipus. She devoured a Theban each day while her famous riddle remained unsolved; Oedipus solved it (775 ff.) before or after he killed his father unknowingly in a quarrel, and was rewarded with the throne and Laius' widow, his own mother, as wife. When his parricide and incest were laid bare, he cursed his progeny, 723–5, 785–90, etc. (see also Introd. 2.2

p. xxix). *for the most missiles to strike this man*: for symbol to turn into reality (cf. 478–9 n.), as defensive Theban missiles hit one of their own Thebans.

545–6 *no petty trafficking in battle*: he takes his trade abroad, like a great merchant, not a local huckster; his trading intends 'wholesale' slaughter; his profit will be the ransack (531). *his long road's journey*: from Arcadia, 547–8; see 553 n.

548 *immigrant*: in Greek a 'metic', one who 'changes his home'. At Athens such persons were granted formal residence in the hope they would help their new country, usually in manufacturing or trade: see n. on *Supp.* 609 (601–14).

552 *all in ruin and in all misery*: echoing formulae from treaty-terms should they be broken.

553 *This…man*, i.e. Arcadian: the emphasis is contemptuous; Arcadians were regarded as uncouth. Parthenopaeus got 'his fine upbringing' at Argos, 548, a detail repeated at Eur. *Suppliants* 890–8.

555 *Actor*: perhaps invented, 504 n.; in other accounts Parthenopaeus is killed by a Theban Periclymenus, e.g. Eur. *Phoenician Women* 1157.

558–61 *monster*: Greek 'biting thing', used of any dangerous creature, even of the husband-killing Clytemnestra at *Ag.* 1232. *constant battering*: Eteocles hopes sardonically for a different effect from the blows intended to fall on the shield-Sphinx's victim (544 n.). [After 558 *to pass* most editors delete 559 'bearing an image on his hostile shield', a line which weakly duplicates 560 'with her bearer'.]

563–7. *His words go through my breast*: the Scout's description of Parthenopaeus pierces home; cf. *LB* 380 'that went sharply right through my ears'. *hair…on end*: cf. *LB* 32, the effect on others of Clytemnestra's screaming nightmare. *great boasting*: 452. *if gods are gods*: cf. *Supp.* 86–7 'Zeus' desire, if Zeus' it really is', Soph. *Oedipus at Colonus* 623 'if Zeus is still Zeus'. *in our land*: that is, 'I wish they all die here, with no return home'. The plots of Aeschylus' lost *Eleusinians* and of Euripides' surviving *Suppliants* concerned the recovery of their unburied bodies from Thebes (49–53 n.).

568–9 *most prudent*: this headline adjective is a powerful surprise after the crazy boasts of the other attackers. *Amphiaraus*: a complex figure, a seer by descent (382 n.), and thus awkwardly prescient of his own future, a great warrior but 'excellent in wisdom and dear to the gods' (Hesiod fr. 25.38). Foreseeing his death at Thebes, he tried vainly to avoid implication in the wrongful attack (Eteocles at 597–619); he foretells that he will be swallowed up in the earth (588, allusively; narrated at Eur. *Suppliants* 500–1). Indeed he enjoyed cult as an underworld power at Thebes (587–9 again; Pindar, *Olympians* 6.13 ff., Herodotus 1.52, 8.134.1), and had an oracle at nearby Oropus (Pausanias 1.34.3). His portrait here has a special function in the play: see Introd. 2.2 p. xxxii. In short: he will be destroyed with his evil companions (597–614), approximately as Eteocles, the virtuous defender of the city, will have no escape from the consequences of his father Oedipus' curse (574) through his brother Polynices' treachery (653–75).

570 *Homoloid Gates*: the name is not certainly identified or understood: it may reflect a cult-title of Zeus at Thebes, or come from a daughter of Niobe (so an ancient commentator), or a Theban hero Homolous (an ancient commentator on Eur. *Phoenician Women* 1119), or a mountain towards which the gates looked.

571–5 *Tydeus... teacher of evil to Argos*: like Polynices he came to Argos from exile; king Adrastus married them both to daughters, and they persuaded him to attack Thebes (573). From the *Iliad* onwards Tydeus is thuggish, aggressive, and bloodthirsty (574, cf. 380, 592–3, and n. on Melanippus at 407–13); so he is *Fury's Summoner*. Aeschylus names this Athenian legal officer who summoned a witness to court, often from abroad: so Tydeus either summons the Fury himself to witness his murderous work, or is the Fury's summoner before she brings it on, precipitating destruction for Thebes and Eteocles through Oedipus' curse and Fury, 70, etc.

576–8 *your brother... his name*: one of the most disputed passages in Aeschylus; both text and translation are everywhere in doubt. The essence of it is, however, clear: Amphiaraus is punning on Polynices' name, Greek *poly-* + *neik-*, 'great' + 'quarrel(er)': Polynices quarrels with his brother Eteocles, and Aeschylus repeats the wordplay at 658, 830, and possibly 935–6; cf. esp. Eur. *Phoenician Women* 636–7. [In 576 *addresses... your brother*, I have substituted a conjecture for corrupt MSS wording which West leaves obelized. In 577, *his eyes turned up in contempt* is doubted because the small action, although conventional, seems incongruous with the violent abuse; some alter 'eyes' to 'name' and translate differently as 'reversing his name', i.e. Greek *neik-* + *poly-*, 'quarrelling greatly'; others make the wordplay explicit by giving the verb *dwelling on* a different sense, 'dividing the name', i.e. into its two Greek parts, 'the great quarreller' (cf. above). In 578 West abandons the MSS *at the end... twice* for a conjecture 'with a twofold ending' which suggests Polynices as both 'the great quarreller' and 'the great abuser' (or 'object of abuse'); the Greek can have both meanings.]

579 *These words pass his lips in speech*: the redundant expression conveys the solemn significance of the seer's condemnation. [The line is sometimes deleted by those who 'emend' 576–8, because the verb 'calls to' which begins it (576 here) destroys the new syntax they introduce.]

580–9 The only 'direct speech' in all seven of the Scout's reports. It is Aeschylus' way of emphasizing its context, anticipatory condemnation of the traitor Polynices. Eteocles does not respond to it when naming Amphiaraus' opponent, but only when he has heard the Scout's description of Polynices' shield-device, in 658–71 answering 642–8.

583 *an army of outsiders*: such an army has no legitimacy in the dynastic conflict at Thebes; cf. 922–5 and the imitative 1019.

584–6 *the life-source of a mother*: i.e. Polynices' motherland, Thebes; cf. Eteocles wording in 16; it is not a metaphor for just the nurturing rivers of Thebes, 308–11.

587–9 *enrich (this land)*: while the verb plays on the idea of life-giving land in 584, Amphiaraus means rather the rich benefit to Thebes of his future cult (above, 568–9 n.); cf. Oedipus' burial in Athenian soil in Soph. *Oedipus at Colonus* 1520 ff. *To battle, then!*: abrupt; Aeschylus wants to emphasize the combination in one man, untroubled by prophetic self-knowledge (590), of deep wisdom (593–4) and supreme courage (592, 569).

591–4 *No device, etc.*: the absence further distinguishes Amphiaraus from the five preceding and boastful attackers. *not the appearance*: he will have no false ostentation on his shield. *crops the deep furrow ... grows*: the imagery of soil and yield (585, 587) takes a further metaphorical turn; it recurs in 600. Cf. also *Pers.* 821–2, the same image of (bad) counsel; 'deep' counsel 142 there, *Supp.* 407.

595–6 *the man who honours god, etc.*: a final distinction between Amphiaraus and the rest: contrast Capaneus 440, Eteoclus 469, Hyperbius 509–20, Parthenopaeus 551.

597 *Ominous, etc.*: Eteocles begins with and concentrates upon Amphiaraus' piety and morality, which draw his strong sympathy, for a good man is often doomed to suffer innocently with the bad. Cf. 568–9 n., at end. The word *ominous* alludes also to Amphiaraus' powers as a seer (569, 588).

600 [*a crop not to be taken in*: followed in the MSS by 601, an interpolated line seemingly intended to amplify the imagery and which is insecurely translated as '(for) the ploughland of ruinous folly reaps death as its crop'; the Greek is anomalous in expression.]

603 *sailors hot upon some villainy*: lit. 'hot sailors and some villainy', apparently a bold hendiadys [but the text has been doubted].

604 *a breed of men the gods abhor*: perhaps an anticipation of Eteocles' own fate: cf. his 653, 691.

607–8 *net*: catching the fated victim, deservingly or not, like Cassandra at *Ag.* 1048, Agamemnon at *LB* 998, *Eum.* 460. *the god's impartial scourge*: that of Zeus, the image as Homer, *Iliad* 12.37, etc., *Ag.* 642.

609–14 An impressive sequence of words and ideas, some deliberately repetitious, most deliberately reflecting those of 598–608; it culminates in a sonorous seven-syllable Greek verb, *he shall be dragged down with them. son of Oicles*: 382 n. *stretch their mission too far to return*: apparently sardonic, but the Greek expression translates with difficulty ['pressing a mission where the return is lengthy' is conjectured]. The mission will end in destruction, 614~608~604.

615–16 *not from lack of heart, etc.*: the Scout's judgement of Amphiaraus at 589, 592; contrast Tydeus' judgement at 382–3.

619 *what hits the mark*: a set phrase, translated in l. 1 as 'what meets the moment', cf. also 65 and e.g. *Supp.* 446, *LB* 582; here is it a euphemism for 'what is inevitable'. Apollo's prophetic voice always hits the mark, for he speaks only of certainties: *LB* 269–70, *Eum.* 615–18 in the *Oresteia*. [Many scholars apply the phrase and the line to the human prophet Amphiaraus, prescient of his imminent death, 587–8, 617; some delete the line altogether.]

620–4 *Lasthenes*: perhaps an invented name; it means 'People's Strength'. Lasthenes' portrait is confined to his prowess in arms (like Actor's, 553–7); because Amphiaraus has no boast on his shield, or moral failing stated (on the contrary), no contrast is required in his designated opponent. *enemy to outsiders*: potential foes; the same word as in 606 'hostile to guests', but less pejorative here. [Individual words in these lines are doubted, esp. *growth*, but it is supported by a papyrus text.]

625 *Yet men's success, etc.*: Eteocles ends with a seeming retreat from confidence; he means perhaps not that Lasthenes' success, as a mere mortal man, may be uncertain, despite Amphiaraus' own certainty that he himself will die, but that everything at Thebes is in the gods' gift: 719.

631–719 The play's crisis, analysed at Introd. 2.2. pp. xxx–xxxiii, with particular attention to Eteocles' speech 653–76.

631–5 *the seventh gates*: the only ones unnamed or unlocated, so that all emphasis falls on the seventh encounter, known to be the last; for 'seventh, last, and implicitly most important' cf. *Pers.* 778, and n. on 800 below. *crying out joyously*: a term from cult, associated esp. with the welcome accorded by ecstatic celebrants to a divine advent: grim, ironic humour for this fatal combat (636, 655, 689, etc.). *victory-hymn*: Iphigenia sang one for her father Agamemnon against Troy, before he left home: *Ag.* 247, cf. also 268–9 n. above. [After 633 West rightly follows some editors in deleting 634 'after mounting the walls and being proclaimed to the land', a line which contradicts fact: he has not yet entered the gates.] *for yourself*: begins Polynices' invocation emphatically: Eteocles is the sole object of his vengeance. [*with living exile ... with expulsion*: sense secure, but text insecure because anomalous in expression.]

642–8 Polynices' device is starkly plain in meaning; it emphasizes the issue of 'justice' between the brothers, taken up by Eteocles at 662, 667, 671; cf. Amphiaraus at 584. *the letters*: cf. 434 n. *possess his father's city and the freedom of his house*: exactly the fugitive matricide Orestes' future when released from the Furies' persecution, *Eum.* 754–8.

649–52 *Those have been the devices these men, etc.*: Aeschylus has the Scout complete his *reports* by referring briefly to the devices of all the attackers; but he finishes allusively by urging Eteocles to choose just one opponent, implicitly for Polynices: the Greek makes this clear with the singular relative pronoun *whom* (I have added *against Polynices* in the translation for clarity). *steer the city's course*: the image with which Eteocles himself began the play, 2–3; the Scout used it too in 62–4. He says 'I have done my job without fault (651–2): now do yours!' [The sudden awkwardness in 650 of *and you yourself must now decide*, but esp. the duplication between it and 652 of *but you yourself must decide*, induce many editors to delete 650 (West does not); the deletion also avoids an unwanted interruption between 'devices' and 'reports'. At the end of 652 a damaged papyrus text appears to attest either 'steer (your) fatherland's course' or 'steer your course back again' (i.e. to safety).]

653–5 *Oh, the family of Oedipus, etc.*: an impassioned outburst, almost lyric in intensity; this opening and the whole tenor of Eteocles' speech resemble a soliloquy. Laius' disregard of Apollo in fathering Oedipus (741–6: see n.; 842) is not described in this play as madness, but both Oedipus' marriage to his mother and his later cursing of his sons are (725, 756, 781): Aeschylus puts this idea firmly in Eteocles' mouth (*family of Oedipus, and mine*), and the Chorus will go on to accuse him of madness himself, 686–7. *their great*

*detestation*: Eteocles again at 691: *now my father's curses ... fulfilment*: unmistakably heralding Eteocles' intention to oppose his brother himself (672–5);
the idea recurs at once in 659, then e.g. 724.

656–7 *give birth to*: a common metaphor, e.g. *Supp.* 498, 770. *grief even harder
to bear*: that of Thebes, Eteocles means, if he fails to save it even at the cost of
fratricide.

658–61 *This man so well named, Polynices*: 576–8 and n. *wittering of wandering wits*: the Greek has a deliberate alliteration, conveying Eteocles' contempt.

662–71 *Justice the maiden daughter of Zeus*: the paternity is as old as Hesiod,
*Works and Days* 256–8. With the etymological play on her name as Zeus'
daughter in 670–1 (also *LB* 949–51), Eteocles distinguishes the true Justice
from the false one on Polynices' shield, 646. *this might perhaps now be so*: this
concession is only a foil to the utter dismissal which follows.

675–6 *greaves ... protection against spear and arrow*: surprising to us, but
apparently accurate to reality: the lower legs, difficult to protect with a shield,
were a favoured target, to bring a man down. The greaves were put on first,
before body-armour, so that Eteocles means that combat is imminent for
himself; perhaps attendants brought on all his armour to underline his final
exchange with the Chorus.

677 *No! Dearest of men, etc.*: the first words spoken, not sung, by the Chorus
since 369–74.

678–80 *that ill-named one*: Polynices again, 658. This translation, rather than
'that one you have spoken ill of', seems indicated by *It is enough, etc.*

682 *no old age for this pollution*: it remains ever fresh, beyond cleansing, cf.
734–9, *LB* 71–4. The expression is typical of folk-wisdom; cf. Eteocles again
at 685 (n.), 719, perhaps indicating stress.

683–5 *If someone really, etc.*: i.e. 'Let me at least die in battle', the soldier's best
chance of fame (first at Homer, *Iliad* 12.322–8, *Odyssey* 24.93–4). Eteocles'
hope for glory is that of saving Thebes; for his *profit*, cf. his 697. By *someone*
is meant Polynices (the indefinite pronoun alludes to an enemy only too
obvious; cf. 402 n.), rather than some anonymous god (despite 689). *you'll
not speak, etc.*: 682 n. [but the text and translation are insecure].

686–711 The Chorus sing in the most excited of Greek lyric metres, dochmiacs (n. on 78–181). They are appalled and desperate to avert the fratricide;
they urge patience upon Eteocles. He answers their alarm in speech, his

four triplets measuring out acceptance of his inevitable fate. For this further 'epirrhematic structure', see 182–286 n.

686 *my son*: a conventional form of address by a chorus, in any mood. *mad ruin*: often personified, e.g. 957, *Pers.* 1007; it is the destructive agent in the house of Atreus in the *Oresteia*, *Ag.* 386, *LB* 1076, etc.

689–91 *Since a god...hurries, etc.*: there is no escape, 719. *line of Laius detested by Apollo*: possibly an allusion to Laius' offence to the gods in abducting the beautiful boy Chysippus (an ancient commentator on Eur. *Phoenician Women* 1760), and almost certainly echoing an emphasis lost to us in the first two plays of the trilogy (see Introd. 2.2 p. xxix and n. 23); 745–8 give only the regular detail that Laius disregarded an oracle of Apollo in fathering Oedipus; but for 'detested' cf. Eteocles at 653. *along with the wind*: accelerating a movement already irresistible, also 854. *Cocytus' wave*: the irresistible flow of Hades' river (*Ag.* 1160); its name means 'Wailing'. Laius' line is doomed to extinction, the 'bitter fruit' of 693–4: see 720.

692–4 *perform*: a term from cult-practice, blackly ironic in implication here; again at 782. *unlawful*: the Greek word registers the prime offence, to the gods.

695–7 *my own father's*: the Greek has these words enclosing *my enemy*, an effect of rhetoric rather than accuracy: Eteocles lamented his descent from Oedipus in 654. *dry, unweeping eyes*: at 653–5 Eteocles had described the curse's effect as 'all the tears to shed'; here he must mean that he himself is beyond tears. *earlier death as profit over later*: that of death without disgrace on the field (684), against one later which might prove shameful. [*black (curse)* is a conjecture, cf. 832, 'black Fury' 988); it is supported too by 'black' in 699 'the Fury cloaked in black storm'. The MSS have a form of the verb 'perform' which has invaded from 693 and which West leaves obelized.]

699–701 *Fury cloaked in black storm*: lit. 'Fury in her black aegis', the potent tasselled shawl-like goatskin distinguishing esp. the goddess Athena (whose rapid flight, like that of the Fury here, it signifies at *Eum.* 406); but the word *aegis* means also 'storm-wind' (*LB* 593). *get your hands' sacrifice*: the hands are unspecified in the Greek [and the expression therefore doubted], but only Eteocles himself could offer sacrifice, as his question in 704 makes plain, 'Why then should I still fawn, etc?'.

703 *favour*: this noun is used of any sacrifice, so that its connotation of 'death' is grimly ironic.

705 *mood*: the gods have this human disposition also at *Supp.* 364. [*Wait*: West's conjecture for MSS 'Now', which lacks syntax; he supports it from 714 'Don't take this road, etc.']

706–8 *late veer... changeable... breath, etc.*: the winds of human fortune changing as the god wills are a common metaphor, e.g. *LB* 1067; the image is renewed from 689–90 'hurries... along with the wind' and 699 'storm'. *storm... boiling*: English too uses this metaphor of the sea; note how it is immediately taken up in 709.

710 *dreams... all too true*: Eteocles has mentioned no dream, but he may have feared the division of Oedipus' wealth by fratricidal sword, 727–30, 788–90; cf. Introd. 2.2. p. xxxi n. 25. For dreams and inevitability in Tragedy, cf. *Pers.* 176–200 and see Introd. 2.1 p. xxvi n. 14.

711–19 Stichomythic form makes this last, brief, and hopeless exchange most effective (see Introd. 3.2 p. lxi).

712–13 *women... although you have no love for them*: Eteocles at 260–4 was rude and impatient with them, before he knew the attackers; now he foresees his fate, he is coldly but briskly polite.

716–17 *victory... even if ignobly won*: the Chorus mean, if they can dissuade Eteocles from the duel; but in 717 he chooses to hear the Chorus literally. A similar conceit at *Ag.* 942–3, when Clytemnestra persuades Agamemnon to walk on the spread purples.

718 *reap... blood*: a vigorous if not unparalleled image, e.g. *Supp.* 637; it may take up the Chorus' 'bitter fruit' of 694.

719 *if the gods give it*: cf. Eteocles at 562 'if the gods will it', but there more hopefully. *you can't escape*: fatalism expressed uncomfortably in an everyday 'second person' axiom; cf. 281 and n.

720–91 Second ode: the history of Oedipus' curse upon his sons. Anxiety that the father's Fury may now divide the sons' inheritance with the sword (720–40) prefaces the account of how Laius fathered Oedipus in defiance of Apollo's oracle that any child would destroy his line (741–9). Oedipus duly became a parricide and the incestuous father of Eteocles and Polynices upon his own mother (750–7); earlier he had reached a zenith of material prosperity, after overcoming the Sphinx (772–7), but on discovering the truth he launched the curse in frenzied despair (778–91). Thus the history is narrated but, in a manner anticipating the *Oresteia*, Aeschylus prefaces Oedipus' prosperity with a moral question: whether prosperity itself predisposes a man to disaster (758–71); indeed the same questioning concludes the

*Agamemnon*'s narrative of Troy's ruin, *Ag.* 750–82. We are in great difficulty to assess both the details narrated here and the background to the question (which is not taken further here) because we have lost both the earlier plays of the trilogy: see Introd. 2.2 p. xxix. A familiar kind of dramaturgical issue also arises from this ode: if the Chorus had such knowledge of Oedipus' curse, why did they not caution Eteocles against fulfilling it (they did not hear his 69–70)? Both question and answer are as irrelevant to Aeschylus' purpose as those concerning Oedipus' seeming ignorance of how and where Laius was killed in Sophocles, *Oedipus Tyrannus* 697 ff. Aeschylus is obeying the needs of his drama, not of real life; cf. n. on *Pers.* 681–851.

The Greek metres are not as varied as in the first ode, but the first pair of stanzas has ionic rhythm, associated with high solemnity (see nn. on *Pers.* 65–101 and 647–702): the Chorus are gravely alarmed, but resigned.

**720–3** *I shudder that the goddess... may fulfil, etc.*: repeated amost exactly when this ode ends, 790–1; much of these lines is echoed also in 941–5 (note too how 723 and 791 bracket the whole ode with the *Fury's* name). *goddess unlike gods... the Fury*: cf. *Eum.* 69–70, 350, 360, the Fury's enforced separation from the Olympian gods. *destroyer of houses*: of criminal ones, *Eum.* 354–5, 421. The string of uncoordinated descriptions is almost matched in the responding stanza at 728–30; for this style, cf. also 916–18, and particularly *Ag.* 738–43.

**725–6** *demented Oedipus*: conscious of, but unhinged by, his catastrophe (778–80), he cursed his sons in frenzy (781–7); cf. n. on 653–5. *destroying sons*: echoing 'destroyer of houses', 720.

**727–30** *the portions*: the Athenians' term for official allocations of land, applied with bleak irony in 731–3; for the figurative language, see Introd. 2.2. p. xxxiv. *Chalybian*: a people near the south shore of the Black Sea, famed for their work with iron, *PB* 715 (where, as here and in 817, they are loosely located in *Scythia*). *Iron*: the metal personified, as in 944; it is often used in metonymy as 'sword', e.g. 788, 817, 883. For 'iron' imagery in the play, see also Introd. 2.2 p. xxxiv.

**732–3** *these great plains*: fertile Boeotia (304–9), the source of royal Theban wealth (730). [The text and syntax of 732 are suspect to many editors.]

**735–8** *Once... earth has drunk... who is to give expiation... release?*: questions to be repeated amid the family killings of the *Oresteia*, *Ag.* 1018–21, *LB* 48. *provide them with release*: so that the pollution does not follow them into Hades, for the Furies persecute after death, *Eum.* 324–40; cf. Clytemnestra's ghost 95–8 there [this wording is inferred from the ancient commentator; the MSS offer 'who is to wash the blood away'].

739 *harsh new*: 'harsh' is idiomatically implicit in the Greek, where *new* is emphasized through the heavy juxtaposition of *ancient*.

744–5 *its penalty swift... to the third generation*: the penalty has followed the transgressions of Laius and Oedipus already and is now certain for the brothers cursed with fratricide, just as Agamemnon must pay for his accursed father Atreus' crime (*Ag.* 1580–2) with one of his own which brings his death.

745–9 *the world's navel*: Delphi, *Eum.* 167. *thrice... without issue*: deliberately 'oracular' language; for the power of the number three, see n. on 43–8. This happens to be the earliest surviving version of Apollo's oracle to Laius; later e.g. Soph. *Oedipus Tyrannus* 711–14.

750 *folly*: the idea returns in 802, 842; but translation of the adjective *pleasing* is insecure, even if it attractively suggests an over-ready self-gratification in Laius' disobedience. West himself offers 'foolish fondness', which reverses the Greek emphasis, others 'his dear ones' folly', alluding to his complicit wife [or editors emend the text to create this last meaning with 'by his dear ones, foolishly'].

753–4 *his mother's sacred tilth*: i.e. forbidden, to prevent incest. The imagery of 'ploughland' in conception is commonplace, e.g. *Supp.* 637.

756–7 *foolhardy! Insanity, etc.*: harsh condemnation of the helpless transgression, mitigated only a little by accompanying madness; the idea is potent in the *Oresteia*, e.g. *Ag.* 218–25, Agamemnon's sacrificial killing of his daughter Iphigenia, where the word-root in 'foolhardy' is used three times with subtle variations of meaning from 'hard' to '(foolhardy) audacity'.

758–61 *waves of trouble*: another commonplace image, e.g. *Supp.* 127, *PB* 886, here combining with that of danger for the ship of state; see next n.

762–3 *wall*: cf. 216, 234, the city's wall 'keeping out' the enemy; the verb there is appropriate also to a ship's sides keeping out water; and so 795–7 below, 208–10 and n. [A senseless MSS text is variously repaired by editors; *of narrow width* is wholly uncertain as an emendation.]

766–71 Exceedingly difficult lines. Text and interpretation are disputed, but the general moralization in 769–71 (*The prosperity... from the stern*) makes it clear that 766–8 are general too, about any inescapable curse, not specifically that of Oedipus (which comes in at 785). The imagery of 767 *settlement* seems to be from money: when 'payment' of the curse falls due, its harshness cannot be deflected; with 'settlement' (also 908) I translate a term taken by many to imply reconciliation. The Chorus appear to vary their assumption of the inevitable: the duel of the brothers is now certain, but not yet its outcome; the curse will be hard to stop. [So West's text. In other reconstructions, 766 *fulfilled* is translated as 'final', as if no avoidance can be expected; but 'fulfilled' for Oedipus' curse appears also in 832, after the deaths are announced.]

769–71 *prosperity . . . fattened to excess must jettison all*: a message repeated with the same imagery from a cargo in *Ag.* 1008–14 (jettison some to save the rest—as the Atreid line is saved in the end); but here safety is hardly foreseen for Oedipus' line, despite his unexampled success with the Sphinx, 772–7.

772–7 *who . . . had such esteem . . . as . . . Oedipus?*:—and fell so far?, ask Pindar, *Olympians* 1.54 and Soph. *Oedipus Tyrannus* 1186–1222. *gods that share the altars here*: 251.

777 *snatcher of our men*: the Sphinx, 539–41 n.

778–91 These lines are marked by a number of verbal repetitions, echoes, and resemblances between the two stanzas, although there are no exact correspondences in position.

778–84 More very difficult lines. *fully conscious of his dreadful marriage*: recovering from the delusive madness in which he entered it, 756–7. *the two evil acts*: parricide and incest with his mother (752–4), the second a consequence of the first—even if both were done in ignorance, 541–4 n. *performed*: for the connotation of this verb see the n. on 693. [West's text rests on this interpretation of *the two acts he had performed* and on his conjecture in 784 *from better judgement*, but is very plausible. Earlier editors had kept MSS 'he performed (or 'fulfilled') two evil acts' in 782, and tried to retain in 784 a mixture of strongly doubted MSS readings and conjectures which gave 'lost his eyes (*or* house) which were superior to children'; then *the two evil acts* were the hideous self-blinding and the pronouncement of the curse itself.]

785–91 *they had not sustained him*: in his blindness; but this is an approximation to the sense, not a translation, for the text of 785–6 is uncertain. The sixth century BC epic poem *Thebais* (very fragmentary) told how Oedipus' sons sent him only poor meat from sacrificial animals, a dereliction of their duty to support a parent and an insult to his royalty. This must have been after his 'evil acts' were revealed (782 and n.). Others have understood the Greek to mean that his anger was for his sons' 'very conception', incestuous:

perhaps, and it may not matter that the equally wretched daughters were not cursed too. [In offering this approximate meaning, I have not translated at all the corrupt word in 785 which appears to duplicate *curses*, and which West leaves obelized.] *divide his possessions with swords of iron in hand*: again at 944–6. *swift-running*: lit. 'leg-flexing', a detail matching artistic representations of a pursuing *Fury*; this significant name is given the final, emphatic place in stanza and ode, as in the *Oresteia* at *Ag.* 748, cf. 59; cf. Ares at 344 above and 910.

792–819 *s.d.*: The Scout: for his identity as the 'messenger' see the n. on the *hypothesis*, p. 160.

Thebes is saved, but Eteocles and Polynices have now killed each other. The scene repeats the curse's origin in Laius' disobedience of Apollo (800–2: 743–52) and the division of Oedipus' property with the sword (816–17: 727–30, 788–90)—but it is the Scout, not the Chorus, who says these things. This different emphasis upon them indicates that the scene prepares concisely for the extended lamentation which now ends the play, and the trilogy: see 822–1004 and n.

792–4 *escaped slavery*: a constant anxiety, 75; cf. 253–4 n. *high and mighty*: translates a single Homeric adjective, applied to Ares the god of war at *Iliad* 5.845. [*noble*: West's conjecture; the MSS have 'daughters reared by (your) mothers', unconvincingly interpreted as 'timid because sheltered by your mothers' (cf. their fear at 78, 182–90, etc.). Some editors suppose the loss of a whole line amplifying the phrase.]

796 *the city has let in no water*: the imagery of 762–3 (n.). The Greek here shows a typical resort to contrast for emphasis where one term (*calm*) is both otiose and unapt; cf. 197 n.

800–2 *leader of all sevens*: a cult 'title' not elsewhere recorded but modelled on others registering the god's sphere, e.g. 'leader of the Muses'. Myth had Apollo born 'on the seventh day' of the month (Hesiod, *Works and Days* 770–1); his festivals were usually held on that day. Aeschylus wishes to emphasize the seventh gate as the site for the fratricidal duel and the end of Laius' male line which became inevitable when he defied Apollo's command to save his city by dying without issue (745, cf. 618). The Greek line is impressively sonorous, adding to this effect. *ancient folly of Laius*: 750.

803–10 A further very brief stichomythia (like 712–19), this time with the function of securing more information. [Its regularity is destroyed by the interpolated line 804 'The city is saved; and the royal brothers'; 804 is almost identical with the similarly interpolated 820: see 816–19 n.]

805 *The men are dead, etc.* and 806 *Who?*: the Scout seems reluctant, even evasive, with the truth after the transparent 800–2; but Aeschylus accommodates the revelation to the Chorus' extreme anxiety (note the Scout's initial 'Take heart!', 792).

809 *felled*: lit. 'made (down) into ash', a vigorous metaphor for physical and mental battering; of a severe storm, *Ag.* 670.

811–12 *too closely kin in blood*: a similar grim wordplay at 940, cf. also 974, 984 [but the phrase is a conjecture here, replacing MSS 'brotherly', to accommodate *too* more effectively. Even so 811–12 remain very weak lines, and editors have made many changes in trying to restore idiom and logic to them]. *the demon*: again at 960, the remorseless spirit of destruction infesting the house of Laius; at 705 it was translated as 'the divine power', not quite equated with the Fury of 700; possibly it was mentioned in one or other of the preceding two lost plays. Aeschylus has a similar 'demon' haunt the house of Atreus, persecuting it through inherited criminality, in the *Oresteia*, e.g. *Ag.* 769, 1468, 1501. Some, however, translate as 'the god', i.e. Apollo, who indeed *consumed the ill-fated family* (801–2); while this translation seems false to Aeschylus' use of the particular Greek noun, it can be supported: the Scout simply repeats his attribution of cause, without emphasizing the curse here but mentioning it at 819.

816–19 *dividing... burial*: recapitulating the Chorus' own 727–33. *what land, etc.*: they get only as much soil as their corpses 'take up', 731–2. [This recapitulation in fact protects 815–17 against suspicion of interpolation, it does not compound it. Line 819 is followed by stronger candidates for deletion, 820–1 'The city is safe; the earth has drunk the blood of two sibling princes through their mutual bloodshed'; these lines weakly duplicate 804–5. West suggests that they were meant to replace all of 805–19, and that this explains the presence of 820 in clumsy adaptation of 804.]

822–1004 Lamentations conclude the play—and the trilogy. A striking aspect of them is that only the Chorus utter them, as one voice (822–60) and then as antiphonal semi-choruses (874–1004); there is no parallel in extant Tragedy. Indeed, what other voice should utter than the one which has heard and talked with Eteocles throughout his last hours? [A fabricator—or two— was nevertheless not deterred from introducing other persons, for theatrical effect if at the cost of dramaturgical harm (unless the fabrication was for a performance of this play in separation from its trilogy): see the nn. on 861– 73, 996–7, 1005–77, and cf. 822–31 n.; Introd. 2.2 p. xxxv.]

First comes a reaction of ambivalence: joy for the city's safety or tears for the royal line now extinguished (822–31), followed by bleak recognition—once again—that the curse is fulfilled (832–47). Then the two corpses are brought in, and the Chorus rouse themselves to grief (848–60); it will be a *kommos* ('beating'), lamentation accompanied by rhythmic striking and tearing of body and dress (n. on *Persians* 908–1077); these acts are explicit in the wording throughout, and announced clearly at the start: see 854–6 and n. This *kommos* resembles that of *Persians* in becoming ever more emotional and fragmented, as the utterances shorten, and echo or take up each other, or share syntax and word-patterns; such effects are most marked after 961: see n. on 961–1004.

West numbers the paired stanzas continuously from 832, but after the prelude (822–31) and the first pair (832–47) the sequence is quite violently interrupted for a brief passage of free lyric (848–60: n.), as the bodies are brought in and the Chorus prepare themselves for the *kommos* proper. The metre of the entire sequence is heavily iambic, frequent in laments of all kinds; this rhythm closes the *Persians* too. We cannot know how the divided stanzas (from 875–960) were performed: did one semi-chorus stand silent when the other danced and sang, or were both in constant movement? In the broken short exchanges of 961–1004 such movement was certain.

822–31 A chanted prelude which summarizes the ensuing long sequence of sung and chanted lament. [In these lines *great* in 822 is suspect in its Greek form; 823 is plausibly and 830 indisputably supplemented by conjecture; in 826 the translation gives only the apparent sense, for both language and metre are at fault in the word translated as *safety*. Some editors believe all ten lines inauthentic; cf. 822–1004 n., end of the first paragraph.]

828 *who leave no children*: an aspect of the brothers' death brought up with remarkable abruptness [some editors therefore obelize the passage]. The idea of the male royal line being extinguished has, however, occurred in Eteocles' self-destructive prayers at 689–91, and in the Scout's statement at 813, and will be resumed in 953–60. Myth, however, named one son for each brother.

829–30 *rightly named*: for Eteocles 'of true glory' see n. on 458, for Polynices 'of much contention' on 576–8.

835–9 *possessed*: abandoning oneself to grief, a metaphor from an ecstatic female worshipper less forceful than at 498 (n.). *evil death... evil omen*: a wordplay typical of extreme lamentation, e.g. 912–13, 941–4. *two spears piping music as one*: the conceit is perhaps eased by preceding *I begin a chant*; and there appears to be a double allusion: their spears played the same music in their duel, and now the same lament begins over their two bodies; funeral music came from a droning pipe.

842 *Laius' disobedient resolve*: again, cf. 743–50, 802.

848 *s.d.*: the approach of the bodies is inferred from *Here* ... in 848 and *two deaths* in 850; they have been set down by 860, and the Chorus address them at once, in 874.

848–60 An interlude of quickly contrasting styles: bleak, terse sentences recognize the full tragedy, 848–53; a single elaborate one invites ritual lament, 854–60. Rhythmic beating of the mourners' hands, expressed in vocabulary common to grief and rowing (854–6), develops into detailed evocation of Charon's boat conveying the dead across Hades' river *Acheron* (a picture similar to that at Eur. *Alcestis* 252–4, 361). [All this is generally clear from a Greek text nevertheless extremely insecure in 849–53 and 857–8, where all editors differ in diagnosis and conjecture.]

853–60 *go along with the wind*: 690 (n.), the destruction of Laius' line. *beat* is lit. 'row with oars', used of the regular beating of the body in grief also at *Pers.* 1046; *steering* is lit. 'conveying by ship'. *the mission ... its canvas black*: black is of course the colour of death (e.g. *Pers.* 1052), but there is here an allusion to Athens' black-sailed ship sent annually to Apollo's sacred island Delos, commemorating the mythical boat which bore fourteen Athenian boys and girls as victims for the Cretan king Minos' Minotaur, and honouring the god for saving them. *the dry shore which Healer Apollo may not tread*: a conventional evocation of Hades' joyless dark; the god's bright and healing power is inimical to death. *where all are received*: ironic as well as euphemistic, for the Greek adjective normally registers agreeable hospitality, 18, *LB* 662.

861–73 Interpolated to prepare for Antigone's part in the fabricated 1005–77; cf. also 996–7, and n. on 1055–77. *without disputing*: unlike their brothers. The erotic interest in the girls' femininity (864–5, 871) suggests a later sensibility, of the mid-fourth century, gratuitous here, although *dressed in deep folds* is a Homeric borrowing (see n. on *Pers.* 155). The tone is quite different from the significant concentration on sexuality at *Supp.* 996–1005 (n.).

868–9 *ill-sounding hymn of the Fury ... hateful paean to Hades*: oxymoron and euphemism for a reversal of happy music: cf. e.g. *Ag.* 645 paean to the Furies, 1190 their 'revel', and *LB* 151 paean to the dead; at *Eum.* 331 the Furies sing their own 'hymn'.

873–4 *truly wail*: emphasis strange in English; cf. 919 'truly streaming tears'.

874–1004 The Chorus now divide again into two voices (as briefly at 369–74); cf. n. on 961–1004.

881–3 *single rule*: which Eteocles had (10, 39, 652, etc.) and Polynices wanted (647–8). *reconciled*: the sword was their 'arbiter', 908, cf. 767 n. [a paraphrase of 883 invaded the MSS after this word; while many early editors retained it, its deletion has caused the subsequent gap in the line-numbering].

886–7 *Oedipus ... Fury*: 723, 791, 976–7 and n. *potent*: lit. 'sovereign, mistress, lady', a form of address to deities (152), dignifies Oedipus' 'shade' at 976, and a Fury also at *Eum.* 951—but there in an optimistic context.

889 *left sides*: unguarded if shields are let drop.

890 *brothers from one womb*: imitated by the fabricator of 1036; cf. 931–4.

896–9 *unspeaking*: the Messenger did not say whether the brothers argued angrily before their duel. There may be an implicit contrast between their silent fight and their *father's* only too violent *curse* (785–7). *fated ... to unity of purpose*: fated to their irreconcilable quarrel, they agreed to resolve it through a duel; cf. 933–6. Others understand this 'unity of purpose' as the divine working of their common fate (812). [Editors have removed some invasive glosses from these lines, and corrected 'division' to *unity* in 899.]

900–2 *Lament*: for the emphatic repetitions of this word cf. *PB* 406–9. *the soil laments for men*: even more strongly at *Persians* 62, 548 and n., 683.

903–5 *successors*: loose in reference, the next rulers of Thebes: see 1005 n. (not the Epigoni, the sons of the defeated Seven, who avenged their fathers upon Thebes: e.g. Euripides, *Suppliants* 1219–26). *death as its end*: a Homeric phrase.

906–10 *equal parts*: death for both, 785–90. *the arbiter*: the sword, 883 n.; paired with *Ares* as 'the evil divider of their property' again in 941–5.

911–14 *Struck by iron*: cf. 730 n. *certain shares—one might say*: bleak humour, for the second 'struck by iron' alludes to graves dug by it; they 'share' *the tombs of their fathers*.

915–21: a typically Aeschylean accumulation of emotive terms. *rending*: only a possible translation [both the preceding and the following line being largely bold conjectural emendation]. The Greek word-root means 'cleaving apart' but describes 'lacerating' grief in Homer; *rending* is similarly uncertain in 918. There may be play too on the iron-struck division of the inheritance, 911–12. *truly streaming tears*: 873 n.

922–5 *One may say, etc.*: a certain caution here, or just understatement? The idiom is slightly different from 'one might say' in 913. *fray*: a Homeric word, only here in Tragedy.

927–8 *mother ... women ... parent*: emphatic redundancy, not rare.

931–2 *killing each other*: further insistence on the fratricide, cf. 850, 888–90.

934 *parting*: i.e. separation, but this translation is disputed. Lit. 'cutting-apart', in which it is difficult not to hear an echo of 'dividing their inheritance with the sword', 816–17, etc.

941–5: repeating much of 727–30 and 906–10. *Harsh... harsh*: a key word, sometimes translated as 'bitter', for the curse and its effects, e.g. 787, 881... *sea-borne*: worked iron imported across the Black Sea and the Aegean; see on 727–30. *leapt from fire*: cf. 207 'born in the fire', of heated horse-bits. *Ares*: see 910 n. In the Greek 'Ares' and 'curse' are juxtaposed in a sound-play (*Ares* : *aran*).

947–50 *portion*: but of what?—seemingly the property, but the word looks forward to *bottomless wealth*, the eternal 'riches' of the grave; for the irony, see 731–3; there is a comparable conceit at *Ag.* 871–2. Greek 'wealth' here (*ploutos*) half-conceals the name of the underworld god Pluto, in black irony: cf. n. on *PB* 806.

951 *crowned... with... sorrows*: a metaphor of grief also at *LB* 150.

957–60 *Ruin*: not personified at 687 (n.), though in this same context. *the demon*: 811–13 n. *ceased*: the 'ceasing' of Ruin is prayed for at the end of *LB*, when the matricidal Orestes' persecution by the Furies begins (1075–6, cf. *Ag.* 1479).

961–1004 Mesode 2 and stanza-pair 6 are a climax of unrestrained but rhythmic grief, with many phrases and sentences of corresponding length both within and across the stanzas; cf. 822–1004 n., and Introd. 3.3 p. lxii, on the *kommos*. The two semi-choruses deal for the most part each with one brother's fate, whereas in 874–960 they sang of them jointly; but while commending Eteocles' preservation of the city (esp. 981), they sympathize with Polynices despite his attack on it (esp. 980). [The MSS are often greatly at variance, and there are a number of corruptions where sure correction is impossible, even if the general sense seems clear, in particular 973–4, 984–5, 1000–4; and most editors interchange 983 and 993. I follow West's edited text throughout, except for two places (973, 984) noted in the Textual Appendix, p. 272. Lines 960–1004 are attributed in part to the brothers' sisters Antigone and Ismene in many MSS (but not in the principal MS, which indicates only change of voice parts); such attributions were almost certainly associated with the fabrication of 861–74, 996–7, and 1005–77: see on 822–1004.]

964 *Let lament come*: self-incitement to grief interrupts constant restatement of its cause; in a *kommos* also e.g. *Pers.* 941–7.

976–7 = 987–8 *potent shade of Oedipus*: a 'shadow' among the dead, but powerful still, like Darius in *Persians*, whose Ghost is summoned up (621, 630, etc.), and Agamemnon in *Libation Bearers* (355–9; he is the object of gifts and prayers both placating him, 23, 44, etc., and exhorting his vengeance, 124 ff., 315 ff.). For the adjective *potent* see the n. on 887. Oedipus is once again equated with his 'black' Curse and the Fury, as in 832–3. *black Fury*: clad in black (*Eum.* 52, 370), as in 'black storm' 699 above; she is 'black' also as the daughter of Night, *Eum.* 745.

985 *triple (blows)*: probably meaning just 'extreme', like the 'triple' wave at 760.

989–91 *at the end of your march:...when you came back to your city*: as Polynices boasted on his shield, 647 n.

995 [The interpolator of 861–74 here inserted two lines for Antigone and Ismene, 996 'But above all for *me*', 997 'And beyond that for *me*'.]

998 [After this line an interpolator inserted 'Eteocles the ruler', defining *lord*.]

1001 *ruinous folly*: cf. 687 n.

1003–4 *honour... greatest*: the Chorus mean that Eteocles, as actual king, and Polynices, as a king's son, deserve the full honour of burial among the royal tombs; but they allow that the dead Oedipus will find it *hurtful* to have the sons he cursed *lie beside* him.

1005–77: 861–74, and perhaps 996–7 were fabricated in association with this whole false play-ending (on which see Introd. 2.2. p. xxxv). 862 names Antigone and Ismene as entering, but they go unmentioned in the genuine scenes of lament which follow 874. In fact only Antigone speaks here, at 1026–52, and is neither addressed by name, nor names herself; nor is Ismene mentioned; see also the s.d. on 1053 and 1077 (n.). Much of 1007–24 resembles Sophocles, *Antigone* 194–210 and Euripides, *Phoenician Women* 1628–34, both of which were later than *Seven*, so that some suppose the fabricator's dependence upon those places.

1005 *present and past decisions*: the apparent sense, the Herald beginning with a solemn statement of his office which reflects the formulae of Athenian democratic consultation and decree; his conclusion is not less formal, 1025; the words are translated less well as 'the wishes and decisions'. In the myth generally, control of Thebes after Eteocles' death passed to Creon, brother of Oedipus' wife and mother Jocasta: 473–4 n. *people's counsellors*: in 1025 they are 'the authorities'.

1009 *(death) within the city*: very flat, unless it anticipates the contrast with Polynices the invader (1019) whose corpse is to be thrown 'outside' (1014) [so 'in the gates' is conjectured, the place where both brothers died (958) or '(chose death) well for the city', anticipating 1011].

1010 *pure... towards its ancestral temples*: unlike Polynices (1016–18), who was accused of intending to ransack them, 582–3.

1011 *where it is honourable for the young to die*: in the front line, Homer, *Iliad* 12.315 ff., Tyrtaeus 10.1–2, 27–31 (a seventh century martial poet). Cf. Eteocles' own words at 683–5, 717.

1014 *to be thrown outside*: outside inhabited or managed land, or perhaps over the border, a regular penalty for executed traitors (in historical times, e.g. Thucydides 1.126.12). *for dogs to seize upon ...(1020) funeral from birds of the air*: the consequence of exposing a corpse, cf. 1035–7, *Supp.* 800–1; a Homeric picture, Iliad 1.4, etc.

1015 and 1018–19: lines composed on the basis of 582–3.

1017 *even in death he shall keep, etc.*: undying punishment for the criminal dead, *Supp.* 228–9, *Eum.* 174–5; cf. 682 and n.

1021 *honour's reward*: sardonic, like 1047–8; the Greek word here for 'reward' normally means 'penalty', as at *Pers.* 823.

1022–3 These lines are so convincingly Aeschylean in diction and feel that one is tempted to think that the fabricator drew them from another play now lost. *hands to work, etc.*: an interdict upon Antigone (who in Sophocles, *Antigone* 384–439 has achieved at least token burial for Polynices; see her 1040 here).

1024 *carried out from home*: for funeral, *LB* 9, 430.

1028–30 *give... given* would be acceptable emphasis, but the effect is weakened when they follow *giving* so closely. *my own brother... defying the city's rule*: similarly Antigone in Sophocles' play, 44–6, 450–6.

1031 *a powerful thing*: this phrase at *PB* 39, of kinship.

1033–4 *unwilling*: factually incorrect (1015 ff.), but the antithesis is automatic rhetoric; cf. 427–8. *my soul*: an elevated form of self-address, very rare in Tragedy except in Euripides (whom Aristophanes mocked for it, e.g. *Acharnians* 450).

1035 *(a line missing)*: such as 'neither dogs nor birds' (1014, 1020)?

1036 *let no one think of that!*: cf. 1040. She repeats and condemns the Herald's 1005, 1008, and esp. 1025.

1037–9 *His funeral ... a woman*: the translation disguises clumsy and possibly corrupt Greek, and there is no grammatical object for *carrying*, so that '*things*' are vaguely 'what is needed for the funeral' [editors tinker with these problems].

1042–53 This brief stichomythic exchange is quite stylish and effective—but not in Aeschylus' typical manner.

1045 *Be harsh!*: perhaps the meaning intended, but the usage of the verb is unparalleled.

1047–8 The text is 1047 is insecure, so that 1048 is hard to interpret except as sardonic: the Herald sees Polynices' 'honour' as the gods punishment: 1021 n. [*Certainly, if*: the two words are conjectural. The MSS have approximately 'He has not already had full honour from the gods', in which 'already' is false to Greek idiom and the whole sentiment incongruous.]

1051 *Strife*: personified by some editors at 726, by almost all at *Ag.* 698, 1461, *LB* 471; there in the *Oresteia*, as here, it represents the fatal conflicts within the family.

1055 *Spirits of Death, you Furies*: equated at Hesiod, *Theogony* 217. The Furies are 'Fates' because persecution by them is fated and inevitable; these identities merge at *PB* 516; cf. *LB* 306, *Eum.* 961. For their relentless persecution of criminal families see *Eum.* 354–5.

1056 *root and branch*: probably an imitation of 71.

1060 [*anger*: a conjectural replacement for the unapt MSS 'fear'.]

1065 *who could believe this?*: translation as 'Who would consent to this?' is possible but rather against idiom; it nevertheless seems to fit the responses in 1069–71.

1071–3 *any city approves what is right differently at times*: Chorus A defies the city's judgement upon Polynices (while allowing it to be right), Chorus B approves it for Eteocles.

1076–7 *swamping by a wave*: seemingly the fabricator of 1055–77 wished to end the play with its opening and repeated metaphor, the ship of state endangered.

1077 *s.d.*: Movement of the two groups in diverging processions may have begun during the last exchange of 1066–77; their parting illustrates the conflict of sympathies and purpose.


## SUPPLIANTS

IMPORTANT preliminary note: the Greek text of *Suppliants* is more desperately damaged than that of any other surviving tragedy. I have therefore confined warnings about insecurities of translation to the worst problems.

For the scarcely tractable problem of the play's date, see Introd. 2.3 p. xxxvi.

1 *s.d.*: *sacred mound*: a collective altar to the city's gods, 189, 222. The naming in 207–21 of individual gods and their emblems invites the spectators to imagine a more elaborate shrine, with recognizable images, cf. 430, 463, and within a precinct, 508–9 (n.). Probably it was represented by the altar central to the *orkhêstra* (see Introd. 2.5 p. liv). *branches which identify suppliants*: 21–2, 191, 241, etc., *Eum.* 43–5.

1–175 Entry of the Chorus (*parodos*) in two parts like that of *Persians* (1–154 and n.): a long, chanted march (1–39) and eight pairs of danced stanzas (40–175). The Chorus tell of their flight from Egypt to Argos, to avoid forcible marriage to their cousins, the sons of king Aegyptus: they detest and fear it; their father Danaus does not approve it; and they have been pursued from Egypt. They will appeal for protection as suppliants, and they have come to the land of their ancestor—Zeus himself, who long ago fathered a child upon the Argive princess Io (1–22). Zeus is the god to whom they appeal first (23–39), then again expressly after they tell the pitiful story of Io (77–110), persecuted by Zeus' wife and transformed into a heifer (40–67), and again in emphatic conclusion (154–75); they appeal also to Zeus' daughter the virgin goddess Artemis, to save their own virginity (144–50). In between they resort helplessly to tearful entreaty (68–76, 112–6).

The *parodos* thus presents the issues which dominate the entire play, through and beyond the Argive king Pelasgus' undertaking to protect them (confirmed in 600–24). The lyric mode here suits the Chorus' emotional narratives and appeals, but Aeschylus later makes them the protagonists in spoken argument too (see Introd. 2.3 p. xxxviii). The Greek metres change gradually, from considerable variety in the first five pairs of stanzas (40–111) to the iambic rhythm for the final three (112–75), which is very common in lamentation (see e.g. *Pers.* 908–1077). The effect is aided by passionate, doubled refrains (*Ephymnia* 1–3, throughout 117–75).

1 *Zeus the god of suppliants*: 347, 478–9, 616. *watch ... over*: 145, 811, etc.

2 *Nile's outer mouth*: where washed-down silt extended the Delta's channels, *PB* 847. *where the sand runs fine*: later remarked by Pliny, *Natural History* 35. 167.

4–5 *Zeus' land*: so named because Egypt possessed a famous oracle of Zeus-Ammon, e.g. Herodotus 2.42.5–6. *whose pastures neighbour Syria*: Aeschylus means the well-watered Nile Delta, and *Syria* refers to all land east and north of it, the Levant.

8–10 *by our own action in flight from men*: the Greek expression is extremely compressed (even for Aeschylus), of just two compound words. The translation given, which is now generally favoured, makes a full contrast with involuntary, public expulson (such as followed homicide: 6–7, 196, and e.g. *Ag.* 1412–13, *LB* 1038); and it gives the motivation of both the daughters and their father Danaus (11) as loathing for the Sons of Aegyptus because of their presumption and potential violence (30, etc.), as well as implying also the daughters' hatred for them as males (393, and n. on 644). An alternative translation was long popular, 'in flight from men, i.e. husbands, of our own race', which was supported by appeal to *PB* 855–6 'in flight from kindred marriage', of this same flight from Egypt, as if the author there reflected our passage in that sense; but see n. on 389–91 below, on the widespread and unexceptionable practice of endogamy. 225 below has also been taken to deprecate such marriage, rather than violent pursuit. *abominate*: a very strong word [*intention*: the missing sense is easily supplied from 108].

11 *group*: the word, different from that translated 'company' in 1 and elsewhere, has a political overtone, suiting a context of exile; it is used of faction at e.g. *Pers.* 715 and (conjecturally) 662 below.

13 *moves to hand*: metaphor from a board-game.

15–19 *where actually our line, etc.*: the ancestry of Danaus and his daughters in the union of Zeus with Io, 295, 535–7, etc.; but the union's location *at Argos* is later abandoned for Egypt itself, where Zeus' *touch* fathered Epaphus, 40–8 and n. 'Touch' is a common image for a god's unseen physical intervention, *PB* 849 also of Io; cf. e.g. *Ag.* 663, *LB* 948, 1059. *gadfly-maddened heifer*: the fly was sent by Zeus' wife Hera to craze and pursue Io to Egypt when the goddess transformed her into the animal through jealousy of her attractiveness to Zeus, 41, 291–309, etc.; Io's whole story fills the episode *PB* 561–886. *his breath*: the divine *afflatus*, impregnating Io; also 44, 577; cf. Aphrodite's breath at 1043.

21–2 *suppliants'... branches*: see n. on the initial s.d. In fact leafy branches or wreaths symbolized any approach under a god's protection, e.g. a messenger reporting victory *Ag.* 493–4.

23–5 *bright water*: significant later: 1024–9. *heroes*: powerful from the grave, and so no less an object of local cult than the gods: see 260–70 n. and e.g. *Ag.* 516, the dead heroes at Argos 'sending' warriors to Troy, and the dead Agamemnon himself at *LB* 483–5. [*to whom the city, etc.*: the Greek syntax is doubted, and editors variously emend this line or suppose the loss of one, e.g. (West) 'O you ancestral deities of Argos'.]

26 *Zeus the saviour and third*: a formula for the last and chief of all gods invoked and thanked, *LB* 244–5, 1073, *Eum.* 759–60.

30 *swarm*: the word is used of 'flocking' doves at 223, but its apparently hostile application here seems to be matched when the Egyptians are allusively hawks in 224, ravens in 751, dogs in 758, spiders in 887, snakes in 895.

37–9 *subject us... to themselves*: at 335 expressed as 'slavery'. *which Right denies them*: this personification also at 360; abstract 'right' at 336, etc. For this ground of appeal, see Introd. 2.3 p. xl.

40–8 A difficult passage. *calf*: the human child of Zeus borne by Io (41, 44), *Epaphus* (48), named as 'calf' also in 314 (cf. 117–21 n. on Apis): this may be a corollary of his mother's being a 'heifer' (43), but it is also a common animal metaphor for a young person, aided here by the apposition of *son* (42). Orestes is a 'colt' at *LB* 794. *my helper beyond the sea*: Epaphus, born and dying long ago in Egypt, is invoked to protect his descendants; note how 40–4 are largely repeated in 49–51. *flower-grazing*: also 539; it marks not so much the heifer Io's special status as the landscape in which she feeds, 50, 540, cf. *PB* 653 (also Io). *touch... Epaphus*: the Greek noun *ephapsis*, like *epaphe* in 16, 'etymologizes' the name; for such wordplays, see 65, 117–21 and nn., and esp. *Seven* 576–8 and n. Text and translation from 44 *her son by his touch* to 47 *duly fulfilled* are insecure; *suitably for his name* seems to mean that the 'touch' led at once to the naming of the child so conceived, and that its later birth confirmed and celebrated its parenthood [some editors emend to 'her fated term aptly fulfilled his naming'].

54–5 *made plain to dwellers in this land*: in 274–6, 291–326. *unexpected*: 277 'incredible'.

57–67 *If some bird-augur, etc.*: the Thracian Tereus took as wife Procne daughter of the Athenian king Pandion; he had her summon her sister

Philomela to Thrace, raped her and cut out her tongue to prevent her informing on him; but she wove or 'embroidered' her story on cloth for Procne. The sisters avenged themselves on Tereus by killing his son by Procne, Itys. Tereus tried to punish them, but all three were turned into birds, Philomela into a swallow, Procne into a lamenting nightingale, Tereus (in most accounts) into a hoopoe—but, uniquely here, into a hawk, a natural predator upon songbirds.

60–2 *hawk-driven*: taken by some to prepare for the hawk-simile of 223–6. [*Tereus' scheming wife crying her sorrow*: text and translation insecure; I offer roughly the paraphrase by the ancient commentator.]

63–4 *leafy rivers*: where poets often located nightingales, and where they are safer from hawks. *unheard-of fate*: both her metamorphosis and what caused it. [*fate* is conjectural in West's text in these lines.]

65 *composing the story of her son's death*: the Greeks heard the sound *itys*, the name of her son Itys (57–67 n.), repeatedly in the nightingale's song, and aetiologized the natural sound from myth: it is a poetic commonplace of extreme grief, e.g. *Ag.* 1142–5.

69–72 *Ionian modes and strains*; the 'Egyptian' Danaids now in Argos adopt trans-Aegean Greek sung lament. *gashing . . . cheek*: a ritual common to both Greeks and Orientals (see on 120–1, and e.g. n. on *Pers.* 1054–7). 'Ionian' may contain an allusion in sound to 'Io' (see 162 and n.), although *flowers of lamentation* is not a reference to her 'flower-grazing' but a regular image, e.g. *LB* 150–1; cf. our 'anthem' (cf. *Seven* 951). Lastly, 'Ionian modes' do not connote Ionic verse-rhythm, which has chiefly solemn associations: see *Pers.* 65–101 and n.

75 *Egypt the land of mists*: over the marshes of the Delta.

78–85 *Now, you gods, etc.*: an appeal to uphold 'right' for the Chorus as suppliants at an altar. It is phrased universally (83–5) but *lustful youth* and *arrogant force* allude to the feared rape by the sons of Aegyptus (105–9) [this approximates to the ancient interpretation, but some modern editors refer 'youthful' to the Danaids and translate 'grant no fulfilment to the taking of young women in marriage'; others emend the text]. *also . . . those fleeing hard-pressed, etc.*: if fugitive soldiers may claim the gods' protection, so no less may we as fugitives (75 'our friendless flight', cf. 5, 13, etc.); cf. the appeal to the god Apollo, also once a fugitive, in 214–15.

86–7 *if Zeus' it really is*: a formula of precautionary reference; for the 'real' identities and names of gods, cf. *Ag.* 160–6, *LB* 948.

93–5 and 88–90 [somehow transposed in the MS tradition, destroying the sequence of ideas; all modern editors accept the rearrangement.]

91–2 *The outcome is sure—no throw on the back!*: a little enigmatic, and no doubt reliant on a common saying. The imagery is from wrestling, as in Zeus' seizure of power at *Ag.* 173, cf. *Eum.* 589. *the nod of Zeus*: famously at Homer, *Iliad* 1.526–7, his assurance of action; similarly Homeric in style is 103 below 'right there from his holy throne' (cf. his high seat at 175, 595–7, *Ag.* 183).

88–90 *blazes out*: Zeus' nod of assurance is like his lightning (*Seven* 513, *PB* 359), unmistakable even in the gloom of mortal misery which prevents men from knowing his intentions (93–5 above. 1057–8).

96–9 *hopes high as towers*: a woman's spirit 'towers' at *Pers.* 192. *makes no armed array*: this battlefield metaphor also at 702.

100 *Among gods all is effortless*: the idea also *Eum.* 650–1, again of Zeus.

105–10 *So let him look, etc.*: the sons of Aegyptus are overcome by the delusion of prospective marriage to their cousins, so that they use violence to achieve it (30, 81, 104, etc.). *stock of Belus*: the Egyptians as descendants of an early, half-divine king, 319 [*Belus* is West's conjecture for the unapt 'mortal (stock)' of the MS; the reference is certainly to a specific family]. *ruin's deceit*: the ruinous folly so prominent in the *Oresteia*, e.g. *Ag.* 386, 771; see *Seven* 601 (n.), 958, 1001 [the translation of l. 110 is only approximate; the MS is damaged and West leaves it obelized].

112–13 *shrill, heavy, all falling tears*: the adjectives describe both the sufferings and the laments they cause.

116 *my laments honour myself—while living!*: pathetic paradox; cf. Clytemnestra at *LB* 926 'singing a dirge to my tomb, but to no effect'.

117–21 *Apis' country*: Argos, named for Apollo's son Apis, a 'doctor-seer' who came and removed a pollution: 262–70 and n. In this play however the name may also suggest the Argive Danaids' ancestor Epaphus (48 n.), who as the heifer Io's calf-son (41) was identified in Egyptian religion with the calf-god Apis (Herodotus 2.38.1, etc.). In *country of hills and cattle* (an expansive English translation, also at 129, 776), the Greek word for 'hills' includes the syllable for 'cow', and seems to allude to Io (Aeschylus is again playing with etymology: 40–8 n.); it seems to be a dialect word (which has survived into modern Greek), like *knows* and *foreign*. Aeschylus invites us to accept that the Chorus here do not use 'real' Greek, but a barbaric sort; a similar play is made with the 'outlandish' Cassandra at *Ag.* 1061. See also on 825–907 below.

*fall on... linen*: demonstrative grief, symbolically damaging one's substance as proof of loss, as gashing the cheek (70) wounds one's living body: Greek at *LB* 27–8, 'barbarian' at *Pers.* 125, 537–8, etc. *Sidonian*: Phoenician linen, famously fine, Homer, *Iliad* 6.289–91, etc., cf. Herodotus 5.29.2.

123–4 *Irreligious rites, etc.*: Greek text and interpretation are very uncertain [many editors obelize the two lines]; seemingly intended (West) is that the gods punish such rites; here, the Chorus mean those of the threatened forcible marriage (80), which they assert that the gods oppose, 9, 37, 78–85. With *if they succeed* (for the Egyptians)... *where death keeps away*, the Chorus are thinking of suicide (154–60, 457–60), but trust that the gods will save them from it.

126–7 *beyond determining*: the language echoes that of public scrutiny at Athens, or that of dreams. *misery... this wave*: metaphor as 470, *Pers.* 433, *Seven* 758.

134–5 *deckhouse... shielding from the sea*: cf. 715 and n. Cf. Xerxes' 'tented carriage' at *Pers.* 1000–1. *all-seeing father*: Zeus, *Eum.* 1045. The Chorus anticipate their concluding appeal to Zeus, 163–75.

141–3 = 151–3 *so very august a mother*: Io was *august* as favoured and literally touched by her divine lover Zeus: 15–19 and n. *unbroken*: the Greek word is repeated in 150, where it is translated as 'unwed'. This metaphor (from livestock) for a still maiden girl begins in Homer, *Iliad* 6.108.

144–50. *chaste daughter of Zeus*: Artemis as virgin goddess is invited to protect the virgin Chorus, cf. 1030–3. *countenance*: a word elsewhere applied to the 'face' of buildings. *rescuing*: here a legal term, 315 n.

154–61 *dark-complexioned, sun-beaten*: this fresh mention of their dark skins appears gratuitous (cf. 70), but may signal again the difficulty their supplication will create in Greek Argos (118–21 = 129–32). At 279–83 Pelasgus comments on the Danaids' Libyan appearance, but at 719–20 the male Egyptians too are distinctive for their dark skins; perhaps the actors' limbs and masks were specially darkened. *that Zeus below the earth*: Hades, 231, also e.g. *Ag.* 1386–7. The idea is that in death they will supplicate Hades to avenge them on their suitors, 230–1. *once we die, etc.*: the Chorus are indeed driven to make this threat at 455–65. *hung nooses*: a common way of suicide for women, also 788, *Ag.* 875.

162–6 = 175a–d *Oh, Io, poor Io*: Aeschylus plays upon an etymology for Io's name in the Greek exclamation *io* 'oh, alas!' (cf. also *PB* 561), just as the tragic hero Ajax's name, *Aias* was heard in *aiai* 'alas!', Sophocles, *Ajax* 431;

their fates require mourning. *know* (*it too well*): Aeschylus uses again the anomalous dialect verb of 130 (117–21 n.). *Zeus' wife triumphant in heaven*: Hera, who regularly out-manoeuvres him (e.g. 296, cf. 302–5). *after a hard gale, etc.*: both gnomic in expression (and often accurate to weather) and pertinent to Io: Hera's anger grew harsher, when Argos the first watcher of Io was succeeded by the tormenting gadfly, 303–8; so now, the Chorus fear for what will follow Zeus' failure to help them. [The MS text in these lines has been much corrected; the ancient commentator appears to give a variant 'lashed' for *hunted*. In 175a–d editors have restored the second Ephymnion 3.]

168–70 *held liable*: political language, cf. 126, 150 (n.). *dishonouring the heifer's son*: that is, in ourselves, as descendants of Epaphus (206, etc.).

173–4 *eyes turned well away*: as Justice rejects the impure, *Ag.* 777.

176–347. First Episode, first part. Two figures are introduced, Danaus the Chorus' father, who directs the whole flight and supplication (176–7, cf. 11–14, 319–20, 970), and Pelasgus the king of Argos, who must decide whether to protect the refugees (333–47).

In the first scene (176–233), Danaus advises the Chorus to be respectful in supplicating the gods of the altar-mound (189, 210–22) and then the approaching Argives (194–203, 232–3); his two speeches surround a brief exchange in which he and they invoke these gods (204–21). In the second scene (234–347) Pelasgus arrives, identifies himself, and learns of the Chorus and their descent from Io, so that he accepts this ground at least for their appeal to him; much of their dialogue runs aptly in 'question and answer' stichomythia (Introd. 3.2 p. lx), and the form returns when the Chorus present their more potent claim: it is for 'right' or 'justice', symbolized in their formal supplication of Argos made under Zeus god of suppliants (328–47). The dialogue exposes for the first time Pelasgus' dilemma: to risk war with the Egyptians or the wrath of Zeus (342, 347: see n. on 348–437).

For Danaus' silence between 234 and 490, see 1–175 n., at end, and Introd. 2.3 p. xxxix).

177 *the captain of your ship*: both literal (2; cf. 503) and metaphorical (12 'leader of our group').

179 *inscribe them in your mind*: similarly Danaus at 991, cf. *PB* 789.

180 *dust … voiceless messenger*: the same conceit at *Seven* 80–2.

181 *wheel-hubs, etc.*: screeching on fixed axles, the picture of *Seven* 153, 205.

183 *round-fronted chariots*: a Homeric description, e.g. *Iliad* 5.231.

186–9 *whetted*: metaphor as at *Seven* 715, *PB* 311. *altar-mound*: see the s.d. on l. 1 and n. *assembled gods*: 242, 333, etc.; all the gods of the community, sharing an altar, 220; invoked again at 209–23 etc. *altar . . . stronger, etc.*: see 85.

191–6 *Hold . . . in your left hands*: to leave the right hands free for formal touching of the one supplicated. *suppliant boughs*: 22 n., etc. *Zeus who ensures respect*: 478, 641. *words deserving respect*: see 455. *flight . . . untainted by bloodshed*: 6–7 and n.

198 *sensibly . . . calm*: Danaus' command also at 724.

203 *Bold words, etc.*: probably a maxim; cf. 489, also at the end of a long speech.

204 *good sense*: emphatic corroboration of Danaus' own words, 176.

210–22 [The MS neither names speakers nor even indicates voice parts, and its order of lines in 207–10 lacks logic. Many remedies have been proposed, none incontrovertible; all require differing interpretation of details; but 210 *Look on us indeed* must follow 206 *look on us*.]

207 *our plan*: submissive supplication, 188–203.

209 [*O Zeus, etc.*: Greek text and syntax disputed; this is the commonest interpretation.]

212–21 See *s.d.* on l. 1.

212–13 *this son of Zeus*: (Apollo 214), identified in 213 the *Sun*: it is one of the earliest such equations, implicit also in *Seven* 859. *god who was an exile from heaven*: Apollo was punished for killing the Cyclopes, who helped make Zeus' lightning-bolts, with one year's servitude to the Thessalian king Admetus (Euripides, *Alcestis* 1–7). [*son* is, however, a much disputed conjecture for MS 'bird', i.e. Zeus' eagle (*PB* 1022); with this reading the Chorus' 213 makes no sense as an answer to Danaus' instruction in 212, but only as a new invocation.]

215 *sympathize with mortals*: i.e. with ourselves, in our exile.

218–19 *trident . . . god*: Poseidon's fish-spear (also 755), with which he ruled the sea (*gave me a good voyage*: 137), as also the land, *Seven* 131, 310 (n.), *PB* 925 (whence *a good welcome on land*).

220 *the herald . . . Greek*: Hermes; cf. 920. Simple statuary often depicted him as phallic, as a god of fertility; hence his recognizability.

**221** *for our freedom*: from the threatened marriage, 807, 811, rather than in general (609).

**223–31** *sit down like doves, etc.*: an extended comparison and lesson; the simile recurs in this same context of supplication at Argos when it is prophesied at *PB* 855–7 (cf. Introd. 3.4 p. lxvi). The simile and the moral appear to echo Hesiod, *Works and Days* 276–9, where Zeus assigns fish, beasts, and birds the habit of eating one another, since they lack the mutual 'justice' which he gives to mankind. *bird eating bird* (226) is as impure as kin forcibly marrying kin (227). Details: *flocking*: the Greek word implies both motion and perching together—like the now seated suppliants. *how could a man … offences*: heavily juridical language. *another Zeus*: Hades, 158 n.

**232–3** *in the manner I have said*: 188–203 [but the translation of the phrase is insecure]. *win well, etc.*: Danaus repeats his 207.

**234** *s.d.*: Pelasgus carries a staff of office (uncertainly identified by the Chorus at 248).

**234–5** *not Greek in clothing, etc.*: unusual costume in drama sometimes prompts a particular direction to the dialogue, esp. when seen or worn by new entrants; here it emphasizes the particular difficulty Pelasgus will face with suppliants from abroad (cf. 496–5030). Aeschylus uses something resembling this device superbly—but in evocative narrative—in the central scenes of *Seven* (n. on 369–685). *headbands*: also 431.

**239** *sponsors*: 419, 491, 830, 919, 920: approximating to modern 'consuls' abroad; they were almost always natives helping foreigners.

**248** *warden with a sacred staff*: a priestly officer supervising the altar-mound.

**249** *Answer accordingly*: Pelasgus is either implicitly confirming 248 'the city's leader' or ignoring the Chorus' 246–8 entirely [some editors move 249 to follow 245 directly].

**250** *Palaechthon*: otherwise unknown. Aeschylus may be inventing a fine-sounding ancestor (the name means 'Ancient of the Land': son … *who was born from it*), but myth generally holds Pelasgus himself to be the founding king, as the next line implies.

**254–9** The geography causes difficulty. *Strymon* was the chief river of Thrace, N. of the Aegean sea (*Pers.* 497); the *Perrhaebians* are attested both in N. Greece, in that direction, but also near the mountain range *Pindus* and the *Paeonians* in W. mainland Greece near *Dodona* (see Map 2); so Pelasgus claims rule over surprisingly much of the mainland. Dodona had a famous oracle (*PB* 658, 830–1), indeed associated with Pelasgus.

260–70 While 254–9 impress on the Chorus the extent of Pelasgus' rule, these lines urge on them the antiquity of his royal seat Argos itself, through the aetiology of its territory's name from *Apis* (262, 269, cf. 260; see 117–21 and n.); the story here seems original to Aeschylus. As a *doctor-seer* Apis cured religious pollution by a mixture of practical and ritual means, just as his father Apollo is given this same title when expected to cleanse his own shrine at Delphi from the polluting matricide Orestes, *Eum.* 62. *Naupactus*: across the Gulf of Corinth from the N. Peloponnese; a harbour still. *remedies... cut*: from roots or herbs, ambiguously to kill or drive out the *snakes* or to cure their victims. *without recrimination*: the people did not suffer. Alternatively and perhaps better, 'without fault', causing no offence to gods or man, so that he *found remembrance... in prayers*, i.e. was heroized and given cult; cf. 23–4 n. [*evil things* and *in anger* in 266 are conjectures for very corrupt wording in the MS which West leaves obelized.]

271–3 *identifications from my side*: at 54–5 the Chorus were expecting to present their own, and these follow in 274–6, 291–324. *no liking for a long speech*: cf. Danaus' advice at 200–1.

276 *graft*: metaphor from tree- or vine-growing [bad MS corruption in this line has been emended].

282–3 *Cyprian character, etc.*: the words *struck, character,* and *forms* are metaphors from coinage; the word *ancestors* seems the best English equivalent for Greek 'craftsmen' or 'architects', which is used metaphorically for Zeus as an 'ancestor' in 594. Not just 'parents' are connoted here, but fathers as the more important, and generative ones rather than the mothers (*Eum.* 658–66). Aeschylus typically elaborates the simple idea, 'your fathers have imprinted an Eastern beauty on you', to make you desirable (*Cyprian*: evocative of Cyprian Aphrodite, 1034, 1041) and as exotic as the women now described in 284–8.

284–6 *Indians... nomadic*: Pelasgus' wonderment that the Chorus have come so far from their home continues in the mention of the *Indians* and their neighbouring *Ethiopians* (located loosely in the East as at *PB* 805–7); so the Chorus share their dark colour. *side-saddle*: the rare Greek word apparently denotes a saddle special to women. [The text is again insecure.]

287–9 *Amazons... no men*: vague, either 'husbandless' or even 'virginal' (they 'hate' men at *PB* 724—not unlike the Danaids, 790–1, 798–9!), or literal, 'with no males'. *live on meat*: Aeschylus is relying on one of two 'folk-etymologies' for the Amazons' name, <u>*a-maz-*</u> 'no-bread'; the other was 'no-breast', from a belief that they amputated one breast in order to use their *bows* more handily. [Text again insecure; some editors suppose loss of a line after *meat*.]

291–335 [The MS does not indicate speaker-parts (cf. 207–22), and their assignment, the extent of textual loss, and the order of lines are much disputed. Early printed editions did not number ll. 294 and 312.]

291–2 *temple-priestess*: lit. 'key-holder to Hera's temple'. Hera would be the more angry at Zeus' union with her priestess; her retaliatory transformation of Io (299) is Aeschylus' invention; in the dominant version Zeus alters her to prevent Hera's discovery of their union, and this may be reflected in 296.

296 *struggle with her*: lit. 'wrestling'; Io resisted Zeus. The same word is used of Cassandra's attempted rape by Apollo at *Ag.* 1206 [but 'wrestling' here is a conjectural replacement of an apparent MS reading 'entanglement', which an ancient scholar paraphrased with 'embrace'].

299 *Argos' goddess*: Hera's cult was very strong there.

300–1 *go with*: as in the English euphemism; also *PB* 897. *fine-horned*: not less attractive to a bull than the girl was to 'human' Zeus: so *mounting a cow*, lit. 'jumping a cow', a verb used of human intercourse at *Eum.* 660. The implication of these lines is that Zeus disguised himself as a bull, but may have been thwarted of the union, so that later he inseminates Io by touch (40–8 n.).

302–5 *Zeus' powerful wife*: 165, cf. 1035; for Hera's persecution of Io, see esp. *PB* 591–2, 599–601, 704. 304 is an awkward line, probably formulated to maintain the stichomythic alternation. *Argos*: a creature variously imagined, with two heads or multiple eyes (*PB* 568, 678–9), some never sleeping. His name appears to have no connection with the city; it was interpreted as 'with brilliant eyes'. *Earth's son*: so also at *PB* 677. Earth generates all monsters, e.g. *PB* 351 Typhon; cf. *LB* 585–6. *that Hermes killed*: quite possibly an element of the story, and done at Zeus' command; but the idea may derive from the Homeric adjective for Hermes *argeiphontēs*, which the ancients etymologized as 'killer of Argos'—but Homer does not elsewhere allude to Argos.

307 [*A line missing*: shown by the break in the stichomythic pattern. Pelasgus requested or gave more information; see the Textual Appendix.]

308–13 [There are textual difficulties whatever order of lines editors adopt. In 310 *too* is particularly in doubt.]

309 *long course*: its length is emphasized at *PB* 591–2.

311 *Canopus*: at the Nile's mouth, where Io's wanderings ended and Zeus 'touched' her; cf. *PB* 846–52. *Memphis*: south of the Delta; it is 'holy' at *Pers.* 36 and possessed a cult of Danaus, to which allusion might have been made later in the trilogy.

313 *Zeus . . . touch*: the Greek has lit. 'Zeus the Toucher', a title invented by Aeschylus, used again at 535.

315 *act of rescue*: a legal term, of reclaiming rights, often implying a duty of protection (150, 324 n.), cf. Zeus 'curing' Io at 586–7, *PB* 848–9. The same legal term has a harsher application at 413, 414, 728, in the sense of seizure of person or property to prevent reprisal; cf. also 924 and n.

316 [*A line missing*: Pelasgus inquired about Epaphus' children.]

317 *Libya*: a daughter, giving her name to the region. [*harvest*]: the most probable supplement; Libya was famous esp. for sheep: Homer, *Odyssey* 4.85–6.

319 *Belus*: Libya's son by the god Poseidon; cf. 105.

320 *all-wise that he is*: a further etymological play, upon Danaus as the 'learned' one (Greek <u>da-</u>). Pelasgus guesses his wisdom from his age (mentioned at 176–7, 602).

321–3 *fifty sons*: the Danaids themselves are fifty in number at *PB* 853. The number is allusive, our 'umpteen'; used notably of Priam of Troy's children. *do not grudge telling*: a formula, also *Seven* 480.

324 *supporting*: lit. 'making stand up', marking the acceptance of suppliants by raising them from their knees [text and translation are insecure in detail, but the overall sense is clear].

327 *how could you brave, etc.*: Pelasgus repeats his question of 238–40.

328–32 *troubles flicker about . . . wings*: flight as image of sudden instability; the language suggests an everyday axiom. *put to trembling flight*: recalling the fearful doves of 223–4.

333–4 *newly cut*: on the spot, since coming ashore; cf. 22 and n. on 508. [Text and translation are insecure in 333.]

335 *slave to Aegyptus*: as a chattel, not a true wife (337).

336 *what right forbids*: 39 (n.). Pelasgus has picked up the hint of 332.

338 *men increase their power*: through calculatingly acquisitive marriage, often to relations (cf. 387–91 n.). *Well, this is the way* recognizes that in such marriages wives do not feel love (so West) [the compression of thought has brought some editors to suppose loss of text after 337].

339–42 *the unfortunate*: either wives or slaves discarded for 'better'. Pelasgus seems to feel implicit criticism of his own power, and in 340 turns abruptly to his dilemma, between the alternatives of 342 and 347. *(unwelcome) war*: again at 439, 950.

343 *Justice*: again at 395; cf. the appeal to 'Right' at 360.

344 *if she is a partner etc.*: Pelasgus' answer shows his misgiving: had the Chorus a good case in law? See his 387–91.

345 *your ship of state*: 438–44 and n.

347 *wrath of Zeus*: the Chorus again at 385–6; Pelasgus at 478–9.

348–437 First Episode, second part. Tension increases towards the first and major crisis of the play, in a mixed lyric sequence. The Chorus plead intensely for Pelasgus to respect his obligations to Zeus' suppliants (348–50, 359–60, 381–6, 395–6); but he fears that helping them will endanger his city, from conflict within and without (356–7, 399–401, 410–17): this is a classic dilemma of 'suppliant' tragedy, recurring in Euripides' *Children of Heracles* and *Suppliant Women*, and in Sophocles' *Oedipus at Colonus*. When he tries to deflect the decision from himself on to the city's public vote (365–9), they presume his authority as king to act alone (370–5, apparently exploiting his statement of wide rule, 250–9). He struggles against their arguments, objecting on religious, moral and political grounds (throughout 354–415), and asking for 'time to think' (406, 417: see 438–523 n.), time which the Chorus fills with a passionate appeal renewed on their earlier grounds, but principally the obligation to suppliants (418–37, 'ring-composition' with 348–50).

Sung stanza-pairs from the Chorus alternate with spoken replies from Pelasgus (348–417: 'epirrhematic' structure, as in e.g. *Seven* 203–44: see n.); they precede two pairs of brief stanzas sung by the Chorus, marking the peak of their anxiety, and ending the sequence as if in a formal ode. The Chorus' uneven Greek metres express their great turmoil, esp. at start and finish of the whole sequence.

351–3 *like a heifer, etc.*: the Chorus implicitly compare their own plight with the heifer Io's wandering (309). *trustful of his aid*: that of Pelasgus, their own *herdsman*; but some translate 'their aid', as if the *crags* were a city wall (cf. *Seven* 762).

354–8 *our citizens from abroad*: Pelasgus accepts the claim of common ancestry (325–6) and later persuades his citizens of it, 618–19. *feuding*: civil faction; cf. 399–401. *unexpected*: cf. the Chorus at 330. *nodding*: the assembled gods, overshadowed by boughs (346, 354), 'assent' because the boughs remain undisturbed [but the word is a conjecture, West himself leaving the impossible MS 'swimming' obelized].

359–60 *Right*: personified: see 38 and n. She and *Zeus* uphold house and family well-being (*hearths*, cf. 372); but Pelasgus will object that the Chorus supplicate not his own hearth, but the city's, 365.

362–4 *the gods ... accepting*: that is, they reward a pure man materially. [The general sense of the text, which is corrupt or defective, is restored from the ancient paraphrase.]

366–75, 366 *community, etc.*: 'anachronistic' democracy; and 370–5, with *the people's voice* and *you preside*, suggest the 'constitutional monarchy' imagined by Athenians for their own mythical king Theseus as 'founder' of their democratic government, as he is portrayed in Euripides' *Suppliant Women* and Sophocles' *Oedipus at Colonus* (see Introd. 1 p. xxi). The Chorus use against Pelasgus his own self-description in 250–9 (n.): he has the real power. *preside*: a term from Athenian politics, over the Council: cf. 667 n. *immune from judgement*: more 'political' vocabulary. *polluted* (366) is countered by *pollution* (375).

376–80 *without harm*: cf. 356 and 359. *of action ... a chance*: translation disputed, but giving better logic than 'both of action or inaction, and of taking a chance', with the last phrase qualifying the previous two.

385–6 *Zeus* (the 'watcher' of 381) ... *implacable*: 646–8; cf. *PB* 34, 184–5.

387–91 *have power ... have ... authority*: synonymous expressions. Aeschylus is borrowing for Egypt a law like that of Athens, in which male heads of family had rights over unmarried women and their (potential) property. He has Pelasgus assume that not Danaus, their blood-father, is head of their family, but Aegyptus, the king (see 321–3).

392–6 *the power of men*: both physically as males and in the legal sense of 391. *I am marking out ... stars above*: the meaning is allusive: rather than marry,

I will flee 'anywhere under heaven'; cf. the Chorus' escape-fantasies of 776–807. *ill-meant marriage*: 9–10, 81, 426, etc. *holy to the gods*: cf. 85.

397–8 *judgement...judge*: the Greek in fact echoes 396 'judgement' three times for emphasis on Pelasgus' dilemma. *I said earlier*: 366–9.

402 *The Zeus of blood-kin...both parties*: Io's descendants are Danaus (331) and his daughters, as well as Aegyptus and his sons (333).

405–6 *Why...weighed impartially, do you grudge*: that is, when bad goes to bad and good goes to good (404), why should you (Pelasgus) not side with the good? [*grudge* is the best available conjecture for MS 'regret', left obelized by West; Pelasgus has done nothing at all as yet.]

407–10 *deep thought*: repeated at 417, the end of Pelasgus' speech (emphasis through 'ring-composition', and then by the Chorus at 418; it recurs in 437 (further 'ring-composition'), and is again taken up by Pelasgus in 438. *like a sponge-diver*: the image was applied by later philosophers trying to fathom the obscure words of Heraclitus (*c*.500 BC); for the language, cf. 1057–8 below. [409 *with eyes...wine* is deleted by some editors, the Greek syntax being difficult and the phrase *clouded by wine* not clearly applicable either to the diver or to Pelasgus.]

412 *Battle*: an Epic word, not personified by Homer but by other poets. *seize us as plunder*: Argives taken so as to force Pelasgus into exchanging them for the Danaids: legal terminology (315 n.).

414–15 *the demon Revenge*: the vindictive, persecuting power haunting Eteocles' family in *Seven*, e.g. 705, 960, and the Atreid family in the *Oresteia*, e.g. *Ag.* 1501, 1508; so it may cause 'bloodshed among kin', 449 below. *heavy housemate*: for the idea cf. 646–51 and the Furies at *Ag.* 1481–2, *LB* 971. *not let the dead go free even in Hades*: the idea of 230–1; cf. *Eum.* 175, 340, the Furies again.

419–20 *sponsor*: 239 n.; the Chorus seem to be answering Pelasgus' fear in 401. *reverence*: cf. Pelasgus' question at 340, and his 941.

432 *like a horse*: of a woman seized in a city's sack at *Seven* 328.

434–5 *whichever...you do...returning an equal due*: either protect suppliants, and fight the Egyptians, or fail suppliants, and fight Zeus' justice (342, 347). Pelasgus grimly repeats these alternatives in 439–40. [*this waits: returning*: the MS is corrupt, and no conjecture confident; but this is the likely sense.]

438–523 First Episode, third part. Pelasgus' 'time to think' (438 'I have indeed thought' picks up 407 (n.) and 417) has only sharpened his dilemma: between war and material loss (439–47) and offence to the gods. He delays by suggesting sacrifices to them to discern their will (450–1), but is pessimistic (454). In a brisk stichomythia the Chorus increase their pressure still more, by threatening suicide within the holy site (455–67), and Pelasgus gives way: anything rather than Zeus' anger (468–89). He sends the long-silent Danaus to the city with suppliant boughs, to predispose the citizens and to avoid blame for himself; Danaus asks for a safe conduct and leaves (490–503). The episode ends with more anxious pleading from the Chorus, and again in stichomythia: how will they be safe when both Danaus and Pelasgus are gone? He entrusts them to the gods in their shrine, and leaves to persuade his citizens (504–23).

This last scene prepares for Argos' full, armed protection of the Chorus; it is reported by Danaus (600–24) and enlarged upon at the play's end (966–1073), once the arriving Egyptians are halted by Pelasgus (710–965). The Chorus' anxiety here at being left alone before the Egyptians are even sighted (this at 710 ff.) recurs more violently in the later scenes (748–9, 776–820), when Danaus leaves them, to fetch armed help (729–33, 774–5).

438–44 *come to land … nails … hull … dock … cables … cargo*: a sustained metaphor for Pelasgus' ship of state (345n.), if it is compelled into war and at risk of losing everything on board (some editors interpret *conclusion* too as 'conclusion of voyage'). *brought into dock*: for fitting out before sailing. [In 443–7 many individual words are conjectural, accompanying the rearrangement of the lines—in which all editors differ.]

446–54 *so too, when a tongue, etc.*: as material loss may be recovered, with Zeus' will (445), so a difference of *sharp-pointed words*, here those between Pelasgus, the Danaids, and eventually the Egyptians, may be resolved peaceably (448–7); the gods' help is needed to prevent a bad quarrel (449–51). Pelasgus hopes still to escape warfare (453–4). *at the wrong moment*: misjudging a crisis; for the idea, see *Seven* 1. *victims … divination*: about war, *Seven* 43, 230–1. *ignorant*: the particular Greek word here is associated with anxieties about divination, e.g. at *Ag.* 1105.

455 *my many words deserving your respect*: Danaus advised these, 194. The Chorus now exploit 'respect' for a harsh warning to Pelasgus if he does not show it towards both suppliants (461) and the gods' statues (463).

457 *breast-bands and a sash*: outside the clothing, 462, *Seven* 872.

460 *Speak out... meaning*: the sense is emphasized by remarkable redundancy in the Greek.

461 *Unless you promise, etc.*: cf. Pelasgus' evasion at 368–9, etc.

463 *unwelcome tablets*: instead of votive messages hanging from the gods' images, expressive corpses: 465.

466 *to lash at my heart*: like a charioteer, to drive it to action; a similar image at *Eum.* 156.

468. [*words missing*: some editors prefer to emend, e.g. to 'Indeed there are issues, etc.']

469–71 *troubles... ocean of bottomless ruin... harbour*: renewing the ship-of-state metaphor, 438–44 n. For this sea-imagery, cf. 126 n.

472–3 *meet this need of yours*: Pelasgus at last concedes the Chorus their insistent claim for respect; cf. 478, and Danaus in 491. *pollution*: of rejecting suppliants, esp. those who are kin. *beyond my range of overcoming*: lit. 'beyond a bowshot', a metaphor used also at *LB* 1033.

476–9 *cost*: language from the counting-house, cf. Pelasgus in 443–4. *men... for women's sake*: for this male valuation, cf. *Ag.* 62, 448, 823, 1453, the Trojan War fought over Helen.

480 *s.d.*: Danaus has been silent since 233: 176–347 n.

481–2 *take these boughs, etc.*: Danaus does not take them all: 506 and n. [The missing line contained probably a simple instruction to leave the shrine.]

485 *people... blame its rulers*: consistent with Pelasgus' concern in 398–401; for such blame cf. *Seven* 5–8.

491 *sponsor*: 239 and n.

494 *altars fronting the temples*: where all will see the boughs, 482–4. [*with many wreaths*: a conjecture for MS 'gods which hold the city', duplicated from 493, which West leaves obelized.]

496–7 *My physical appearance differs*: Danaus is dark-skinned (cf. Pelasgus at 279–81, of his daughters), and his arrival 'from overseas' (503) will be explained. *Inachus*: the river of Argos, and the name of its mythical king, *PB* 590, 663 and nn.

498–9 *boldness, etc.*: that of Pelasgus, in sending an obvious foreigner into the city, even escorted; *fear ... ignorance*: potentially those of the citizens.

502–3 *not talk much, etc.*: only to confirm his identity as *from overseas* (the Greek is lit. 'sailor').

506 *Leave your boughs where they are*: cf. 481–4. With this gesture Pelasgus visibly acknowledges his obligation to the suppliants: see 324 and n.

508–9 *grove*: the sacred precinct of the altar-mound; perhaps where they cut the boughs, 334? Aeschylus is about to 'free' the Chorus for their next danced ode, 524–99; probably they do no more than stand up from the central altar (see *s.d.* on l. 1).

510–11 *winged things ... serpents*: both literal (potentially alarming) and allusive: Pelasgus reassures the Chorus that they will not be like birds at risk from hawks (cf. Danaus' fear in 223), but in their panic they fantasize a worse enemy, serpents with wings, just as later they imagine the Egyptians as bogey-creatures, 761; cf. 30 n.

512 *good words from me*: his promise of 510.

514 [*in the defenceless*: West's own plausible conjecture for MS 'of kings' (only a single letter is involved); also conjectured are 'Women's fear ...' (cf. *Seven* 238) and 'It is the part of kings to undo immoderate fear'.]

518 [*I go*: West prints the best conjecture for hopeless damage in the MS.]

519 *teach your father, etc.*: in fact Pelasgus does the important talking himself, 615–24.

524–99 First choral ode: another impassioned appeal to Zeus, as supreme god and as the Chorus' ancestor through Io (first stanza-pair, 524–37, an appeal emphatically repeated in the last stanza, 590–9). In between is a vivid narrative of the transformed Io's frenzied wanderings, her arrival in an astonished Egypt, and her release and insemination with Epaphus by Zeus's touch (538–89, cf. 535 too for Epaphus: 40–8 n.). The Chorus naturally repeat prayers from their entry-song (91–175), just as they will sing gratitude to Zeus and voice fresh prayers to protect Argos in their next ode (625–709: n.). Their final tribute here to Zeus' omnipotence (590–9) has immediate and apt confirmation when Danaus reports that all has gone well in the city (600–24, ending with 624 'Zeus ... ratified the outcome'). Once more very mixed lyric metres help to express the Chorus' urgency.

524–6 *King of kings*: a natural address to the supreme god, as to a supreme mortal king, that of Persia, *Pers.* 24. *most perfect of the perfect*: lit. 'greatest fulfiller', the title of Zeus at *Ag.* 973, etc., of gods in general *Seven* 167.

529–30 *sea purpled with storm*: Homer's colour for it, *Iliad* 16.391, etc. *black-built vessel of ruin*: Ruin's emotive hue at *Ag.* 770, cf. 'black Curse' at *Seven* 832 (n.). So the Egyptians' ship, if it reaches Argos, is potentially the suppliants' ruin, or the ruin is the Egyptians' own, the fruit of their mad folly (for 'ruin', Greek *atê*, in this sense, see 100 n. above).

532–5 *your kindness to a woman...your touch to Io*: releasing her from her madness and transformed body, and generating Epaphus, 16–19, etc., 310 and n., cf. *PB* 848–9. So the Chorus *proudly claim their descent* from Io, 584–9.

538–46 *I have moved*: i.e. come here from Egypt. *her ancient tracks...torment*: repeating details from 43, 50–1, cf. *PB* 645–81; see Map 5. *many tribes of men*: a Homeric phrase. *cleaving...torment*: Io apparently swims the strait separating Europe and Asia, and Greek myth named it for her as the Bosporus, 'The Cow's Crossing' (but the ancient etymology *bos-poros* is doubted by modern philology: see n. on *PB* 733). [*in her cruel torment* is an insecure conjectural replacement for two disputable Greek expressions in the MS which West leaves obelized, '(cleaving...) apart' and the final phrase 'as destined'.]

547–55 *hurls*: Io's frenzied speed, 562, 599–600, etc., *PB* 600. *Teuthras*: mythical first king of Mysia. This one personal name in the geography of 543–64 may be accidental, or reflect the popularity of the myth of Mysian Telephus, about whom Euripides later wrote a famous but now fragmentary tragedy. Io's path is clear enough [despite further difficulties of text and metre], although the *Pamphylians'* fertility (552–4) belonged historically to the *Cilicians* (551). *Aphrodite's land*: Phoenicia, an exporter of corn (555); the Greek goddess was identified in the Phoenician Astarte, Herodotus 1.105.2.

556–7 *her winged cowherd*: the gadfly, 541, who succeeded the first cowherd, Argos the watcher, 304. [*comes...coming*: an unstylish repetition perplexing to editors since antiquity; some obelize.]

558–61 *Zeus' plain*: habitable Egypt, made fertile by the Nile, cf. 4–5, 855–8, 1024–8, cf. *Pers.* 34, *PB* 812. *meadow fed by snow*: most Greeks, but not Egyptians, believed that the Nile's constant flow was melt-water, e.g. Aeschylus fr. 193a and Euripides *Helen* 2–3; contested by Herodotus 2.22–5, who partly anticipates modern meteorological theory. *Typhon*: an elemental figure of storm (whence our 'typhoon': n. on *Seven* 493–4; for his story, see *PB* 351–72); whether storm-winds and their rain are meant here by *his might*, or great heat (*PB* 370–1), his supposed contribution to fertility is not understood; but the *Nile* was famous for its pure waters (above).

564 *Hera's maenad*: associative metaphor. The goddess's torment of frenzied wandering makes Io like a woman possessed by Dionysus, a bacchant ranging open country (*Seven* 497 n.); the image is used of a distraught woman at *Seven* 836.

568–70 *creature, human hybrid*: in both literature and art Io was depicted either as wholly animal (she is just 'heifer' at 17, 44, and 'flower-grazing' at 539) or as human but with horns (*PB* 588). [*beholding*: good sense, but seemingly at odds with the ancient paraphrase and giving impossible Greek metre; West obelizes.]

571 *who was it healed*? rhetorical question, as in 586–7, followed there by the same answer as here in 576: who else but Zeus? The device recurs in 590–4.

574–80 *Ruling throughout unending life*: Zeus still, probably named in the missing line as well as in 576. *unharming power of Zeus*: 532–5 n.

580 *Zeus' freight*: translation insecure (I have added *in her womb* for clarity); this metaphor from a ship's ballast for 'embryonic child' is unparalleled. *the tale is true*: see 584–5, 589.

582 *whose life, etc.*: the rare over-run across stanzas (Introd. 3.3 p. lxi) helps to mark the contrast-in-correspondence between the first lines of each: Zeus' own endless life (574) generates lengthy life in his son by a mortal woman.

586–90 *afflictions*: lit. 'diseases', a very broad metaphor; of Io's plight also *PB* 597, 632. They are *vengeful* because Hera punishes Zeus' love for Io, 302, 306.

592–4 *his own hand*: with his touch, 535, cf. 45 n. *planting*: metaphor echoing 584 'makes life grow'. *architect*: metaphor for engendering as (allusively) in 283: see n. [*[our] father [himself]*: wording restored from the ancient commentator.]

595–7 *command… powerful… strong… power*: the repetition of these ideas is remarkable, and there can be no thought of any god *seated above* Zeus (see 524–6); so just 'above our human world' may be meant [the Greek expression too is very difficult, so that text and meaning are insecure and partly conjectural]. *deed… swift as his word*: a proverbial expression, e.g. Herodotus 3.134.6. *What of things here, etc.*: cf. 823–4, *Ag.* 1485–8 [again, the text and punctuation are insecure].

600–24 Second Episode. Danaus reports that Argos has confirmed that it will give protection from the Egyptians; Pelasgus' oratory was persuasive, esp. his warning against Zeus' anger if suppliants and fellow-citizens are rejected (615–24; cf. 524–99 n., at end).

The extreme brevity of this 'episode' is matched at *Pers.* 598–622 and *Seven* 793–821 (Introd. 3.2 p. lviii), the latter also a report-scene and also beginning with the words 'Have confidence, my children'.

601–14 *the people have resolved, etc.*: how they did so is revealed only in 615–24. Both Danaus and Chorus use Athenian 'democratic' vocabulary throughout these lines and in 621–4; e.g. in 604 *people's sovereign (hands)* is the earliest express collocation in Greek of the two words later making 'democracy', *demo-* 'people' and *krat-* 'power'; and *hands voted* is just 'hands' in the Greek, as in 621, cf. 607. *immigrants*: Aeschylus applies the analogy of resident foreigners at Athens ('metics') also in 994, *Seven* 548 (cf. the 'immigrant' Furies at Athens in *Eum.* 1011). These lacked full *citizen-rights* (614, cf. 699), but were *not subject to legal seizure* (see 412 n.); Pelasgus in 964 repeats that the Chorus will enjoy *defence* (613) by the Argive people.

602 *sir*: lit. 'old man', with wisdom from experience recognized by both daughters (11–13, 204–6) and Pelasgus (320, 480); a similar connotation at *Pers.* 840.

606 *make me young again in my old heart*: cf. 775. In the sister-play *Daughters of Danaus* Danaus is 'purged' of his old age, fr. 45.

615–17 *let it grow full*: lit. 'fatten', a metaphor picked up in *nourishment* in 620; it is used of prosperity at *Seven* 770. *at some later time*: i.e. incurring 'later punishment', attributed to Zeus at *Ag.* 59, 703, *LB* 383: cf. Introd. 1 p. xix.

618–20 *strangers and citizens together*: Pelasgus acknowledged the Danaids' double identity at 356, the risk of *double pollution* similarly at 473 [*through the city's action*: translation insecure; some editors alter to 'in front of the city', i.e. outside it at the common shrine].

621–4 *without a herald's call*: they voted before procedural invitation (another echo of Athenian democracy), so *good and persuasive* were the arguments. *turns*: the plural means probably that despite Pelasgus' immediate persuasion, other voices agreed; some understand it to suggest particularly persuasive turns of argument in his single speech. *Zeus... ratified the outcome*: as Danaus and Chorus hoped (210 ff.); Aeschylus makes Danaus speak as if he had heard the passionate appeal to Zeus in 524–99, esp. 599 itself.

625–709 Second choral ode. Danaus remains to hear and then applaud (710) the Chorus' grateful prayers to Zeus and the gods, first to recognize Argos' protection of suppliants (625–55), and second to protect it in turn against war's destruction, with security for its future generations of wise leaders, its fertility, and its honour for the gods (656–709). All the issues of the plot so far are here reviewed; they are mostly laid aside in the excitement which follows, as the Egyptians are sighted and prepare to land, to seize the Chorus (730–964); they recur only briefly even in the thanksgiving when that immediate threat is deferred (966–1073).

This ode is the second longest lyric system of the play (after the entry-song 40–175); its metres are again very mixed, but generally more settled.

626 *good . . . good*: ritual doubling in a prayer, also at 966.

627–9 *strangers*: 618 (n.), cf. 202, 277. In securing their reception in Argos (641, 652–3), *Zeus who protects strangers* (also 670) must now ensure their proper gratitude. [*so that it proves true . . . without fault*: only an approximation to what Aeschylus may have written, the MS being corrupt and left obelized by West.]

630–2 *gods, Zeus-born*: pious exaggeration, for not all the Olympians were Zeus' children; similarly *Seven* 301. *for my race*: the Chorus identify wholly with Argos-Pelasgia (635) now it has accepted them as residents (609, 618) and kin (651). [*my voice*: conjectural, the MS giving no sense and left obelized by West.]

634–6 *insatiably crying war*: like Homeric warriors, *Iliad* 13.621. *lustful*: the word hints at the Chorus' fear of rape, cf. 819–21. *harvests . . . crop in others' fields*: killing the sons of others' loins (cf. 664–6). [The text here is again greatly corrected by editors.]

644 *on the side of men*: the Sons of Aegyptus: 393, 426, 487, etc.

646–51 *Zeus' exactor, etc.*: 'the demon Revenge', 414–5 and n., the agent of their punishment. [Again the MS has needed wide correction, esp. in *would be cheered to have* replacing 'would have polluting it'.]

656–62 *blessings*: as in 628. *in wreaths' shadow*: those of suppliants (346). *empty . . . of its men*: loss pictured as at *Pers.* 118, 549, etc. *[faction]*: also 661, catastrophic from its bloodshed, 678–83, as in *Eum.* 977–83; coupled with *pestilence* in 684–5, as in *Pers*. 715. It was feared by Pelasgus at 358, 410–15, 449. [*faction* is therefore a more apt supplement than e.g. 'war'].

**664–6** *bloom...unculled...shear...flower*: not empty repetition, for the Chorus wish that Argos' youth should not be cut off by early death, and war not deprive Argos of men in their prime, the fathers of future generations through *Aphrodite's* work of love. The Greek imagery is common, e.g. *Pers.* 60, 252, etc.; 'shear' of *Ares* also *Pers.* 952; as *Aphrodite's bedmate* he famously cuckolded Hephaestus, Homer, *Odyssey* 8.267–70.

**667–75** *For those dignified...well governed*: a prayer for successive generations of effective senior counsellors: cf. the elders at *Pers.* 1–7, 682, etc. Pelasgus himself is tactfully addressed as such, 361. *altars...blazing*: in celebration, as at *Ag.* 91. An Athenian audience would think of the rituals surrounding its official 'presidents' in the Council (cf. 371 and n.). *age-old law*: for the idea, cf. Sophocles, *Antigone* 456–8, the immemorial law of funeral. [The text of 667–9 is insecure.]

**676–7** *Artemis*: the goddess of *childbirth* (e.g. *Ag.* 134), despite her own virginity (144–50 and n.). She is *far-shooting* like her brother Apollo (686); the Chorus pray that she does not shoot her lethal arrows (*Seven* 149) to harm the newborn.

**678** *havoc*: expressly recalling Ares' work, 665; 'war' follows in 681–3.

**681–3** *war...no dancing...no lyre...tears...civil strife*: 635. Such dangers destroy the arts (see 694–7) and bring barbarism, like the Furies within a house *Ag.* 990–2, *Eum.* 331–3, etc. For the 'tears of war', see Homer, *Iliad* 3.132; cf. *Pers.* 134, war's widows. *clamour*, possibly an echo of Ares' joy in the war-cry, 635 again [but the word is insecure, and 'violence' has been conjectured].

**684–5** *diseases...swarm, settle*: pictured as pestiferous birds or insects, or even crop-blight (*Eum.* 942).

**686** *the Lycean one*: Apollo, the archer god (cf. 675 n.), visiting plague and death on his victims, Homer, *Iliad*, 1.43–57; in war, *Seven* 146. *show favour to* therefore means 'not kill'. Apollo was a patron-god of Argos (214), with his own precinct in the city, Sophocles, *Electra* 7. One popular interpretation of the name *Lycean* was '(slayer of) wolves', Greek *lyk-* (cf. 760–1 and n.); for other etymologies, see n. on *Seven* 146–9.

**689–93** *full yielding...thrive*: similar prayers at *Eum.* 921–6, 944–8. *outside the walls*: let loose to graze, cf. *Ag.* 127–9. The alternative translation is 'prime beasts', i.e. their excellence marks them out for divine sacrifice.

694–7 *singers, etc.*: both in thanks and prayerful anticipation. Probably dancing singers are meant (like the play's chorus); for such celebration, cf. 1022–4, *Ag.* 23. *friendship with the lyre*: such as war destroys (681 n.).

698–703 Lines suddenly different in tone, full of 'political' language familiar to an Athenian audience.

698–700 *the body public*: reflecting 366 and 370–2 (n.), and wishing an anachronistic 'constitutional monarchy' to continue successfully in Argos (cf. Introd. 1 p. xxi); cf. Pelasgus above at 369, 518, and Danaus' report at 621–4. *counsel for the common good*: the Furies' gift at *Eum.* 984–6.

701–3 Lines resembling the terms of state-treaties, e.g. Thucydides 4.118; but the idea of resolving disputes without war begins in Hesiod, *Works and Days* 225–7. *rights... to plead cases*: as Pelasgus allowed Danaus to appear before the people, 480–503.

704–6 *native gods who hold their land*: heavy emphasis, drawing attention yet again to the common altar which is the scene (222, 242). *bearing bays*: ritual emblems, wreaths sacred esp. to Apollo (686 n.). *sacrificing oxen*: indicative of special, lavish offerings, *PB* 531; to dead heroes *LB* 261, 483–5.

707–9 *Respect for parents... third*: seemingly after the first duty, to strangers (698–703), and the second, to gods (704–6). Other such 'trinities' often include law, personified here in *Justice*; she is supremely important in the *Oresteia* (*Ag.* 383 has 'her great altar'). Her name in 709 has the same place in the stanza as the abstract 'justice' in 703.

710–75. Third Episode. There is sudden alarm: Danaus sees the first Egyptian ships mooring (it is a 'mirror-scene' of his sighting the approach of Pelasgus at 176–80: so Taplin, *Stagecraft* 210). He tries to calm his daughters by saying that he will go for help (726–34, cf. 774–5) and that problems of landing will delay an attack (764–72); they must again trust to protection from the shrine (725, 730–1, 773; cf. earlier 188–96, 222–5, 348–66).

Two longish speeches by Danaus surround a more excited exchange, the Chorus singing, Danaus speaking reassurance (734–61; 'epirrhematic' structure once again: 348–417 in 348–437 n.). The Chorus' new panic is expressed in the most irregular of Greek metres, the dochmiac (736–8 = 743–5, 750–2 = 757–9; cf. 827–42). Danaus counters their colourful fear of the Egyptians' barbaric intentions (750–2, 755–9, 762–3) with confidence in Argos and its hardened soldiers (739–40, 746–7, 760–1).

711 *but now don't be afraid, etc.*: dramatic conventions require the Chorus' grateful song to end before, but not to be cut short by, Danaus' abrupt sight of danger.

715–20 *side screens*: protecting against thrown-up water, or even missiles; cf. 134–5 n. *prow with its eyes*: painted on, regularly depicted on vases—and on warships, whence *such a ship could not be friendly*. These painted eyes may also have been symbolically deterrent, glaring danger; cf. 742–3. *obeying too well*: their pursuit has been only too fast; cf. 1045–6 and n.

721 *all their support*: a similar is term used at *Pers.* 731, 903.

726 *advocates to aid your case*: Athenian forensic terminology. Danaus means Pelasgus, who intervenes both with argument and arms at 911.

728 *make seizures to prevent reprisal*: once they have abducted you; cf. 412 n.

732 *Have confidence*: so Danaus already at 600, and again at 740, cf. Pelasgus at 955; grimly reversed perhaps at 907, cf. 1015. *the day appointed*; another quasi-legal term, used of inevitable punishment at *Ag.* 766, *LB* 612.

734–61. It cannot be known whether the first two lines of each stanza were spoken or sung; if the second (as West indicates), probably the whole stanza, and not just the last three lines, was danced as well.

735 *no long interval*: between our arrival here, and theirs.

739 *vote had full authority*: Danaus repeats his 601.

741 *Quite accursed*: a term from curse-formulae, cf. *Seven* 552. *lust-mad*: also 758, 762; cf. 635 on Ares (n.).

743–5 *dark-eyed vessels... dark-skinned men*: repeating 716–20; Aeschylus makes the suppliants forget they are themselves dark-skinned (n. on 496–7). *splashing haste*: the noise of their oars (723) [but *splashing* is a conjecture for 'anger'].

746–7 *well-toughened by midday heat*: Danaus parries the Chorus' fear like a native Greek, no less used than Egyptians were to fighting under the sun; similar contempt in 760–1. *well-toughened*: like hardened leather, the material of many soldiers' armour or shields [it is a conjecture for MS 'well-filed', i.e. 'lean and fit'].

749 *no war is in her*: seemingly a stock phrase, e.g. of old men at *Ag.* 79.

751–2 *like ravens*: birds regularly scavenging from altars.

754 *your hatred for them*: 332, 511, etc.; other men too might share it, 486–7. *shared by the gods*: if offended by the Egyptians' violation of your sanctuary.

755 *these tridents*: Poseidon's (218 n.).

757–9 *bold as dogs*: shameless; sexual aggression may be hinted too, cf. 762–3. The words occupy the same position in the stanza as 'like ravens' in 751.

760–1 *a saying, etc.*: Aeschylus often resorts to folk-sayings, e.g. 598, *Pers.* 162 and n. *wolves*: i.e. the Argives, who used the animals on their coinage (see the note on Apollo 'slayer of wolves' at 686); the 'dogs' are the Egyptians. *papyrus as a harvest-crop*: Herodotus 2.92.5, etc. The contempt for Egyptian diet is repeated at 953.

762–3 *unholy*: recapitulating 751–9. [*speedily*: a conjecture induced by 'speedy' in Danaus' reply, 764; the MS have a doubtful Greek form meaning 'strongly'; West simply obelizes.]

764–73 *despatching… the gods!*: Danaus attempts reassurance by stating the practical problems which will delay the Egyptians from coming ashore, but in 773 can only repeat his advice to trust to heaven while he fetches help (724–31).

774–5 *The city will not fault a messenger, etc.*: Danaus relies on the earlier favour of the Argive assembly (605–24). *old but has youth's vigour*: a similar pairing at *Seven* 662. [*after securing help* shows that the missing line had Danaus as its grammatical subject: cf. his 726.]

776–824. Third choral ode. A song of despair: how after all can we now escape the threatened marriage (790–1, 798–9, 804–7, 811–12)? The Chorus long to hide (777–8), or to be transformed into smoke or dust carried up to heaven (779–83, cf. 792–3), or to reach inaccessible heights (794–8) before the suicide which seems inevitable (784–91, 796–9; earlier, they threatened it in order to persuade Pelasgus, 455–67). They will accept even exposure of their dead bodies as carrion (800–1), for death at least gives freedom (802–3). This is the earliest occurrence of a Tragic commonplace: the wish, in the face of impossible danger, for miraculous escape or oblivion. These fantasies (cf. 392–5 n.) fill the first three stanza-pairs; the striking picture of the elements in 778–83 is continued in 792–3 and developed into one from a rocky landscape in 794–6. In the last pair of stanzas (808–24), the Chorus return to their familiar invocation of the gods, Zeus above all (in the last lines of each stanza, 811–16, 823–4). The lyric metre, despite the despairing panic, is largely that frequent in lamentations, iambic, e.g. *Pers.* 1002–77, *Seven* 832–1004.

The ode runs directly into a wholly lyric scene, of extreme excitement, 825–907 (n.).

776 *O country of hills and cattle*: 118 n.

778–83 *dark hiding place*: underground; Hades itself at *PB* 219. *smoke*: a detail absent from many fantasies, but a parody of these scenes at Aristophanes, *Wasps* 324 suggests it was not rare. *die*: anticipating 789, 796–7, 802–4.

785 *heart...darkness*: without light, and hope lost amid fear: *Pers.* 115, *LB* 410–13; a Homeric picture, *Iliad* 1.103 (anger).

787–91 *noose*: 160; used as a threat at 465. *before any detested man, etc.*: the prayer of 392–3, cf. 1062–4. *Hades my lord*: i.e. marriage to Death rather than to a man; see n. on 1033.

792–9 *water-clouds become snow*: familiar to anyone climbing high. *bare...vultures*: in Aeschylus' Greek a string of uncoordinated adjectives like *Seven* 722–3, 728–30, 916–18; *too sheer for goats* and *mind-lonely* echo Homeric vocabulary not surely understood [and are therefore suspect to editors, but not, rightly, to West]; *mind-lonely* may be inspired particularly by *Iliad* 24.614, where Niobe mourns and broods, solitary on a mountain. *vultures*: for their high nests, see *Ag.* 50–3; they do not necessarily anticipate the carrion-birds of 801. *before my heart, etc.*: the idea of 'before' matches 790–1, and is echoed in 804–7. *torn in two by...marriage*: a powerful paradox. Note that the wished-for alternative, 'to free me from marriage', fills l. 807 in the corresponding stanza.

800–1 *prey and food for the dogs, etc.*: a Homeric horror, *Iliad* 1.4–5, etc., sometimes taken up by Tragedy, e.g. *Seven* 1014.

802–3 *death does liberate*: translation insecure. *evils loved by grief*: cf. 69, *Seven* 917–18.

808 [*Wail out*: only the probable sense; West leaves the words obelized.]

812–15 *Watch over me...Zeus*: the theme of 381–6. *protector of this land*: the place of their ancestry through Zeus himself, 15–26, etc.; *in all your might, Zeus*; 437, 526, a frequent title, e.g. *Seven* 255. The Chorus appeal to Zeus here almost exactly as they appealed to Pelasgus as ruler (423–7). [The text in 811–12 is widely conjectural.]

816–21 *Aegyptus' line, in its men...outrage*: yet another recall of 30, cf. 790 in this same ode; 426, 487, etc. *lewdness* 762 and n. *take me by violence*: i.e.

'rape'; the word *violence* has the same place as in the responding stanza at 813.

**822–4** *the balance and its beam*: Zeus' scales of justice, 403, 405–6. *without you, what is fulfilled*: cf. 599 (n.).

**825–907** Fourth Episode (825–965), first part: an excited lyric scene. Egyptians (but not the Sons of Aegyptus themselves) burst in, to seize the Chorus and drag them off to their ships (826, 836 etc.); then a Herald from the Sons (see 951) repeats this intention (882–4, 909, etc.). The first moments are free lyric (825–42); then lyric 'dialogue' begins, alternating Egyptian threats and the Chorus' prayers throughout one lyric stanza-pair (843–65), after which the Herald enters and answers three further stanza-pairs from the Chorus with speech (866–907; 'epirrhematic' structure once again: 348–417 in 348–437 n.). The Herald's sinister physical appearance (887–91, 895–901) drives the Chorus into frantic appeals for rescue, by the absent Danaus (885), by the gods (890–2 = 900–2, a sort of refrain), and by Pelasgus (905, 908)—who appears on cue (911).

This fast-moving scene is vigorous theatrically. The Egyptians form a second chorus; they are given exotic cries and a simulated 'foreign' dialect like that of the Chorus themselves at 118–19 (n.), and resembling effects invented sporadically for the excited satyrs searching in Sophocles' *Trackers* 80–204; cf. also the dialects in Aristophanes, *Acharnians* 100–4, 860 ff. The meaning of some of the cries can only be guessed. The language is very colourful throughout, with threats and panic alternating. Metre too is extraordinarily excited, probably to accompany dance-movements suggesting menace. [All this strangeness caused extreme difficulty for scribes, and textual damage is extreme; wording has been lost, many passages are corrupt beyond repair, the line order is disrupted, and indications of the voice-parts are missing. Different editors have taken very different views too about the assignment of the parts; e.g. Taplin, *Stagecraft* 217 ff. suggests that 825–35 are the Chorus' own alarmed anticipation of seizure, and that from 836 the Herald alone sings or speaks, accompanied by armed men.]

**828–34** *back again*: 'to the sea', suggests West—to be drowned (843–6, cf. the Chorus at 32–6)? *prelude*: a common metaphor, grim at *PB* 741 too. *for my sponsor*: Pelasgus [but the word is West's conjecture for meaningless letters in the MS]. *safe protection*: the altar-mound: cf. Danaus at 725, etc. *unendurable*: the Egyptians also at 818. The Chorus know their violence from Egypt itself; now they fear it from the voyage back there as captives.

836–41 *Hurry, hurry, etc.*: repeated doubling of words indicates violent passion; cf. *Pers.* 1010, 1039. *bark*: 882, 873; an Egyptian word (Herodotus 2.96.5), used also at *Pers.* 553, 1075. *branding*: runaway slaves were branded in Persian practice (Herodotus 7.35.1). *heads hacked off*: also a Persian practice (*Pers.* 371); an exaggeration to terrify women. *to the cutter*: the English noun marks a grim pun even more explicitly than in the Greek; the Greek noun is rare [and restored here by conjecture, as in 847]; it occurs also in Aeschylus fr. 214, where the sources define it as a ship which 'cuts, reaps' the sea; a cognate verb occurs in metaphor at *Pers.* 822.

847–53 [*All blood... pious men*: the MS has been heavily emended by editors with the aid of the ancient paraphrase; much remains insecure in sense.]

850 *Longing*: the Greek word is of uncertain form and meaning, and unique, and its point here lost amid the textual damage.

855–8 *waters that make cattle thrive*: the Nile of the fertile Delta, cf. 561 and n. *men's blood, etc.*: this easy equation of blood and life-spirit is found in contemporary Greek scientific speculation.

859–62 *ilk*: Aeschylus may have borrowed from what seems to be dialect, as in *willy-nilly*. [*warfare's man*: West's plausible conjecture for an unknown word.]

863–5 *Force enforces much!*: text again conjectural [West], but apt as a recourse to a folk-axiom amid extreme excitement (cf. 760–1).

868–71 *plain of the... sea*: cf. *Pers.* 111. *Syrian winds... Sarpedon's great bank*: i.e. wrecked on the S. coast of Asia Minor, against Cape Sarpedon in Cilicia, on the long coastal and circular voyage back to Egypt. Zeus' son Sarpedon, fighting the Greeks at Troy, was carried home on swift winds for funeral by Sleep and Death (Homer, *Iliad* 16.671–5).

882–4 *speedy (bark)*: only a possible meaning; the ancient translation was 'well-found'. *no one*: of clear reference in a threat, like 903, cf. 924. *Dragging... hair*: as if the Herald had heard the Egyptians at 839; the threat recurs at 909. [Editors are forced to interchange 882–4 and 872–5 by the sequence of ideas; comparable disruption in 905–7.]

877–81 [*This outrage... lost to sight*: even the words translated are uncertain, and have been much emended by conjecture, particularly by West.]

875 *Your wailing... the pain itself*: the 'translation' approximates to the ancient paraphrase [the line is hopelessly corrupt in the MS, and left obelized by West].

885–8 *Father*: the absent Danaus. *help from the statue*: to which each has fled, 832, cf. Danaus at 192, and before his departure, 731, 773; the Chorus themselves at 463. *seaward*: a further Homeric word. *like a spider walking*: imagining the Egyptians as many-legged, perhaps, dragging their prey, or the Herald alone?—for 895 has a 'snake with two feet'. *a black nightmare*: black may hint the Egyptian's dark skin (719 n.); nightmare visions also at *Ag.* 1218, *LB* 523–4.

890–2 = 900–2 For such a refrain, cf. 141–3 = 151–4. *Mother Earth*: invoked to avert harm e.g. *Seven* 69, but here perhaps as herself the mother of all monsters (*LB* 585–6). [*monster*: I have substituted this English word for a corrupt Greek one left obelized by West; he himself conjectured 'spectre'.] *father*: putative translation of a monosyllabic and probably dialect form. *Zeus, Earth's child*: perhaps an identification of Rhea, Zeus' mother, with Earth; at Aeschylus fr. 70 Zeus is equated with earth and heaven, his domains.

894 [*I'll not grow old*: West's own conjecture for apparent 'I would not have grown old' in the MS].

895 *Raging*: yet another Homeric word. *a snake with two feet*: the bloodstained Clytemnestra is a 'lioness with two feet' at *Ag.* 1258.

903 *someone*: i.e. 'you', threatening: cf. 883 n.

905, 909–10, 908, 906–7. [The order 908 + 906–7 (= Str. 4), 905 + 909–10 (= Ant. 4) is advocated by some editors.]

908–65 Fourth Episode, second part. In a spoken scene Pelasgus defies the Egyptians; there is a hostile stichomythia (916–29: n.), and the Egyptians withdraw now that war is inevitable (949–53). Pelasgus tells the Chorus to be ready to go to the city, where comfortable homes await them; repeating his assurance that Argos will protect them, he begins to leave (954–65).

908 *my lord*: not Zeus, but, following 905 'city-leaders', Pelasgus—who now appears.

912–13 *land of men ... city of women*: cf. the womanly coward Aegisthus *Ag.* 1224, *LB* 305.

914–15 *barbarian*: the Greek word is itself a near-barbarism, used contemptuously also at *Ag.* 1061; it is the word translated 'foreigner' at 118 = 130 above. The assumption that *Greeks* are superior to, and should therefore rule, non-Greeks is recurrent in literature; cf. Pelasgus again at 952–3 (n.) and Introd. 2.3 p. xxxviii n. 33. The reverse assumption naturally underlies

Persian arrogance in *Persians*, e.g. 50, 858–902. *done nothing correct*: not followed the Greek courtesies of diplomacy, 917.

916–29 *But what have I done, etc.*: a particularly good example of stichomythia (Introd. 3.2 p. lx) used to build differing attitudes into total hostility; cf. *PB* 964–86.

917 *how strangers should behave*: contrast Danaus' advice to his daughters, 194–203. Pelasgus means the Herald does not realize that as a stranger he has no legal standing: 919.

919–20 *sponsors*: 239 (n.); but the Herald uses the word generally. *Hermes* is the patron of heralds (*Ag.* 515), and as *god of lucky searches* he alone received words from this Herald (931) because the Herald has already found what he wanted (918).

921–2 *no reverence for those gods*: cf. the Herald at 894–5 (not heard by Pelasgus).

924–5 *removes them from me*: an Athenian legal concept and term for placing in temporary neutral hands runaway slaves which a master wishes to 'remove', i.e. recover, and which another person of legal standing claims now to be 'free'; cf. also n. on 412. The Herald treats the Chorus as such slaves of Aegyptus; Pelasgus resents the pre-emption of his own authority over the suppliants (925; contrast his initial wish to wash his hands of them, throughout 365–417).

927 *those who despoil the gods*: robbing them of suppliants in their protection: Danaus at 188–92, Pelasgus at 333–47.

929 *brood upon it*: a metaphor from watching over cattle: *Ag.* 669, *Eum.* 78.

932–3 *should I say, etc.*: to his Egyptian masters. *women-cousins*: cf. 8, Danaus at 984 *taken from me*: the 'legal' verb of 924; such language continues in 934–5.

934–7 *accepting silver*: settlement in money rather than by repossession. *their spasms*: a Homeric picture of the dying, e.g. *Iliad* 10.521, cf. *Ag.* 1293. [The Herald's plain threat of war is felt by some editors to be premature, and they move 934–7 to follow 949 in the Herald's mouth or 950 in that of Pelasgus; others suppose loss of text before 934.]

938–41 *you'll learn and know it well enough*: harshly colloquial, like 949 'take yourself off'. *fellow-traders*: contemptuous; a similar metaphor from trade at *Seven* 545. The Herald and his masters are seen as mere ship-borne traffickers. *some reverent words*: Pelasgus defies the Herald's irreligion (921–3). [The missing line may have been 'but you will not take them against their will': so West.]

942–3 *unanimous vote, etc.*: reported at 601–5.

944–9 *This is final, etc.*: the solemnity of the people's decision is conveyed through images, familiar to Athenians, of public edicts inscribed and securely bolted up; Pelasgus communicates it in speech, however, rather than by handing the Herald an official reply concealed in writing-tablets or rolled parchment or the like.

950–1 *unwelcome war*: as Pelasgus feared, 342. *victory and full power*: the Herald's language is (ironically) that of Danaus' contrary wish at 207, 233.

951–2 *men...real men*: the abusive exchange ends where Pelasgus began it, in 912–13; cf. Danaus at 746–7. *barley-beer*: derisive: cf. Danaus at 761. Herodotus 2.77.4 explains Egyptian beer as made in default of grapes for wine. Angry or ominous words are often hurled at departing stage-persons (examples in Taplin, *Stagecraft* 221–2); hurled by the departing e.g. *PB* 1071–7.

954 *your dear servants*: Pelasgus intends kindness. This reference is the first indication in the play text that the Chorus may have had women servants with them from the beginning [but editors have emended the MS gender of the servants from male to female]; the one certain indication is at 977. We cannot know how numerous these silent servants ('extras') would have been, where they may have been since the play's start, whether they joined the Chorus in dancing, or whether and how they moved position at 979. Taplin, *Stagecraft* 222–38 argues strongly that 966–79 may be an interpolated passage (substituted for a full ode), and that the maids may best be eliminated from the play altogether; but this brief passage of anxiety creates a certain urgency before Danaus' last entry at 980.

956 *towers contrived for height*: alternative and more difficult translation 'towers contrived by deep thought' (for the latter, cf. 407).

957–62 *Houses too there are, etc.*: Pelasgus offers the Chorus various housing, which they refer to their father's decision, 970–4—and which he already knows of, 1009–11. *public lodgings*: found already in Homer's world, *Odyssey* 20.264–5. *with many others*: sharing with other tenants, or just among themselves?

963 *pick the best*: the Greek metaphor is from flowers.

963–5 *champion*: at Athens this word was either the technical term for the legal sponsor of immigrants, which the Danaids will be (602–14 n.), or the unofficial term for the most prominent politician claiming to represent the common interest of all enfranchised *citizens*: whence *greater authority*: cf. 739, 942–3.

966–1073 Final scenes (*exodos*). As Pelasgus begins to leave, the Chorus chant grateful prayers for Argos' well-being (966–79; cf. 625–709 n.); in 978 they name Danaus, who like Pelasgus at 911 enters on cue. The spoken scene which follows (980–1017) is almost entirely his monologue, confirming Pelasgus' generosity (980–90, 1006–11) but charging the Chorus with strict sexual morality (991–1005, 1012–13). This surprising redirection of their antipathy to men and marriage is some kind of trailer for the next play in the trilogy. It is not transient, moreover: while it is followed at once by more jubilation from the Chorus (one stanza-pair, 1018–33), a further, separate chorus formed from the Men of Argos who returned with Danaus (985) sobers their joy: 'women must not scorn marriage, even you—for why else has Zeus brought the Egyptians safely here?' (one stanza-pair, 1034–51). The Chorus repel this advice, trusting still to Zeus to save them from the forcible marriage (two stanza-pairs, the first shared with the Argives, 1052–73). The play therefore ends with two issues unresolved: will Pelasgus defeat the Egyptians? whether he does or not, will the Chorus maintain their total hostility to men, to both Egyptian and potentially Argive husbands? See Introd. 2.3 p. xxxvii n. 32.

966–7 *good things . . . goodness*: 626 and n. *most glorious of Pelasgians*: Homeric in tone; exaggerated, but matching Danaus' grand comparison of Pelasgus to the gods in 980–2; cf. Pelasgus' dominions in 250–9.

968–70 *have our father sent here*: delaying their departure at once to safety in the city (954–6). *prudent . . . leader, etc.*: as in 12.

971–4 *a friendly place*: one where *foreigners* will not be criticized, 973–4, cf. Danaus at 993–5. *may it be for the best*: possibly a distrustful echo of Pelasgus' words in 962; but such a wish is a cliché, e.g. 454.

979 *dowry of servants*: they would be war-captives, and therefore mere chattels, as much indicative of wealth as useful to their mistresses. The idea of 'dowry' conflicts, however, with the women's flight from marriage, or at least from the Egyptian marriage; Aeschylus may hint at the coming pressure from the Argives that they should marry like other women, 1050–1 (n.), or he may be using a common association between a young mistress and her servants.

**980–1016** *My children, etc.*: Danaus returns after Pelasgus, although he had gone to fetch his aid (774). He fulfils his daughters' hopes of wise advice (969–76) as if he had heard them himself, given their fear of abuse as foreigners in Argos; in particular, they must want to be accepted (993), and know that tongues may be unkind (994–5). Pelasgus' offer of housing of their choice is known to Danaus too (1009–11, cf. 957–65).

**980–2** *(to the people)...as if to Olympian gods*: an extreme comparison, intended to register Danaus' excited relief. *saviours* echoes the regular title and address of gods, e.g. 213 the Sun, and esp. Zeus himself (26 and n., *Seven* 520, etc.). The victorious Agamemnon is uncomfortable with similar adulation with *Ag.* 921–2.

**987** *everlasting burden*: of pollution, if as a suppliant Danaus were abducted or killed: cf. Pelasgus at 365–7, 376, 473, 619. [Loss of text is shown by the lack of a 'nor'-clause corresponding with 'neither' in 987.]

**990** [The words *we must pay* and *respectful* are West's replacement of MS corruption which he leaves obelized.]

**991–5** *write this in your minds*: the notion is common enough (179 n.), for Aeschylus to omit 'in your minds' here; no recall of Pelasgus' language to the Herald (946–7) seems intended. *immigrant*: 609 n.

**996–1005** *with your young beauty...longing overcomes him*: a threefold illustration of dangerous sexual attraction, from (1) ripe fruits (997–8), (2) animals naturally 'in season' (999–1002), and (3) lovely girls drawing admirers' eyes (1003–5, repeating 997). The passage is a remarkable flight by Aeschylus, matched for colour in this play only by Danaus' pictures of navigation at 714–22 and 764–70 and by the Chorus' imagination of Io's wanderings at 538–64 and of remote solitude at 791–4. Details: *ruin it*: the verb has connotations of rape. *turns men's eyes*: as splendid children do, *LB* 350; cf. *shoots a glance* in 1004–5. *Creatures...that fly and walk the ground*: also in a 'natural' illustration at *LB* 591. *Cypris*: Aphrodite, the sexual instinct; cf. 1034–42. *ripe readiness*: a slightly coy translation. The Greek has 'dripping fruitfulness', an image from fruits ripe for picking, but in this context of animals, Aeschylus almost certainly means 'dripping' to connote animal oestrus. [The text in 1002 *half-heating...with desire* depends heavily on West's own conjectures.]

**1006–8** *what...to avoid, and why, etc.*: forcible marriage, although they are ripe for it (996–1005). *great effort...great sea*: in the Greek these phrases differ by only one letter, and are juxtaposed, a device of heavy emphasis. *pleasure for my enemies*: the worst hurt, *Pers.* 1034, cf. *PB* 159. Danaus does say 'my', not 'our'.

1011 *living...free from payment*: immigrants at Athens ('metics', 609 n.) could inhabit only rented property.

1012–15 *observe these instructions of your father*: 'ring-composition' with 992–3; similarly *the Olympian gods* recalls the start of Danaus' long speech, 981. *be quite confident*: true to the quality they praised in him (970); cf. his 600 to them. *I will not turn aside, etc.*: another pointer forward to the rest of the trilogy. Cf. Introd. 2.3 p. xxxvii.

1018–21 *celebrate*: the apparent meaning [of an anomalous verb-form which West leaves obelized]; cf. 'praise' in 1023. *Erasinus*: a much smaller companion river at Argos to the Inachus (497), but precious for its constant flow; cf. n. on 1024–9.

1022 *Take up our song, you escorts*: those provided by Pelasgus to Danaus (985); they are the Men of Argos who sing in 1034–51 (see 1034 n.), natives accepting incomers' praise, a polite commentary on the Danaids' anxiety about their reception, 973–6, 994–5.

1024–9 *Nile*: the Danaids now 'forget' Egypt, and instead of evoking that river's nutritive excellence (561 n.) they extol similar qualities in the rivers of Argos, 1027–8, such as the Erasinus (1020).

1030–3 *May holy Artemis...watch over*: the same appeal as in 144–50 (n.), to safeguard their virginity. *Cytherean rite*: marriage, a phrase of Homeric colour. This cult-title of Aphrodite (1034, cf. 1001; first at Homer, *Odyssey* 8.288) is not certainly explained, but seems to relate to the island of Cythera off the S. Peloponnese. *prize*: of securing me as bride, another Homeric phrase (of Penelope, *Odyssey* 21.73). *(prize for) Styx*: the underworld river: i.e. 'may I die first!' in marriage to Death (791, 804–5); this conceit is a cliché in Tragedy for the unwed girl who is to die, voluntarily or not.

1034 *s.d.* MEN OF ARGOS: modern editors introduce here a further subsidiary chorus (see 825–907 n., on the Egyptians) because the praise of sexual love in 1034–42 cannot come from the Danaids after their words in 1030–3. In view of the political sentiments voiced in 1043–51, etc., the chorus is more safely identified as the Argive men escorting Danaus (985), than as the Danaids' women servants (977). Translation with *a...law* in 1034 goes with this identification, better than with 'our...theme' ['our well-meaning company', is also conjectured; many MS errors throughout 1034–42 have been corrected].

1034–7 *Cypris...Hera...Zeus*: the trinity of powers overseeing loving, stable, and socially fundamental marriage, *Eum.* 213–18. *wiles*: for Aphrodite's arts, see esp. Homer, *Iliad* 14.214 ff., her deception of Zeus himself. *holy rites*: love's consummation, guaranteeing fresh generations of children (1008).

1038–42 *Sharing...love*: almost a description of the 'rites' of 1037, and almost matched in *PB* 649–54, Zeus' captivation by Io. *Desire*: 87, but personified here (but not an alias of Eros as Aphrodite's son). *Persuasion*: often personified by Aeschylus, both happily and darkly in the *Oresteia*; for sexual charming here cf. 1055, cf. 1004 and n. *Harmony*: another companion, or sometimes daughter, of Aphrodite (Hesiod, *Theogony* 937, cf. *Homeric Hymn to Aphrodite* 194). One god may have a share in another's essential power: Aphrodite unites lovers. *whispering paths of love*: scholars dispute how explicit the Greek words are; Aeschylus is unafraid of such directness: see nn. on 296, 1001.

1043–4 *those fleeing her breath*: i.e. yourselves; cf. the corresponding verse 1034. For *breath*, rationalizing invisible divine intervention, cf. 577; similarly 'touch', 18 and n.

1045–6 *Why, why, etc.*: except to bring war (1044): the Egyptians' *swift pursuit* must be with the will of the gods.

1047–9 *what is fated will happen*: a frequent axiom, e.g. *Seven* 281. *circumventing Zeus' great mind*: cf. *PB* 550–2; but the Greek verb implies 'transgressing, disobeying', as at *Ag.* 59.

1050–4 Text and translation are most insecure, frustrating inference, how the trilogy developed (see on 966–1073, at end). A wish here by the Men for the Danaids' marriage can only be in their general acceptance of Aphrodite's power; a wish for their marriage to Aegyptus' sons is implied when the translation is *This indeed would be for the best*, or contradicted by the equally possible translation 'That indeed...', i.e. 1050–1—but 1055–6 accommodate both outcomes.

1055 *You'd try charming, etc.*: cf. 1040. I translate this line as an allusive generality, suiting 1056; some translate as 'You'd try charming (him) who cannot be charmed', i.e. Zeus (1052).

1057–8 *Why am I to look, etc.*: how can I be expected to know Zeus' mind? (cf. 1048–9; earlier, 93–5). *beyond fathom*: lit. 'depthless'; the mind's depths at 407 (n.), cf. *Seven* 593.

1061 *do nothing in excess*: a maxim attributed to the sixth-century Spartan 'sage' Chilon; but all excess is regularly deprecated in poetry, e.g. *Pers.* 820, 827.

1062 *marriage to an evil man*: cf. 394 and e.g. 9–10, 37, 332.

1064–7 *set Io free*: 571–9. The play ends by recalling the suppliants' chief claim upon Argos through their ancestress. *checking... healing
hand... kindness*: of the same incident, *PB* 848–9.

1068 *grant women victory*: if, or when, war comes (1044), reversing the
Herald's prayer for 'the men' (951 and n.). The line echoes the Chorus' 524–
31, 643–6.

1069–73 *better part*: euphemistic, as in English, i.e. 'the bigger', defined in the
Greek idiom as *two parts out of three*, also euphemistic and almost certainly
also a folk-saying, as at e.g. Pindar, *Pythians* 3.80 ff. The Chorus mean, the
residual third, namely the smaller 'good': escape from the marriage will be
better for them than the 'larger' *Evil*, namely subjection to men. *justice to
follow justice*: just victory to follow just rejection of marriage [but this is
only one emendation of the corrupt MS, which West leaves obelized]. *release
devised by god*: the concluding two stanzas, and particularly this line, again
trail the tense issues of the following play, *The Egyptians*: see 966–1073 n.
above and Introd. 2.3 p. xxxvii. Cf. the heavily anticipatory final lines of
*Agamemnon* and *Libation Bearers*.


## PROMETHEUS BOUND

THE medieval manuscripts offer a *hypothesis* ('introduction') written at their
date partly in the style of Aristophanes of Byzantium (see on *Persians*, p. 130),
but to a larger scale: 'Prometheus is in Scythia, in bonds because of his theft
of fire. Io learns from him (*words missing*) in her wanderings, and that as a
result of Zeus' touch she will give birth to Epaphus. Hermes is brought on to
threaten Prometheus with lightning unless he says what the future destines
for Zeus. At the end amid thunder Prometheus is lost to sight. The story
occurs incidentally in Sophocles' *Women of Colchis*, but is wholly absent
from Euripides. The scene of the play is set in Scythia in the mountains of
Caucasus. The chorus is composed of the daughters of Oceanus, who are
nymphs. The main issue is Prometheus' being put in bonds.' There follows a
list of the characters.

The summary of content omits Oceanus' attempt to intervene (ll. 276–
396); only something short is lost from the sentence about Io, perhaps 'how
many lands she will visit' (so West). Io's story (561–886 and n.) provides
background for Aeschylus' *Suppliant Women* (15–19, etc.; see Introd. 2.3
p. xlii). Sophocles' *Women of Colchis* is a very fragmentary play, said to have
dramatized Medea's help to Jason in recovering the Golden Fleece from the
mythical land of Colchis; its date is unknown.

For the play's theatrical aspects, see the Introd. 2.4 Appendix, p. lii.

1 *s.d.*: *near the sea*: see 573, where Io seems to have come from a shore.

1–87 Prologue, first scene. Prometheus is fettered to the ravine-face by Hephaestus, who is overseen by Power (77); it is Zeus' punishment for his theft of fire from heaven to give to mortal man (7–11). Hephaestus works reluctantly (12–20, 39, 45, 51), while Power is merciless (36, 42, 78).

Power and Force are personified abstractions, a type of figure infrequent upon the tragic stage, if frequent on the comic. We may compare the ogre Death who comes to fetch Alcestis at the start of Euripides' mythic tragicomedy (name play), but there is nothing of the fairy tale about our opening scene. Power's mute companion, his near-namesake Force, compounds this effect, for both were no doubt costumed impressively (for Power see 78). Prometheus stays silent until he is abandoned in his fetters (after 87).

The scene contains stichomythia in the rare form of alternating single lines from Hephaestus and couplets from Power (36–81: see Introd. 3.2 p. lxi). The inequality may express a contrast between the former's weakness and the latter's dominance.

2 *Scythia*: loosely the area of the modern Ukraine and eastward round the Black Sea; cf. 417–19, *Seven* 728; see Map 5.

4 *father Zeus*: just 'father' in the Greek, as his adherents call him: 17, 40, 53, etc., 947, 984, etc.

5 *harness*: the metaphor also at 618; see Introd. 2.4 p. xlix.

10 *rule*: the Greek noun *tyrannis* expresses absolutism, and became pejorative, our 'tyranny'. It is not so here, nor in 310, probably (Oceanus, cf. his 324, Greek 'monarch'); at 49 and 958 Zeus simply 'rules'; but Prometheus uses *tyrann-* frequently, perhaps pejoratively at 222, 224, 305, 357 (cf. Io at 761), certainly so at 736, 756, 909, 942, 957, 996. For tyranny in the play, see Introd. 2.4 p. xlviii and n. 44.

18 *Son of Themis right in her counsel*: a contrast of her prudence with her son's arrogance. Her name personifies 'right, ordinance, law' (Greek *the-*, the abstract form of it occurring at *Supp.* 39, 332). She knows the future, so that she indeed 'counsels rightly': 209–11, 873–4 and nn. *over-lofty in your designs*: dangerously ambitious and defiant, so that his punishment is appropriately 'lofty' too. Here even the sympathetic Hephaestus recognizes the fault in Prometheus' high intelligence; cf. Oceanus at 328, and 308, who marks Prometheus' arrogance at 318–20.

24–5 *night's starry cloak*: cf. *Seven* 400–1 (on a decorated shield); a clear night, therefore, leading to *dawn frost*.

27 *the one who is to alleviate it is not yet born*: but he will be: Heracles, alluded to in 871–3, 1026–9 (n.).

30 *beyond what was just*: similarly Prometheus' help to men is described at 507 with 'unduly'; Hephaestus may mean no more than 'against the natural distinction between god and man', and not that defiance of Zeus' rule is objectively criminal (although Power regards it so, 5, 9, etc.).

31–2 *guard*: bleakly ironic allusion to the way a guard must stand on watch, often immobile. Prometheus speaks of himself as a guard at 143.

35 *every ruler new to power is harsh*: 96 and n.

38 *prerogative*: as 82, 107, 229, 439; cf. 'privileges' in 30, 946.

39 *Kinship…powerful*: a cliché: Oceanus at 290, Prometheus at 347, 635–6, cf. *Seven* 1031. *comradeship*: through their association with fire, 7–8. The two gods shared cult and ritual at Athens.

45 *the worth of my hands*: as metal-smith, 366–7; cf. 619.

55–77 Hephaestus moves down from Prometheus' shoulders to his feet when shackling and even (64–8) transfixing him. Sonorous and varied vocabulary suggest sustained violence.

62 *for all his cleverness*: cf. Hermes' abuse at 944, 1011—and Prometheus' sad comment on himself at 470–1. The Greek word here gives us our 'sophist(ry)'; in Aeschylus' life time it was still acquiring a pejorative implication, changing from mere 'wisdom' or 'cleverness'. Power repeats this mockery at 85–7 (n.).

65 *right through his chest*: literally, it would seem. Since Prometheus is immortal (753, 933, 1052), he could withstand such violence; later he is to endure repeated laceration of his entrails (1022–3).

73 *urge…on loudly*: this verb, also 277, 393, 1041, expresses any forceful command; it is a metaphor from a hunstman shouting on his hounds.

76–7 *cross-fetters*: some translate 'pierced fetters', i.e. with holes for driving spikes through; either sense suits the bonds put round his legs in 74.

78 *voice's tone matches your appearance*: they both convey violence (cf. 42); Power's theatrical costume, perhaps an exaggerated bodysuit, and mask would suggest his cruelty.

82–4 *gods' prerogatives*: fire chiefly is meant (7–9, cf. 38 and n.) and its companion metal-working (500–2), rather than e.g. divination (447–54, 484–99); but there is allusion also to Prometheus' attempt to cheat Zeus of the meat in divine sacrifice, Hesiod, *Theogony* 521–616: see 493–9 n. and Introd. 2.4 p. xliii. *What... can mortal men make lighter for you?*: see the Chorus at 546–7. *make lighter*: lit. 'bail out, drain away', metaphor from a ship's bilge, used as 'endure to the dregs' at 375.

85–6 *Prometheus, but the name is false, etc.*: it etymologizes as 'man of foreknowledge or foresight', as is spelled out in 86 [where *foresight* is an editor's correction of MSS 'one with foresight', i.e. Prometheus' name without a 'capital P']; a similar nameplay in 506. For *false* in such nameplay, cf. 717, and for the whole, frequent phenomenon e.g. *Seven* 576–8 and n.

88–126 Prologue, second scene. Prometheus is left alone, to endless torment. He speaks and chants in despairing protest (88–100), quickly sobers into speech again as his foreknowledge reminds him that he cannot escape (101–13), and then briefly sings astonishment as his senses herald an unexpected visitor (114–19) before once more chanting his misery and alarm (120–7). This quick alternation of theatrical voices conveys Prometheus' immediate confusion; it has no certain parallel in surviving Tragedy, but Io later moves from chanting to singing within her entry monody (562–608 n.).

88–90 *O sky divine, etc.*; the regular Tragic idiom, in which despairing appeal is made to nature's elements to witness disaster (Prometheus again at 1091–3), here acquires ironic truth: they are Prometheus' only company. In the Greek the effect is enhanced by alliteration on the letters 'p' and 't'—as again in 98–100. *waves' bright laughter*: glittering, an effect of light not sound: so the earth laughs under glinting weaponry, first in Homer, *Iliad* 19.362. The phrase *beyond counting* is forceful: it is figuratively apt for *waves*.

93–4 *look upon... See*: the language used in calling upon legal witnesses; cf. the crag witnessing a fatal leap at *Supp.* 797–8.

96 *new captain*: ruthless, therefore (35, 149, 310, etc.).

100 *limit for my agonies*: cf. 183, 257, 755, 1026.

101 *I have accurate foreknowledge*: from his mother Themis, 209–11, cf. 873–4; she told him also that superior powers (i.e. Zeus) could be overcome only by guile, not force (212–13): hence his 'theft' in 110.

109 *fennel-stalk*: its dry pith would smoulder, permitting fire to be carried.

112–13 *wrongdoings*: sardonic; contrast Power at 9, even the Chorus at 260— and Prometheus himself at 266: Introd. 2.4 p. xlvii. *under the open sky*: cf. 15 'ravine beaten by storms', 22–5. Line 113 (*under…fast*) has just three words in the Greek, a powerfully sounding conclusion to the speech; this effect occurs in mid-speech at e.g. 711, 799.

114–26 *s.d.*: *an imminent arrival*: the Chorus of Oceanus' daughters begin their entry. They are 'flying' (128–30); however this entry was managed in the theatre (see Introd. 2.4 Appendix, p. lii), their initial invisibility (115, 123–4) to the immobile Prometheus is plausible.

116–17 *god, or…men*: The Oceanids possess divine 'winged' transport like their father (287), but in other respects behave like shy (134) but sympathetic girls (160–3, etc.). [*someone*: without this supplement, there is no personal subject to the sentence, only the 'sound' or 'scent' of 115.]

118 *to view my misery*: like a theatre spectator, an allusion used similarly at *LB* 246; see below, on 299–302.

119 *See me in bonds, etc.*: Prometheus' first words set the tone of his continuous resentment.

126 *All that approaches*: ambiguous; both persons and the future itself (272) may be meant.

127–92. Entry of the Chorus (*parodos*); for realization in the theatre, see Introd. 2.4 Appendix p. lii. A remarkable aspect of the entry is that the Chorus only sing, without dance, for only at 278 do they dismount: see Taplin, *Stagecraft* 252–60.

The Chorus explain their coming rather improbably: deep in their caverns where their father Oceanus' stream bounds the earth (139–40) they heard the echo of Hephaestus' hammering (133–4); but the picture may derive from Thetis and the Nereids hearing from the depths of the sea her son Achilles' loud grief for Patroclus, Homer, *Iliad* 18.35 ff. More important is the Oceanids' motive, which their father will share: friendly sympathy for Prometheus (128, 144–6, etc.; cf. Oceanus at 289, 295–7, etc.); and Io's accidental encounter with him prompts her sympathy too, for she suffers from gods as well, fettered metaphorically to pain (588–9), as he is literally (cf. 561–886 n., Introd. 2.4 p. xlix).

This *parodos* is not a continuous song by the chorus as found in all six authentic Aeschylean plays. They sing two pairs of responding stanzas, with each stanza answered by Prometheus with chanted anapaests: their surprise and emotion are countered by his more controlled self-pity (on the Greek lyric metre of 128–35 = 144–51 see 397–435 n., at end). Prometheus, however, quickly begins a theme which provides him with confident resistance to Zeus, and dominates much of the play: his eventual release is as predestined as his bonds, for he has foreknowledge which will secure it for him from Zeus (85–6 n.).

128 *formation*: a naval or military term, perhaps apt to a tightly organized entry by the Chorus. *as friends*: like their father Oceanus (290). The Oceanids helped celebrate Prometheus' wedding (556–60).

133–5 *shocked me out of my shy reserve*: they are like ordinary unmarried Athenian girls, socially 'invisible' and wholly dependent on their legal guardian (cf. e.g. *Supp.* 204–5 and 391 n.); for their *caves*, cf. 300–1.

138–40 *Tethys of the many children and ... Oceanus*: primeval parents of gods and powers, Homer, *Iliad.* 14.201; and esp. of river-deities and nymphs (Hesiod, *Theogony* 337–70 advances the number 3,000 for the nymphs alone); for Tethys and rivers, see also *Seven* 311. *coils round all the earth*: a picture formed from the experience of oceans apparently limitless to West and East, and from 'geography' which imagined the earth almost as a floating dish.

143 *unenviable guard*: cf. Hephaestus at 31.

148 *wither*: as 269; at *LB* 296 a polluted outlaw must starve and then 'mummify'.

149–51 *Olympus' helm*: see *Seven* 2 and n. for the metaphor. *laws ... without due base*: emphatic paradox; Zeus' autocracy without 'constitutional' sanction recurs at 403, cf. 187, 324. *what was mighty before*: Zeus' own father Cronus (185, cf. 907–12), and then the Titans, overthrown, and with the Titan Prometheus' help (201–21).

152–4 *down ... into boundless Tartarus*: at play-end Prometheus will repeat this wish, inviting Zeus' cataclysm to send him even that deep, 1051; cf. Hermes at 1027–9.

159 *for my enemies' delight*: the idea is continued in 160–1; cf. *Supp.* 1008 and n.

163–7 *rancorous*: a god's vindictive anger, e.g. Hera's against Io at 602. *unbending in purpose*: 34, 185, *Supp.* 385–6, etc. *the race of Ouranos*: father of Cronus (149–51 n.). *by some ruse, etc.*: the Greek word covers both cunning and force. *the rule ... hard to attain*: over the gods.

168–71 *the blessed ones*: *Seven* 97, *Supp.* 524, etc. *president*: the word for an appointed officer at Athens (also *Supp.* 371)—but Zeus is an absolute ruler, 10 n. *new plan*: the adjective is 'sinister' (cf. 'fresh' in 150). The poet begins here upon Prometheus' secret knowledge how Zeus may fall (cf. 188–9); it is through his own design, a marriage which Prometheus knows will recoil on him: 511–25, 761–5, 907–12 and nn., Introd. 2.4 p. xlvii.

173 *cower*: as he had not before punishment, 29, and will not again, 960.

183–5 *come ashore*: i.e. in safety, the idea semi-metaphorical at *Supp.* 337; to uncertainty, 438 there. Alternative translation: 'wherever in this pain ... and see its end'. *inexorable heart*: cf. 164.

187–9 *keeps justice to himself*: see on 150. *in this way*: a loose back-reference to 170–1, it appears. *smashed*: a surprisingly strong verb; it is used of Zeus' own intention against men at 236.

191–2 *bond of friendship*: echoing a Homeric expression, *Iliad* 7.302. Cf. 169.

193–396 First episode. In its first scene (193–276) Prometheus' preceding words on Zeus' harsh injustice to him but destined reconciliation lead the Chorus to ask why Zeus punished him as he did. In a long speech (198–241), then dialogue (242–62) and a shorter speech (263–76), he explains the theft of fire and why his punishment is so severe. The Chorus seek to learn more (277–83, lyric interlude), only for their father Oceanus to enter abruptly and make the episode's second scene (286–396); it is unconnected with the first, except through the motif of sympathy; Oceanus does not mention his daughters, and they are silent throughout. Oceanus offers the help due from kin to kin (289–97); he will try to intercede with Zeus, but Prometheus repels him, saying that Zeus is inflexible and citing his similarly harsh retaliation upon Atlas and Typhon, Titans like himself (his long speech 340–77 answers that of Oceanus 307–29). In a brief stichomythia, Prometheus mixes concern for Oceanus, that he should not share Zeus' displeasure, with a sharp dismissal (378–96). In this episode the poet is beginning to characterize Prometheus with the obduracy which dismays all who may sympathize with him, including at play-end the Chorus (1036–7); the term becomes frequent: 436 n., Introd. 2.4 p. xlvii.

Like his daughters the Chorus before him, Oceanus does not enter speaking: he chants, they sang; and the next entrant, Io, will chant before singing (561 ff.).

196–8 *even to speak ... pain*: Prometheus repeats his 106–7; but the Chorus' *you are hurt* in 196 makes the words ambiguous of physical pain as well; cf. 238, 261.

199–205 *divine powers... angry... faction*: from mutual jealousy, Hesiod, *Theogony* 617–38. *Titans, children of Heaven and Earth*: *Theogony* 644.

209–11 *my mother Themis and Earth, one form with many names*: one or more divine identities fuse; such syncretism, poetic or pragmatic for worship, is a marked feature of Greek religion (cf. 516 n.). Here the poet wishes to impress Prometheus' pedigree upon the Chorus (and the audience); as Earth, his mother bore all manner of creatures (*LB* 127); as Themis, she owned, and passed to him, prophetic powers (211, 873–4, cf. esp. *Eum.* 2–4, where she is Earth's daughter and once controlled Delphi and its oracle). Accordingly he can foretell the future (604–7, 622–30, 824–6) and pass skill in divination to men (484, etc.).

217–21 *join my mother... to aid... Zeus*: she is already his ally at Hesiod, *Theogony* 901 ff. *through my counsels*: at *Theogony* 624–8 it is Earth (see 209–10 n.) who advises Zeus in his triumph over violent strength. *Tartarus conceal... Cronus*: when deposed by Zeus; cf. Homer, *Iliad* 8.479–80 (where Prometheus is said to be in Tartarus, and will indeed go in our play, 1029, 1050).

223 *reward*: grim irony; the Greek word, like a synonym at *Pers.* 823, *Seven* 1021, can also mean 'punishment' (and in the chief MS it has been replaced by a gloss with this meaning).

230 *assigned... prerogatives*: the poet follows Hesiod, *Theogony* 73–4.

231–6 *mortals... obliterate their whole race*: probably a loose reference to the myth of the Ages of Man in Hesiod's *Works and Days*, successively destroyed by Zeus. *set men free, etc.*: also loose, for if the poet is following Hesiod for the fifth, last and worst Age, that of Iron, as that to which Prometheus gave fire (*Works and Days* 49–52), Hesiod says only that Zeus will destroy it (180), not that Prometheus thwarted him (235).

237–43 *bent... brought... into line*: grimly said: the 'bending' of Prometheus in his fetters (306, 513, cf. 995) does not 'bring him into line' in the sense of correcting him; the second Greek verb carries also the sense 'given this shape'. *not... getting (pity)*: cf. Power's jibe at 68. *ruthlessly*: 240–1 answers the Chorus' 194–5 explicitly; with their *share resentment* in 243 they repeat 162 (cf. Prometheus himself at 303).

246–60 This brief stichomythia serves to lift Prometheus' benefits to men clear of his offences to Zeus and punishment, which dominate the episode after the Chorus' request at 193–5; cf. 273–5.

246 *friends*: 128.

248–50 *from foreseeing their death*: this 'benefit' (251) is said at Plato, *Gorgias* 523d to have been given at Zeus' own prompting. *blind hopes*: possibly an allusion to Zeus' gift of Pandora's jar, in which only hope remained once she released all the evils, Hesiod, *Works and Days* 96 ff.; cf. Introd. 2.4. p. xliii. Hope is seldom presented favourably in early Greek thought, e.g. 'empty hopes' *Pers.* 804, *Supp.* 96.

253–4 *ephemeral men*: 82–4 n. *learn ... crafts*: 110, 477, etc.

257 *no end set*: cf. Prometheus himself at 100, 755.

259 *What hope is there?*: do the Chorus here see any hope for Prometheus as 'blind' (250)? At 509 they have 'good hopes' for him.

263 *with his feet out of harm's way*: an everyday expression, *LB* 697.

265–6 *Everything of this I knew*: in advance, he said at 101. *I did wrong willingly*: repudiating the Chorus' oblique criticism at 260–1. The doubling of *willingly* nears pathos, evident in the doubling of 'let me persuade you' in 274. It is possible, but no more, that the wording reflects the paradox attributed to Socrates, 'No one does wrong willingly'.

269 *withering away*: the Chorus' words at 147.

272 *step down*: from their winged 'carriages', 279–80; see 127–92 n.

274 *Let me persuade you*: reversed at 1039, when the Chorus plead with Prometheus.

275–6 *for misery ... now upon another*: hinting to the Chorus that even they may suffer from a tyranny like that of Zeus [*for* is West's conjecture (although he does not print it), and makes the best connection between the two clauses; the MSS are unsatisfactory].

278 *with light step*: self-referential, a decorative adjective for a nymph; cf. 125 'light beat of wings'.

284 *s.d.*: Oceanus' entry is as abrupt as Io's at 561. He rides a griffin, a four-legged 'bird', 395 (n.), a creature also employed by Zeus (802–4 and n.); for the staging, see Introd. 2.4 Appendix p. lii. Prometheus does not voice surprise until 298, and speaks as if he had not heard Oceanus' first words, which suggests that Oceanus is still out of his view (cf. the Chorus at 114–26). The text does not reveal whether Oceanus dismounts at all, and at 396 he leaves as abruptly as he came.

284–396 Oceanus' arrival pre-empts Prometheus' narrative promised to the Chorus (272–3, 282). He comes, like his daughters, in true sympathy and friendship (289, 297); as Prometheus' former helper (331) he will try to help again, to seek mercy from Zeus (312–13, 325–6, 338–9, 381–5). Prometheus will have none of it (333–5, 340–4, 383–92); he is as resentful of his own punishment as of Zeus' cruelty to his cousins Atlas and Typhon (346–72).

290 *kinship*: Oceanus is a half-brother of Prometheus (559–60), and his daughters the Chorus are relatives by marriage too (558); cf. 'friends', 128, 246. Cf. Hephaestus at 14 and 39 (n.).

299–302 *view ... observe*: verbs with overtones, the first suggestive of viewing by a privileged few (as at a mystery-cult), the second connoting either official visitation or theatrical spectating—as Prometheus anticipated at 119(n.); 'look at the sight' in 304 may have the same allusion. *stream named for you*: remote Ocean, bounding the world, 140; for the *caverns*, see 137. *land that mothers iron*: Scythia (2): 714–15, *Seven* 728 (n.).

308 *ingenious*: the Greek word has a pejorative tone: cf. 328 'extreme intelligence'. Oceanus hopes that this very cleverness nevertheless recognizes there is room for help.

309 *Learn to know yourself!*: slightly varied in implication from the famous Delphic maxim 'Know thyself'.

310 *new ... new*: juxtaposed in the Greek for effect. Oceanus repeats Hephaestus' warning of 35.

312 *Zeus ... seated ... higher*: in the sky; of the gods generally, *Supp.* 597.

314–17 *child's play*: a surprisingly rare metaphor, whereas *old-fashioned*, i.e. 'an old fool', is quite common.

318–19 *tongue too lofty*: cf. 327, 360; 'over-lofty' also in Hephaestus' criticism at 18. Cf. the Chorus at 180, and their 'yield not at all' in 179.

323–4 *kick against the pricks*: this maxim also at *Ag.* 1624. *monarch*: see 10 n. *answerable*: an expression from Athenian public life: *Pers.* 213 and n.

328–9 *extreme intelligence*: 308 and n.

331 *you have shared everything courageously with me*: translation disputed; besides, Prometheus claimed sole opposition to Zeus at 234 [therefore the line is suspect to editors, and often emended (e.g. to 'when you have not had the courage to share everything with me'), or deleted].

333 *Zeus ... not easily persuaded*: 164 and n.

336 *Facts, not words*: a contrast so common in all registers of language that it becomes trite, not always accurately employed: Oceanus may mean, the sight of Prometheus' fetters is stronger evidence of his folly even than his words; but in Prometheus' immobility, his words are the only reality.

339 *release from this ordeal*: Oceanus repeats his 316, 326.

342-3 *effort ... no help, etc.*: as Power told Prometheus, 44. The triple repetition of 'effort' seems clumsy to us, but the Greek verb has the same root as 'ordeal' in 339, and Prometheus may be intending a rhetorical play.

344 *No, stay quiet*: hurling Oceanus' own advice back at him: 327.

346 *harm as few as possible*: the apparent implication, for the Greek expression jars awkwardly, lit. 'I would not wish harm to as many as possible'; but perhaps it simply negates what Prometheus may be expected to wish, that as many others as possible suffer like himself.

347-50 *my brother Atlas*: like Prometheus' half-brother Typhon (351-72: n.), and like Prometheus himself, punished by Zeus with tortured immobility. *supporting ... earth's and heaven's pillar*: imprecise, as in 429-30, for in myth and art Atlas supports only the heaven, because he stands on the earth (these lines are based upon Hesiod, *Theogony* 517-18); at Homer, *Odyssey* 1.52-4 he 'has' the pillar; at Herodotus 4.184.4 he is himself the pillar (in the form of Atlas the mountain). So the picture here may be of Atlas seeming to join heaven as the pillar's capital to earth as its base. *not easy for the arms*: when they are flexed to hold in place what the neck and shoulders bear. [Minor MSS give 347-72 to Oceanus, which is not impossible ('brother' in 347 can be accommodated), but much less apt for the sympathies towards like sufferers: 331.]

351-72 *Typhon* (354, 370) who opposed Zeus (358) is blasted and crushed with a brutality which Prometheus' own punishment will reproduce (1015-19); he is 'buried' like Zeus' other foes (219-20, cf. 151). The author paints Typhon's agonies with vivid relish and resonance, very much in Aeschylus' style (see below); he draws many details from Hesiod, *Theogony* 820 ff. and Pindar, *Pythians* 1.15-28.

351-4 *child of earth*: primeval, *monstrous*, like Io's watcher the many-eyed Argos (568, 677-9; cf. *Supp.* 303); so Typhon sprang from, and lived in, *caves*. [*stood against all the gods*: metrically corrupt in the MSS and not yet emended, but the general sense is certain.]

355–7 *hissing terror...flashed a fierce gleam*: for the imagery, cf. the mixture of terrifying sights and sounds marking the shields and their bearers in *Seven*, e.g. Typhon at 493–6, 511, cf. 385, 537. *intent on the violent ruin*: again cf. *Seven* 427, 467.

359–60 *lightning which descends*: the Greek evokes this idea through Zeus' cult-title 'Descender'. *lofty boastings*: again cf. *Seven*, e.g. 551, 794.

361 *to the very soul of his being*: see n. on 881 'inside me'.

363–72 *sea-narrows*: the modern Straits of Messina. *crushed*: the Greek word is very rare, and derives here probably from Pindar, *Olympians* 4.7–8, who describes this same retaliation by Zeus upon Typhon. *Hephaestus*: the still active volcano Etna was imagined as the fire-god's forge. Hephaestus fetters *Typhon* like Prometheus, but with fire; the already incinerated but likewise immortal Typhon, buried beneath Etna, nevertheless spews out his rage in lava.

373–6 *save yourself as you know how*: a bitter reference to 330–1. *endure...to the dregs*: for the image, see 34 n. *until Zeus, etc.* 257–8, cf. 27.

377–93 This brief exchange, some of it in tense stichomythia (Introd.3.2 p. lx), shows Prometheus so contemptuous of help (383, 392) that Oceanus feels dismissed (387, 393). It exposes Prometheus' extreme resentment and self-pity even more than his last speech to the Chorus at 263–76.

377–8 *temper*: the Greek word (80) has the same ambiguity as the English. *sick*: for this nearly 'dead' metaphor, cf. 384, 685, 698, 977–8; cf. Introd. 2.4 p. xlix.

379–80 *softens...reduce swollen*: medical vocabulary; cf. 473–5 and n.

389 *newly seated, etc.*: he is harsh in consequence, 35, 310–14, etc.

394–6 *bird-like steed*: lit. 'four-limbed bird', the griffin, 286 n. The strange emphasis on the creature's impatience to leave may be intended to herald a further demonstrative theatrical effect, reversing Oceanus' sudden entry at 284: see n. there.

397–435 First choral ode; it is very brief, like the other two (526–60, 887–906: see Introd. 2.4 p. 1). The Chorus briefly renew their sympathy, decorate it by listing the peoples outside Greece who share it, and end by adding to these the sea and rivers; these natural elements are the ones they know best, as the daughters of Oceanus, 133–40. Zeus' arrogant rule (402–5) and his 'fettering' of Atlas (425–30, already cited by Prometheus at 347–50) illuminate what the world 'laments'; the Greek word-root 'lament pervades the ode (397 = 435 in 'ring-composition'; 407, 409, 413, 432). Poetic colour is attempted briefly with the Amazons (415–16) and the high-castled warlike 'Arabs' (420–4); these brief images may anticipate the much more detailed and vivid geographies of Io's wanderings (707–852); for their geographical imprecision, see Introd. 2.4 p. xlviii and n. 45. [For the problematic text of 425–35, see n. on 425–30.]

The Greek ionic metre of the first pair of stanzas (397–414) repeats that of the first pair of the *parodos* (128–35 = 144–51), and is normally associated with solemn or ritual themes (see n. on *Pers.* 65); but, as in 128–51, such tones are absent here.

398–401 *lament... tears... in their wet flow*: typical redundancy in emphatic statements of sorrow; the Chorus' true sympathy shows when they share Prometheus' destruction, 1064–70.

402–5 *unsparingly*: translation insecure. The Greek word means usually 'unenviable (as at *Supp.* 642), unenvying'; the nuance here is perhaps 'showing no envious regard for any other', because of his absolute power. *with private laws* and *those former gods*: for both phrases see 150–1 and n.

406–10 *The whole earth*: but only Asia is meant (413), where Prometheus is fettered. Its peoples catalogued in 411–24 as sympathetic to Prometheus were legendary for their hard ferocity. *your magnificence... ancient*: while he was Zeus' ally, 216–23 [loss of text is shown by defective metrical correspondence with 400; West suggests 'now smashed', others '(lament)... with tears']. *your blood-kin*: Atlas and Typhon, 347–72.

411–13 *inhabiting homes settled*: the redundancy is in the Greek, but has no point, unlike the repetition of 'lament' (397–435 n.). *sacred Asia*: the adjective often honours major natural phenomena, e.g. a mountain at *Pers.* 49, rivers at 434, 812 below and *Pers.* 497, etc.

415–19 *maidens fearless in battle*: the Amazons, whom Prometheus will name in his prophecies of Io's wanderings (723–8), again as near *Maeotis' lake* (73: see Map 5).

420–4 *Arabia*: the name stands loosely for 'the East', like 'Ethiopia' in *Supp.* 286; editors cite Plautus, *Trinummus* 933–4 'A:... on our way to the Black Sea we sailed to Arabia.' B: 'Hey, is Arabia actually on the Black Sea?' *flower, its warriors*: metaphor as *Pers.* 59, etc. *Caucasus*: the whole area around the modern Sea of Azov, not our Georgia; the play's ancient 'hypothesis' (p. 238) locates Prometheus himself in the Caucasus, but at 719 he speaks of it as distant from him. *roar*: as Tydeus roars at the prospect of battle, *Seven* 378.

425–30 [*supports... like a covering roof*: only the probable meaning of an apparent conjecture in a single late MS, adopted by West: the older MSS have 'groans beneath'. The words *who* and *earth* appear to be certain supplements. The text of the final lines, 425–35, is damaged or defective, and not all editors have formed them into a pair of stanzas. Some editors believe them to be so irreparably damaged, and the sufferings of Atlas to interrupt the concentration upon sympathy for Prometheus so severely, that they resort to deletion, either leaving 425–30 as an 'epode', or removing 425–35 entirely.]

436–525 Second Episode. Prometheus narrates his services to mankind, in two long speeches, interrupted but not deflected by the Chorus' puzzled observation that his inventiveness could not save himself (471–5 between 436–70 and 476–506). This topic resumes the earlier anxieties of the Chorus (e.g. 181–5, 262) and of Oceanus (e.g. 295, 315–16), and occupies the episode's end, in a short exchange (507–25); and it continues in the ode 526–60: see n.

Prometheus' benefits to men (the term occurs at 251, 501, 613): in the fifth century BC theories of human progress not only began but multiplied and varied. They moved away from earlier attributions of man's whole condition to the gift of gods (or their punishment: Hesiod, *Works and Days* 109–211, the successively worsening 'Ages of Man'); through conceptions of advance as initiated by gods but developed by men; to rationalization of conditions and progress as man's own achievement. Prometheus in this play favours mankind (11, 28, etc.); as well as removing their foreknowledge of death, and imbuing them with hope, his chief gift is of fire, the element which 'teaches' (110) men how to 'learn' (254) practical and technological skills, once he has enabled their intelligence (443–4). Through this last, they master other 'skills' (477, 506) to which he 'shows them the way' (498): the natural calendar, number, writing, animal husbandry, ships, medicine, and divination (454–99; see too the nn. on 459–61, 462–6, 467–8). Fifth-century Tragedy contains two other striking accounts of human progress: Sophocles, *Antigone* 332–75, a 'hymn to man's pure inventiveness' (*c*.440 BC, very close to the *Prometheus* in date), and Euripides, *Suppliants* 201–15, man's advance from bestial chaos to orderly communication (late 420s). Excellent summary discussions by Griffith in his edition (1982), 166–8 and Podlecki (2005), 116–27; earlier e.g. Conacher (1980), 82–97.

436–7 *I keep silent, etc.*: Prometheus has necessarily been silent during the Chorus' ode, but a longer silence seems implied here, which he fears the Chorus will interpret wrongly. Probably the actor stayed silent until the Chorus moved towards him. *obduracy*: of Prometheus at 907, 964, 1012, 1034, 1037.

439–40 *prerogatives for these new gods*: see n. on 230.

448–9 *like dream-shapes*: i.e. ineffectually; the idea also at 549.

452 *scurrying*: the Greek adjective is lit. 'light as air'.

455–6 *fruitful summer*: the period for taking any ripe crop, including our autumn.

458 *the risings . . . of the stars*: possibly an echo of *Ag.* 7, a verse of disputed authenticity.

459–61 *Number*: an invention commonly associated with the human Palamedes, e.g. in the now lost nameplays by Sophocles and Euripides. *letters*: also attributed to Palamedes; Euripides, *Palamedes* fr. 582 has them as 'remedy' against forgetfulness: cf. *record of all things* here. *mother and crafter of poetry*: 'Crafter' was a cult-title of Athena, a patroness of both arts and crafts (Sophocles fr. 844); for 'mother' in metaphor, cf. 301 (the earth, of iron), *Pers.* 614 (the grape, of wine).

462–6 *yoking, etc.*: of beasts for heavy work (464), while *horses* were for the rich, to ride or to pull carriages or chariots (465–6). *yoke-loops*: attached to the T-bar across the animals' shoulders (*Pers.* 191–2). *chariot . . . luxury*: for the link, cf. *Pers.* 607–8. The domestic use of such vehicles was condemned as un-Athenian, e.g. at Demosthenes 42.24. [*saddles* is an emendation of MSS 'bodies', as in 'take over with their bodies from men'.]

467–8 *ships*: Prometheus' son was Deucalion, who built the first 'ark' to escape the flood. For ships as men's own invention see Sophocles, *Antigone* 334–7.

473–5 *you cannot discover . . . cure yourself*: 'Physician, heal thyself.' The Greek is phrased so as to emphasize 'cure', thus resuming the entire simile in 473–4. Oceanus had made the same bleak comment (335–6). Here, Prometheus ignores the Chorus' thrust, and immediately states his mastery of real medicine (478–83): dramatist's irony?

484–99 *many ways of divination*: a remarkably detailed exposition: why? Probably because Prometheus himself heard and learned prophecy from his mother Themis (209–11 n.) and relies on her confident prediction of his ultimate release (873–4). Also, he will prophesy to Io her future, tormented wanderings (604–8, etc.).

485–6 *judged from dreams what must be reality*: alluding probably to the famous Homeric picture of false and true dreams, *Odyssey* 19.547, 20.90.

486–92 *omens from people's remarks*: unconsidered or involuntary revelations ('people's' is not in the Greek). *signs met on their journeys*: in Aeschylus, famously Zeus' eagles sent to encourage Agamemnon at Aulis, *Ag.* 111–59. *birds of prey...perchings together*: suggestive or determinative analogies for human behaviour: see the meaning of the simile *Supp.* 223–8(n.).

493–9 *entrails, etc.*: from their shape and colour, and afterwards the manner of their burning. There is comparable detail in a sacrifice narrated at Euripides, *Electra* 827–9. *thigh-bones...in fat*: Prometheus presents favourably what Hesiod, *Theogony* 535–57 portrayed as his deception of Zeus, and a cause of Zeus' anger: men sacrificing treated the animal's bones in this way, but kept the flesh for themselves; the story became a comfortable explanation of a puzzling ritual (cf. 82–4 n. and Introd. 2.4. p. xliii).

500–4 *silver and gold*: the formulaic, precious pair are distinguished from the utilitarian other metals as early as Homer, *Iliad* 6.48.

505–6 *all their skills from Prometheus!*: a very pointed ending, with a play on his own name like the cruel one by Power in 85–6 (n.).

507–10 *unduly*: see n. on 30. *hopes that you will yet be freed*: matching their father Oceanus' confidence, 338–9. *and be no less strong than Zeus*: the poet is making the Chorus build a lot on what they have heard from Prometheus at 168–9 (n.).

513 *bent like this*: 237 n.

515–21 A very brief stichomythia ends this episode, as it did the last (377–93 n.), expressing once again Prometheus' obduracy.

515 *the helm of the inevitable*: a variation on the image of 149 (n.).

516 *Fates and...Furies*: overlapping identities (cf. 209–11 n. on Themis-Earth); they are identical at *Seven* 1055, sisters at *Eum.* 961. They are often associated in their working (esp. in accursed families *Seven* 975, *LB* 910–11), because retribution from the Furies is fated and inevitable; Prometheus is emphasizing Zeus' helplessness against inevitability, 518. *ever-mindful*: borrowed from references to their relentlessness at *Ag.* 155, *Eum.* 383. *three*: a canonical number for supernatural beings, e.g. the Phorcides at 795; cf. Geryon's three bodies at *Ag.* 870. The alliteration on 'f' in this line follows that of the Greek.

519 *Zeus except to rule...?*: cf. 757.

520 *You'll learn nothing further, etc.*: Prometheus clings to his secret knowledge (168–76; cf. 377–8 and n.), even to friends—but see 769 ff. (to Io) and 907 ff. (to the Chorus again).

526–60 Second choral ode. The first pair of stanzas (526–44) states the insuperable power of Zeus: the Chorus fear it for themselves, Prometheus suffers for his lack of fear. The second pair (545–60) develops this concern, in more human and intimate terms: men cannot return Prometheus' favours with help against Zeus; and in their sympathy the Chorus recall their closeness to him at his wedding.

The deeper emotion thus suddenly expressed may aim to prepare for the pathos of the following episode with Io (561–886 and n.); but the Greek metre of this ode is associated particularly with hymnic or celebratory verse (see n. on *Pers.* 532–97), and seems appropriate only in the first pair of stanzas; see however on the metre of both the first ode (397–435) and the third (887–906).

530–1 *feasts where oxen are killed*: special and extravagant gestures of honour: *Supp.* 706, *LB* 261. *Oceanus' unquenchable stream*: 'unsleeping' at 139.

534 *I wish this remains firm*: never to offend Zeus, 526–33.

541 [Defective metrical responsion alone reveals the loss of words; the sense is complete, so that supplementation would be mere guesswork.]

542 *no fear of Zeus*: so Prometheus himself at 174, 960.

543–7 *regard...for...men...is too high*: cf. Power at 11. *What aid...from ephemeral men?*: Power at 84.

549–50 *dream-like*: see on 449. *blindness*: from which Prometheus claimed to have rescued them (447).

552 *ordered government*: lit. 'harmony', imposed by Zeus' mind (526) which it is impossible to escape, 907, *Supp.* 1049.

557–60 *wedding-hymn beside bath and bed*: in ritual procedures, as the bride bathed before she left her father's house (e.g. Euripides, *Medea* 1026–7, *Phoenician Women* 348) and as the bridal pair entered the bedroom (e.g. *Ag.* 707). *led in*: as the groom taking the bride to her new home. *Hesione*: in early myth Prometheus has no wife, or she is named as Pyrrha.

561–886 Third Episode: Io's story and her importance to Prometheus; on this difficult episode, see Introd. 2.4 p. xlv. Io is the third visitor for Prometheus, both unexpected and with an unexpected link to him; he knows her story and her future (589–92, 609–12, 617, etc.) and they bear on his own (see below). Daughter of Inachus king of Argos, she caught Zeus' roving eye (654), but the jealousy of Zeus' wife Hera drove her from home, partly transformed into a cow, harried jointly by a maddening cattle-fly and a constant watcher, the many-eyed Argos (673–9); in the play, her actor wore a head-mask with a cow's horns (588: cf. n., and Introd. 2.5 p. lv.) Her frenzied flight takes her round much of N. Greece, our Balkans, S. Russia, the Caucasus, and the nearer Middle East to Egypt: see Map 5. Her story is told in less detail in *Suppliants* (274–325, 538–89, cf. 15–19, 40–8).

She has supernatural motion and speed, and mountains and waters are no obstacle (e.g. 722, 729–34). So her passing through these mountains is at least explicable; Prometheus at first only hints her importance to him (at 611 she is a 'friend'), but he has foreknowledge that one of her distant descendants will free him from his bonds (771–4)—and his prophecy of this ends the episode (869–73), at last satisfying the Chorus' anxiety to know this detail (785, 821–2, cf. 259, 521).

Much of the episode is filled out with long narratives by Io of her past (640–86) and by Prometheus of her future (700–41, 786–818, 823–76). After his prophecy the episode ends as abruptly as it begins, with Io's renewed seizure by her frenzy, which in 877–86 carries her violently away; as soon as she enters, it seizes her in a short paroxysm of pain and bitterness. Her entry-monody (566–608) conveys this cruel torment much more vividly than her own narrative; the monody moves in mid-sentence (573–4) from free lyric into a pair of long responding stanzas, all written in very irregular rhythms; the two stanzas are capped each by spoken lines from Prometheus (566–88 + 589–603 = 593–608 + 609–12). In the second stanza Io's language, if not the rhythm, is more calm; this prepares for her questioning of Prometheus, in only slightly irregular stichomythic dialogue (613–30, and later 742–79). In their second exchange, after he tells her of her future wanderings (700–41), she is able to check her dismay sufficiently to ask him about his own release. (This monody is unique in the complete plays attributed to Aeschylus: we do not know whether Aeschylus himself ever used the form.) The skilled deployment of varying formal resources creates outward dramatic order for a remarkable episode.

561 *Whom do I see, should I say, etc.*: to know his name, in order to address him effectually with her appeal of 604–8; Prometheus anticipates her own name, 589–90, cf. 593. Cf. Prometheus' own apprehension of the unseen Chorus at 114–26.

563 *storm-beaten*: partly literal (cf. 22–5, 113), primarily metaphorical: 1015, cf. 838 of Io herself.

564 *For what crime, etc.*: Io repeats her question at 620; cf. Prometheus' own 112.

568–72 *that cowherd...passed from the dead below*: at 680–1 Io relates how Argos, the watcher set over her by Hera, was killed by the god Hermes (cf. *Supp.* 305 and n.); is she hallucinating in her frenzy, and taking the gadfly to be Argos tormenting her from Hades? If so, the reed-pipe he plays in 574–5 is part of her hallucination. *cunning in his look*: probably alluding to Argos' ability to keep at least some of his *countless eyes* (678–9) open at all times [but some editors are unhappy, and read 'with his eyes at a slant': he sees without looking 'straight'].

573 *in hunger*: cf. 598–9, endlessly seeking new grazing; cf. *Supp.* 539–42. *over the sand by the sea*: taken to indicate the setting of the play near the sea: see s.d. on 1, and 713 below.

574–5 *wax-bound reed-pipe*: the pastoral 'Pan-pipes', the syrinx, of reeds set together and waxed to a frame. For music warding off sleep see *Ag.* 16–17 [but *to destroy my sleep* is a conjecture adopted by West instead of the converse 'to give me sleep']: Io's torment is sleepless wandering, Prometheus' is sleepless immobility (32).

579 *yoke...under...torments*: a yoke is not inappropriate for Io transformed into a heifer, but the metaphor is often 'dead'; at 108 it is partly alive for Prometheus' 'bonds', cf. Introd. 2.4. p. xlix.

580 *derange*: a torture of the Furies, *Eum.* 329.

582–3 *Burn me, etc.*: death-wishes are frequent in Tragic extremity: Io again at 747–51, cf. *Supp.* 787–806. *sea-creatures*: ultimate terrors, *LB* 587–8. *devour*: an ugly word in Greek, used of Thyestes' eating his children's flesh, *Ag.* 1597.

588 *horned like a cow*: also 674. Later art depicted her thus (like Isis in Egyptian cult: Herodotus 2.41.2), earlier art showed her completely transformed (perhaps implied by *Supp.* 299–301).

589 *Inachus' daughter*: see 705.

591–2 *Hera*: 600, 704, 900; for her vindictive torment of Io, see *Supp.* 290–309, 562–4, 586–7. *weariness...course*: the metaphor from athletic training is fuller here than in 586.

595 *Who are you, etc.*: Io knows very well who Prometheus is, for at 605 she asks for his prophecy. Perhaps the author is continuing her initial disorientated surprise (561 ff.).

598 *wastes me away*: from hunger (573); the Furies too harry their victims into starved debility, *Eum.* 139, 267. Prometheus also is to 'wither', 147, 269.

599–601 *wild bucking*: like the heifer she partly is; also 675. *headlong speed*: this detail also at *Supp.* 547. *rancorous ... [Hera]*: see on 591–2 [the name is supplied from the ancient commentary; defective metre reveals its loss].

604–8 *tell me clearly ... if you know*: Io asked in 593–7 how he knew her name, and now guesses his prophetic knowledge too.

610–11 *riddles ... plain words*: the author likes this contrast: 949, cf. 775, 833. Here it marks the change from Io's wild singing to measured dialogue, and heralds the emphasis on facts and clarity in this episode (Io at 605 and 640–1, both she and Prometheus throughout 613–27), avoiding the enigmas invariably associated with prophecy (cf. Cassandra at *Ag.* 1183). *friends*: Prometheus has never met Io but at once acknowledges sympathy from a fellow-victim of Zeus.

613–30 A quickly moving stichomythic exchange in which Io successfully presses Prometheus to reveal her future, as she has just asked, 604–8.

613 *O you who appeared, etc.*: Io's first spoken words are suddenly elevated in tone; 'appear' often registers a divine or extraordinary manifestation, e.g. 1028, *Pers.* 354, 666. *mankind's common benefactor*: unlike so many gods who help only individuals.

622–3 *Well ... will be*: such double-line interruptions to stichomythia often accompany a sudden new tone or topic.

631–4 *No, not yet!, etc.*: a further, dramatically motivated postponement of Prometheus' prophecies; cf. 282, where Oceanus' entry interrupted them.

635–6 *It's your job*: an everyday expression, colloquial. *your father's sisters*: Io's father Inachus (590) was held, as a river-god, to be descended from Oceanus the father of the Chorus (140).

649–54 *Zeus has been inflamed, etc.*: as Prometheus knew, 590. *Lerna's deep meadow*: well-watered, 677; it was to be the setting for Zeus' attraction to her (*Supp.* 539–42, cf. 43). Meadows, grassy and flowery, often have erotic connotations, as do the *eyes* (*Zeus'* here), e.g. Helen's eyes at *Ag.* 742.

655–7 *dreams ... every night ... dreams ... in the night*: repetition uncomfortable to us (and cf. 645 already), but the author is emphasizing that Io's (eventual) fate was the inescapable if forewarned will of gods; for such dreams see Introd. 2.1 p. xxvi n. 14.

658 *Pytho*: the oracle at Delphi, which in some accounts Apollo had taken over after killing its guardian 'snake' (cf. 'python'), whence his title 'Pythian', *Seven* 748, etc. Ancient folk-etymology explained the name from the rotting (Greek <u>*pyth*</u>-) of the dead snake, *Homeric Hymn to Apollo* 372–4; modern philology is baffled. *Dodona*: in upland W. mainland Greece, roughly N. of Delphi. The oracle of Zeus there (also 830) was famous and believed to be the oldest in use (Herodotus 2.52.2, cf. Hom. *Od.* 14.327–8).

666–8 *let loose to wander*: anticipating her transformation into the heifer: animals were often turned loose, for a god to accept as sacrifice or not: cf. *Supp.* 691 and n. *should he not be willing, etc.*: such threatening tones occur in Apollo's oracle to Orestes about the matricide, *LB* 269–74, etc., *Eum.* 465–7. Like Inachus here (699), Orestes was 'persuaded' by the oracle, *LB* 297–8, *Eum.* 84. *Zeus*: Io here attributes both the threats to her father and her own suffering wholly to Zeus himself.

669–72 *Loxias*: for this name of Apollo, see *Seven* 618 and n. *against my will, and his will too*: for this verbal conceit, cf. 19, *Supp.* 227, etc. *Zeus' curb compelled*: cf. the metaphor from forcible harnessing used for Agamemnon's surrender to Artemis in sacrificing Iphigenia at Aulis, *Ag.* 218 'put on the yoke-strap of compulsion'.

676 *Cerchne*: an area W. of Argos.

677–9 *born from the earth*: cf. 351, and 209–11n. *clustered eyes*: 568 and n.

680–2 *sudden death*: see 570 n. *god's scourge*: *Seven* 608; a Homerism, e.g. *Iliad* 12.27 (Zeus). [The MS text in 680 *sudden* is unmetrical, but easily corrected. West however leaves it obelized.]

684–6 *don't ... out of pity ... vice*: recalling Prometheus' promise at 610.

687–95 Brief, passionate lyrics from the Chorus divide Io's pathetic narrative (640–86) from Prometheus' long forecasts of her future suffering (696–876); this separating device is used repeatedly in *Seven* 369–685 (see Introd. 3.3 p. lxii). [Unfortunately the Greek text and metre are insecure in 692–3 and left obelized by West; with *strike* in the translation of 692 I follow an editor's emendation, approved but not printed by West, which is based upon comparable imagery from chariot-driving at *Eum.* 156–7.]

707–11 *turn yourself from here*: for the apparent course of Io's wandering, see Map 5. Many of the place names seem inaccurate, for the author locates to the West of the Crimea and the Sea of Azov some places which are East or South of it, or not even on the Black Sea at all: see the n. on 420–4 [some editors have moved 717–28 to follow 791 to ease the problems]. *towards the sun's rising*: for a Greek the Caucasus (719; also 420–4 n.) lay far to the N., so that Io must go both E. and S. *unploughed lands... the nomadic Scythians*: their life on *carts* is described with wonder by Herodotus 4.46.

713 *keep close to the... sea*: very confusing, but the author at least places Scythia to the N. of the Black Sea. Cf. 573 and n.

714–16 *the Chalybes, workers with iron*: 133, *Seven* 728 (n.). They are here moved far eastward from their traditional home on the S. shore of the Black Sea.

717 *Hybristes—not falsely named!*: i.e. the '(River) Outrager', defying or destroying would-be crossers; for such punning, see 85 and n. This river is cautiously identified on grounds of location and torrential character (720) with the Hypanis, which flowed into the N. Black Sea near the Cimmerian Bosporus (730); the name Hybristes is similar in sound and may be an invention both to create the pun and to extend the idea of the 'uncivilized' Chalybes.

723–8 *Amazons*: located in Colchis in 415–16, approximately the same area as here. At *Supp.* 287–8 (n.) they are 'meat-eaters', and archers (like *Eum.* 628). *Themiscyra* and *Thermodon* were historically on the S. coast of the Black Sea. *Salmydessus*: the long and dangerous coastline of the S.-W. Black Sea; the author has again moved it to the S. coast and eastward. *stepmother evil*: 'evil' is not in the Greek, and has been added for clarity; this pejorative image of the stepmother was common to many cultures. *and very gladly*: as men-hating women (724, cf. *Supp.* 287) they are sympathetic to another woman ill-used by the male Zeus (Io's view: 671–2).

729–34 *the Cimmerian isthmus*: the Crimea; Lake *Maeotis* behind it (418) is the Sea of Azov. *Bosporus... called after your name*: the name Bosporus was understood in antiquity, perhaps from this passage, as 'the crossing of the ox' (or 'cow', for Io is here the 'cow' or 'heifer'; modern scholars doubt the etymology (see n. on *Supp.* 543–5). The better-known Bosporus was and is still at the entrance to the Black Sea (*Pers.* 746 and n.); in variations upon Io's myth she crosses into Asia at that point by swimming (*Supp.* 544–81), rather than at the Crimea; but it is not said here how she crosses the *Maeotic basin*.

735 *Europe... Asia*: the Greeks set Asia's beginning either at the E. Black Sea (as here, and e.g. Herodotus 4.45.2) or at the Turkish Bosporus (*Pers.* 799, *Supp.* 547).

736–41 *weighed... down on her*: the verb suggests the image of the weighing scale, e.g. *Seven* 21, *Supp.* 405 [but it is an editor's alteration of MSS 'hurled down']. *A cruel suitor, etc.*: the Greek appears to emphasize the cruelty with a harsh assonance in this sentence. The Greek adjective here translated as *cruel* often describes persons in whom their true nature comes out only later, e.g. 944 ('extreme' there), or the unexpectedly harsh recoil on them of their own actions, *Seven* 730; 941–5 and n. *prelude*: for this metaphor applied to suffering, cf. *Supp.* 830.

742 *Oh! ... No!*: these ejaculations stand here outside the verse-line; as such they are very rare and strongly dramatic, e.g. from Cassandra in sudden prophetic seizure at *Ag.* 1214 (950 below is not an example).

746 *sea ... of torment*: cf. Io's use of 'storm' at 643, Hermes' at 1015.

747–51 *What use for me to live then?*: for such death-wishes, see 582–3 n.

753 *not my destiny to die*: repeated at 933, cf. 1052.

756 *until Zeus is thrown, etc.*: Prometheus opens this outcome to Io as a further sympathetic visitor, just as he had to the Chorus (168 ff.); but here he gives details he earlier withheld.

757–79 Line 757 signals the ensuing stichomythia; it is long, initially interrogative, and then informative; it both frustrates Io and promises her the reassurance which at last follows in 823–76.

760 [*rejoice*: an editor's correction of 'learn (the facts)'.]

762 *His very own empty-headed designs*: revealed in the following lines; but 170 already alluded to them.

764–8 *such a marriage*: again at 907–10. *one who will bear a son mightier than his father*: Thetis, competed for by Zeus and Poseidon, to whom Prometheus' mother Themis made this prophecy (Pindar, *Isthmians* 3.26 ff., cf. 924–5 below). *wife*: see n. on 'partner' in 834.

771 *if Zeus is unwilling*: circular in logic, since Zeus will certainly not be willing (770), but Prometheus is sure (764 n.), so that Zeus' fall is certain unless ... ['while Zeus rules' has been conjectured, however].

772 *one of your descendants*: Heracles: see n. on 1026–9.

774 *third ... after ten others*: 'thirteen' is 'lucky' here, but less evidently for Aegisthus at *Ag.* 1605.

775 *prophecy*: Prometheus will reveal 'fate' (772); Io reacts as if to an enigmatic oracle replying to her questions; both the mention of her descendants and the number 'thirteen' (772, 774) baffle her, despite Prometheus' promise of clarity at 620 (n.).

776 *do not seek to learn ... either*: rather like Prometheus' prevarication before (see on 757–79); but he quickly gives way (786 ff.), as he did earlier to Io after due warning (622–30: with 786 cf. 630).

790–2 *the flow bounding the continents*: the Cimmerian Bosporus, 730 and (n.) 785 [*make your way ... rising*: the MSS text has needed correction; some editors have supposed loss of text, or brought in 717–28 to follow 791].

792–800 *the Gorgon plains ... the Phorcides*: Io will now enter a purely mythical area, inhabited by monstrous beings. *Phorcides*: also called the Graeae or 'Ancient Ones', *long-lived* like those other female horrors, the never-ageing 'maidens' the Furies (*Eum.* 68–9). They are named the Gorgons' guardians in Aeschylus' lost satyr-play *Phorcides* (frs. 261–2), in which Perseus stole their single eye and so eluded their watch, in order to kill the Gorgon Medusa; since her eyes turned men to stone (800 *no one who sees them, etc.*), he caught her look in his polished shield. *Cisthene*: a notional place here, proverbially a remote mountain; there were in fact historical places with this name. *three*: for the canonical number, see 516 n. *hair white as swans*: this is how most scholars understand the Greek, which is lit. '(maidens) swan-formed' and for which no explanation has been suggested; for *Phorcides* is from a word-root meaning 'white (haired)'. *neither sun nor moon, etc.*: another supernatural abnormality, for the Phorcides' one eye is for keeping watch, just as the Furies apparently see amid their constant darkness, *LB* 285; cf. the Cimmerians at Homer, *Odyssey* 11.14–19—whose territory Io passes here, 730. *snake-haired Gorgons*: Orestes uses this detail to evoke his hallucination by the Furies, *LB* 1048–50. The name *Gorgon* baffles etymologists, for it seems to be itself the root-form of many derivatives connoting something terrifying with its look, or to another's gaze; it may be formed from an inarticulate or child's name for such a horror.

801–4 *garrison*: translation disputed, for an ancient commentator understood the word here to mean 'place against which one must be on guard' [and some editors emend the word to give 'such is the prelude to what I tell you']. *sight*: the word is that of 118(n.). *griffins*: 286 n.; *unbarking hounds*: a 'kenning' like 'bird-like steed' at 395; cf. 'winged hound' of Zeus' eagle at 1022. Aeschylus fr. 422 apparently described a 'griffin-eagle', made in bronze on a shield; the word was mocked by Aristophanes, *Frogs* 927.

804–7 *one-eyed Arimaspian horse-riders*: a fabulous people, probably made 'one-eyed' here to match the Phorcides of 794; *horse-riders* too may duplicate the nomadic Scythians of 709, and recall the Indians of *Supp.* 284. *Pluto*: a name invented to go with *golden*; it means 'Wealth(y)'. The underworld deity Pluto was so named, with euphemistic irony, as king of a featureless realm.

807–9 *black race, etc.*: the further south, the darker the skin, an age-old observation. Io's son Epaphus, to be born in Egypt, will have this colour, 851. *river Ethiops*: the Upper Nile is meant.

810–14 *Nile…pure flow*: good for drinking, fertile: *Supp.* 1024–9, *Pers.* 611 and nn. *revered*: for holy rivers, see e.g. *Pers.* 497. *Bybline*: another appropriated or imaginary name; the historical Egyptian Byblos was a town in the Nile valley. *far-distant colony*: 846–7. But some translate 'long-lived', for Io's line will be absent from Greece for many generations (cf. 774, 853–4); Io's mother is 'ancient' in *Supp.* 51.

816–17 *indistinctly*: lit. 'lispingly'. *doubling back*: probably a metaphor from the return-leg of a race (*Ag.* 344).

825–6 *I shall tell what she has endured, etc.*: true seers 'knew' the past, and such knowledge made their prophecy of the future credible (cf. 835); cf. the Chorus and Cassandra at *Ag.* 1199–201.

828 *very end*: Prometheus appears to mean the end of Io's wanderings in mainland Greece before she was driven round the Black Sea, as she herself told, 571–5 [but the phrase is suspect to editors after 'entire end' in 823].

829–35 *Molossian regions*: N. W. Greece (Epirus), and far from Io's home in Argos. For the oracle at *Dodona*, see 658 n. *Thesprotia* was a coastal area. *speaking oak-trees*: the oracle's priestesses interpreted the sounds of their moving branches or leaves. *by which you were told*: Prometheus repeats Io's own narrative from 658–9. *with no riddling*: again, cf. 610 (n.). *partner of Zeus*: the Greek word implies a 'lawful' wife, but this was Hera (*Supp.* 296, 1035); the oracle therefore meant that Io would be specially privileged by her union with him—as her dream had first told her (645–54). When Prometheus prophesied Zeus' disastrous union with Thetis at 764 (cf. 909), the Chorus used the same word 'wife' of her in 767.

835 *does anything… win your belief?*: 825–6 n.

836–41 *Rhea*: Zeus' mother. This gulf, the S. Adriatic, also bore his father Cronus' name, but why, is not known, unless myth gave it a part in Rhea's attempt to hide the infant Zeus from Cronus' assault, for his destruction by Zeus was prophesied (cf. 201–2). In making Io the eponym of the *Ionian* sea (the same S. Adriatic), the author is abusing tradition (the name came from the Ionian Greeks). The Cimmerian Bosporus is named from Io's crossing (732–4 and n.).

844–5 *tell you and Io jointly*: cf. 784–5. Past narrative now returns to future, picking up 810–14, Io's arrival in Egypt; here she will bear Zeus' son Epaphus

(851 n.), from whom Prometheus' rescuer Heracles will descend (1026–9 n.); and this will answer the Chorus' questions too.

846–69 This account of how Io's descendants, the fifty daughters of Danaus, were pursued to Argos by their fifty suitors, the sons of Aegyptus, summarizes the action of *Suppliants*, except that there the women are promised help to avoid marriage by 'Pelasgus' land' (860 below); here they themselves act, murderously. See Introd. 2.2 p. xxxvii.

846–7 *Canopus*: Io's destination in Egypt also at *Supp.* 311. *Nile's...banked-up silt*: the Delta: *Supp.* 3 and n.

848–52 *touch of a...hand...named...[Epaphus]*: the etymological 'aetiology' of his name reproduces that of *Supp.* 15–18, 45–7 (n.), 313–15.

856–8 *hawks...doves*: this image for the suitors' 'hunt' appears too at *Supp.* 223–4 (n.).

860–3 *two-edged*: lit. 'twice-whetted', i.e. sharpened on both sides. [Not all editors suppose loss of text; but *will accept* is problematic because in *Suppliants* 'Pelasgus' land' accepts Io's descendants before any bloodshed. Accordingly, 'will be soaked' is conjectured in replacement.]

864–5 *I wish Aphrodite...my enemies*: Prometheus hopes for this outcome for Zeus from his bride (764–8 and n.). *one of the daughters*: Hypermnestra, who spared Lynceus (Introd. 2.2. p. xxxvii). This motif is found in another story of murderous brides, those of Lemnos (*LB* 631–4).

871–3 *one bold...with his bow*: Heracles (1026–9 n.). He gave his bow to his friend Philoctetes, and it was needed for the capture of Troy (see Sophocles' *Philoctetes*: the plays of Aeschylus and Euripides with this subject are both very fragmentary). [The Greek text is strained in expression, and a line may have been lost after *bold* in 871.]

873–4 *oracle...Themis*: see on 209–11.

877–86 These lines are a remarkable example of bodily self-description to supplement, indeed almost to replace, realistic 'acting'. Some of the vocabulary here is 'medical', but comparable evocations of madness are not rare in poetry; in Tragedy Eur. *Heracles* 931 ff. is notable, cf. 867–70. *Onward!*: an exhortation used in war, appropriate for a deranged person about to launch forward; but the ancient commentator says that here, as elsewhere, it expressed just distress [in some MSS the two exclamations are violently expanded]. *spear-point*: a very rare Greek noun, but suiting martial *Onward!* [its rarity induces most editors to retain MSS 'unfired' where West adopts the conjecture *fiery*; then 'unfired spearpoint' is the gadfly's sting, in yet another 'kenning' (e.g. 801–4 and n.)]. *inside me*: evades the literal translation '(kicking) my diaphragm', of a suddenly thumping 'heart' (as in 361 'the very soul of his being').

887–906 Third choral ode: a brief meditation on the perils of 'marriage' with partners, especially gods, who are incomparably greater. The Chorus even as nymphs fear it, Io as mortal woman suffers cruelly from it. The ode forces the myth to suit the world of the Athenian spectators: the terrible example of Zeus and Io (894–900, 906) illustrates awkwardly the everyday human truth (and Greek custom) that marriage among equals works best: the artisan should not aspire to wed above himself (890–3, 901); Io deserves the love of a man, not of a god (899). The Chorus' sympathy for Io reminds them of Prometheus' marriage (553–60); and the Greek metre of the stanza-pair here is repeated from that almost 'hymnic' ode (see 526–60 n.); the similar elevation of tone is conveyed also by the triadic form here, epodes (901–6) being regular in such hymns.

[The text of 894–906 has needed considerable correction by editors, mostly for metrical reasons; see esp. on 894–6.]

889 *Wise indeed, yes, wise*: the doubling is pointedly emphatic, and matched in the responding stanza at 894; cf. on 891–3.

892–3 *either made effete... or vaunting, etc.*: these two lines in the Greek are markedly similar in phrasing and sound, a further device aiming at solemnity; cf. 901–6 n.

894–6 *Fates*: dispensers of human destiny, *Eum.* 724—but also of divine, above 516. [*text missing*: revealed by metrical inequivalence with 888, where some editors therefore delete words; others supplement here, e.g. with 'who bring all to fulfilment', applied to the Fates in 511.]

897–900 *Io hating her husband*: Io is still a maiden, hating the 'husband' who desired her and brought her misery, Zeus (see her cry at 578–81); the Chorus pray to avoid that (906), for as nymphs they could expect divine suitors. *wandering, her ordeal from Hera*: 599–601, cf. 592; also *Supp.* 564.

901–6 *For me... Zeus' design*: the Greek has marked assonances in 901 and 904, probably another effect like that of 891–3. *escape Zeus' design*: cf. 552 (also the Chorus).

907–1093 Final scenes (*exodos*). Prometheus' exchanges with Io, and revelation of their linked destinies, only increase his defiance of Zeus, voiced in a monologue and exchange with the Chorus (907–40): 'Zeus will not rule the gods for long', 940. Pat on cue comes Zeus' messenger Hermes, to demand Prometheus' secret knowledge of how Zeus is endangered by his planned marriage (947–8; cf. 168–71 n.); deliberately or not, this plays ironically upon the Chorus' deprecation of Zeus as marriage-partner (894–7). Hermes and Prometheus are contemptuous of each other's arrogance; Hermes matches Prometheus' threat to Zeus with Zeus' threat of even worse violence yet to come: lengthy imprisonment beneath a cataclysm of stone when Zeus' lightning destroys the ravine, and a return to the light only to be perpetually eaten alive by Zeus' eagle until some god takes Prometheus' place (1014–29; there is more irony here, for Hermes threatens only what Prometheus knows of his release, 871–3). Their fruitless, ever more divisive altercation is carried in a natural-feeling dialogue which varies single speeches and angry stichomythia (941–1035).

The Chorus echo the last advice of Hermes, for 'wise deliberation' (1038, from 1035), urging it one final time upon Prometheus, only for him to scorn absolutely the threatened cataclysm. This extreme defiance is marked by change from speech to chanting (from 1040), in which Hermes and the Chorus join as the god tries to detach them from Prometheus; Hermes fails, and he leaves (1054–79). The cataclysm begins, in which the Chorus share Prometheus' fate (1080–93). Mythology—or poetic invention—can be appropriately extreme too.

907–11 *Zeus shall yet…I swear*: the wording of 168, Prometheus' response to the Chorus' first incredulity about his fall. *the marriage*: enlarging on Prometheus' prophecy of 764 ff. (n.); the 'son' of this marriage (768) is described in 920–2 in more portentous terms. *curse of his father Cronus*: not otherwise known to myth. One senses here the author's imitation of the paternal curses of Oedipus (*Seven* 70, 723 ff.) or Thyestes (*Ag.* 1600).

913 *No god but I, etc.*: earlier at 440, 770.

916 *(Zeus') thunder*: 923, 1062, 1081–2.

920–5 *strong…rival in the ring*: lit. 'wrestler', the image used of Cronus' fall to Zeus at *Ag.* 171. *portentous, etc.*: the wording here is very similar to that of Pindar, *Isthmians* 8.31–5a, where the prophecy is attributed to Themis: see 873–4. The colourful language of 922–4 seems to anticipate the descriptions of storm and earthquake in 992–4, 1015–19, 1043–9, 1080–90.

924–5 *disturbance*: lit. 'disease', i.e. an abnormality of nature, an earthquake created by Zeus' new 'rival' (920) in Poseidon's own realm *the sea* to destroy his power, of which his *three-tined spear* (or trident) was the emblem, 925

(*Supp.* 218, *Seven* 133); and Poseidon is Zeus' brother [but 'disease' is a remarkable metaphor, preserved by some editors like West only at the cost of emending the MSS in 925]. This vivid passage may owe much to Hesiod's account of Zeus overwhelming the Titans with lightning and storm, *Theogony* 687–710.

933 *I am not fated to die*: 753, 1052.

936 *Nemesis*: the Greek name here is <u>*Adrasteia*</u>, 'She from whom there is no running away'; Plato too uses it.

937 *Go on, pay your honours, etc.*: cf. Prometheus' abrupt dismissal of Oceanus' pragmatism at 391–2.

941 *runner*: derogatory; cf. Prometheus at 966 and Hermes' hurt pride in 986–7. *servant*: milder, cf. 954, 983.

944–6 *You...I mean you!*: aggressive, abusive, and semi-colloquial lines. Hermes' tone at once establishes his crude arrogance, with his pompous selfishness in 950–1. As Zeus' herald he is characterized as unfavourably as such human officers often are in Tragedy (and were no doubt felt to be in life); cf. the Egyptian herald at *Supp.* 882–953. *the clever one*: Power scorned Prometheus's 'cleverness' at 62. *extreme...for his own good*: cf. n. on 308, and on 739 'cruel'. *giving ephemeral men privileges*: 82–3. *thief of fire*: 7–8, cf. Prometheus himself at 109–10.

947–8 *what marriage, etc.*: Zeus and Hermes are well aware of this aspect of Prometheus' prophecies (764, 908–27).

949 *with no riddling*: the author repeats his 610 (n.).

955–6 *You are all new, new to power*: 35, 96, 149, etc. *citadel free of sorrow*: the imagined bliss of the gods, e.g. *Supp.* 524–5; the earliest such picture is at Homer, *Odyssey* 6.42–6.

957–9 *two tyrants expelled*: before Zeus, his father Cronus (195, 280, 911, *Ag.* 171, *Eum.* 641) and grandfather Ouranos (205, *Ag.* 158–9). *watch*: for the nuance of this verb see n. on 299 'view'. *most shamefully and most speedily*: the translation imitates the Greek rhythm and assonance, typical of a half-colloquial curse-formula.

960 *cowering*: the expected attitude of submission (Power at 29), already repudiated by Prometheus (174).

965 *anchor in these torments*: cf. the Chorus at 183.

968 *servitude to this rock*: cf. Hephaestus at 31.

971 *luxuriate*: cf. 436, and for the oxymoron, cf. perhaps *Supp*. 833.

975–6 *gods who came off well*: after Prometheus helped Zeus overcome Cronus, 218–20.

977–8 *the madness in you*: of hating the gods (976), but madder still is not *loathing one's enemies* (cf. 1041–2, and 970); the first may seem irreligious, not to do the second is against personal and public duty (cf. 1069). The tripling *illness … ill … ill* is rather contrived, although 'sickness' is a very common metaphor for any dangerous abnormality (see n. on 'disturbance', 924): see Introd. 2.4. p. xlix.

980 *Alas for me!*: momentary self-pity, emphasized by the very unusual division of a single verse-line in a stichomythia [some editors therefore isolate Prometheus' exclamation, and repeat it for Hermes before 'That is a word, etc.', in an effect like 971–2, or give 980–1 wholly to Prometheus].

985 *And yet if, etc.*: sarcasm in this line provokes 986; but the translation is not sure. Prometheus seems to confirm that he will say nothing (cf. 963), but the sarcasm may depend on a different meaning here, 'since I owe …'.

989–91 *There is no torment … released*: so Prometheus as early as 173–5.

992–4 *his blazing flame … snowstorm … thunderings in the earth*: Zeus as master of destructive nature, 358–9, 563, 916, etc.; an anonymous god, *Pers*. 496. *feathery white snowstorm*: the literal translation: Herodotus 4.31.2 tells of 'feathers' in the Scythians' description of snowflakes; but our line may mean 'snowstorm on wings of white'. *embroil and confound*: a pairing from everyday speech, frequent in Aristophanes.

997–8 *Now see if, etc.*: normally a half-colloquial caution, here carrying malicious expectation, to which Prometheus replies knowingly.

1001–6 *like advising a sea-wave*: it is deaf and inflexible; a frequent image, like that of unyielding rock (242). *in womanly fear*: cf. Eteocles' condemnation at *Seven* 182–95, esp. 195.

1007–11 *like a colt new to harness … reins*: simile running into metaphor. For Prometheus 'harnessed' in his bonds, see 5, 618, etc., Introd. 2.4. p. xlix. *stratagem*: his silence; cf. 470. The Greek word echoes Hermes' 'You, the clever one' at 944.

1015 *huge wave*: lit. 'triple wave': *Seven* 760 and n.

1016–19 This threatened cataclysm begins at 1080. Prometheus will emerge from it into the light (1021), but still need a rescuer who will succeed to his miseries by entering the underworld (1028–9): this is Heracles (n. on 1026–9).

1020–5 *winged hound... eagle*: cf. 803 (griffin) and n. *tawny*: probably the meaning of the Greek adjective, for Aeschylus calls eagles 'fiery-red' in fr. 160; but the word can mean also 'bloodthirsty'. *banqueter*: horrific application of human imagery to animal, not rare in bloody allusions, e.g. of the eagle's feast at *Ag.* 138; cf. *Supp.* 801. *every day*: this translation seems forced by *approaching*, but some translate 'all day long', comparing Prometheus' agony at Hesiod, *Theogony* 525. *blackened with its gnawing*: the dark of clotted blood, *Seven* 736, etc.

1026–9 *some god... to succeed*: a supposed impossibility intended as a final taunt; but Heracles, who was Zeus' son and became a demi-god after his death, indeed went down to Hades. Our author seems to cast Heracles as Prometheus' saviour, as one of his descendants (771–4); and Heracles was famous as an archer (872–3). In some accounts the centaur Chiron (half-man, half-horse, also a god's son, and another benefactor of mankind) surrenders his immortality in favour of Prometheus: see Introd. 2.4 p. li n. 49, on the *Prometheus Unbound*. *Tartarus*: 219; 'dark' at 1051.

1031–3 *spoken all too surely*: 'surely' is not in the Greek, and this translation is therefore doubted [some editors emend to 'all too true']. *Zeus' lips... fulfilled*: cf. *Eum.* 615–21, Apollo's assertion that as Zeus' prophet he may speak only the certain truth. For Zeus the 'fulfiller', cf. *Supp.* 524–6 (n.).

1034 *Look about you*: perhaps literal, perhaps loose for 'consider widely'; cf. Prometheus advice to Oceanus at 334 'keep looking out for yourself'.

1036–9 *To us, Hermes seems, etc.*: the Chorus appear to sympathize with Hermes' arguments as prudent, fearing further punishment for Prometheus, but at 1064–70 they reject his advice to themselves to abandon Prometheus as morally unthinkable ('cowardice', 1066).

1040–2 *nothing unseemly, etc.*: a rejoinder to the Chorus' rebuke of his unrelenting animosity with 'shameful' (1039). *enemy suffering badly from enemies*: 977–8 (n.).

1043–9 *the double fiery flare*: Zeus' lightning, 358–9, 917, sometimes pictured by artists and sculptors as a bolt flaming at both ends. *flare* is lit. 'curl of (long) hair', a metaphor for forked lightning; cf. 'branches' in 1083. *ocean-wave . . . block . . . the . . . stars*: the watery complement to the uprooted earth; cf. 1088 'heaven is confounded with ocean'; no doubt ancient sailors too told of such giant waves, if not as large as those now firmly attested for the world's oceans, not to speak of tsunamis which follow earthquakes. All the extreme phenomena of 1043–9, like those of 1016–19, begin in 1080–7.

1051–3 *cruel spirals*: lit. 'solid whirlpools'. The adjective is not rare metaphorically, the noun is used both literally and figuratively of disaster at *Eum.* 559. *compulsion*: the word often nears 'fate' in sense (cf. 105, 514–15, and n. on 673 'curb'). *killing me, etc.*: Prometheus is immortal: see 65 and n.

1054–62 *Exactly the . . . resolve, etc.*: Hermes tries to spare the Chorus from Prometheus' ruinous folly (1059, cf. 1067) in defiance of Zeus (1071–9).

1056 *hit the wrong note*: translation insecure, but probably a metaphor from music (and apt therefore to the *vow* of 1052). Although the Greek verb in 1055 'stricken minds' is different, a secondary wordplay may be intended.

1061 *bellowing*: metaphor from cattle, repeated at 1083.

1063–5 *what will actually persuade me*: to stand by Prometheus, not abandon him (*the word* of 1060, 'go quickly away somewhere'). *slipped in*: insecure translation of a metaphor seemingly from sweeping one thing along with others, in order to slip it past. Some take the image to be of things swept along incidentally, like flotsam on the main stream.

1069–70 *traitors*: the Chorus identify Hermes with the gods who betrayed Prometheus' help, 438–40. *abominate*: lit. 'spit from me', a vigorous, almost colloquial idiom, nevertheless at home in high poetry, e.g. *Ag.* 1192.

1073–9 *hunted down . . . entangled . . . net*: linked imagery; for *ruin's net*, cf. *Ag.* 360–1 (Troy's, in Zeus' net); the ominous term 'ruin', often personified, e.g. *Pers.* 1007, *Seven* 957, is doubled here (1073, 1078), at start and end of Hermes' final threat. For *inescapable* (or 'with no way through') as the net's adjective in 1079, cf. *Ag.* 1382 (Clytemnestra snares Agamemnon in his robing).

1080 *s.d. noisily*: Prometheus cries out as the cataclysm begins. How the play's end was managed in the theatre is conjectural: see Introd. 2.4 Appendix pp. lii–liii.

1080–90 *Here is the reality*: Prometheus' description of the storm now all about him ends with this same emphasis, 1090 *too clearly*. Much of the

vocabulary for nature's upheaval here is repeated from Prometheus' defiance of Hermes in 1016–19 and 1043–9. It appeared in the Io-episode in
metaphor for her frenzied suffering (n. on 563), and helps to link her fate
with Prometheus' as victims of Zeus; note esp. *leap wildly about*, the image
from an animal's 'bucking' used of Io's frenzied rushing at 599, 675.

1091–3 *most holy mother*: Themis, invoked here both as primeval diety and
prophet (209–11 n.): 'can you tolerate this outrage to your son? will your
foreknowledge not stand by me again?' *heaven revolving the light*: paraphras-
ing a conventional appeal to the Sun, who illuminates and witnesses all (91,
cf. *Supp.* 213 for the Sun's powers of salvation); the Sun 'revolves' his chariot
of light across the heaven. *how unjustly I suffer*: last at 976, first at 93.

# Textual Appendix

A list of conjectural readings taken from West's *apparatus* to replace words which he retains in his edited text but marks as corrupt, and of other differences. The line-numbers are those of the Greek text.

## PERSIANS

110–11 πνεύμασι λάβροισι περᾶν Enger: πνεύματι λάβρωι†ἐσορᾶν†
281 Πέρσαις φίλοις West (*apparatus*): †Πέρσαις δαίοις†
288 πολλὰς Περσίδων MSS: πολλοὺς σπερμάτων West (conjecture in text)
656 ηὐοδώκει West (*apparatus*), translated approximately: †εὖ ἐποδώκει†
732 ιηῆδέ τις πέμ Gomperz: †οιῆδέ τις γέρων†
859 λοχίσματα West (*apparatus*): †νομί(σ)ματα†
900 the entire line is obelized by West; translation is approximate
925 Ἀιδοβάται Passow: ἀγδαβάται
967 <βόα>, πού σοι Hermann: †πού δέ † σοι
997 καὶ Δαδάκαν Wilamowitz: †κηγδαδάταν†
1002 οἷπερ MSS: τοῖπερ West (conjecture in text)

## SEVEN AGAINST THEBES

137 φύτωρ (Weil) ἐπώνυμον Κάδμου (MS M): †φεῦ φεῦ ἐπώνυμον Κάδμου†
162 παῖ Διὸς (Westphal) ὅθεν (Van den Bergh): †καὶ Διόθεν†
221–2 κἀκ στρατοῦ δαπτομέναν Hutchinson after Prien: †στράτευμ' ἁπτόμενον†
364 τλαμόνως <φέρουσιν> εὐνὰν {αἰχμάλωτον} West (*apparatus*; translated approximately): †τλήμονες εὐνὰν αἰχμάλωτον†
435 φωτὶ πέμπε, editors: φωτί, πέμπε Pauw
576 προσθροῶν (Francken) ὁμόσπορον (Burges): †πρὸς μόραν ἀδελφεόν†
695 μέλαιν' Weil: †τελεῖ †
785 the translation ignores †ἀραίας†
792 εὐγενῶν West (*apparatus*): †μητέρων†
824 <μεμέλησθε> West (*apparatus*): only loss of wording is marked in his text
826 †σωτῆρι† approximately translated
849 δίδυμα γοερὰ Brown: δίδυμ' †ἀνορέα†

973 the translation ignores †τοίων†
984 δύστονα κῆδε᾽ (MSS) ὁμαίμονα (Haupt): †δύστονα κῆδε᾽ ὁμώνυμα†

## SUPPLIANTS

22a West's supplement <ἀλλ᾽ ὦ πάτριοι δαίμονες Ἄργους> is translated only in the Explanatory Note
110 ἄτας δ᾽ἀπάταν Westphal is translated approximately: †ἄται δ᾽ἀπάται†
212 ἶνιν Kiehl ... 214 γ᾽ Page: ὄρνιν ... 214 τ᾽ MS
266 μηνίσασ᾽ ἄχη Martin: †μηνεῖται ἄκη†
307 Χο. βοηλάτην μύωπα κινητήριον MS (followed by 'a line missing'): 307 Χο. βοηλάτην <ἔπεμψεν ἐπτερωμένον. | 307a Πε. βοῶν λέγεις> μύωπα κινητήριον supplemented conjecturally by West and put in his text
355 νεύονθ᾽ Bamberger: †νέονθ᾽†
363–4 the translation relies heavily on οὐ πτωχεύσεις, the ancient paraphrase of originally lengthier wording, and †ἱεροδόκα† is translated only approximately: οὐ λιπερ<νὴς⏑ ⏑⏑>†ἱεροδόκα† West
405–6 μεγαίρεις Stadtmüller: †μεταλγεῖς†
435 δεῖ ᾽κτίνειν Whittle is approximately translated: †δρεικ†τίνειν
494 πολυστεφεῖς Butler: †πολισσούχων†
514 ἀνάλκτων West (_apparatus_): †ἀνάκτων†
544–5 δύαι ... ἐν ἀικεῖ West (_apparatus_): †διχῇι† ··· †ἐν αἴσαι†
568 †ἐσορῶντες† translated despite the problems: see Explanatory Note
628–9 †ἀπ᾽ἀληθείαι | τερμόν᾽ἀμέμπτων πρὸς ἅπαντα† is paraphrased approximately
630 ὅπ᾽ἐμὰν Badham: †ὅτε καί†
661 <στάσις> Bamberger: only loss of wording is marked in West's text
763 τάχος Tucker: †κράτος†
808 ἵυζε δ᾽(Arsenius) {ὀμφάν} (del. Haupt): †ἵυζεν δ᾽ὀμφάν†
842 {ὀλόμεν᾽} (del. Robortelli) ἐπ᾽ ἀμάδα West (_apparatus_) after Schütz (ἀμάδα): †ὀλόμεν᾽ἐπαμίδα†
875 καὶ αὐτῶν τῶν ἀχέων πικρότερα ἵυζε (the scholiast's apparent paraphrase) is translated approximately: †πικρότερ᾽ ἀχέων οἰζύος ὄνομ᾽ ἔχων†
890 = 900 †βοάν† is represented by 'monster' in the translation
990 τιμίαν ἡμᾶς χρεών West (_apparatus_): †τιμιωτέραν ἐμοῦ†
1019 †γαναέντες† translated despite its anomalous form
1071 δίκαι δίκαν Haupt: †δίκα δίκας†

**PROMETHEUS**

275 μογοῦντι ταῦτ᾽, ἐπεὶ West (*apparatus*): μογοῦντι· πάντα (Herwerden: ταῦτα MSS) τοι

680 αἰφνίδιος αὐτὸν Porson: αὐτὸν †αἰφνίδιος†

693 τύψειν Wilamowitz: ψύχειν (and all of 691–3) obelized

# Index

This index covers both this volume and its predecessor *Aeschylus, Oresteia* (2002). It is a very selective index to their **Introductions** and **Explanatory Notes** alone, not to Aeschylus' translated text; many names and topics which occur only once in the Introductions or Notes are not included. The only text-critical discussions indexed are of interpolation.

References are by **page-numbers**, to the **Introductions** through **Roman** numerals, to the **Explananatory Notes** through **Arabic** numerals. References to **this volume** are made in plain type, to the *Oresteia* in italic type; when both are indexed, references to this volume always come first. A figure in round brackets following a page-number indicates that there is more than one reference on that page to the name or topic. A few important discussions are indicated by inclusive page-numbers (e.g. xii–vii, *145–51*) or by an asterisk (e.g. 230*, *xxvi**).

**American Literature**

**British and Irish Literature**

**Children's Literature**

**Classics and Ancient Literature**

**Colonial Literature**

**Eastern Literature**

**European Literature**

**Gothic Literature**

**History**

**Medieval Literature**

**Oxford English Drama**

**Poetry**

**Philosophy**

**Politics**

**Religion**

**The Oxford Shakespeare**